# China's Ethnic Minorities

The majority of China's population is the Han. Up to now, China has officially identified, except for other unknown ethnic groups and foreigners with Chinese citizenship, 55 ethnic minorities. Ethnic minorities vary widely in size in China. With a population of more than 15 million, the Zhuang have been the largest minority group, and the Lhoba, with only 2,000 or more, the smallest. China's ethnic diversity has resulted in a special socioeconomic landscape of China itself. This book sets out to collect and estimate a full set of data on the socioeconomic situations of China's ethnic minorities.

Until the present, a complete socioeconomic picture of China's ethnic groups still remains unclear from China's official sources. How different have China's ethnic minorities been in every sphere of daily life and economic development during the country's fast transition period? In order to answer this question, we need a detailed and comparable set of data for each of China's ethnic minorities.

The book provides, in an easy-to-use format, a broad collection of data on China's 55 ethnic minorities. It is a resource book that profiles the demography, employment and wages, livelihood, agriculture, industry, education, science and technology, culture, sports, and public health for each of these ethnic minorities. These indicators, estimated by the author based on materials gathered from a variety of sources and clearly presented in one volume, will be of great value to researchers, businesses, government agencies, and news media.

**Rongxing Guo** is Professor and Head of the Regional Economics Committee, Regional Science Association of China (RSAC) at Peking University, Beijing. He has served with the OECD in Paris and at the Brookings Institution in Washington, DC. He has taught at China University of Mining and Technology, Korea University, Trier University in Germany, and Gakushuin University in Tokyo.

# China's Ethnic Minorities

## Social and economic indicators

**Rongxing Guo**

Routledge
Taylor & Francis Group

LONDON AND NEW YORK

First published 2013
by Routledge
2 Park Square, Milton Park, Abingdon, Oxfordshire OX14 4RN

Simultaneously published in the USA and Canada
by Routledge
711 Third Avenue, New York, NY 10017

First issued in paperback 2014

*Routledge is an imprint of the Taylor and Francis Group, an informa business*

*British Library Cataloguing in Publication Data*
A catalogue record for this book is available from the British Library

*Library of Congress Cataloging in Publication Data*
Guo, Rongxing.
  China's ethnic minorities : social and economic indicators / by Rongxing Guo.
    pages cm. – (Routledge studies in the modern world economy ; 114)
  Includes bibliographical references and index.
  1. Minorities–China–Economic conditions.   2. Minorities–China–Social conditions.   3. Economic indicators–China.   4. Social indicators–China.   I. Title.
  HC427.95.G8626 2013
  330.9510089–dc23
  2012034589

ISBN 978-0-415-81015-9 (hbk)

ISBN 978-1-138-91034-8 (pbk)

ISBN 978-0-203-58436-1 (ebk)

Typeset in Times New Roman by
Newgen Imaging Systems

This book is dedicated to my friends Eui-Gak and Young-Ja Hwang (Seoul, South Korea), from whom I learnt how to write books in English during the early period of my academic career.

# Contents

# Preface

The objective of this book is to collect and estimate a full set of data on the socioeconomic situations of China's ethnic minorities.

Although the majority of China's population is of the Han nationality (which accounts for more than 90 percent of China's population), the non-Han ethnic groups have a population of more than 100 million. China has officially identified, except for other unknown ethnic groups and foreigners with Chinese citizenship, 55 ethnic minorities. In addition, ethnic minorities vary widely in size. With a population of more than 15 million, the Zhuang have the largest ethnic minority, and the Lhoba, with only 2,000 or more, the smallest. China's ethnic diversity has resulted in a special socioeconomic landscape of China itself.

A complete socioeconomic picture of China's ethnic groups still remains unclear. How different have China's ethnic minorities been in every sphere of daily life and economic development during China's fast transition period? In order to answer this question, we need a detailed and comparable set of data for each of China's ethnic minorities.

There has not been any official statement of China's socioeconomic development from a multi-ethnic dimension. The only official data released can be found in the *China Ethnic Statistical Yearbook* (released by the State Commission of Ethnic Affairs of the People's Republic of China since 1994). However, as this *Yearbook* has only reported the socioeconomic statistics for the minority-based autonomous areas, a complete set of China's multi-ethnic data cannot be derived from it. For instance, only five provincial-level minority-based autonomous regions (Inner Mongolia, Tibet, the Zhuang-based Guangxi, the Hui-based Ningxia, and the Uygur-based Xinjiang) and all other subprovincial-level autonomous prefectures and counties, which cover 19 provinces, were included in this *Yearbook*. All of these minority-based autonomous areas, however, account for less than two-thirds of the total population of the ethnic minorities in China, while the remaining one-third population is included in the Han majority-based administrative areas.

Another reason why the data of an ethnic-based area do not represent those of that ethnic people stems from two facts in China: first, there usually exist two or more ethnic peoples in each ethnic-based area; second, each ethnic minority is usually included geographically in at least two adminis-trative divisions (provinces, prefectures, counties, and others). For instance, according to the composition of the population, the Mongol people have now become a true minority in Inner Mongolia, hometown of the ethnic Mongols, as a result of the large-scale Han immigration during the twentieth century.

## Organization of this book

This book sets out to present, in an easy-to-use format, a broad collection of social and economic indicators on China's 55 ethnic minorities. It is a databook that profiles population, employment and income distribution, people's livelihood, agriculture and rural economy, education, science and technology, and culture and public health for each of these ethnic minorities. These indicators are estimated by using the methodology shown in Appendix A and the regional and local data gathered from a variety of sources. This book is organized as follows.

This book contains six chapters, including (1) population; (2) employment and income distribution; (3) people's livelihood; (4) agriculture and rural economy; (5) education and science and technology; and (6) culture and public health. At the beginning of each chapter, there is a brief introduction to data sources, statistical coverage, and statistical methods. In addition, some explanatory notes on main indicators are presented, where necessary, at the end of each table.

In addition to the data on each of the 55 minority ethnic groups, this book also provides two sets of data (all marked in italic in the text): one for China as a whole (sometimes this set includes the data of 2005 as well as of the pre-ceding years) and one for the Han ethnic majority. This will then provide useful benchmarks for different research purposes.

At the end of this book, there are five appendices. In Appendix A, the methodology by which to estimate multi-ethnic data is briefly described. Appendix B provides China's ethnic population shares for its 31 provinces, autonomous regions, and municipalities. In order to provide more infor-mation about China's ethnic minorities, the minority-based administra-tive divisions at different levels (including the autonomous regions as the first-class administrative divisions; cities, prefectures, autonomous prefec-tures, and *meng*s as the second-class administrative divisions; and cities, counties, autonomous counties, *Qi*s, and autonomous *Qi*s as the third-class administrative divisions) are listed in Appendix C. In addition, Appendix D provides selected indicators on social and economic development in ethnic minority autonomous areas and Appendix E shows the geocultural condi-tions of the 55 ethnic minorities in China.

**Acknowledgments**

During the whole process of this research, we received generous offers and help from the following organizations:

- Department of Financial Management, Ministry of Culture
- Department of Financial Management, State Administration of Broadcasting, Film and Television
- Department of Financial Management, State Agency of News and Publication
- Department of Planning and Development, Ministry of Education
- Department of Population and Employment Statistics of the National Bureau of Statistics
- Department of Urban Socio-economic Survey, National Bureau of Statistics
- Information Center, Ministry of Public Health
- State Intellectual Property Office
- Ministry of Public Health
- Rural Socio-economic Survey Organization, National Bureau of Statistics
- State Administration for Industry and Commerce
- State Agency of News and Publication

This book has also benefited from the skillful assistance of the following individuals: Bian Lihua, Cai Qixin, Chen Yueyue, Deng Weiping, Dong Lihua, Du Yan, Feng Nailin, Guan Xiaojing, Guo Dong, Hao Shenglong, Hou Rui, Huang Pei, Jin Zhaofeng, Ju Chuanling, Li Huimin, Li Junbo, Li Min, Li Suoqiang, Li Xiaowei, Liang Erwei, Long Ling, Luan Jinhui, Meng Hehe, Que Xiaoqing, Song Shaoying, Tang Ping, Tie Bing, Wang Ping, Wang Xiaohong, Xiao Li, Xu Hui, Xu Lan, Xu Xiongfei, Ye Liqi, Ye Shifang, Zhai Shangqing, Zhang Xin, Zhao Huiyun, Zheng Xuegong, Zheng Zexiang, Zhou Xuewen, and Zhu Weisheng.

During the review and revision stage, the feedback and encouragement received from Lam Yong Ling (Commissioning Editor, Routledge, Singapore) enabled me to finalize this project without delay. In addition, Penny Harper, Alison Evans, and Luc (Chang'lei) Guo also provided superb editorial assistance during the production stage. I am especially grateful to three anonymous reviewers whose comments and suggestions have helped me refine many parts of the manuscript. However, all views and errors in this book certainly are mine only and not necessarily those of the organizations and individuals who provided the original data.

Rongxing Guo, Qiaozi, Huairou, Beijing, 2012
(www.amazon.com/Rongxing-Guo/e/B001H6MWNY)

# Notes on the text

(a) Unless stated otherwise, all data reported in this book are as of 2005.

(b) The ethnic minorities and their socioeconomic indicators monitored in this book are only based on the geographical scope of mainland China.

(c) All national-level data in this book (marked in italic) also include those of unknown ethnic groups and foreigners with Chinese citizenship.

(d) The Chinese currency is renminbi (RMB). The official exchange rate of RMB yuan to US dollar is approximately 8.2:1 as of 2005.

(e) Unless stated otherwise, the monetary values are measured at current prices.

(f) Statistical discrepancies due to rounding are not adjusted in the book.

(g) If a table occupies more than one page, the footnotes pertaining to the table are placed at the end of the table.

(h) Blank space indicates that the figure is not large enough to be measured with the smallest unit in the table, or data are unknown or are not available.

(i) The data of the Han majority are included in the text (marked in italic).

(j) Due to reasons that are beyond our control, estimation errors may exist in the indicators reported in the book.

# 1 Population

Data in this chapter show some demographic conditions of China's ethnic minorities, such as population, urban population and rural population, birth rates, death rates, natural growth rates, dependency ratio, household size, and education attainment in 2005.

The data are estimated based on the data provided by the Department of Population and Employment Statistics of the National Bureau of Statistics. Specifically, data in Table 1.1 are estimates from the 2005 National Sample Survey of 1% of Population. Data in Table 1.2 are from the national and provincial communiqués of the key results of the 2005 National Sample Survey of 1% of Population. Data in Table 1.3 are compiled from the 1990 and 2000 population censuses. Data in Tables 1.4–1.14 are the sample results of the 2005 National Sample Survey of 1% of Population.

The National Sample Survey of 1% of Population adopted a multi-stage stratified systematic probability-proportional-to-size ("PPS") cluster sampling scheme, in which the selection probability for each element is set to be proportional to its size measure, up to a maximum of 1. In this PPS scheme, the whole nation is taken as the population, and each province, autonomous region, or municipality as the sub-population.

A total of 16.99 million people were selected from 77,417 survey districts in 21,181 townships (towns and urban neighborhood committees) in 2,869 counties (including country-level cities and districts) of the 31 provinces, autonomous regions, and municipalities. The weighted estimation procedure suggested that the birth rate was 12.40 per thousand, the death rate was 6.51 per thousand, and the natural growth rate was 5.89 per thousand for China in 2005.

*Table 1.1* Total population and birth rate, death rate, and natural growth rate

| Ethnic group | Total population (1,000 persons) | Birth rate (‰) | Death rate (‰) | Natural growth rate (‰) |
|---|---|---|---|---|
| *National total* | *1,307,560* | *12.40* | *6.51* | *5.89* |
| Achang | 35.65 | 14.68 | 6.74 | 7.94 |
| Bai | 1,946.00 | 14.43 | 6.78 | 7.65 |
| Baonan | 17.13 | 12.84 | 6.50 | 6.34 |
| Blang | 96.47 | 14.66 | 6.74 | 7.92 |
| Buyi | 3,142.97 | 14.47 | 7.15 | 7.32 |
| Dai | 1,217.06 | 14.66 | 6.75 | 7.92 |
| Daur | 137.29 | 9.59 | 5.38 | 4.21 |
| Deang | 18.84 | 14.70 | 6.75 | 7.96 |
| Derung | 7.76 | 13.94 | 6.61 | 7.33 |
| Dong | 3,078.16 | 13.52 | 6.86 | 6.66 |
| Dongxiang | 534.01 | 13.03 | 6.39 | 6.64 |
| Ewenki | 31.34 | 9.90 | 5.46 | 4.45 |
| Gaoshan | 4.63 | 11.48 | 6.14 | 5.34 |
| Gelao | 612.93 | 14.50 | 7.16 | 7.34 |
| *Han* | *1,173,257.85* | *11.08* | *6.14* | *4.95* |
| Hani | 1,512.05 | 14.68 | 6.75 | 7.94 |
| Hezhe | 4.88 | 8.16 | 5.30 | 2.86 |
| Hui | 10,377.47 | 13.09 | 5.94 | 7.15 |
| Jing | 23.91 | 14.15 | 6.12 | 8.03 |
| Jingpo | 138.81 | 14.68 | 6.74 | 7.94 |
| Jino | 21.95 | 14.67 | 6.74 | 7.93 |
| Kazak | 1,361.37 | 16.40 | 5.05 | 11.36 |
| Kirgiz | 175.04 | 16.32 | 5.04 | 11.28 |
| Korean | 1,969.82 | 7.97 | 5.43 | 2.54 |
| Lahu | 476.45 | 14.67 | 6.74 | 7.93 |
| Lhoba | 3.13 | 17.42 | 7.07 | 10.35 |
| Li | 1,363.91 | 14.60 | 5.79 | 8.82 |
| Lisu | 665.86 | 14.54 | 6.75 | 7.79 |
| Manchu | 10,922.18 | 8.63 | 5.99 | 2.64 |
| Maonan | 113.74 | 14.30 | 6.40 | 7.90 |
| Miao | 9,244.80 | 13.39 | 6.85 | 6.55 |
| Monba | 9.44 | 17.55 | 7.10 | 10.45 |
| Mongol | 5,968.89 | 10.03 | 5.61 | 4.42 |
| Mulao | 220.18 | 14.19 | 6.21 | 7.97 |
| Naxi | 323.95 | 14.55 | 6.75 | 7.80 |
| Nu | 30.21 | 14.70 | 6.74 | 7.96 |
| Oroqen | 8.52 | 9.00 | 5.38 | 3.62 |

*Table 1.1* (*cont.*)

| Ethnic group | Total population (1,000 persons) | Birth rate (‰) | Death rate (‰) | Natural growth rate (‰) |
|---|---|---|---|---|
| Pumi | 35.28 | 14.64 | 6.74 | 7.90 |
| Qiang | 305.48 | 9.75 | 6.79 | 2.96 |
| Russian | 16.61 | 13.67 | 5.27 | 8.40 |
| Salar | 116.28 | 15.29 | 6.21 | 9.08 |
| She | 745.04 | 11.90 | 5.84 | 6.05 |
| Shui | 430.45 | 14.50 | 7.13 | 7.37 |
| Tajik | 44.58 | 16.23 | 5.08 | 11.15 |
| Tatar | 5.31 | 16.03 | 5.14 | 10.89 |
| Tibetan | 5,715.51 | 14.97 | 6.81 | 8.16 |
| Tu | 267.05 | 15.03 | 6.23 | 8.79 |
| Tujia | 7,925.32 | 11.05 | 6.43 | 4.62 |
| Uygur | 9,142.97 | 16.38 | 5.05 | 11.34 |
| Uzbek | 13.46 | 16.32 | 5.06 | 11.26 |
| Va | 416.19 | 14.60 | 6.73 | 7.87 |
| Xibe | 194.12 | 8.95 | 5.79 | 3.16 |
| Yao | 2,758.90 | 13.45 | 6.22 | 7.23 |
| Yi | 8,046.63 | 13.29 | 6.81 | 6.49 |
| Yugur | 14.20 | 12.67 | 6.51 | 6.16 |
| Zhuang | 17,183.88 | 14.17 | 6.09 | 8.08 |

*Notes:* (i) Military personnel were included in the national total population, but excluded in that of each ethnic group. (ii) The national total population excluded the population of Hong Kong, Macau, and Taiwan. (iii) Data of total population are based on the 2005 National Sample Survey of 1% of Population with consideration of floating population. So the data in some regions are not comparable with the preceding year.

"Birth rate" (or "crude birth rate") refers to the ratio of the number of births to the average population (or mid-period population) during a certain period of time (usually a year), expressed in ‰. Birth rate in the chapter refers to annual birth rate. The following formula is used:

$$\text{Birth rate} = \frac{\text{Number of births}}{\text{Annual average population}} \times 1000‰$$

Number of births in the formula refers to live births, i.e. when a baby has breathed or showed any vital phenomena regardless of the length of pregnancy. Annual average population is the average of the number of population at the beginning of the year and that at the end of the year. Sometimes it is substituted by the mid-year population.

"Death rate" (or "crude death rate") refers to the ratio of the number of deaths to the average population (or mid-period population) during a certain period of time (usually a year), expressed in ‰. Death rate in the chapter refers to annual death rate. The following formula is used:

$$\text{Death rate} = \frac{\text{Number of deaths}}{\text{Annual average population}} \times 1000‰$$

## 4   Population

"Natural growth rate of population" refers to the ratio of natural increase in population (number of births minus number of deaths) in a certain period of time (usually a year) to the average population (or mid-period population) of the same period, expressed in ‰. The following formula is applied:

$$\text{Natural growth rate of population} = \frac{\text{Number of births} - \text{Number of deaths}}{\text{Annual average population}} \times 1000‰$$

*Table 1.2* Population by urban and rural residence

| Ethnic group | Urban population | | Rural population | |
|---|---|---|---|---|
| | Population (1,000 persons) | Proportion (%) | Population (1,000 persons) | Proportion (%) |
| National total | 561,570.00 | 42.99 | 744,710.00 | 57.01 |
| Achang | 10.56 | 29.68 | 25.02 | 70.32 |
| Bai | 584.47 | 30.08 | 1,358.42 | 69.92 |
| Baonan | 5.27 | 30.76 | 11.85 | 69.24 |
| Blang | 28.63 | 29.73 | 67.67 | 70.27 |
| Buyi | 870.67 | 27.74 | 2,268.12 | 72.26 |
| Dai | 360.45 | 29.67 | 854.55 | 70.33 |
| Daur | 67.38 | 49.09 | 69.88 | 50.91 |
| Deang | 5.56 | 29.59 | 13.24 | 70.41 |
| Derung | 2.53 | 32.64 | 5.22 | 67.36 |
| Dong | 978.91 | 31.84 | 2,095.65 | 68.16 |
| Dongxiang | 165.25 | 30.97 | 368.29 | 69.03 |
| Ewenki | 15.08 | 48.12 | 16.26 | 51.88 |
| Gaoshan | 1.94 | 41.89 | 2.69 | 58.11 |
| Gelao | 168.80 | 27.58 | 443.31 | 72.42 |
| *Han* | *515,778.11* | *44.00* | *656,498.90* | *56.00* |
| Hani | 447.72 | 29.66 | 1,061.78 | 70.34 |
| Hezhe | 2.59 | 53.00 | 2.29 | 47.00 |
| Hui | 4,177.45 | 40.30 | 6,188.89 | 59.70 |
| Jing | 8.14 | 34.11 | 15.74 | 65.89 |
| Jingpo | 41.13 | 29.68 | 97.44 | 70.32 |
| Jino | 6.50 | 29.67 | 15.41 | 70.33 |
| Kazak | 505.38 | 37.16 | 854.74 | 62.84 |
| Kirgiz | 65.29 | 37.33 | 109.59 | 62.67 |
| Korean | 1,053.54 | 53.51 | 915.45 | 46.49 |
| Lahu | 141.11 | 29.67 | 334.54 | 70.33 |
| Lhoba | 0.88 | 28.11 | 2.25 | 71.89 |
| Li | 605.18 | 44.46 | 756.01 | 55.54 |
| Lisu | 197.76 | 29.75 | 466.99 | 70.25 |
| Manchu | 5,782.17 | 52.96 | 5,134.83 | 47.04 |

*Table 1.2* (*cont.*)

| Ethnic group | Urban population | | Rural population | |
|---|---|---|---|---|
| | Population (1,000 persons) | Proportion (%) | Population (1,000 persons) | Proportion (%) |
| Maonan | 36.47 | 32.10 | 77.14 | 67.90 |
| Miao | 2,962.48 | 32.08 | 6,271.25 | 67.92 |
| Monba | 2.64 | 28.03 | 6.77 | 71.97 |
| Mongol | 2,850.93 | 47.77 | 3,116.96 | 52.23 |
| Mulao | 73.87 | 33.59 | 146.07 | 66.41 |
| Naxi | 96.35 | 29.79 | 227.06 | 70.21 |
| Nu | 8.98 | 29.78 | 21.18 | 70.22 |
| Oroqen | 4.31 | 50.57 | 4.21 | 49.43 |
| Pumi | 10.48 | 29.76 | 24.74 | 70.24 |
| Qiang | 101.17 | 33.14 | 204.15 | 66.86 |
| Russian | 6.97 | 42.00 | 9.63 | 58.00 |
| Salar | 44.60 | 38.39 | 71.57 | 61.61 |
| She | 353.65 | 47.51 | 390.72 | 52.49 |
| Shui | 119.31 | 27.75 | 310.57 | 72.25 |
| Tajik | 16.65 | 37.38 | 27.89 | 62.62 |
| Tatar | 1.99 | 37.50 | 3.31 | 62.50 |
| Tibetan | 1,791.21 | 31.40 | 3,912.60 | 68.60 |
| Tu | 102.77 | 38.52 | 164.03 | 61.48 |
| Tujia | 3,072.68 | 38.80 | 4,846.22 | 61.20 |
| Uygur | 3,398.46 | 37.20 | 5,736.10 | 62.80 |
| Uzbek | 5.03 | 37.38 | 8.42 | 62.62 |
| Va | 124.34 | 29.93 | 291.15 | 70.07 |
| Xibe | 104.37 | 53.79 | 89.67 | 46.21 |
| Yao | 1,001.62 | 36.34 | 1,754.29 | 63.66 |
| Yi | 2,437.15 | 30.33 | 5,598.77 | 69.67 |
| Yugur | 4.36 | 30.76 | 9.83 | 69.24 |
| Zhuang | 5,911.37 | 34.44 | 11,253.35 | 65.56 |

*Notes:* (i) "Urban population" refers to all people residing in cities and towns, while "rural population" refers to population other than urban population. (ii) Data in this table are obtained from the *Communiqué* on major figures of the 2005 National Sample Survey of 1% of Population.

*Table 1.3* Population life expectancy

| Ethnic group | Life expectancy in 1990 | Male | Female | Life expectancy in 2000 | Male | Female |
|---|---|---|---|---|---|---|
| *National total* | 68.55 | 66.84 | 70.47 | 71.40 | 69.63 | 73.33 |
| Achang | 63.54 | 62.12 | 65.04 | 65.57 | 64.31 | 66.98 |
| Bai | 63.88 | 62.47 | 65.38 | 66.03 | 64.72 | 67.50 |
| Baonan | 66.80 | 65.90 | 67.82 | 67.43 | 66.67 | 68.30 |
| Blang | 63.39 | 61.98 | 64.88 | 65.60 | 64.34 | 67.01 |
| Buyi | 64.45 | 63.17 | 65.82 | 66.22 | 64.77 | 67.85 |
| Dai | 63.53 | 62.11 | 65.02 | 65.58 | 64.32 | 67.00 |
| Daur | 66.15 | 64.86 | 67.74 | 70.74 | 69.02 | 72.77 |
| Deang | 63.50 | 62.09 | 64.99 | 65.53 | 64.28 | 66.93 |
| Derung | 63.31 | 61.88 | 64.83 | 66.73 | 65.37 | 68.25 |
| Dong | 65.78 | 64.36 | 67.33 | 68.24 | 66.65 | 70.04 |
| Dongxiang | 66.70 | 65.83 | 67.67 | 67.47 | 66.69 | 68.38 |
| Ewenki | 65.98 | 64.71 | 67.56 | 70.25 | 68.61 | 72.21 |
| Gaoshan | 67.97 | 66.20 | 69.93 | 71.58 | 69.73 | 73.58 |
| Gelao | 64.33 | 63.06 | 65.69 | 66.16 | 64.72 | 67.79 |
| *Han* | *67.29* | *65.56* | *69.20* | *71.89* | *70.05* | *73.89* |
| Hani | 63.51 | 62.09 | 65.00 | 65.56 | 64.30 | 66.97 |
| Hezhe | 67.14 | 65.66 | 68.89 | 72.38 | 70.44 | 74.62 |
| Hui | 67.02 | 65.66 | 68.53 | 69.97 | 68.44 | 71.66 |
| Jing | 68.43 | 66.86 | 70.06 | 71.04 | 68.89 | 73.42 |
| Jingpo | 63.56 | 62.14 | 65.05 | 65.57 | 64.31 | 66.98 |
| Jino | 63.44 | 62.03 | 64.93 | 65.56 | 64.30 | 66.97 |
| Kazak | 62.61 | 61.97 | 63.28 | 67.42 | 65.99 | 69.14 |
| Kirgiz | 62.65 | 62.00 | 63.33 | 67.47 | 66.03 | 69.21 |
| Korean | 68.15 | 66.76 | 69.79 | 72.97 | 71.17 | 74.99 |
| Lahu | 63.50 | 62.09 | 65.00 | 65.58 | 64.32 | 66.99 |
| Lhoba | 59.93 | 57.98 | 61.82 | 64.89 | 63.06 | 66.69 |
| Li | 69.74 | 66.76 | 72.90 | 72.59 | 70.37 | 74.90 |
| Lisu | 63.62 | 62.21 | 65.11 | 65.73 | 64.45 | 67.16 |
| Manchu | 69.50 | 67.94 | 71.29 | 72.89 | 71.07 | 74.92 |
| Maonan | 67.46 | 65.99 | 69.02 | 69.76 | 67.78 | 71.97 |
| Miao | 61.74 | 60.41 | 63.20 | 68.01 | 66.45 | 69.76 |
| Monba | 60.00 | 58.02 | 61.92 | 64.78 | 62.93 | 66.57 |
| Mongol | 66.41 | 65.12 | 67.99 | 70.48 | 68.84 | 72.41 |
| Mulao | 68.17 | 66.63 | 69.79 | 70.62 | 68.51 | 72.96 |
| Naxi | 63.58 | 62.16 | 65.07 | 65.72 | 64.44 | 67.16 |
| Nu | 63.53 | 62.11 | 65.04 | 65.62 | 64.34 | 67.04 |
| Oroqen | 66.62 | 65.25 | 68.30 | 71.34 | 69.55 | 73.44 |

*Table 1.3* (*cont.*)

| Ethnic group | Life expectancy in 1990 | Male | Female | Life expectancy in 2000 | Male | Female |
|---|---|---|---|---|---|---|
| Pumi | 63.57 | 62.15 | 65.06 | 65.62 | 64.36 | 67.03 |
| Qiang | 66.26 | 64.99 | 67.63 | 71.17 | 69.23 | 73.36 |
| Russian | 64.23 | 63.30 | 65.31 | 68.75 | 67.23 | 70.56 |
| Salar | 61.51 | 60.29 | 62.84 | 66.34 | 64.95 | 67.92 |
| She | 68.95 | 66.98 | 71.18 | 72.27 | 70.27 | 74.49 |
| Shui | 64.56 | 63.27 | 65.93 | 66.31 | 64.85 | 67.96 |
| Tajik | 62.53 | 61.85 | 63.23 | 67.57 | 66.12 | 69.31 |
| Tatar | 62.95 | 62.26 | 63.69 | 67.61 | 66.19 | 69.32 |
| Tibetan | 62.18 | 60.61 | 63.79 | 66.67 | 64.98 | 68.43 |
| Tu | 62.01 | 60.74 | 63.40 | 66.60 | 65.19 | 68.19 |
| Tujia | 54.83 | 53.54 | 56.29 | 70.22 | 68.53 | 72.12 |
| Uygur | 62.62 | 61.97 | 63.30 | 67.44 | 66.01 | 69.17 |
| Uzbek | 62.74 | 62.08 | 63.45 | 67.51 | 66.07 | 69.25 |
| Va | 63.44 | 62.02 | 64.94 | 65.73 | 64.45 | 67.15 |
| Xibe | 68.53 | 67.19 | 70.06 | 72.12 | 70.37 | 74.10 |
| Yao | 68.08 | 66.45 | 69.83 | 70.78 | 68.79 | 72.98 |
| Yi | 64.38 | 63.03 | 65.83 | 67.18 | 65.71 | 68.83 |
| Yugur | 67.09 | 66.19 | 68.11 | 67.56 | 66.81 | 68.40 |
| Zhuang | 68.47 | 66.88 | 70.13 | 70.95 | 68.79 | 73.33 |

*Note:* Life expectancy in 2000 is calculated by the death data of 2000's Population Census, which is modified by the mortality rates from the annual national sample surveys on population changes since 1990.

*Table 1.4* Household, population, and household size

| Ethnic group | Number of households (households) | Family households | Collective households | Family household population (persons) | Average family size (persons/ household) |
|---|---|---|---|---|---|
| *National total* | *5,391,013* | *5,286,554* | *104,459* | *16,570,406* | *3.13* |
| Achang | 132 | 130 | 2 | 464 | 3.58 |
| Bai | 7,286 | 7,183 | 103 | 25,336 | 3.54 |
| Baonan | 62 | 61 | 1 | 225 | 3.66 |
| Blang | 356 | 351 | 5 | 1,255 | 3.58 |
| Buyi | 12,077 | 11,990 | 87 | 41,275 | 3.44 |
| Dai | 4,495 | 4,426 | 69 | 15,828 | 3.58 |
| Daur | 613 | 607 | 6 | 1,795 | 2.96 |
| Deang | 69 | 68 | 1 | 245 | 3.59 |
| Derung | 30 | 29 | 0 | 101 | 3.49 |

*Table 1.4 (cont.)*

| Ethnic group | Number of households (households) | Family households | Collective households | Family household population (persons) | Average family size (persons/household) |
|---|---|---|---|---|---|
| Dong | 12,189 | 12,073 | 117 | 40,270 | 3.34 |
| Dongxiang | 1,939 | 1,923 | 16 | 7,009 | 3.65 |
| Ewenki | 141 | 139 | 2 | 408 | 2.93 |
| Gaoshan | 19 | 19 | 0 | 60 | 3.21 |
| Gelao | 2,352 | 2,336 | 17 | 8,050 | 3.44 |
| *Han* | *4,954,698* | *4,855,207* | *99,492* | *15,133,860* | *3.14* |
| Hani | 5,581 | 5,495 | 86 | 19,664 | 3.58 |
| Hezhe | 22 | 21 | 0 | 64 | 2.99 |
| Hui | 40,854 | 40,355 | 499 | 135,542 | 3.38 |
| Jing | 94 | 92 | 1 | 313 | 3.38 |
| Jingpo | 512 | 504 | 8 | 1,805 | 3.58 |
| Jino | 81 | 80 | 1 | 285 | 3.58 |
| Kazak | 5,194 | 5,149 | 45 | 17,884 | 3.47 |
| Kirgiz | 669 | 663 | 6 | 2,299 | 3.46 |
| Korean | 8,480 | 8,420 | 61 | 25,815 | 3.07 |
| Lahu | 1,759 | 1,732 | 27 | 6,196 | 3.58 |
| Lhoba | 9 | 9 | 0 | 41 | 4.86 |
| Li | 4,718 | 4,614 | 105 | 17,598 | 3.81 |
| Lisu | 2,472 | 2,435 | 37 | 8,663 | 3.57 |
| Manchu | 47,767 | 47,344 | 424 | 143,023 | 3.03 |
| Maonan | 442 | 438 | 4 | 1,489 | 3.40 |
| Miao | 36,641 | 36,278 | 363 | 120,903 | 3.34 |
| Monba | 26 | 25 | 0 | 124 | 4.93 |
| Mongol | 26,507 | 26,190 | 317 | 77,863 | 2.98 |
| Mulao | 860 | 850 | 10 | 2,877 | 3.38 |
| Naxi | 1,201 | 1,183 | 18 | 4,214 | 3.57 |
| Nu | 111 | 110 | 2 | 393 | 3.60 |
| Oroqen | 38 | 38 | 0 | 111 | 2.95 |
| Pumi | 130 | 128 | 2 | 459 | 3.58 |
| Qiang | 1,368 | 1,360 | 9 | 4,013 | 2.96 |
| Russian | 68 | 67 | 1 | 217 | 3.25 |
| Salar | 421 | 414 | 7 | 1,513 | 3.66 |
| She | 3,278 | 3,150 | 128 | 9,431 | 3.01 |
| Shui | 1,653 | 1,641 | 12 | 5,654 | 3.44 |
| Tajik | 171 | 169 | 2 | 585 | 3.46 |
| Tatar | 20 | 20 | 0 | 70 | 3.46 |
| Tibetan | 19,258 | 19,072 | 186 | 74,837 | 4.10 |

Table 1.4  (cont.)

| Ethnic group | Number of households (households) | Family households | Collective households | Family household population (persons) | Average family size (persons/ household) |
|---|---|---|---|---|---|
| Tu | 972 | 955 | 17 | 3,468 | 3.64 |
| Tujia | 33,487 | 33,125 | 362 | 103,395 | 3.12 |
| Uygur | 34,900 | 34,598 | 302 | 120,103 | 3.47 |
| Uzbek | 51 | 51 | 0 | 177 | 3.47 |
| Va | 1,542 | 1,519 | 24 | 5,413 | 3.57 |
| Xibe | 849 | 842 | 7 | 2,546 | 3.03 |
| Yao | 10,912 | 10,727 | 186 | 35,738 | 3.33 |
| Yi | 31,527 | 31,162 | 366 | 105,058 | 3.39 |
| Yugur | 51 | 51 | 0 | 186 | 3.65 |
| Zhuang | 66,874 | 65,975 | 899 | 223,969 | 3.39 |

*Note:* Data in this table are obtained from the 2005 National Sample Survey of 1% of Population. The sampling fraction is 1.325%.

Table 1.5  Population and sex ratio

| Ethnic group | Population (persons) | Male | Female | Sex ratio (female=100) |
|---|---|---|---|---|
| *National total* | *16,985,766* | *8,584,882* | *8,400,884* | *102.19* |
| Achang | 472 | 243 | 228 | 106.52 |
| Bai | 25,759 | 13,273 | 12,486 | 106.29 |
| Baonan | 227 | 114 | 112 | 101.87 |
| Blang | 1,277 | 659 | 618 | 106.48 |
| Buyi | 41,601 | 21,407 | 20,194 | 106.01 |
| Dai | 16,110 | 8,308 | 7,802 | 106.49 |
| Daur | 1,817 | 925 | 892 | 103.74 |
| Deang | 249 | 129 | 121 | 106.53 |
| Derung | 103 | 53 | 50 | 105.70 |
| Dong | 40,744 | 20,933 | 19,811 | 105.65 |
| Dongxiang | 7,068 | 3,568 | 3,500 | 101.94 |
| Ewenki | 415 | 212 | 203 | 104.36 |
| Gaoshan | 61 | 31 | 30 | 103.04 |
| Gelao | 8,113 | 4,176 | 3,937 | 106.05 |
| *Han* | *15,530,212* | *7,842,038* | *7,688,176* | *102.01* |
| Hani | 20,015 | 10,323 | 9,691 | 106.52 |
| Hezhe | 65 | 33 | 32 | 102.45 |
| Hui | 137,359 | 69,429 | 67,929 | 102.22 |
| Jing | 316 | 164 | 153 | 107.30 |

*Table 1.5 (cont.)*

| Ethnic group | Population (persons) | Male | Female | Sex ratio (female=100) |
|---|---|---|---|---|
| Jingpo | 1,837 | 948 | 890 | 106.52 |
| Jino | 291 | 150 | 141 | 106.52 |
| Kazak | 18,004 | 9,124 | 8,879 | 102.76 |
| Kirgiz | 2,315 | 1,173 | 1,142 | 102.76 |
| Korean | 26,074 | 13,204 | 12,871 | 102.59 |
| Lahu | 6,307 | 3,253 | 3,054 | 106.50 |
| Lhoba | 41 | 21 | 21 | 98.48 |
| Li | 18,054 | 9,463 | 8,590 | 110.15 |
| Lisu | 8,814 | 4,542 | 4,272 | 106.30 |
| Manchu | 144,576 | 72,773 | 71,803 | 101.35 |
| Maonan | 1,506 | 778 | 727 | 107.08 |
| Miao | 122,370 | 62,807 | 59,562 | 105.41 |
| Monba | 125 | 62 | 63 | 98.18 |
| Mongol | 79,017 | 40,237 | 38,780 | 103.77 |
| Mulao | 2,915 | 1,508 | 1,407 | 107.21 |
| Naxi | 4,288 | 2,209 | 2,079 | 106.29 |
| Nu | 400 | 206 | 194 | 106.34 |
| Oroqen | 113 | 57 | 55 | 103.35 |
| Pumi | 467 | 241 | 226 | 106.46 |
| Qiang | 4,044 | 2,017 | 2,027 | 99.52 |
| Russian | 220 | 112 | 108 | 103.29 |
| Salar | 1,540 | 778 | 762 | 102.12 |
| She | 9,862 | 4,986 | 4,876 | 102.24 |
| Shui | 5,698 | 2,933 | 2,765 | 106.07 |
| Tajik | 590 | 299 | 291 | 102.76 |
| Tatar | 70 | 36 | 35 | 102.72 |
| Tibetan | 75,661 | 37,782 | 37,879 | 99.74 |
| Tu | 3,536 | 1,787 | 1,749 | 102.21 |
| Tujia | 104,905 | 53,482 | 51,424 | 103.95 |
| Uygur | 120,913 | 61,280 | 59,633 | 102.76 |
| Uzbek | 178 | 90 | 88 | 102.79 |
| Va | 5,509 | 2,840 | 2,669 | 106.39 |
| Xibe | 2,569 | 1,292 | 1,277 | 101.19 |
| Yao | 36,519 | 18,819 | 17,700 | 106.32 |
| Yi | 106,511 | 54,440 | 52,071 | 104.52 |
| Yugur | 188 | 95 | 93 | 101.88 |
| Zhuang | 227,460 | 117,743 | 109,718 | 107.32 |

*Note:* Data in this table are obtained from the 2005 National Sample Survey of 1% of Population. The sampling fraction is 1.325%.

*Table 1.6* Age composition of population

| Ethnic group | Population (persons) | Age 0–14 | Age 15–64 | Age 65 and over |
|---|---|---|---|---|
| *National total* | *16,985,766* | *3,321,029* | *12,123,681* | *1,541,056* |
| Achang | 472 | 114 | 323 | 36 |
| Bai | 25,759 | 6,207 | 17,543 | 2,009 |
| Baonan | 227 | 53 | 157 | 16 |
| Blang | 1,277 | 307 | 873 | 97 |
| Buyi | 41,601 | 11,614 | 26,561 | 3,426 |
| Dai | 16,110 | 3,876 | 11,016 | 1,218 |
| Daur | 1,817 | 301 | 1,375 | 142 |
| Deang | 249 | 60 | 171 | 19 |
| Derung | 103 | 24 | 71 | 8 |
| Dong | 40,744 | 10,048 | 27,066 | 3,630 |
| Dongxiang | 7,068 | 1,656 | 4,908 | 504 |
| Ewenki | 415 | 70 | 312 | 33 |
| Gaoshan | 61 | 12 | 44 | 5 |
| Gelao | 8,113 | 2,278 | 5,168 | 667 |
| *Han* | *15,530,212* | *2,997,457* | *11,113,711* | *1,419,045* |
| Hani | 2,0015 | 4,816 | 13,688 | 1,511 |
| Hezhe | 65 | 10 | 50 | 5 |
| Hui | 137,358 | 29,748 | 97,056 | 10,554 |
| Jing | 316 | 75 | 212 | 30 |
| Jingpo | 1,837 | 442 | 1,256 | 139 |
| Jino | 291 | 70 | 199 | 22 |
| Kazak | 18,004 | 4,237 | 12,599 | 1,168 |
| Kirgiz | 2,315 | 543 | 1,622 | 150 |
| Korean | 26,074 | 3,831 | 20,146 | 2,098 |
| Lahu | 6,307 | 1,517 | 4,314 | 476 |
| Lhoba | 41 | 11 | 28 | 3 |
| Li | 18,054 | 4,304 | 12,210 | 1,540 |
| Lisu | 8,814 | 2,114 | 6,026 | 673 |
| Manchu | 144,576 | 22,051 | 109,600 | 12,925 |
| Maonan | 1,506 | 376 | 992 | 137 |
| Miao | 122,370 | 30,046 | 81,535 | 10,788 |
| Monba | 125 | 34 | 83 | 8 |
| Mongol | 79,017 | 13,566 | 59,012 | 6,439 |
| Mulao | 2,915 | 706 | 1,937 | 272 |
| Naxi | 4,288 | 1,029 | 2,932 | 327 |
| Nu | 400 | 96 | 273 | 30 |
| Oroqen | 113 | 18 | 86 | 9 |
| Pumi | 467 | 112 | 320 | 35 |

*Table 1.6* (*cont.*)

| Ethnic group | Population (persons) | Age 0–14 | Age 15–64 | Age 65 and over |
|---|---|---|---|---|
| Qiang | 4,044 | 884 | 2,720 | 440 |
| Russian | 220 | 46 | 158 | 16 |
| Salar | 1,540 | 368 | 1,076 | 96 |
| She | 9,862 | 1,907 | 7,059 | 897 |
| Shui | 5,698 | 1,584 | 3,643 | 471 |
| Tajik | 590 | 138 | 413 | 39 |
| Tatar | 70 | 16 | 49 | 5 |
| Tibetan | 75,661 | 18,857 | 51,254 | 5,549 |
| Tu | 3,536 | 841 | 2,469 | 226 |
| Tujia | 104,905 | 21,984 | 72,868 | 10,053 |
| Uygur | 120,913 | 28,431 | 84,628 | 7,854 |
| Uzbek | 178 | 42 | 125 | 12 |
| Va | 5,509 | 1,319 | 3,772 | 418 |
| Xibe | 2,569 | 417 | 1,922 | 230 |
| Yao | 36,519 | 8,159 | 24,944 | 3,417 |
| Yi | 106,511 | 25,487 | 71,957 | 9,067 |
| Yugur | 188 | 44 | 131 | 14 |
| Zhuang | 227,460 | 53,783 | 152,463 | 21,214 |

*Note:* Data in this table are obtained from the 2005 National Sample Survey of 1% of Population. The sampling fraction is 1.325%.

*Table 1.7* Dependency ratio of population

| Ethnic group | Gross dependency ratio (%) | Children dependency ratio (%) | Old dependency ratio (%) |
|---|---|---|---|
| National total | 40.10 | 27.39 | 12.71 |
| Achang | 46.22 | 35.18 | 11.04 |
| Bai | 46.84 | 35.38 | 11.45 |
| Baonan | 44.04 | 33.73 | 10.31 |
| Blang | 46.20 | 35.14 | 11.05 |
| Buyi | 56.63 | 43.73 | 12.90 |
| Dai | 46.24 | 35.19 | 11.06 |
| Daur | 32.21 | 21.87 | 10.34 |
| Deang | 46.24 | 35.22 | 11.02 |
| Derung | 44.86 | 33.53 | 11.33 |
| Dong | 50.53 | 37.12 | 13.41 |
| Dongxiang | 44.01 | 33.74 | 10.27 |
| Ewenki | 33.06 | 22.46 | 10.59 |
| Gaoshan | 40.37 | 27.91 | 12.46 |

*Table 1.7* (cont.)

| Ethnic group | Gross dependency ratio (%) | Children dependency ratio (%) | Old dependency ratio (%) |
|---|---|---|---|
| Gelao | 56.99 | 44.07 | 12.91 |
| *Han* | *39.74* | *26.97* | *12.77* |
| Hani | 46.22 | 35.18 | 11.04 |
| Hezhe | 29.64 | 19.54 | 10.10 |
| Hui | 41.52 | 30.65 | 10.87 |
| Jing | 49.59 | 35.49 | 14.10 |
| Jingpo | 46.23 | 35.20 | 11.03 |
| Jino | 46.22 | 35.19 | 11.04 |
| Kazak | 42.90 | 33.63 | 9.27 |
| Kirgiz | 42.74 | 33.47 | 9.27 |
| Korean | 29.43 | 19.01 | 10.41 |
| Lahu | 46.20 | 35.16 | 11.04 |
| Lhoba | 49.62 | 40.06 | 9.56 |
| Li | 47.86 | 35.25 | 12.61 |
| Lisu | 46.25 | 35.08 | 11.17 |
| Manchu | 31.91 | 20.12 | 11.79 |
| Maonan | 51.83 | 37.96 | 13.86 |
| Miao | 50.08 | 36.85 | 13.23 |
| Monba | 49.66 | 40.17 | 9.49 |
| Mongol | 33.90 | 22.99 | 10.91 |
| Mulao | 50.45 | 36.42 | 14.02 |
| Naxi | 46.28 | 35.11 | 11.16 |
| Nu | 46.21 | 35.17 | 11.04 |
| Oroqen | 31.21 | 20.87 | 10.34 |
| Pumi | 46.17 | 35.11 | 11.06 |
| Qiang | 48.67 | 32.50 | 16.17 |
| Russian | 38.90 | 28.90 | 10.00 |
| Salar | 43.11 | 34.19 | 8.92 |
| She | 39.71 | 27.01 | 12.70 |
| Shui | 56.41 | 43.49 | 12.92 |
| Tajik | 42.85 | 33.46 | 9.39 |
| Tatar | 42.70 | 33.25 | 9.44 |
| Tibetan | 47.62 | 36.79 | 10.83 |
| Tu | 43.18 | 34.05 | 9.14 |
| Tujia | 43.97 | 30.17 | 13.80 |
| Uygur | 42.88 | 33.60 | 9.28 |
| Uzbek | 42.86 | 33.53 | 9.33 |
| Va | 46.06 | 34.97 | 11.10 |
| Xibe | 33.64 | 21.69 | 11.95 |
| Yao | 46.41 | 32.71 | 13.70 |

*Table 1.7 (cont.)*

| Ethnic group | Gross dependency ratio (%) | Children dependency ratio (%) | Old dependency ratio (%) |
|---|---|---|---|
| Yi | 48.02 | 35.42 | 12.60 |
| Yugur | 43.96 | 33.55 | 10.41 |
| Zhuang | 49.19 | 35.28 | 13.91 |

*Notes:* Data in this table are obtained from the 2005 National Sample Survey of 1% of Population. The sampling fraction is 1.325%. "Gross dependency ratio," also called gross dependency coefficient, refers to the ratio of non-working-age population to working-age population, expressed in percent. Describing in general the number of non-working-age people that every 100 people at working age will take care of, this indicator reflects the basic relation between population and economic development from the demographic perspective. The gross dependency ratio is calculated with the following formula:

$$GDR = \frac{P_{0-14} + P_{65+}}{P_{15-64}} \times 100\%,$$ where: GDR is the gross dependency ratio, $P_{0-14}$ is the population

of children aged 0–14, $P_{65+}$ is the elderly population aged 65 and over, and $P_{15-64}$ is the working-age population aged 15–64. "Old dependency ratio," also called old dependency coefficient, refers to the ratio of the elderly population to the working-age population, expressed in percent. It describes the number of elderly people that every 100 people at working age will take care of. Old dependency ratio is one of the indicators reflecting the social implication of population aging from the economic perspective. The old dependency

ratio is calculated with the following formula: $ODR = \frac{P_{65+}}{P_{15-64}} \times 100\%$, where: ODR is the old

dependency ratio, $P_{65+}$ is the elderly population aged 65 and over, and $P_{15-64}$ is the working-age population aged 15–64. "Children dependency ratio," also called children dependency coefficient, refers to the ratio of the child population to the working-age population, expressed in percent. It describes the number of children that every 100 people at working age will take care of. The children dependency ratio is calculated with the following formula:

$$CDR = \frac{P_{0-14}}{P_{15-64}} \times 100\%,$$ where: CDR is the children dependency ratio, $P_{0-14}$ is the child

population aged 0–14, and $P_{15-64}$ is the working-age population aged 15–64.

*Table 1.8* Population by sex and marital status

| Ethnic group | Population aged 15 and over | Male | Female |
|---|---|---|---|
| National total | 13,664,737 | 6,786,677 | 6,878,061 |
| Achang | 358 | 183 | 175 |
| Bai | 19,552 | 9,969 | 9,584 |
| Baonan | 174 | 86 | 87 |
| Blang | 970 | 496 | 474 |
| Buyi | 29,987 | 15,149 | 14,839 |
| Dai | 12,234 | 6,253 | 5,981 |

*Table 1.8 (cont.)*

| Ethnic group | Population aged 15 and over | Male | Female |
|---|---|---|---|
| Daur | 1,517 | 768 | 748 |
| Deang | 189 | 97 | 93 |
| Derung | 79 | 40 | 39 |
| Dong | 30,697 | 15,479 | 15,218 |
| Dongxiang | 5,412 | 2,691 | 2,721 |
| Ewenki | 345 | 175 | 170 |
| Gaoshan | 49 | 24 | 25 |
| Gelao | 5,835 | 2,948 | 2,887 |
| *Han* | *12,532,754* | *6,216,809* | *6,315,945* |
| Hani | 15,199 | 7,770 | 7,429 |
| Hezhe | 55 | 28 | 27 |
| Hui | 107,611 | 53,665 | 53,945 |
| Jing | 241 | 122 | 119 |
| Jingpo | 1,395 | 713 | 682 |
| Jino | 221 | 113 | 108 |
| Kazak | 13,767 | 6,954 | 6,812 |
| Kirgiz | 1,772 | 895 | 877 |
| Korean | 22,244 | 11,188 | 11,055 |
| Lahu | 4,790 | 2,448 | 2,342 |
| Lhoba | 30 | 15 | 15 |
| Li | 13,750 | 7,066 | 6,683 |
| Lisu | 6,700 | 3,421 | 3,279 |
| Manchu | 122,525 | 61,121 | 61,404 |
| Maonan | 1,129 | 572 | 557 |
| Miao | 92,323 | 46,568 | 45,755 |
| Monba | 91 | 45 | 47 |
| Mongol | 65,450 | 33,117 | 32,334 |
| Mulao | 2,209 | 1,120 | 1,089 |
| Naxi | 3,259 | 1,664 | 1,595 |
| Nu | 304 | 155 | 149 |
| Oroqen | 95 | 48 | 47 |
| Pumi | 355 | 181 | 174 |
| Qiang | 3,160 | 1,547 | 1,612 |
| Russian | 174 | 88 | 86 |
| Salar | 1,172 | 586 | 585 |
| She | 7,955 | 3,947 | 4,009 |
| Shui | 4,113 | 2,079 | 2,035 |
| Tajik | 451 | 228 | 224 |
| Tatar | 54 | 27 | 27 |

*Table 1.8* (*cont.*)

| Ethnic group | Population aged 15 and over | Male | Female |
|---|---|---|---|
| Tibetan | 56,804 | 28,027 | 28,777 |
| Tu | 2,695 | 1,348 | 1,347 |
| Tujia | 82,921 | 41,500 | 41,422 |
| Uygur | 92,482 | 46,715 | 45,767 |
| Uzbek | 136 | 69 | 67 |
| Va | 4,190 | 2,140 | 2,050 |
| Xibe | 2,152 | 1,074 | 1,078 |
| Yao | 28,360 | 14,334 | 14,026 |
| Yi | 81,024 | 40,891 | 40,133 |
| Yugur | 144 | 72 | 73 |
| Zhuang | 173,677 | 88,108 | 85,569 |

| Ethnic group | Never married | Male | Female |
|---|---|---|---|
| National total | 2,619,360 | 1,524,886 | 1,094,474 |
| Achang | 69 | 44 | 25 |
| Bai | 3,739 | 2,360 | 1,379 |
| Baonan | 34 | 20 | 14 |
| Blang | 186 | 118 | 68 |
| Buyi | 5,415 | 3,387 | 2,028 |
| Dai | 2,343 | 1,488 | 855 |
| Daur | 254 | 152 | 102 |
| Deang | 36 | 23 | 13 |
| Derung | 15 | 9 | 6 |
| Dong | 5,925 | 3,645 | 2,280 |
| Dongxiang | 1,054 | 616 | 438 |
| Ewenki | 58 | 35 | 23 |
| Gaoshan | 10 | 6 | 4 |
| Gelao | 1,054 | 660 | 395 |
| Han | 2,395,186 | 1,389,492 | 1,005,694 |
| Hani | 2,913 | 1,850 | 1,063 |
| Hezhe | 9 | 5 | 4 |
| Hui | 20,558 | 11,946 | 8,612 |
| Jing | 55 | 34 | 21 |
| Jingpo | 268 | 170 | 98 |
| Jino | 42 | 27 | 15 |
| Kazak | 2,945 | 1,761 | 1,184 |
| Kirgiz | 378 | 226 | 152 |
| Korean | 3,844 | 2,223 | 1,621 |

*Table 1.8* (cont.)

| Ethnic group | Never married | Male | Female |
|---|---|---|---|
| Lahu | 918 | 583 | 335 |
| Lhoba | 10 | 6 | 5 |
| Li | 3,539 | 2,158 | 1,381 |
| Lisu | 1,276 | 810 | 466 |
| Manchu | 21,003 | 12,026 | 8,977 |
| Maonan | 244 | 152 | 92 |
| Miao | 17,375 | 10,748 | 6,627 |
| Monba | 31 | 17 | 14 |
| Mongol | 11,212 | 6,694 | 4,518 |
| Mulao | 494 | 308 | 187 |
| Naxi | 623 | 395 | 228 |
| Nu | 59 | 37 | 22 |
| Oroqen | 16 | 9 | 6 |
| Pumi | 68 | 43 | 25 |
| Qiang | 472 | 290 | 182 |
| Russian | 34 | 20 | 14 |
| Salar | 227 | 133 | 93 |
| She | 1,587 | 922 | 666 |
| Shui | 748 | 469 | 280 |
| Tajik | 96 | 58 | 39 |
| Tatar | 11 | 7 | 5 |
| Tibetan | 14,314 | 8,063 | 6,251 |
| Tu | 523 | 308 | 215 |
| Tujia | 15,145 | 9,217 | 5,928 |
| Uygur | 19,785 | 11,831 | 7,954 |
| Uzbek | 29 | 17 | 12 |
| Va | 802 | 508 | 294 |
| Xibe | 364 | 211 | 153 |
| Yao | 6,342 | 3,873 | 2,469 |
| Yi | 14,489 | 9,122 | 5,367 |
| Yugur | 28 | 16 | 12 |
| Zhuang | 39,762 | 24,702 | 15,060 |

| Ethnic group | First married | Male | Female |
|---|---|---|---|
| National total | 9,824,784 | 4,801,807 | 5,022,977 |
| Achang | 257 | 126 | 130 |
| Bai | 13,988 | 6,882 | 7,106 |
| Baonan | 125 | 60 | 64 |
| Blang | 695 | 342 | 353 |

*Table 1.8* (*cont.*)

| Ethnic group | First married | Male | Female |
|---|---|---|---|
| Buyi | 21,512 | 10,480 | 11,032 |
| Dai | 8,765 | 4,318 | 4,446 |
| Daur | 1,128 | 562 | 566 |
| Deang | 136 | 67 | 69 |
| Derung | 57 | 28 | 29 |
| Dong | 21,747 | 10,617 | 11,130 |
| Dongxiang | 3,845 | 1,866 | 1,978 |
| Ewenki | 259 | 129 | 129 |
| Gaoshan | 35 | 17 | 18 |
| Gelao | 4,184 | 2,038 | 2,146 |
| *Han* | *9,031,477* | *4,413,234* | *4,618,244* |
| Hani | 10,889 | 5,366 | 5,524 |
| Hezhe | 41 | 20 | 21 |
| Hui | 77,108 | 37,762 | 39,346 |
| Jing | 165 | 81 | 85 |
| Jingpo | 999 | 492 | 507 |
| Jino | 158 | 78 | 80 |
| Kazak | 8,522 | 4,144 | 4,378 |
| Kirgiz | 1,099 | 535 | 564 |
| Korean | 16,342 | 8,122 | 8,220 |
| Lahu | 3,432 | 1,691 | 1,741 |
| Lhoba | 17 | 8 | 9 |
| Li | 9,235 | 4,569 | 4,666 |
| Lisu | 4,803 | 2,365 | 2,438 |
| Manchu | 90,191 | 44,601 | 45,590 |
| Maonan | 782 | 381 | 401 |
| Miao | 65,765 | 32,124 | 33,641 |
| Monba | 51 | 25 | 26 |
| Mongol | 48,638 | 24,207 | 24,432 |
| Mulao | 1,517 | 739 | 779 |
| Naxi | 2,334 | 1,149 | 1,185 |
| Nu | 217 | 107 | 110 |
| Oroqen | 71 | 35 | 36 |
| Pumi | 254 | 125 | 129 |
| Qiang | 2,309 | 1,110 | 1,199 |
| Russian | 117 | 58 | 59 |
| Salar | 817 | 401 | 416 |
| She | 5,686 | 2,791 | 2,895 |
| Shui | 2,947 | 1,436 | 1,511 |
| Tajik | 281 | 137 | 144 |

*Table 1.8* (cont.)

| Ethnic group | First married | Male | Female |
|---|---|---|---|
| Tatar | 34 | 16 | 17 |
| Tibetan | 36,489 | 17,749 | 18,741 |
| Tu | 1,886 | 926 | 960 |
| Tujia | 59,408 | 28,979 | 30,428 |
| Uygur | 57,267 | 27,851 | 29,416 |
| Uzbek | 85 | 41 | 43 |
| Va | 3,003 | 1,479 | 1,524 |
| Xibe | 1,549 | 765 | 785 |
| Yao | 19,500 | 9,527 | 9,973 |
| Yi | 58,381 | 28,537 | 29,844 |
| Yugur | 104 | 50 | 53 |
| Zhuang | 118,774 | 57,874 | 60,901 |

| Ethnic group | Re-married | Male | Female |
|---|---|---|---|
| *National total* | *301,209* | *138,947* | *162,262* |
| Achang | 9 | 4 | 4 |
| Bai | 486 | 245 | 241 |
| Baonan | 4 | 2 | 2 |
| Blang | 24 | 12 | 12 |
| Buyi | 820 | 424 | 396 |
| Dai | 302 | 153 | 149 |
| Daur | 43 | 21 | 23 |
| Deang | 5 | 2 | 2 |
| Derung | 2 | 1 | 1 |
| Dong | 754 | 374 | 380 |
| Dongxiang | 148 | 75 | 73 |
| Ewenki | 8 | 4 | 5 |
| Gaoshan | 1 | 0 | 1 |
| Gelao | 160 | 83 | 77 |
| *Han* | *266,268* | *121,279* | *144,990* |
| Hani | 375 | 190 | 185 |
| Hezhe | 2 | 1 | 1 |
| Hui | 3,097 | 1,559 | 1,539 |
| Jing | 4 | 2 | 2 |
| Jingpo | 34 | 17 | 17 |
| Jino | 5 | 3 | 3 |
| Kazak | 1,324 | 727 | 597 |
| Kirgiz | 169 | 93 | 76 |
| Korean | 603 | 287 | 316 |

*Table 1.8* (cont.)

| Ethnic group | Re-married | Male | Female |
|---|---|---|---|
| Lahu | 118 | 60 | 58 |
| Lhoba | 0 | 0 | 0 |
| Li | 192 | 101 | 91 |
| Lisu | 166 | 84 | 83 |
| Manchu | 3,182 | 1,489 | 1,693 |
| Maonan | 21 | 11 | 10 |
| Miao | 2,354 | 1,160 | 1,194 |
| Monba | 1 | 1 | 1 |
| Mongol | 1,714 | 787 | 926 |
| Mulao | 37 | 18 | 18 |
| Naxi | 81 | 41 | 40 |
| Nu | 7 | 4 | 4 |
| Oroqen | 3 | 1 | 1 |
| Pumi | 9 | 4 | 4 |
| Qiang | 98 | 42 | 56 |
| Russian | 11 | 6 | 5 |
| Salar | 43 | 22 | 21 |
| She | 147 | 66 | 80 |
| Shui | 111 | 58 | 54 |
| Tajik | 42 | 23 | 19 |
| Tatar | 5 | 3 | 2 |
| Tibetan | 1,334 | 654 | 680 |
| Tu | 91 | 47 | 44 |
| Tujia | 2,140 | 993 | 1,147 |
| Uygur | 8,881 | 4,878 | 4,003 |
| Uzbek | 13 | 7 | 6 |
| Va | 103 | 52 | 51 |
| Xibe | 86 | 43 | 42 |
| Yao | 502 | 242 | 260 |
| Yi | 2,165 | 1,047 | 1,118 |
| Yugur | 3 | 1 | 2 |
| Zhuang | 2,697 | 1,337 | 1,360 |

| Ethnic group | Divorced | Male | Female |
|---|---|---|---|
| *National total* | *135,625* | *81,486* | *54,139* |
| Achang | 3 | 2 | 1 |
| Bai | 191 | 114 | 77 |
| Baonan | 2 | 1 | 1 |
| Blang | 9 | 5 | 4 |
| Buyi | 323 | 205 | 118 |

*Table 1.8 (cont.)*

| Ethnic group | Divorced | Male | Female |
|---|---|---|---|
| Dai | 118 | 69 | 49 |
| Daur | 22 | 13 | 9 |
| Deang | 2 | 1 | 1 |
| Derung | 1 | 0 | 0 |
| Dong | 309 | 197 | 112 |
| Dongxiang | 60 | 35 | 25 |
| Ewenki | 4 | 3 | 2 |
| Gaoshan | 0 | 0 | 0 |
| Gelao | 63 | 40 | 23 |
| *Han* | *120,896* | *73,281* | *47,615* |
| Hani | 146 | 86 | 60 |
| Hezhe | 1 | 1 | 0 |
| Hui | 1,316 | 716 | 600 |
| Jing | 2 | 1 | 1 |
| Jingpo | 13 | 8 | 6 |
| Jino | 2 | 1 | 1 |
| Kazak | 382 | 182 | 200 |
| Kirgiz | 49 | 23 | 26 |
| Korean | 369 | 215 | 155 |
| Lahu | 46 | 27 | 19 |
| Lhoba | 1 | 0 | 0 |
| Li | 94 | 60 | 34 |
| Lisu | 65 | 38 | 27 |
| Manchu | 1,957 | 1,093 | 864 |
| Maonan | 10 | 6 | 4 |
| Miao | 960 | 602 | 358 |
| Monba | 2 | 0 | 1 |
| Mongol | 857 | 497 | 360 |
| Mulao | 19 | 12 | 7 |
| Naxi | 32 | 19 | 13 |
| Nu | 3 | 2 | 1 |
| Oroqen | 1 | 1 | 1 |
| Pumi | 3 | 2 | 1 |
| Qiang | 38 | 23 | 15 |
| Russian | 4 | 2 | 2 |
| Salar | 23 | 11 | 12 |
| She | 68 | 44 | 25 |
| Shui | 44 | 28 | 16 |
| Tajik | 12 | 6 | 6 |
| Tatar | 1 | 1 | 1 |

*Table 1.8* (*cont.*)

| Ethnic group | Divorced | Male | Female |
|---|---|---|---|
| Tibetan | 941 | 367 | 575 |
| Tu | 49 | 24 | 25 |
| Tujia | 875 | 543 | 332 |
| Uygur | 2,565 | 1,223 | 1,343 |
| Uzbek | 4 | 2 | 2 |
| Va | 40 | 24 | 17 |
| Xibe | 44 | 23 | 21 |
| Yao | 242 | 154 | 88 |
| Yi | 844 | 503 | 341 |
| Yugur | 1 | 1 | 1 |
| Zhuang | 1,411 | 899 | 512 |

| Ethnic group | Widowed | Male | Female |
|---|---|---|---|
| *National total* | *783,760* | *239,551* | *544,209* |
| Achang | 21 | 7 | 14 |
| Bai | 1,149 | 368 | 781 |
| Baonan | 10 | 3 | 7 |
| Blang | 56 | 18 | 38 |
| Buyi | 1,917 | 652 | 1,266 |
| Dai | 706 | 224 | 482 |
| Daur | 69 | 21 | 48 |
| Deang | 11 | 3 | 7 |
| Derung | 5 | 1 | 3 |
| Dong | 1,961 | 645 | 1,316 |
| Dongxiang | 305 | 99 | 206 |
| Ewenki | 15 | 5 | 11 |
| Gaoshan | 3 | 1 | 2 |
| Gelao | 374 | 127 | 247 |
| *Han* | *718,923* | *219,526* | *499,397* |
| Hani | 876 | 278 | 598 |
| Hezhe | 3 | 1 | 2 |
| Hui | 5,531 | 1,683 | 3,848 |
| Jing | 15 | 5 | 11 |
| Jingpo | 80 | 26 | 55 |
| Jino | 13 | 4 | 9 |
| Kazak | 593 | 139 | 454 |
| Kirgiz | 76 | 18 | 58 |
| Korean | 1,086 | 342 | 744 |
| Lahu | 276 | 88 | 188 |

*Table 1.8* (cont.)

| Ethnic group | Widowed | Male | Female |
|---|---|---|---|
| Lhoba | 2 | 1 | 1 |
| Li | 690 | 178 | 512 |
| Lisu | 389 | 124 | 265 |
| Manchu | 6,192 | 1,912 | 4,280 |
| Maonan | 73 | 23 | 50 |
| Miao | 5,869 | 1,934 | 3,935 |
| Monba | 6 | 2 | 4 |
| Mongol | 3,030 | 932 | 2,098 |
| Mulao | 142 | 43 | 99 |
| Naxi | 189 | 60 | 129 |
| Nu | 18 | 6 | 12 |
| Oroqen | 4 | 1 | 3 |
| Pumi | 20 | 6 | 14 |
| Qiang | 242 | 82 | 160 |
| Russian | 8 | 2 | 6 |
| Salar | 63 | 19 | 44 |
| She | 467 | 124 | 343 |
| Shui | 263 | 89 | 174 |
| Tajik | 20 | 5 | 15 |
| Tatar | 2 | 1 | 2 |
| Tibetan | 3,724 | 1,195 | 2,529 |
| Tu | 146 | 44 | 102 |
| Tujia | 5,353 | 1,768 | 3,586 |
| Uygur | 3,984 | 933 | 3,051 |
| Uzbek | 6 | 1 | 5 |
| Va | 242 | 77 | 165 |
| Xibe | 109 | 32 | 77 |
| Yao | 1,774 | 539 | 1,235 |
| Yi | 5,145 | 1,682 | 3,463 |
| Yugur | 8 | 3 | 6 |
| Zhuang | 11,033 | 3,296 | 7,737 |

*Note:* Data in this table are obtained from the 2005 National Sample Survey of 1% of Population. The sampling fraction is 1.325%.

*Table 1.9* Population by sex and educational attainment

| Ethnic group | Population aged 6 and over | Male | Female |
|---|---|---|---|
| *National total* | *15,878,355* | *7,975,386* | *7,902,969* |
| Achang | 430 | 221 | 209 |
| Bai | 23,521 | 12,070 | 11,451 |
| Baonan | 211 | 106 | 105 |
| Blang | 1,165 | 599 | 566 |
| Buyi | 37,830 | 19,318 | 18,512 |
| Dai | 14,695 | 7,554 | 7,141 |
| Daur | 1,719 | 874 | 845 |
| Deang | 227 | 117 | 110 |
| Derung | 94 | 48 | 46 |
| Dong | 37,346 | 19,041 | 18,305 |
| Dongxiang | 6,575 | 3,302 | 3,273 |
| Ewenki | 392 | 200 | 192 |
| Gaoshan | 57 | 29 | 28 |
| Gelao | 7,375 | 3,766 | 3,609 |
| *Han* | *14,534,128* | *7,292,674* | *7,241,454* |
| Hani | 18,255 | 9,385 | 8,870 |
| Hezhe | 61 | 31 | 30 |
| Hui | 127,223 | 63,969 | 63,254 |
| Jing | 290 | 149 | 141 |
| Jingpo | 1,676 | 862 | 814 |
| Jino | 265 | 136 | 129 |
| Kazak | 16,522 | 8,364 | 8,157 |
| Kirgiz | 2,125 | 1,076 | 1,049 |
| Korean | 24,791 | 12,524 | 12,267 |
| Lahu | 5,752 | 2,957 | 2,795 |
| Lhoba | 37 | 19 | 19 |
| Li | 16,684 | 8,680 | 8,003 |
| Lisu | 8,044 | 4,131 | 3,913 |
| Manchu | 137,009 | 68,734 | 68,276 |
| Maonan | 1,375 | 706 | 668 |
| Miao | 112,243 | 57,206 | 55,037 |
| Monba | 113 | 56 | 57 |
| Mongol | 74,547 | 37,887 | 36,661 |
| Mulao | 2,666 | 1,371 | 1,295 |
| Naxi | 3,913 | 2,010 | 1,904 |
| Nu | 365 | 187 | 177 |
| Oroqen | 107 | 54 | 53 |

*Table 1.9* (*cont.*)

| Ethnic group | Population aged 6 and over | Male | Female |
| --- | --- | --- | --- |
| Pumi | 426 | 219 | 207 |
| Qiang | 3,769 | 1,869 | 1,900 |
| Russian | 204 | 104 | 101 |
| Salar | 1,413 | 711 | 702 |
| She | 9,210 | 4,628 | 4,582 |
| Shui | 5,181 | 2,647 | 2,534 |
| Tajik | 541 | 274 | 267 |
| Tatar | 65 | 33 | 32 |
| Tibetan | 69,111 | 34,377 | 34,735 |
| Tu | 3,249 | 1,634 | 1,614 |
| Tujia | 97,745 | 49,484 | 48,260 |
| Uygur | 110,967 | 56,177 | 54,789 |
| Uzbek | 163 | 83 | 81 |
| Va | 5,027 | 2,583 | 2,444 |
| Xibe | 2,429 | 1,219 | 1,210 |
| Yao | 33,599 | 17,203 | 16,396 |
| Yi | 97,680 | 49,700 | 47,980 |
| Yugur | 175 | 88 | 87 |
| Zhuang | 208,216 | 107,165 | 101,051 |

| Ethnic group | No schooling | Male | Female |
| --- | --- | --- | --- |
| *National total* | *1,646,360* | *450,088* | *1,196,272* |
| Achang | 77 | 24 | 53 |
| Bai | 4,057 | 1,256 | 2,801 |
| Baonan | 39 | 12 | 26 |
| Blang | 208 | 66 | 142 |
| Buyi | 6,893 | 1,839 | 5,054 |
| Dai | 2,630 | 833 | 1,797 |
| Daur | 153 | 47 | 106 |
| Deang | 41 | 13 | 28 |
| Derung | 15 | 5 | 11 |
| Dong | 5,229 | 1,381 | 3,848 |
| Dongxiang | 1,138 | 359 | 779 |
| Ewenki | 39 | 12 | 27 |
| Gaoshan | 6 | 1 | 4 |
| Gelao | 1,349 | 359 | 990 |
| *Han* | *1,478,395* | *39,9512* | *1,078,883* |
| Hani | 3,270 | 1,036 | 2,234 |

*Table 1.9* (cont.)

| Ethnic group | No schooling | Male | Female |
|---|---|---|---|
| Hezhe | 4 | 1 | 3 |
| Hui | 16,918 | 5,137 | 11,781 |
| Jing | 25 | 6 | 19 |
| Jingpo | 300 | 95 | 205 |
| Jino | 47 | 15 | 32 |
| Kazak | 1,340 | 522 | 818 |
| Kirgiz | 171 | 67 | 105 |
| Korean | 1,510 | 452 | 1,058 |
| Lahu | 1,029 | 326 | 703 |
| Lhoba | 16 | 6 | 10 |
| Li | 1,512 | 362 | 1,150 |
| Lisu | 1,433 | 453 | 980 |
| Manchu | 8,117 | 2,227 | 5,890 |
| Maonan | 153 | 39 | 114 |
| Miao | 16,512 | 4,517 | 11,995 |
| Monba | 49 | 20 | 30 |
| Mongol | 7,262 | 2,193 | 5,069 |
| Mulao | 253 | 63 | 189 |
| Naxi | 701 | 222 | 479 |
| Nu | 66 | 21 | 45 |
| Oroqen | 9 | 3 | 6 |
| Pumi | 76 | 24 | 52 |
| Qiang | 559 | 166 | 393 |
| Russian | 18 | 6 | 12 |
| Salar | 304 | 99 | 205 |
| She | 1,084 | 255 | 829 |
| Shui | 931 | 249 | 682 |
| Tajik | 44 | 17 | 27 |
| Tatar | 5 | 2 | 3 |
| Tibetan | 21,018 | 7,813 | 13,205 |
| Tu | 686 | 222 | 464 |
| Tujia | 11,050 | 2,928 | 8,122 |
| Uygur | 8,976 | 3,494 | 5,482 |
| Uzbek | 13 | 5 | 8 |
| Va | 892 | 282 | 610 |
| Xibe | 139 | 42 | 98 |
| Yao | 2,955 | 768 | 2,187 |
| Yi | 16,724 | 5,120 | 11,603 |
| Yugur | 32 | 10 | 22 |
| Zhuang | 18,153 | 4,618 | 13,535 |

*Table 1.9* (cont.)

| Ethnic group | Primary school | Male | Female |
| --- | --- | --- | --- |
| *National total* | *5,285,045* | *2,581,633* | *2,703,412* |
| Achang | 204 | 109 | 96 |
| Bai | 10,847 | 5,748 | 5,099 |
| Baonan | 78 | 39 | 39 |
| Blang | 552 | 294 | 259 |
| Buyi | 16,767 | 8,904 | 7,863 |
| Dai | 6,975 | 3,710 | 3,265 |
| Daur | 491 | 237 | 253 |
| Deang | 108 | 57 | 51 |
| Derung | 42 | 22 | 20 |
| Dong | 15,078 | 7,807 | 7,271 |
| Dongxiang | 2,418 | 1,207 | 1,212 |
| Ewenki | 110 | 54 | 57 |
| Gaoshan | 19 | 9 | 10 |
| Gelao | 3,274 | 1,739 | 1,534 |
| *Han* | *4,779,772* | *2,325,120* | *2,454,653* |
| Hani | 8,667 | 4,610 | 4,057 |
| Hezhe | 18 | 8 | 9 |
| Hui | 42,177 | 20,992 | 21,185 |
| Jing | 115 | 57 | 58 |
| Jingpo | 795 | 423 | 372 |
| Jino | 126 | 67 | 59 |
| Kazak | 5,772 | 2,849 | 2,924 |
| Kirgiz | 741 | 366 | 375 |
| Korean | 7,314 | 3,499 | 3,816 |
| Lahu | 2,728 | 1,451 | 1,277 |
| Lhoba | 16 | 9 | 7 |
| Li | 5,262 | 2,570 | 2,692 |
| Lisu | 3,807 | 2,023 | 1,784 |
| Manchu | 38,548 | 18,353 | 20,195 |
| Maonan | 564 | 286 | 278 |
| Miao | 46,595 | 24,244 | 22,351 |
| Monba | 48 | 27 | 21 |
| Mongol | 21,405 | 10,430 | 10,975 |
| Mulao | 1,070 | 536 | 534 |
| Naxi | 1,852 | 984 | 867 |
| Nu | 172 | 92 | 81 |
| Oroqen | 30 | 15 | 16 |
| Pumi | 202 | 107 | 94 |

*Table 1.9* (cont.)

| Ethnic group | Primary school | Male | Female |
| --- | --- | --- | --- |
| Qiang | 1,629 | 839 | 789 |
| Russian | 65 | 32 | 33 |
| Salar | 488 | 257 | 232 |
| She | 3,405 | 1,663 | 1,742 |
| Shui | 2,294 | 1,217 | 1,078 |
| Tajik | 189 | 93 | 96 |
| Tatar | 22 | 11 | 11 |
| Tibetan | 28,108 | 15,276 | 12,832 |
| Tu | 1,131 | 593 | 538 |
| Tujia | 35,855 | 18,044 | 17,812 |
| Uygur | 38,748 | 19,119 | 19,629 |
| Uzbek | 57 | 28 | 29 |
| Va | 2,369 | 1,258 | 1,111 |
| Xibe | 701 | 336 | 365 |
| Yao | 12,841 | 6,398 | 6,443 |
| Yi | 44,903 | 23,692 | 21,211 |
| Yugur | 64 | 32 | 32 |
| Zhuang | 83,247 | 41,477 | 41,771 |

| Ethnic group | Junior secondary school | Male | Female |
| --- | --- | --- | --- |
| *National total* | *6,088,659* | *3,316,912* | *2,771,747* |
| Achang | 107 | 65 | 43 |
| Bai | 6,152 | 3,664 | 2,487 |
| Baonan | 61 | 35 | 26 |
| Blang | 290 | 175 | 115 |
| Buyi | 10,266 | 6,231 | 4,035 |
| Dai | 3,654 | 2,202 | 1,452 |
| Daur | 689 | 379 | 310 |
| Deang | 56 | 34 | 22 |
| Derung | 26 | 15 | 11 |
| Dong | 12,046 | 6,907 | 5,139 |
| Dongxiang | 1,959 | 1,112 | 847 |
| Ewenki | 152 | 85 | 67 |
| Gaoshan | 23 | 12 | 10 |
| Gelao | 1,996 | 1,213 | 783 |
| *Han* | *5,629,861* | *3,060,481* | *2,569,379* |
| Hani | 4,536 | 2,734 | 1,801 |
| Hezhe | 26 | 14 | 12 |

*Table 1.9* (*cont.*)

| Ethnic group | Junior secondary school | Male | Female |
|---|---|---|---|
| Hui | 44,563 | 24,713 | 19,850 |
| Jing | 109 | 61 | 47 |
| Jingpo | 417 | 251 | 166 |
| Jino | 66 | 40 | 26 |
| Kazak | 5,949 | 3,197 | 2,752 |
| Kirgiz | 767 | 412 | 355 |
| Korean | 10,546 | 5,632 | 4,914 |
| Lahu | 1,433 | 863 | 570 |
| Lhoba | 4 | 2 | 2 |
| Li | 6,677 | 3,728 | 2,949 |
| Lisu | 2,014 | 1,210 | 805 |
| Manchu | 60,769 | 32,264 | 28,505 |
| Maonan | 479 | 275 | 204 |
| Miao | 34,723 | 19,992 | 14,731 |
| Monba | 11 | 6 | 5 |
| Mongol | 29,199 | 16,128 | 13,071 |
| Mulao | 977 | 555 | 422 |
| Naxi | 977 | 587 | 390 |
| Nu | 90 | 54 | 36 |
| Oroqen | 44 | 24 | 20 |
| Pumi | 106 | 64 | 42 |
| Qiang | 1,154 | 624 | 530 |
| Russian | 75 | 41 | 34 |
| Salar | 368 | 216 | 152 |
| She | 3,176 | 1,802 | 1,374 |
| Shui | 1,418 | 859 | 559 |
| Tajik | 195 | 105 | 90 |
| Tatar | 23 | 12 | 11 |
| Tibetan | 13,442 | 7,651 | 5,791 |
| Tu | 859 | 503 | 356 |
| Tujia | 34,825 | 19,179 | 15,646 |
| Uygur | 39,995 | 21,490 | 18,506 |
| Uzbek | 59 | 32 | 27 |
| Va | 1,267 | 761 | 506 |
| Xibe | 1,054 | 557 | 497 |
| Yao | 12,632 | 7,008 | 5,624 |
| Yi | 26,049 | 15,212 | 10,837 |
| Yugur | 51 | 29 | 22 |
| Zhuang | 77,685 | 43,884 | 33,801 |

*Table 1.9 (cont.)*

| Ethnic group | Senior secondary school | Male | Female |
| --- | --- | --- | --- |
| *National total* | *1,975,098* | *1,120,964* | *854,134* |
| Achang | 27 | 15 | 12 |
| Bai | 1,642 | 932 | 711 |
| Baonan | 24 | 14 | 10 |
| Blang | 75 | 42 | 33 |
| Buyi | 2,613 | 1,555 | 1,058 |
| Dai | 936 | 527 | 410 |
| Daur | 257 | 139 | 118 |
| Deang | 14 | 8 | 6 |
| Derung | 7 | 4 | 3 |
| Dong | 3,547 | 2,077 | 1,470 |
| Dongxiang | 745 | 439 | 305 |
| Ewenki | 60 | 33 | 27 |
| Gaoshan | 7 | 4 | 3 |
| Gelao | 507 | 302 | 205 |
| *Han* | *1,833,693* | *1,041,422* | *792,271* |
| Hani | 1,163 | 654 | 509 |
| Hezhe | 9 | 5 | 4 |
| Hui | 15,364 | 8,536 | 6,827 |
| Jing | 29 | 17 | 12 |
| Jingpo | 107 | 60 | 47 |
| Jino | 17 | 9 | 7 |
| Kazak | 2,016 | 1,055 | 961 |
| Kirgiz | 260 | 136 | 124 |
| Korean | 3,673 | 1,985 | 1,689 |
| Lahu | 367 | 207 | 161 |
| Lhoba | 2 | 1 | 1 |
| Li | 2,339 | 1,490 | 849 |
| Lisu | 516 | 290 | 226 |
| Manchu | 19,120 | 10,227 | 8,892 |
| Maonan | 125 | 75 | 50 |
| Miao | 10,107 | 5,878 | 4,229 |
| Monba | 3 | 2 | 1 |
| Mongol | 10,917 | 5,932 | 4,985 |
| Mulao | 259 | 155 | 104 |
| Naxi | 251 | 141 | 110 |
| Nu | 23 | 13 | 10 |
| Oroqen | 16 | 9 | 7 |

*Table 1.9*  (*cont.*)

| Ethnic group | Senior secondary school | Male | Female |
|---|---|---|---|
| Pumi | 27 | 15 | 12 |
| Qiang | 294 | 164 | 130 |
| Russian | 28 | 15 | 13 |
| Salar | 156 | 84 | 71 |
| She | 1,091 | 636 | 454 |
| Shui | 360 | 214 | 146 |
| Tajik | 66 | 35 | 31 |
| Tatar | 8 | 4 | 4 |
| Tibetan | 4,320 | 2,375 | 1,946 |
| Tu | 357 | 195 | 162 |
| Tujia | 11,578 | 6,677 | 4,901 |
| Uygur | 13,551 | 7,094 | 6,457 |
| Uzbek | 20 | 10 | 10 |
| Va | 327 | 184 | 143 |
| Xibe | 331 | 175 | 156 |
| Yao | 3,746 | 2,201 | 1,545 |
| Yi | 6,655 | 3,759 | 2,896 |
| Yugur | 20 | 12 | 8 |
| Zhuang | 20,696 | 12,344 | 8,352 |

| Ethnic group | College and higher level | Male | Female |
|---|---|---|---|
| *National total* | *883,192* | *505,789* | *377,404* |
| Achang | 15 | 8 | 6 |
| Bai | 823 | 471 | 352 |
| Baonan | 10 | 6 | 4 |
| Blang | 40 | 22 | 17 |
| Buyi | 1,290 | 788 | 502 |
| Dai | 499 | 282 | 217 |
| Daur | 130 | 72 | 58 |
| Deang | 8 | 4 | 3 |
| Derung | 4 | 2 | 2 |
| Dong | 1,446 | 869 | 577 |
| Dongxiang | 315 | 186 | 129 |
| Ewenki | 31 | 17 | 14 |
| Gaoshan | 3 | 2 | 1 |
| Gelao | 250 | 153 | 97 |

*Table 1.9* (cont.)

| Ethnic group | College and higher level | Male | Female |
|---|---|---|---|
| *Han* | *812,404* | *466,133* | *346,271* |
| Hani | 620 | 350 | 270 |
| Hezhe | 4 | 2 | 2 |
| Hui | 8,201 | 4,590 | 3,611 |
| Jing | 12 | 7 | 5 |
| Jingpo | 57 | 32 | 25 |
| Jino | 9 | 5 | 4 |
| Kazak | 1,444 | 742 | 702 |
| Kirgiz | 185 | 95 | 90 |
| Korean | 1,747 | 957 | 790 |
| Lahu | 195 | 110 | 85 |
| Lhoba | 1 | 0 | 0 |
| Li | 895 | 531 | 364 |
| Lisu | 273 | 154 | 119 |
| Manchu | 10,456 | 5,662 | 4,794 |
| Maonan | 53 | 31 | 22 |
| Miao | 4,306 | 2,575 | 1,732 |
| Monba | 1 | 1 | 1 |
| Mongol | 5,764 | 3,204 | 2,561 |
| Mulao | 107 | 62 | 45 |
| Naxi | 133 | 75 | 58 |
| Nu | 12 | 7 | 5 |
| Oroqen | 8 | 4 | 3 |
| Pumi | 15 | 8 | 6 |
| Qiang | 133 | 76 | 57 |
| Russian | 17 | 9 | 8 |
| Salar | 98 | 55 | 43 |
| She | 455 | 271 | 183 |
| Shui | 177 | 108 | 69 |
| Tajik | 47 | 24 | 23 |
| Tatar | 6 | 3 | 3 |
| Tibetan | 2,224 | 1,262 | 962 |
| Tu | 216 | 122 | 94 |
| Tujia | 4,436 | 2,657 | 1,779 |
| Uygur | 9,696 | 4,981 | 4,715 |
| Uzbek | 14 | 7 | 7 |
| Va | 172 | 97 | 75 |
| Xibe | 203 | 109 | 94 |

*Table 1.9* (*cont.*)

| Ethnic group | College and higher level | Male | Female |
|---|---|---|---|
| Yao | 1,426 | 827 | 598 |
| Yi | 3,349 | 1,917 | 1,432 |
| Yugur | 8 | 5 | 3 |
| Zhuang | 8,435 | 4,842 | 3,592 |

*Note:* Data in this table are obtained from the 2005 National Sample Survey of 1% of Population. The sampling fraction is 1.325%.

*Table 1.10* Illiterate population aged 15 and over by sex

| Ethnic group | Population aged 15 and over | Male | Female |
|---|---|---|---|
| National total | 13,664,737 | 6,786,677 | 6,878,061 |
| Achang | 358 | 183 | 175 |
| Bai | 19,552 | 9,969 | 9,584 |
| Baonan | 174 | 86 | 87 |
| Blang | 970 | 496 | 474 |
| Buyi | 29,987 | 15,149 | 14,839 |
| Dai | 12,234 | 6,253 | 5,981 |
| Daur | 1,517 | 768 | 748 |
| Deang | 189 | 97 | 93 |
| Derung | 79 | 40 | 39 |
| Dong | 30,697 | 15,479 | 15,218 |
| Dongxiang | 5,412 | 2,691 | 2,721 |
| Ewenki | 345 | 175 | 170 |
| Gaoshan | 49 | 24 | 25 |
| Gelao | 5,835 | 2,948 | 2,887 |
| *Han* | *12,532,754* | *6,216,809* | *6,315,945* |
| Hani | 15,199 | 7,770 | 7,429 |
| Hezhe | 55 | 28 | 27 |
| Hui | 107,611 | 53,665 | 53,945 |
| Jing | 241 | 122 | 119 |
| Jingpo | 1,395 | 713 | 682 |
| Jino | 221 | 113 | 108 |
| Kazak | 13,767 | 6,954 | 6,812 |
| Kirgiz | 1,772 | 895 | 877 |
| Korean | 22,244 | 11,188 | 11,055 |

*Table 1.10 (cont.)*

| Ethnic group | Population aged 15 and over | Male | Female |
|---|---|---|---|
| Lahu | 4,790 | 2,448 | 2,342 |
| Lhoba | 30 | 15 | 15 |
| Li | 13,750 | 7,066 | 6,683 |
| Lisu | 6,700 | 3,421 | 3,279 |
| Manchu | 122,525 | 61,121 | 61,404 |
| Maonan | 1,129 | 572 | 557 |
| Miao | 92,323 | 46,568 | 45,755 |
| Monba | 91 | 45 | 47 |
| Mongol | 65,450 | 33,117 | 32,334 |
| Mulao | 2,209 | 1,120 | 1,089 |
| Naxi | 3,259 | 1,664 | 1,595 |
| Nu | 304 | 155 | 149 |
| Oroqen | 95 | 48 | 47 |
| Pumi | 355 | 181 | 174 |
| Qiang | 3,160 | 1,547 | 1,612 |
| Russian | 174 | 88 | 86 |
| Salar | 1,172 | 586 | 585 |
| She | 7,955 | 3,947 | 4,009 |
| Shui | 4,113 | 2,079 | 2,035 |
| Tajik | 451 | 228 | 224 |
| Tatar | 54 | 27 | 27 |
| Tibetan | 56,804 | 28,027 | 28,777 |
| Tu | 2,695 | 1,348 | 1,347 |
| Tujia | 82,921 | 41,500 | 41,422 |
| Uygur | 92,482 | 46,715 | 45,767 |
| Uzbek | 136 | 69 | 67 |
| Va | 4,190 | 2,140 | 2,050 |
| Xibe | 2,152 | 1,074 | 1,078 |
| Yao | 28,360 | 14,334 | 14,026 |
| Yi | 81,024 | 40,891 | 40,133 |
| Yugur | 144 | 72 | 73 |
| Zhuang | 173,677 | 88,108 | 85,569 |

| Ethnic group | Illiterate population | Male | Female |
|---|---|---|---|
| *National total* | *1,508,706* | *397,877* | *1,110,828* |
| Achang | 72 | 22 | 49 |
| Bai | 3,757 | 1,128 | 2,629 |

*Table 1.10* (cont.)

| Ethnic group | Illiterate population | Male | Female |
|---|---|---|---|
| Baonan | 36 | 11 | 25 |
| Blang | 193 | 60 | 134 |
| Buyi | 6,261 | 1,592 | 4,670 |
| Dai | 2,442 | 752 | 1,690 |
| Daur | 140 | 41 | 99 |
| Deang | 38 | 12 | 26 |
| Derung | 14 | 4 | 10 |
| Dong | 4,761 | 1,199 | 3,562 |
| Dongxiang | 1,050 | 322 | 728 |
| Ewenki | 37 | 11 | 26 |
| Gaoshan | 5 | 1 | 4 |
| Gelao | 1,225 | 310 | 914 |
| *Han* | *1,357,235* | *354,481* | *1,002,754* |
| Hani | 3,037 | 935 | 2,102 |
| Hezhe | 4 | 1 | 3 |
| Hui | 15,554 | 4,585 | 10,970 |
| Jing | 22 | 5 | 17 |
| Jingpo | 278 | 86 | 193 |
| Jino | 44 | 14 | 30 |
| Kazak | 1,151 | 433 | 719 |
| Kirgiz | 147 | 55 | 92 |
| Korean | 1,345 | 387 | 958 |
| Lahu | 956 | 294 | 661 |
| Lhoba | 13 | 5 | 8 |
| Li | 1,406 | 314 | 1,093 |
| Lisu | 1,331 | 409 | 922 |
| Manchu | 7,340 | 1,942 | 5,398 |
| Maonan | 138 | 33 | 105 |
| Miao | 15,090 | 3,957 | 11,133 |
| Monba | 39 | 14 | 25 |
| Mongol | 6,719 | 1,969 | 4,750 |
| Mulao | 227 | 52 | 174 |
| Naxi | 650 | 200 | 450 |
| Nu | 61 | 19 | 42 |
| Oroqen | 8 | 2 | 6 |
| Pumi | 71 | 22 | 49 |
| Qiang | 523 | 152 | 372 |
| Russian | 16 | 5 | 11 |
| Salar | 269 | 84 | 185 |
| She | 1,002 | 224 | 778 |

*Table 1.10* (*cont.*)

| Ethnic group | Illiterate population | Male | Female |
| --- | --- | --- | --- |
| Shui | 846 | 215 | 631 |
| Tajik | 38 | 14 | 24 |
| Tatar | 5 | 2 | 3 |
| Tibetan | 17,525 | 6,006 | 11,519 |
| Tu | 609 | 188 | 420 |
| Tujia | 10,200 | 2,611 | 7,589 |
| Uygur | 7,712 | 2,897 | 4,815 |
| Uzbek | 11 | 4 | 7 |
| Va | 829 | 255 | 574 |
| Xibe | 124 | 35 | 88 |
| Yao | 2,675 | 653 | 2,022 |
| Yi | 15,516 | 4,612 | 10,904 |
| Yugur | 29 | 9 | 20 |
| Zhuang | 16,306 | 3,831 | 12,475 |

| Ethnic group | % to total aged 15 and over | Male | Female |
| --- | --- | --- | --- |
| *National total* | *11.04* | *5.86* | *16.15* |
| Achang | 19.96 | 12.02 | 28.26 |
| Bai | 19.22 | 11.32 | 27.43 |
| Baonan | 20.48 | 12.57 | 28.30 |
| Blang | 19.93 | 12.00 | 28.22 |
| Buyi | 20.88 | 10.51 | 31.47 |
| Dai | 19.96 | 12.02 | 28.26 |
| Daur | 9.24 | 5.39 | 13.20 |
| Deang | 20.01 | 12.06 | 28.33 |
| Derung | 18.07 | 10.78 | 25.61 |
| Dong | 15.51 | 7.75 | 23.40 |
| Dongxiang | 19.40 | 11.96 | 26.75 |
| Ewenki | 10.60 | 6.14 | 15.21 |
| Gaoshan | 10.36 | 5.33 | 15.36 |
| Gelao | 20.99 | 10.52 | 31.67 |
| *Han* | *10.83* | *5.70* | *15.88* |
| Hani | 19.98 | 12.03 | 28.29 |
| Hezhe | 6.54 | 3.67 | 9.44 |
| Hui | 14.45 | 8.54 | 20.33 |
| Jing | 9.28 | 4.20 | 14.51 |
| Jingpo | 19.95 | 12.01 | 28.25 |

*Table 1.10* (*cont.*)

| Ethnic group | % to total aged 15 and over | Male | Female |
|---|---|---|---|
| Jino | 19.98 | 12.03 | 28.28 |
| Kazak | 8.36 | 6.22 | 10.55 |
| Kirgiz | 8.31 | 6.18 | 10.49 |
| Korean | 6.05 | 3.46 | 8.66 |
| Lahu | 19.95 | 12.02 | 28.24 |
| Lhoba | 41.72 | 30.83 | 52.22 |
| Li | 10.23 | 4.44 | 16.35 |
| Lisu | 19.87 | 11.97 | 28.11 |
| Manchu | 5.99 | 3.18 | 8.79 |
| Maonan | 12.19 | 5.72 | 18.84 |
| Miao | 16.35 | 8.50 | 24.33 |
| Monba | 43.00 | 31.96 | 53.63 |
| Mongol | 10.27 | 5.95 | 14.69 |
| Mulao | 10.26 | 4.68 | 16.00 |
| Naxi | 19.96 | 12.04 | 28.21 |
| Nu | 20.21 | 12.24 | 28.53 |
| Oroqen | 8.46 | 4.84 | 12.17 |
| Pumi | 19.92 | 12.00 | 28.19 |
| Qiang | 16.56 | 9.80 | 23.05 |
| Russian | 9.36 | 6.18 | 12.61 |
| Salar | 22.97 | 14.31 | 31.64 |
| She | 12.60 | 5.68 | 19.41 |
| Shui | 20.56 | 10.35 | 30.99 |
| Tajik | 8.42 | 6.19 | 10.69 |
| Tatar | 8.85 | 6.40 | 11.35 |
| Tibetan | 30.85 | 21.43 | 40.03 |
| Tu | 22.58 | 13.95 | 31.22 |
| Tujia | 12.30 | 6.29 | 18.32 |
| Uygur | 8.34 | 6.20 | 10.52 |
| Uzbek | 8.35 | 6.17 | 10.58 |
| Va | 19.77 | 11.90 | 28.00 |
| Xibe | 5.75 | 3.30 | 8.19 |
| Yao | 9.43 | 4.55 | 14.42 |
| Yi | 19.15 | 11.28 | 27.17 |
| Yugur | 20.30 | 12.41 | 28.09 |
| Zhuang | 9.39 | 4.35 | 14.58 |

*Notes:* Data in this table are obtained from the 2005 National Sample Survey of 1% of Population. The sampling fraction is 1.325%. "Illiterate population" in this table refers to the population aged 15 and over who are unable or find it very difficult to read.

*Table 1.11* Family households by size

| Ethnic group | Number of family households | One person | Two persons | Three persons | Four persons | ≥Five persons |
|---|---|---|---|---|---|---|
| *National total* | 5,286,554 | 567,455 | 1,294,464 | 1,577,147 | 1,014,177 | 833,311 |
| Achang | 130 | 10 | 21 | 31 | 35 | 32 |
| Bai | 7,183 | 601 | 1,260 | 1,747 | 1,884 | 1,691 |
| Baonan | 61 | 4 | 10 | 16 | 14 | 17 |
| Blang | 351 | 28 | 58 | 83 | 96 | 86 |
| Buyi | 11,990 | 1,036 | 2,454 | 3,080 | 2,695 | 2,725 |
| Dai | 4,426 | 357 | 731 | 1,051 | 1,207 | 1,080 |
| Daur | 607 | 49 | 166 | 236 | 94 | 61 |
| Deang | 68 | 5 | 11 | 16 | 19 | 17 |
| Derung | 29 | 2 | 5 | 7 | 7 | 6 |
| Dong | 12,073 | 1,175 | 2,621 | 3,190 | 2,634 | 2,454 |
| Dongxiang | 1,923 | 130 | 328 | 505 | 443 | 516 |
| Ewenki | 139 | 12 | 38 | 54 | 22 | 13 |
| Gaoshan | 19 | 2 | 4 | 6 | 4 | 3 |
| Gelao | 2,336 | 201 | 478 | 599 | 525 | 533 |
| *Han* | 4,855,207 | 526,992 | 1,200,682 | 1,454,458 | 924,977 | 748,099 |
| Hani | 5,495 | 442 | 905 | 1,305 | 1,501 | 1,343 |
| Hezhe | 21 | 2 | 6 | 8 | 3 | 2 |
| Hui | 40,355 | 3,406 | 8,499 | 11,867 | 8,474 | 8,110 |
| Jing | 92 | 10 | 19 | 23 | 20 | 20 |
| Jingpo | 504 | 41 | 83 | 120 | 138 | 123 |
| Jino | 80 | 6 | 13 | 19 | 22 | 19 |
| Kazak | 5,149 | 428 | 1,017 | 1,499 | 1,021 | 1,183 |
| Kirgiz | 663 | 55 | 132 | 194 | 131 | 151 |
| Korean | 8,420 | 578 | 2,177 | 3,255 | 1,342 | 1,067 |
| Lahu | 1,732 | 139 | 286 | 412 | 473 | 423 |
| Lhoba | 9 | 1 | 1 | 1 | 2 | 4 |
| Li | 4,614 | 433 | 722 | 988 | 971 | 1,499 |
| Lisu | 2,435 | 200 | 410 | 582 | 657 | 586 |
| Manchu | 47,344 | 3,901 | 12,703 | 17,240 | 7,724 | 5,777 |
| Maonan | 438 | 46 | 90 | 109 | 96 | 97 |
| Miao | 36,278 | 3,550 | 7,838 | 9,574 | 7,982 | 7,334 |
| Monba | 25 | 2 | 3 | 4 | 5 | 13 |
| Mongol | 26,190 | 2,249 | 7,058 | 9,875 | 4,266 | 2,741 |
| Mulao | 850 | 93 | 175 | 211 | 185 | 186 |
| Naxi | 1,183 | 97 | 199 | 283 | 319 | 286 |
| Nu | 110 | 9 | 18 | 26 | 30 | 27 |

Table 1.11 *(cont.)*

| Ethnic group | Number of family households | One person | Two persons | Three persons | Four persons | ≥Five persons |
|---|---|---|---|---|---|---|
| Oroqen | 38 | 3 | 10 | 15 | 6 | 4 |
| Pumi | 128 | 10 | 21 | 31 | 35 | 31 |
| Qiang | 1,360 | 191 | 372 | 385 | 229 | 183 |
| Russian | 67 | 6 | 16 | 22 | 12 | 11 |
| Salar | 414 | 32 | 68 | 111 | 94 | 109 |
| She | 3,150 | 461 | 804 | 874 | 564 | 447 |
| Shui | 1,641 | 142 | 334 | 420 | 370 | 374 |
| Tajik | 169 | 14 | 34 | 49 | 33 | 38 |
| Tatar | 20 | 2 | 4 | 6 | 4 | 5 |
| Tibetan | 19,072 | 1,665 | 3,301 | 4,360 | 3,719 | 6,027 |
| Tu | 955 | 75 | 159 | 255 | 217 | 248 |
| Tujia | 33,125 | 3,637 | 8,241 | 9,540 | 6,550 | 5,157 |
| Uygur | 34,598 | 2,884 | 6,845 | 10,077 | 6,859 | 7,933 |
| Uzbek | 51 | 4 | 10 | 15 | 10 | 12 |
| Va | 1,519 | 123 | 254 | 364 | 411 | 367 |
| Xibe | 842 | 72 | 228 | 307 | 128 | 107 |
| Yao | 10,727 | 1,189 | 2,273 | 2,728 | 2,339 | 2,198 |
| Yi | 31,162 | 3,099 | 6,309 | 7,904 | 7,343 | 6,507 |
| Yugur | 51 | 3 | 9 | 13 | 12 | 14 |
| Zhuang | 65,975 | 7,291 | 13,350 | 16,235 | 14,556 | 14,543 |

*Note:* Data in this table are obtained from the 2005 National Sample Survey of 1% of Population. The sampling fraction is 1.325%.

Table 1.12 Singletons aged 0–30

| Ethnic group | Singletons aged 0–30 | | | As percentage of the same age (%) | | |
|---|---|---|---|---|---|---|
| | Total | Male | Female | Total | Male | Female |
| *National total* | *2,098,947* | *1,188,145* | *910,801* | *29.30* | *32.02* | *26.38* |
| Achang | 37 | 19 | 18 | 16.06 | 15.86 | 16.28 |
| Bai | 2,106 | 1,110 | 996 | 16.97 | 17.05 | 16.87 |
| Baonan | 20 | 11 | 9 | 19.86 | 21.26 | 18.39 |
| Blang | 101 | 52 | 48 | 16.15 | 15.96 | 16.36 |
| Buyi | 3,392 | 1,852 | 1,540 | 16.79 | 17.37 | 16.14 |
| Dai | 1,267 | 656 | 611 | 16.12 | 15.92 | 16.34 |
| Daur | 290 | 160 | 130 | 40.20 | 43.21 | 37.01 |

*Table 1.12* (cont.)

| Ethnic group | Singletons aged 0–30 | | | As percentage of the same age (%) | | |
|---|---|---|---|---|---|---|
| | *Total* | *Male* | *Female* | *Total* | *Male* | *Female* |
| Deang | 20 | 10 | 9 | 16.01 | 15.79 | 16.25 |
| Derung | 9 | 5 | 4 | 18.71 | 19.00 | 18.40 |
| Dong | 3,779 | 2,122 | 1,658 | 20.22 | 21.52 | 18.76 |
| Dongxiang | 641 | 351 | 290 | 19.83 | 21.18 | 18.42 |
| Ewenki | 64 | 35 | 28 | 38.26 | 41.13 | 35.22 |
| Gaoshan | 7 | 4 | 3 | 27.49 | 29.73 | 25.06 |
| Gelao | 657 | 359 | 298 | 16.64 | 17.21 | 16.02 |
| *Han* | *1,942,306* | *1,102,233* | *840,072* | *29.87* | *32.74* | *26.78* |
| Hani | 1,570 | 813 | 758 | 16.07 | 15.87 | 16.29 |
| Hezhe | 11 | 6 | 5 | 46.91 | 50.63 | 42.99 |
| Hui | 15,237 | 8,364 | 6,873 | 24.32 | 26.01 | 22.55 |
| Jing | 26 | 15 | 12 | 17.94 | 18.66 | 17.11 |
| Jingpo | 144 | 75 | 69 | 16.05 | 15.85 | 16.27 |
| Jino | 23 | 12 | 11 | 16.09 | 15.88 | 16.32 |
| Kazak | 1,921 | 991 | 930 | 21.06 | 21.43 | 20.67 |
| Kirgiz | 249 | 129 | 120 | 21.26 | 21.66 | 20.85 |
| Korean | 4,602 | 2,595 | 2,008 | 47.10 | 51.71 | 42.24 |
| Lahu | 495 | 257 | 239 | 16.10 | 15.90 | 16.31 |
| Lhoba | 3 | 2 | 2 | 14.62 | 14.22 | 15.03 |
| Li | 1,467 | 799 | 668 | 16.24 | 16.43 | 16.02 |
| Lisu | 708 | 367 | 341 | 16.55 | 16.39 | 16.72 |
| Manchu | 23,525 | 13,340 | 10,185 | 43.25 | 47.96 | 38.33 |
| Maonan | 123 | 68 | 55 | 17.35 | 18.00 | 16.60 |
| Miao | 11,637 | 6,463 | 5,174 | 20.76 | 21.90 | 19.48 |
| Monba | 10 | 5 | 5 | 14.48 | 13.98 | 15.00 |
| Mongol | 11,928 | 6,629 | 5,298 | 37.49 | 40.50 | 34.30 |
| Mulao | 240 | 133 | 107 | 17.63 | 18.33 | 16.83 |
| Naxi | 345 | 179 | 166 | 16.54 | 16.37 | 16.72 |
| Nu | 32 | 16 | 15 | 16.15 | 15.97 | 16.34 |
| Oroqen | 19 | 10 | 8 | 42.73 | 46.07 | 39.20 |
| Pumi | 37 | 19 | 18 | 16.21 | 16.03 | 16.41 |
| Qiang | 587 | 316 | 271 | 37.32 | 39.41 | 35.16 |
| Russian | 28 | 15 | 13 | 27.02 | 28.33 | 25.66 |
| Salar | 166 | 86 | 80 | 21.96 | 22.42 | 21.50 |
| She | 1,109 | 664 | 445 | 25.93 | 30.12 | 21.47 |
| Shui | 463 | 253 | 211 | 16.76 | 17.31 | 16.14 |
| Tajik | 63 | 33 | 31 | 21.28 | 21.72 | 20.83 |
| Tatar | 8 | 4 | 4 | 21.44 | 21.92 | 20.94 |

*Table 1.12* (*cont.*)

| Ethnic group | Singletons aged 0–30 | | | As percentage of the same age (%) | | |
|---|---|---|---|---|---|---|
| | Total | Male | Female | Total | Male | Female |
| Tibetan | 7,651 | 3,939 | 3,711 | 20.21 | 20.46 | 19.95 |
| Tu | 377 | 196 | 181 | 21.86 | 22.40 | 21.31 |
| Tujia | 12,594 | 7,164 | 5,430 | 29.16 | 31.64 | 26.43 |
| Uygur | 12,919 | 6,669 | 6,251 | 21.09 | 21.47 | 20.70 |
| Uzbek | 19 | 10 | 9 | 21.12 | 21.51 | 20.71 |
| Va | 438 | 228 | 210 | 16.36 | 16.24 | 16.50 |
| Xibe | 422 | 238 | 184 | 42.73 | 47.29 | 37.99 |
| Yao | 3,312 | 1,863 | 1,449 | 19.96 | 21.18 | 18.59 |
| Yi | 10,286 | 5,437 | 4,849 | 20.93 | 21.21 | 20.61 |
| Yugur | 17 | 9 | 8 | 19.94 | 21.40 | 18.40 |
| Zhuang | 18,608 | 10,303 | 8,305 | 17.53 | 18.17 | 16.79 |

*Note:* Data in this table are obtained from the 2005 National Sample Survey of 1% of Population. The sampling fraction is 1.325%.

*Table 1.13* Number of households by sources of housing

| Ethnic group | Total number of households | Self-built house | Purchasing commercial building | Purchasing economically affordable housing |
|---|---|---|---|---|
| *National total* | 5,277,716 | 3,644,340 | 367,737 | 152,584 |
| Achang | 129 | 103 | 3 | 3 |
| Bai | 7,169 | 5,686 | 164 | 175 |
| Baonan | 61 | 45 | 3 | 3 |
| Blang | 350 | 280 | 7 | 8 |
| Buyi | 11,974 | 9,208 | 346 | 334 |
| Dai | 4,419 | 3,529 | 92 | 107 |
| Daur | 606 | 301 | 86 | 31 |
| Deang | 68 | 55 | 1 | 2 |
| Derung | 29 | 22 | 1 | 1 |
| Dong | 12,041 | 9,292 | 371 | 293 |
| Dongxiang | 1,920 | 1,381 | 100 | 88 |
| Ewenki | 139 | 71 | 19 | 5 |
| Gaoshan | 19 | 13 | 1 | 1 |
| Gelao | 2,333 | 1,794 | 67 | 65 |
| *Han* | 4,847,163 | 3,345,231 | 341,843 | 137,493 |
| Hani | 5,486 | 4,382 | 114 | 133 |

*Table 1.13* (cont.)

| Ethnic group | Total number of households | Self-built house | Purchasing commercial building | Purchasing economically affordable housing |
|---|---|---|---|---|
| Hezhe | 21 | 10 | 3 | 1 |
| Hui | 40,304 | 26,678 | 3,081 | 1,654 |
| Jing | 92 | 73 | 2 | 2 |
| Jingpo | 504 | 402 | 10 | 12 |
| Jino | 80 | 64 | 2 | 2 |
| Kazak | 5,146 | 2,833 | 329 | 450 |
| Kirgiz | 663 | 364 | 43 | 58 |
| Korean | 8,413 | 4,377 | 1,173 | 572 |
| Lahu | 1,729 | 1,382 | 36 | 42 |
| Lhoba | 9 | 7 | 0 | 0 |
| Li | 4,608 | 3,060 | 130 | 192 |
| Lisu | 2,431 | 1,941 | 53 | 59 |
| Manchu | 47,312 | 25,524 | 6,773 | 2,060 |
| Maonan | 437 | 345 | 11 | 8 |
| Miao | 36,191 | 27,806 | 1,214 | 918 |
| Monba | 25 | 21 | 0 | 0 |
| Mongol | 26,152 | 13,772 | 3,499 | 1,026 |
| Mulao | 848 | 669 | 22 | 15 |
| Naxi | 1,181 | 942 | 26 | 28 |
| Nu | 109 | 87 | 2 | 3 |
| Oroqen | 38 | 19 | 6 | 2 |
| Pumi | 128 | 102 | 3 | 3 |
| Qiang | 1,355 | 1,063 | 66 | 25 |
| Russian | 67 | 36 | 6 | 4 |
| Salar | 413 | 262 | 28 | 22 |
| She | 3,145 | 2,033 | 213 | 57 |
| Shui | 1,639 | 1,264 | 46 | 45 |
| Tajik | 169 | 94 | 11 | 14 |
| Tatar | 20 | 11 | 1 | 2 |
| Tibetan | 18,972 | 14,548 | 731 | 502 |
| Tu | 953 | 611 | 64 | 48 |
| Tujia | 33,030 | 24,501 | 1,515 | 849 |
| Uygur | 34,575 | 19,045 | 2,211 | 3,018 |
| Uzbek | 51 | 28 | 3 | 4 |
| Va | 1,516 | 1,210 | 33 | 37 |
| Xibe | 841 | 416 | 130 | 42 |
| Yao | 10,696 | 8,331 | 330 | 193 |

*Table 1.13* (cont.)

| Ethnic group | Total number of households | Self-built house | Purchasing commercial building | Purchasing economically affordable housing |
|---|---|---|---|---|
| Yi | 31,095 | 24,602 | 941 | 715 |
| Yugur | 51 | 37 | 3 | 2 |
| Zhuang | 65,844 | 52,103 | 1,685 | 1,074 |

| Ethnic group | Purchasing former public-owned building | Renting public-owned building | Renting commercial building | Others |
|---|---|---|---|---|
| *National total* | *461,939* | *172,499* | *301,799* | *176,818* |
| Achang | 7 | 4 | 3 | 6 |
| Bai | 398 | 199 | 192 | 355 |
| Baonan | 6 | 2 | 1 | 1 |
| Blang | 19 | 10 | 9 | 17 |
| Buyi | 620 | 330 | 441 | 695 |
| Dai | 239 | 122 | 109 | 220 |
| Daur | 106 | 17 | 45 | 20 |
| Deang | 4 | 2 | 2 | 3 |
| Derung | 2 | 1 | 1 | 1 |
| Dong | 720 | 347 | 435 | 582 |
| Dongxiang | 207 | 55 | 47 | 42 |
| Ewenki | 23 | 4 | 12 | 5 |
| Gaoshan | 2 | 1 | 1 | 1 |
| Gelao | 120 | 65 | 85 | 136 |
| *Han* | *420,947* | *157,436* | *283,849* | *160,364* |
| Hani | 297 | 152 | 135 | 273 |
| Hezhe | 4 | 1 | 1 | 1 |
| Hui | 4,515 | 1,482 | 1,764 | 1,131 |
| Jing | 6 | 3 | 3 | 3 |
| Jingpo | 27 | 14 | 12 | 25 |
| Jino | 4 | 2 | 2 | 4 |
| Kazak | 916 | 206 | 237 | 176 |
| Kirgiz | 118 | 26 | 31 | 23 |
| Korean | 1,272 | 323 | 442 | 254 |
| Lahu | 94 | 48 | 42 | 86 |
| Lhoba | 0 | 0 | 0 | 0 |
| Li | 429 | 281 | 224 | 292 |
| Lisu | 132 | 67 | 60 | 119 |

*Table 1.13* (*cont.*)

| Ethnic group | Purchasing former public-owned building | Renting public-owned building | Renting commercial building | Others |
|---|---|---|---|---|
| Manchu | 7,085 | 2,190 | 2,673 | 1,007 |
| Maonan | 25 | 15 | 14 | 19 |
| Miao | 2,141 | 1,052 | 1,286 | 1,774 |
| Monba | 1 | 1 | 1 | 1 |
| Mongol | 4,177 | 788 | 2,074 | 817 |
| Mulao | 51 | 30 | 28 | 33 |
| Naxi | 64 | 33 | 30 | 58 |
| Nu | 6 | 3 | 3 | 5 |
| Oroqen | 7 | 1 | 3 | 1 |
| Pumi | 7 | 4 | 3 | 6 |
| Qiang | 82 | 33 | 42 | 43 |
| Russian | 11 | 2 | 4 | 2 |
| Salar | 51 | 17 | 15 | 19 |
| She | 169 | 88 | 356 | 230 |
| Shui | 85 | 46 | 59 | 94 |
| Tajik | 30 | 7 | 8 | 6 |
| Tatar | 3 | 1 | 1 | 1 |
| Tibetan | 1,199 | 696 | 556 | 740 |
| Tu | 111 | 38 | 37 | 44 |
| Tujia | 2,461 | 1,120 | 1,240 | 1,343 |
| Uygur | 6,144 | 1,381 | 1,593 | 1,183 |
| Uzbek | 9 | 2 | 2 | 2 |
| Va | 83 | 42 | 38 | 75 |
| Xibe | 140 | 45 | 50 | 18 |
| Yao | 680 | 357 | 399 | 406 |
| Yi | 1,736 | 832 | 864 | 1,405 |
| Yugur | 5 | 1 | 1 | 1 |
| Zhuang | 3,991 | 2,392 | 2,127 | 2,473 |

*Note:* Data in this table are obtained from the 2005 National Sample Survey of 1% of Population. The sampling fraction is 1.325%.

*Table 1.14* Number of rooms and floor space of family households

| Ethnic group | Number of family households (households) | Population in family households (persons) | Number of rooms per household (rooms/ household) | Floor space of housing per capita (sq.m/ person) | Number of rooms per capita (rooms/ person) |
|---|---|---|---|---|---|
| National total | 5,286,554 | 16,570,406 | 3.05 | 28.69 | 0.97 |
| Achang | 130 | 464 | 2.80 | 24.29 | 0.78 |
| Bai | 7,183 | 25,336 | 2.85 | 25.09 | 0.81 |
| Baonan | 61 | 225 | 3.95 | 20.81 | 1.08 |
| Blang | 351 | 1,255 | 2.80 | 24.35 | 0.78 |
| Buyi | 11,990 | 41,275 | 2.80 | 24.74 | 0.82 |
| Dai | 4,426 | 15,828 | 2.80 | 24.34 | 0.78 |
| Daur | 607 | 1,795 | 2.33 | 22.27 | 0.79 |
| Deang | 68 | 245 | 2.80 | 24.26 | 0.78 |
| Derung | 29 | 101 | 2.82 | 24.82 | 0.81 |
| Dong | 12,073 | 40,270 | 3.03 | 28.08 | 0.91 |
| Dongxiang | 1,923 | 7,009 | 3.89 | 20.94 | 1.06 |
| Ewenki | 139 | 408 | 2.39 | 22.64 | 0.81 |
| Gaoshan | 19 | 60 | 3.13 | 27.94 | 0.97 |
| Gelao | 2,336 | 8,050 | 2.80 | 24.66 | 0.81 |
| Han | 4,855,207 | 15,133,860 | 3.08 | 29.03 | 0.98 |
| Hani | 5,495 | 19,664 | 2.80 | 24.30 | 0.78 |
| Hezhe | 21 | 64 | 2.20 | 21.78 | 0.74 |
| Hui | 40,355 | 135,542 | 3.15 | 24.01 | 0.93 |
| Jing | 92 | 313 | 3.21 | 27.66 | 0.95 |
| Jingpo | 504 | 1,805 | 2.80 | 24.28 | 0.78 |
| Jino | 80 | 285 | 2.80 | 24.29 | 0.78 |
| Kazak | 5,149 | 17,884 | 2.79 | 22.50 | 0.80 |
| Kirgiz | 663 | 2,299 | 2.78 | 22.50 | 0.80 |
| Korean | 8,420 | 25,815 | 2.31 | 22.22 | 0.75 |
| Lahu | 1,732 | 6,196 | 2.81 | 24.31 | 0.78 |
| Lhoba | 9 | 41 | 3.69 | 24.27 | 0.77 |
| Li | 4,614 | 17,598 | 2.46 | 20.87 | 0.64 |
| Lisu | 2,435 | 8,663 | 2.81 | 24.59 | 0.79 |
| Manchu | 47,344 | 143,023 | 2.51 | 23.92 | 0.82 |
| Maonan | 438 | 1,489 | 3.10 | 26.78 | 0.92 |
| Miao | 36,278 | 120,903 | 2.98 | 27.95 | 0.90 |
| Monba | 25 | 124 | 3.73 | 24.19 | 0.76 |
| Mongol | 26,190 | 77,863 | 2.47 | 23.12 | 0.83 |
| Mulao | 850 | 2,877 | 3.17 | 27.31 | 0.94 |
| Naxi | 1,183 | 4,214 | 2.82 | 24.59 | 0.79 |

*Table 1.14 (cont.)*

| Ethnic group | Number of family households (households) | Population in family households (persons) | Number of rooms per household (rooms/ household) | Floor space of housing per capita (sq.m/ person) | Number of rooms per capita (rooms/ person) |
|---|---|---|---|---|---|
| Nu | 110 | 393 | 2.82 | 24.37 | 0.78 |
| Oroqen | 38 | 111 | 2.29 | 22.23 | 0.78 |
| Pumi | 128 | 459 | 2.81 | 24.34 | 0.78 |
| Qiang | 1,360 | 4,013 | 3.14 | 34.61 | 1.07 |
| Russian | 67 | 217 | 2.66 | 22.85 | 0.82 |
| Salar | 414 | 1,513 | 3.19 | 20.24 | 0.87 |
| She | 3,150 | 9,431 | 3.18 | 35.27 | 1.06 |
| Shui | 1,641 | 5,654 | 2.81 | 24.78 | 0.82 |
| Tajik | 169 | 585 | 2.80 | 22.71 | 0.81 |
| Tatar | 20 | 70 | 2.84 | 22.60 | 0.82 |
| Tibetan | 19,072 | 74,837 | 3.48 | 25.44 | 0.87 |
| Tu | 955 | 3,468 | 3.20 | 20.72 | 0.88 |
| Tujia | 33,125 | 103,395 | 3.11 | 32.70 | 1.00 |
| Uygur | 34,598 | 120,103 | 2.79 | 22.54 | 0.80 |
| Uzbek | 51 | 177 | 2.80 | 22.60 | 0.80 |
| Va | 1,519 | 5,413 | 2.81 | 24.42 | 0.79 |
| Xibe | 842 | 2,546 | 2.37 | 23.55 | 0.78 |
| Yao | 10,727 | 35,738 | 3.22 | 29.05 | 0.97 |
| Yi | 31,162 | 105,058 | 2.89 | 27.19 | 0.86 |
| Yugur | 51 | 186 | 3.98 | 20.87 | 1.09 |
| Zhuang | 65,975 | 223,969 | 3.19 | 27.40 | 0.94 |

*Note:* Data in this table are obtained from the 2005 National Sample Survey of 1% of Population. The sampling fraction is 1.325%.

# 2 Employment and income distribution

Data in this chapter show the basic conditions of China's labor economy, including the main data of labor statistics.

Data on basic conditions of employment and the total wage bill of workers and staff are collected and compiled through the *Comprehensive Labor Statistics Reporting System*, the *Sample Survey on Population Changes*, and the *Rural Social and Economic Survey* by the Department of Population and Employment Statistics of the National Bureau of Statistics. The *Comprehensive Labor Statistics Reporting System* covers corporate enterprises, institutions, and administrative agencies (excluding township enterprises, private units, or self-employed businesses). The *Sample Survey on Population Changes* covers and estimates the population aged 16 and over of the whole country. The *Rural Social and Economic Survey* covers all rural areas below township level in China.

Data on the number of persons employed in private enterprises and self-employed persons in industry and commerce are provided by the State Administration for Industry and Commerce. The *Statistical Reporting System on Training and Employment* covers all agencies and units providing employment services. The *Statistical Reports on Private Enterprises and Individual Industrial and Commercial Business* cover the whole society.

A complete reporting from lower to higher levels is used in the labor statistics reporting system. Surveys on population changes and labor force surveys are conducted according to the sampling scheme designed by the National Bureau of Statistics. Statistics on training, employment, private enterprises, and self-employed individuals are collected and compiled on the basis of administrative records.

*Table 2.1* Number of employed persons at the year-end by three industries

| Ethnic group | Total | Composition in percentage | | |
| --- | --- | --- | --- | --- |
| | Employed persons (1,000 persons) | Primary industry | Secondary industry | Tertiary industry |
| National total | 75,825.0 | 44.8 | 23.8 | 31.4 |
| Achang | 20 | 69.1 | 10.1 | 20.7 |
| Bai | 1,087 | 66.5 | 10.8 | 22.7 |
| Baonan | 9 | 56.7 | 13.9 | 29.4 |
| Blang | 53 | 69.0 | 10.2 | 20.8 |
| Buyi | 1,860 | 56.9 | 10.9 | 32.1 |
| Dai | 673 | 69.1 | 10.1 | 20.8 |
| Daur | 60 | 51.0 | 17.8 | 31.2 |
| Deang | 10 | 69.3 | 10.0 | 20.7 |
| Derung | 4 | 64.9 | 12.3 | 22.8 |
| Dong | 1,795 | 55.1 | 13.3 | 31.6 |
| Dongxiang | 269 | 56.7 | 13.8 | 29.5 |
| Ewenki | 14 | 52.3 | 16.7 | 31.0 |
| Gaoshan | 3 | 47.0 | 22.2 | 30.7 |
| Gelao | 363 | 57.0 | 10.8 | 32.3 |
| Han | 622,869 | 43.9 | 24.6 | 31.4 |
| Hani | 836 | 69.2 | 10.1 | 20.7 |
| Hezhe | 2 | 46.8 | 21.2 | 32.0 |
| Hui | 5,298 | 49.3 | 20.5 | 30.2 |
| Jing | 14 | 55.8 | 11.8 | 32.4 |
| Jingpo | 77 | 69.1 | 10.1 | 20.8 |
| Jino | 12 | 69.2 | 10.1 | 20.7 |
| Kazak | 518 | 53.2 | 13.3 | 33.4 |
| Kirgiz | 67 | 53.2 | 13.4 | 33.4 |
| Korean | 839 | 45.1 | 20.6 | 34.3 |
| Lahu | 264 | 69.1 | 10.2 | 20.7 |
| Lhoba | 2 | 60.1 | 10.2 | 29.7 |
| Li | 632 | 56.7 | 10.9 | 32.4 |
| Lisu | 368 | 68.6 | 10.4 | 21.0 |
| Manchu | 5,130 | 40.3 | 25.0 | 34.6 |
| Maonan | 66 | 56.2 | 11.3 | 32.6 |
| Miao | 5,362 | 56.1 | 13.4 | 30.5 |
| Monba | 5 | 60.2 | 10.0 | 29.7 |
| Mongol | 2,683 | 50.3 | 18.0 | 31.7 |
| Mulao | 128 | 55.6 | 11.7 | 32.7 |

Table 2.1 *(cont.)*

| Ethnic group | Total | Composition in percentage | | |
| --- | --- | --- | --- | --- |
| | Employed persons (1,000 persons) | Primary industry | Secondary industry | Tertiary industry |
| Naxi | 179 | 68.5 | 10.4 | 21.1 |
| Nu | 17 | 68.7 | 10.3 | 21.0 |
| Oroqen | 4 | 49.6 | 19.1 | 31.3 |
| Pumi | 20 | 69.0 | 10.2 | 20.8 |
| Qiang | 171 | 50.6 | 18.4 | 31.0 |
| Russian | 7 | 51.4 | 15.5 | 33.1 |
| Salar | 57 | 50.0 | 16.9 | 33.1 |
| She | 416 | 36.0 | 31.7 | 32.3 |
| Shui | 254 | 57.2 | 10.8 | 32.0 |
| Tajik | 17 | 52.9 | 13.7 | 33.4 |
| Tatar | 2 | 52.7 | 13.9 | 33.5 |
| Tibetan | 2,960 | 56.0 | 13.6 | 30.4 |
| Tu | 133 | 49.9 | 17.3 | 32.8 |
| Tujia | 4,410 | 49.5 | 17.8 | 32.7 |
| Uygur | 3,485 | 53.2 | 13.4 | 33.4 |
| Uzbek | 5 | 53.0 | 13.5 | 33.5 |
| Va | 230 | 68.6 | 10.5 | 20.9 |
| Xibe | 87 | 40.0 | 23.0 | 37.0 |
| Yao | 1,577 | 54.7 | 14.2 | 31.1 |
| Yi | 4,501 | 62.8 | 12.4 | 24.9 |
| Yugur | 7 | 56.6 | 13.9 | 29.5 |
| Zhuang | 9,880 | 56.2 | 11.9 | 32.0 |

*Notes:* "Employed persons" refers to persons aged 16 and over who are engaged in work permitted by law and receive remuneration payment or earn business income. This indicator reflects the actual utilization of total labor force during a certain period of time and is often used for the research on China's economic situation and national power. "Primary industry" refers to agriculture, forestry, animal husbandry, and fishery, and services in support of these industries. "Secondary industry" refers to mining and quarrying, manufacturing, production and supply of electricity, water, and gas, and construction. "Tertiary industry" refers to all other economic activities not included in the primary or secondary industries.

*Table 2.2* Number of employed persons in urban units at the year-end by sector (unit: 1,000 persons)

| Ethnic group | Total | Agriculture, forestry, animal husbandry, and fishing | Mining | Manufacturing | Production and supply of electricity, gas, and water |
|---|---|---|---|---|---|
| National total | 114,040.3 | 4,462.6 | 5,092.0 | 32,109.0 | 2,999.5 |
| Achang | 2.0 | 0.1 | 0.0 | 0.4 | 0.1 |
| Bai | 111.0 | 6.2 | 3.0 | 20.8 | 3.1 |
| Baonan | 1.3 | 0.1 | 0.1 | 0.3 | 0.0 |
| Blang | 5.4 | 0.4 | 0.1 | 1.0 | 0.2 |
| Buyi | 181.6 | 2.9 | 8.9 | 37.3 | 5.5 |
| Dai | 68.0 | 4.4 | 1.7 | 12.4 | 1.9 |
| Daur | 15.5 | 2.3 | 1.2 | 3.0 | 0.5 |
| Deang | 1.1 | 0.1 | 0.0 | 0.2 | 0.0 |
| Derung | 0.5 | 0.0 | 0.0 | 0.1 | 0.0 |
| Dong | 189.5 | 4.1 | 7.1 | 40.2 | 5.4 |
| Dongxiang | 42.9 | 3.4 | 2.2 | 8.8 | 1.4 |
| Ewenki | 3.3 | 0.4 | 0.2 | 0.6 | 0.1 |
| Gaoshan | 0.4 | 0.0 | 0.0 | 0.1 | 0.0 |
| Gelao | 35.3 | 0.5 | 1.8 | 7.2 | 1.1 |
| *Han* | *105,198.6* | *3,699.1* | *4,693.6* | *30,334.9* | *2,738.7* |
| Hani | 84.4 | 5.5 | 2.1 | 15.4 | 2.4 |
| Hezhe | 0.6 | 0.1 | 0.1 | 0.1 | 0.0 |
| Hui | 991.6 | 65.5 | 57.4 | 216.8 | 33.7 |
| Jing | 1.5 | 0.1 | 0.0 | 0.3 | 0.0 |
| Jingpo | 7.8 | 0.5 | 0.2 | 1.4 | 0.2 |
| Jino | 1.2 | 0.1 | 0.0 | 0.2 | 0.0 |
| Kazak | 165.6 | 41.5 | 10.8 | 16.8 | 3.8 |
| Kirgiz | 21.3 | 5.3 | 1.4 | 2.2 | 0.5 |
| Korean | 214.3 | 20.4 | 13.0 | 51.2 | 6.5 |
| Lahu | 26.6 | 1.7 | 0.7 | 4.9 | 0.8 |
| Lhoba | 0.2 | 0.0 | 0.0 | 0.0 | 0.0 |
| Li | 121.1 | 28.7 | 1.9 | 12.4 | 3.2 |
| Lisu | 37.3 | 2.4 | 0.9 | 6.9 | 1.1 |
| Manchu | 1,222.2 | 81.1 | 72.2 | 324.3 | 38.8 |
| Maonan | 6.9 | 0.3 | 0.2 | 1.4 | 0.2 |
| Miao | 572.2 | 15.5 | 21.4 | 120.9 | 16.3 |
| Monba | 0.6 | 0.0 | 0.0 | 0.0 | 0.0 |

Table 2.2 (cont.)

| Ethnic group | Total | Agriculture, forestry, animal husbandry, and fishing | Mining | Manufacturing | Production and supply of electricity, gas, and water |
|---|---|---|---|---|---|
| Mongol | 618.0 | 67.3 | 41.3 | 125.2 | 21.7 |
| Mulao | 13.6 | 0.6 | 0.3 | 2.9 | 0.4 |
| Naxi | 18.2 | 1.2 | 0.5 | 3.3 | 0.5 |
| Nu | 1.7 | 0.1 | 0.0 | 0.3 | 0.0 |
| Oroqen | 1.0 | 0.1 | 0.1 | 0.2 | 0.0 |
| Pumi | 2.0 | 0.1 | 0.0 | 0.4 | 0.1 |
| Qiang | 19.2 | 0.4 | 0.8 | 4.4 | 0.6 |
| Russian | 1.9 | 0.4 | 0.1 | 0.3 | 0.1 |
| Salar | 9.4 | 0.6 | 0.4 | 1.5 | 0.4 |
| She | 76.0 | 1.3 | 0.9 | 32.9 | 1.6 |
| Shui | 24.7 | 0.4 | 1.2 | 5.0 | 0.8 |
| Tajik | 5.4 | 1.3 | 0.3 | 0.6 | 0.1 |
| Tatar | 0.6 | 0.2 | 0.0 | 0.1 | 0.0 |
| Tibetan | 392.7 | 13.6 | 9.7 | 52.0 | 15.0 |
| Tu | 21.2 | 1.1 | 0.8 | 3.7 | 0.8 |
| Tujia | 582.0 | 18.1 | 18.4 | 142.9 | 15.4 |
| Uygur | 1,112.0 | 278.4 | 72.4 | 113.3 | 25.6 |
| Uzbek | 1.6 | 0.4 | 0.1 | 0.2 | 0.0 |
| Va | 23.5 | 1.5 | 0.6 | 4.4 | 0.7 |
| Xibe | 23.2 | 2.4 | 1.4 | 5.9 | 0.7 |
| Yao | 178.3 | 6.8 | 3.5 | 39.8 | 4.8 |
| Yi | 465.8 | 21.5 | 14.9 | 92.4 | 13.5 |
| Yugur | 1.1 | 0.1 | 0.1 | 0.2 | 0.0 |
| Zhuang | 1,070.6 | 51.2 | 19.4 | 225.6 | 29.7 |

| Ethnic group | Construction | Transport, storage, and post | Information transmission, computer service and software | Wholesale and retail trade | Hotels and catering services |
|---|---|---|---|---|---|
| National total | 9,265.9 | 6,138.7 | 1,301.0 | 5,440.4 | 1,812.5 |
| Achang | 0.1 | 0.1 | 0.0 | 0.1 | 0.0 |
| Bai | 9.3 | 5.8 | 1.3 | 5.2 | 1.7 |
| Baonan | 0.1 | 0.1 | 0.0 | 0.1 | 0.0 |
| Blang | 0.4 | 0.3 | 0.1 | 0.2 | 0.1 |

*Table 2.2  (cont.)*

| Ethnic group | Construction | Transport, storage, and post | Information transmission, computer service and software | Wholesale and retail trade | Hotels and catering services |
|---|---|---|---|---|---|
| Buyi | 20.2 | 7.7 | 1.5 | 10.2 | 2.4 |
| Dai | 5.1 | 3.6 | 0.8 | 3.1 | 1.1 |
| Daur | 1.0 | 1.0 | 0.2 | 0.6 | 0.2 |
| Deang | 0.1 | 0.1 | 0.0 | 0.0 | 0.0 |
| Derung | 0.0 | 0.0 | 0.0 | 0.0 | 0.0 |
| Dong | 21.2 | 9.2 | 1.8 | 9.3 | 2.9 |
| Dongxiang | 3.0 | 2.5 | 0.5 | 1.8 | 0.5 |
| Ewenki | 0.2 | 0.2 | 0.0 | 0.1 | 0.0 |
| Gaoshan | 0.0 | 0.0 | 0.0 | 0.0 | 0.0 |
| Gelao | 3.9 | 1.5 | 0.3 | 2.0 | 0.5 |
| *Han* | *8,565.2* | *5,649.0* | *1,201.9* | *5,066.7* | *1,681.7* |
| Hani | 6.3 | 4.5 | 1.0 | 3.9 | 1.3 |
| Hezhe | 0.0 | 0.0 | 0.0 | 0.0 | 0.0 |
| Hui | 70.7 | 56.0 | 12.5 | 45.7 | 15.7 |
| Jing | 0.1 | 0.1 | 0.0 | 0.1 | 0.0 |
| Jingpo | 0.6 | 0.4 | 0.1 | 0.4 | 0.1 |
| Jino | 0.1 | 0.1 | 0.0 | 0.1 | 0.0 |
| Kazak | 10.9 | 7.9 | 1.5 | 5.1 | 1.9 |
| Kirgiz | 1.4 | 1.0 | 0.2 | 0.7 | 0.2 |
| Korean | 12.8 | 13.8 | 2.5 | 8.6 | 2.6 |
| Lahu | 2.0 | 1.4 | 0.3 | 1.2 | 0.4 |
| Lhoba | 0.0 | 0.0 | 0.0 | 0.0 | 0.0 |
| Li | 8.7 | 6.7 | 1.5 | 4.7 | 4.9 |
| Lisu | 2.9 | 2.0 | 0.4 | 1.7 | 0.6 |
| Manchu | 75.9 | 77.8 | 14.9 | 51.0 | 17.4 |
| Maonan | 0.6 | 0.4 | 0.1 | 0.3 | 0.1 |
| Miao | 63.9 | 28.2 | 5.5 | 27.7 | 8.7 |
| Monba | 0.0 | 0.0 | 0.0 | 0.0 | 0.0 |
| Mongol | 35.7 | 39.6 | 6.7 | 21.3 | 7.4 |
| Mulao | 1.1 | 0.8 | 0.2 | 0.7 | 0.2 |
| Naxi | 1.4 | 1.0 | 0.2 | 0.8 | 0.3 |
| Nu | 0.1 | 0.1 | 0.0 | 0.1 | 0.0 |
| Oroqen | 0.1 | 0.1 | 0.0 | 0.0 | 0.0 |
| Pumi | 0.1 | 0.1 | 0.0 | 0.1 | 0.0 |
| Qiang | 2.8 | 0.9 | 0.2 | 0.7 | 0.2 |
| Russian | 0.1 | 0.1 | 0.0 | 0.1 | 0.0 |
| Salar | 0.6 | 0.7 | 0.2 | 0.4 | 0.1 |

*Table 2.2* (cont.)

| Ethnic group | Construction | Transport, storage, and post | Information transmission, computer service and software | Wholesale and retail trade | Hotels and catering services |
|---|---|---|---|---|---|
| She | 7.5 | 3.0 | 0.7 | 2.5 | 1.1 |
| Shui | 2.7 | 1.1 | 0.2 | 1.4 | 0.3 |
| Tajik | 0.4 | 0.3 | 0.0 | 0.2 | 0.1 |
| Tatar | 0.0 | 0.0 | 0.0 | 0.0 | 0.0 |
| Tibetan | 28.7 | 20.4 | 5.7 | 14.7 | 6.2 |
| Tu | 1.5 | 1.6 | 0.4 | 0.8 | 0.2 |
| Tujia | 67.4 | 32.1 | 5.7 | 26.8 | 8.7 |
| Uygur | 73.1 | 53.0 | 9.9 | 34.6 | 12.6 |
| Uzbek | 0.1 | 0.1 | 0.0 | 0.1 | 0.0 |
| Va | 1.8 | 1.2 | 0.3 | 1.1 | 0.4 |
| Xibe | 1.4 | 1.4 | 0.2 | 0.8 | 0.3 |
| Yao | 16.2 | 10.3 | 2.2 | 7.9 | 3.2 |
| Yi | 46.7 | 23.1 | 5.1 | 20.9 | 6.4 |
| Yugur | 0.1 | 0.1 | 0.0 | 0.0 | 0.0 |
| Zhuang | 84.2 | 64.5 | 13.6 | 51.3 | 18.6 |

| Ethnic group | Financial intermediation | Real estate | Leasing and business services | Scientific research, technical services, and geological prospecting | Management of water conservancy, environment, and public facilities |
|---|---|---|---|---|---|
| National total | 3,592.9 | 1,465.1 | 2,185.4 | 2,277.3 | 1,803.9 |
| Achang | 0.1 | 0.0 | 0.0 | 0.0 | 0.0 |
| Bai | 3.2 | 1.1 | 1.2 | 2.4 | 1.7 |
| Baonan | 0.0 | 0.0 | 0.0 | 0.0 | 0.0 |
| Blang | 0.2 | 0.0 | 0.1 | 0.1 | 0.1 |
| Buyi | 4.3 | 3.2 | 2.2 | 3.1 | 2.2 |
| Dai | 1.9 | 0.6 | 0.7 | 1.5 | 1.1 |
| Daur | 0.5 | 0.1 | 0.2 | 0.3 | 0.3 |
| Deang | 0.0 | 0.0 | 0.0 | 0.0 | 0.0 |
| Derung | 0.0 | 0.0 | 0.0 | 0.0 | 0.0 |
| Dong | 5.2 | 3.0 | 2.5 | 3.2 | 2.7 |
| Dongxiang | 1.3 | 0.3 | 0.5 | 1.0 | 0.8 |
| Ewenki | 0.1 | 0.0 | 0.0 | 0.1 | 0.1 |
| Gaoshan | 0.0 | 0.0 | 0.0 | 0.0 | 0.0 |

*Table 2.2 (cont.)*

| Ethnic group | Financial intermediation | Real estate | Leasing and business services | Scientific research, technical services, and geological prospecting | Management of water conservancy, environment, and public facilities |
|---|---|---|---|---|---|
| Gelao | 0.8 | 0.6 | 0.4 | 0.6 | 0.4 |
| *Han* | *3,332.6* | *1,362.0* | *2,040.1* | *2,096.3* | *1,646.9* |
| Hani | 2.4 | 0.7 | 0.9 | 1.9 | 1.4 |
| Hezhe | 0.0 | 0.0 | 0.0 | 0.0 | 0.0 |
| Hui | 31.8 | 12.5 | 20.7 | 24.2 | 19.4 |
| Jing | 0.0 | 0.0 | 0.0 | 0.0 | 0.0 |
| Jingpo | 0.2 | 0.1 | 0.1 | 0.2 | 0.1 |
| Jino | 0.0 | 0.0 | 0.0 | 0.0 | 0.0 |
| Kazak | 3.9 | 1.6 | 2.7 | 3.0 | 2.9 |
| Kirgiz | 0.5 | 0.2 | 0.4 | 0.4 | 0.4 |
| Korean | 6.9 | 2.5 | 3.4 | 4.8 | 4.8 |
| Lahu | 0.8 | 0.2 | 0.3 | 0.6 | 0.4 |
| Lhoba | 0.0 | 0.0 | 0.0 | 0.0 | 0.0 |
| Li | 3.0 | 2.3 | 2.2 | 2.4 | 3.3 |
| Lisu | 1.1 | 0.3 | 0.4 | 0.8 | 0.6 |
| Manchu | 41.8 | 16.2 | 26.3 | 26.6 | 24.8 |
| Maonan | 0.2 | 0.1 | 0.1 | 0.1 | 0.1 |
| Miao | 15.8 | 8.7 | 7.2 | 10.2 | 8.1 |
| Monba | 0.0 | 0.0 | 0.0 | 0.0 | 0.0 |
| Mongol | 20.4 | 5.0 | 9.0 | 11.5 | 14.1 |
| Mulao | 0.4 | 0.2 | 0.3 | 0.3 | 0.2 |
| Naxi | 0.5 | 0.2 | 0.2 | 0.4 | 0.3 |
| Nu | 0.0 | 0.0 | 0.0 | 0.0 | 0.0 |
| Oroqen | 0.0 | 0.0 | 0.0 | 0.0 | 0.0 |
| Pumi | 0.1 | 0.0 | 0.0 | 0.0 | 0.0 |
| Qiang | 0.6 | 0.2 | 0.2 | 0.4 | 0.3 |
| Russian | 0.1 | 0.0 | 0.0 | 0.0 | 0.0 |
| Salar | 0.3 | 0.1 | 0.1 | 0.4 | 0.2 |
| She | 2.2 | 1.0 | 1.3 | 0.9 | 0.8 |
| Shui | 0.6 | 0.4 | 0.3 | 0.4 | 0.3 |
| Tajik | 0.1 | 0.1 | 0.1 | 0.1 | 0.1 |
| Tatar | 0.0 | 0.0 | 0.0 | 0.0 | 0.0 |
| Tibetan | 12.9 | 1.5 | 3.5 | 12.0 | 5.4 |
| Tu | 0.7 | 0.1 | 0.3 | 0.8 | 0.4 |
| Tujia | 17.1 | 8.3 | 7.1 | 10.5 | 9.0 |
| Uygur | 26.3 | 10.7 | 18.4 | 20.0 | 19.4 |

*Table 2.2* (*cont.*)

| Ethnic group | Financial intermediation | Real estate | Leasing and business services | Scientific research, technical services, and geological prospecting | Management of water conservancy, environment, and public facilities |
|---|---|---|---|---|---|
| Uzbek | 0.0 | 0.0 | 0.0 | 0.0 | 0.0 |
| Va | 0.7 | 0.2 | 0.2 | 0.5 | 0.4 |
| Xibe | 0.8 | 0.3 | 0.5 | 0.5 | 0.5 |
| Yao | 5.3 | 2.4 | 3.3 | 3.1 | 3.0 |
| Yi | 13.7 | 4.4 | 5.1 | 10.1 | 7.0 |
| Yugur | 0.0 | 0.0 | 0.0 | 0.0 | 0.0 |
| Zhuang | 30.3 | 12.5 | 22.0 | 20.2 | 19.0 |

| Ethnic group | Services to households and other services | Education | Health, social securities, and social welfare | Culture, sports, and entertainment | Public management and social organization |
|---|---|---|---|---|---|
| *National total* | *539.3* | *14,832.5* | *5,089.0* | *1,225.2* | *12,408.2* |
| Achang | 0.0 | 0.4 | 0.1 | 0.0 | 0.3 |
| Bai | 0.3 | 20.5 | 5.6 | 1.5 | 17.2 |
| Baonan | 0.0 | 0.2 | 0.1 | 0.0 | 0.2 |
| Blang | 0.0 | 1.0 | 0.3 | 0.1 | 0.8 |
| Buyi | 0.7 | 32.2 | 7.7 | 1.8 | 27.4 |
| Dai | 0.1 | 12.9 | 3.4 | 0.9 | 10.6 |
| Daur | 0.1 | 1.8 | 0.6 | 0.2 | 1.7 |
| Deang | 0.0 | 0.2 | 0.1 | 0.0 | 0.2 |
| Derung | 0.0 | 0.1 | 0.0 | 0.0 | 0.1 |
| Dong | 0.6 | 32.3 | 9.2 | 1.9 | 27.7 |
| Dongxiang | 0.1 | 6.6 | 1.7 | 0.6 | 5.9 |
| Ewenki | 0.0 | 0.4 | 0.1 | 0.0 | 0.4 |
| Gaoshan | 0.0 | 0.1 | 0.0 | 0.0 | 0.0 |
| Gelao | 0.1 | 6.3 | 1.5 | 0.3 | 5.3 |
| *Han* | *508.5* | *13,525.9* | *4,667.3* | *1,119.8* | *11,267.9* |
| Hani | 0.2 | 16.0 | 4.3 | 1.2 | 13.2 |
| Hezhe | 0.0 | 0.1 | 0.0 | 0.0 | 0.1 |
| Hui | 4.8 | 129.1 | 43.6 | 13.1 | 118.2 |
| Jing | 0.0 | 0.3 | 0.1 | 0.0 | 0.2 |
| Jingpo | 0.0 | 1.5 | 0.4 | 0.1 | 1.2 |
| Jino | 0.0 | 0.2 | 0.1 | 0.0 | 0.2 |

*Table 2.2* (cont.)

| Ethnic group | Services to households and other services | Education | Health, social securities, and social welfare | Culture, sports, and entertainment | Public management and social organization |
|---|---|---|---|---|---|
| Kazak | 0.2 | 21.6 | 7.3 | 1.7 | 20.5 |
| Kirgiz | 0.0 | 2.8 | 0.9 | 0.2 | 2.6 |
| Korean | 1.3 | 25.4 | 10.0 | 2.6 | 21.0 |
| Lahu | 0.1 | 5.0 | 1.3 | 0.4 | 4.2 |
| Lhoba | 0.0 | 0.0 | 0.0 | 0.0 | 0.1 |
| Li | 0.1 | 14.6 | 4.8 | 2.0 | 13.7 |
| Lisu | 0.1 | 7.0 | 1.9 | 0.5 | 5.8 |
| Manchu | 7.6 | 137.6 | 52.6 | 14.4 | 120.8 |
| Maonan | 0.0 | 1.3 | 0.4 | 0.1 | 0.9 |
| Miao | 1.7 | 97.0 | 27.3 | 5.9 | 82.2 |
| Monba | 0.0 | 0.1 | 0.0 | 0.0 | 0.2 |
| Mongol | 2.5 | 80.1 | 26.8 | 7.7 | 74.4 |
| Mulao | 0.0 | 2.5 | 0.8 | 0.2 | 1.7 |
| Naxi | 0.0 | 3.4 | 0.9 | 0.3 | 2.8 |
| Nu | 0.0 | 0.3 | 0.1 | 0.0 | 0.3 |
| Oroqen | 0.0 | 0.1 | 0.0 | 0.0 | 0.1 |
| Pumi | 0.0 | 0.4 | 0.1 | 0.0 | 0.3 |
| Qiang | 0.1 | 3.0 | 1.0 | 0.2 | 2.3 |
| Russian | 0.0 | 0.2 | 0.1 | 0.0 | 0.2 |
| Salar | 0.1 | 1.4 | 0.5 | 0.1 | 1.5 |
| She | 0.2 | 8.4 | 2.8 | 0.7 | 6.3 |
| Shui | 0.1 | 4.4 | 1.1 | 0.2 | 3.7 |
| Tajik | 0.0 | 0.7 | 0.2 | 0.1 | 0.7 |
| Tatar | 0.0 | 0.1 | 0.0 | 0.0 | 0.1 |
| Tibetan | 1.0 | 63.7 | 23.2 | 8.2 | 94.8 |
| Tu | 0.1 | 3.1 | 1.1 | 0.3 | 3.3 |
| Tujia | 1.6 | 85.7 | 28.6 | 5.8 | 72.8 |
| Uygur | 1.4 | 145.3 | 49.2 | 11.2 | 137.3 |
| Uzbek | 0.0 | 0.2 | 0.1 | 0.0 | 0.2 |
| Va | 0.1 | 4.4 | 1.2 | 0.3 | 3.6 |
| Xibe | 0.1 | 2.5 | 1.0 | 0.2 | 2.3 |
| Yao | 0.5 | 31.0 | 10.0 | 2.0 | 23.1 |
| Yi | 1.3 | 82.8 | 23.3 | 5.7 | 67.8 |
| Yugur | 0.0 | 0.2 | 0.0 | 0.0 | 0.2 |
| Zhuang | 2.9 | 200.2 | 62.1 | 12.4 | 130.9 |

*Note:* "Employed persons" in urban units doesn't include those in private enterprise and self-employed individuals.

*Table 2.3* Number of staff and workers at the year-end by sector (unit: 1,000 persons)

| Ethnic group | Total | Agriculture, forestry, animal husbandry, and fishing | Mining | Manufacturing | Production and supply of electricity, gas, and water |
|---|---|---|---|---|---|
| National total | 108,503.1 | 4,142.2 | 4,975.9 | 30,964.5 | 2,937.3 |
| Achang | 1.9 | 0.1 | 0.1 | 0.4 | 0.1 |
| Bai | 105.8 | 5.7 | 6.1 | 20.2 | 3.0 |
| Baonan | 1.3 | 0.1 | 0.1 | 0.3 | 0.0 |
| Blang | 5.2 | 0.3 | 0.3 | 1.0 | 0.1 |
| Buyi | 174.1 | 2.7 | 8.8 | 36.3 | 5.3 |
| Dai | 64.9 | 4.0 | 4.0 | 12.0 | 1.8 |
| Daur | 14.9 | 2.0 | 1.3 | 2.9 | 0.5 |
| Deang | 1.0 | 0.1 | 0.1 | 0.2 | 0.0 |
| Derung | 0.5 | 0.0 | 0.0 | 0.1 | 0.0 |
| Dong | 180.0 | 3.7 | 7.0 | 38.8 | 5.2 |
| Dongxiang | 41.7 | 3.4 | 3.5 | 8.6 | 1.4 |
| Ewenki | 3.2 | 0.4 | 0.2 | 0.6 | 0.1 |
| Gaoshan | 0.4 | 0.0 | 0.0 | 0.1 | 0.0 |
| Gelao | 33.8 | 0.5 | 1.7 | 7.0 | 1.0 |
| Han | 100,052.9 | 3,407.4 | 4,078.0 | 29,251.0 | 2,682.4 |
| Hani | 80.6 | 5.0 | 5.0 | 14.9 | 2.3 |
| Hezhe | 0.6 | 0.1 | 0.1 | 0.1 | 0.0 |
| Hui | 945.4 | 63.8 | 75.0 | 209.8 | 33.2 |
| Jing | 1.4 | 0.1 | 0.0 | 0.3 | 0.0 |
| Jingpo | 7.4 | 0.5 | 0.5 | 1.4 | 0.2 |
| Jino | 1.2 | 0.1 | 0.1 | 0.2 | 0.0 |
| Kazak | 160.9 | 41.2 | 41.2 | 16.5 | 3.8 |
| Kirgiz | 20.7 | 5.3 | 5.3 | 2.1 | 0.5 |
| Korean | 206.0 | 18.1 | 12.9 | 49.7 | 6.4 |
| Lahu | 25.4 | 1.6 | 1.6 | 4.7 | 0.7 |
| Lhoba | 0.2 | 0.0 | 0.0 | 0.0 | 0.0 |
| Li | 117.7 | 28.2 | 1.9 | 11.9 | 3.0 |
| Lisu | 35.6 | 2.2 | 2.2 | 6.7 | 1.0 |
| Manchu | 1,166.4 | 74.9 | 71.6 | 313.0 | 38.3 |
| Maonan | 6.5 | 0.2 | 0.2 | 1.4 | 0.2 |
| Miao | 544.8 | 14.4 | 23.0 | 116.6 | 15.7 |
| Monba | 0.6 | 0.0 | 0.0 | 0.0 | 0.0 |
| Mongol | 602.8 | 66.3 | 44.4 | 123.0 | 21.5 |

*Table 2.3 (cont.)*

| Ethnic group | Total | Agriculture, forestry, animal husbandry, and fishing | Mining | Manufacturing | Production and supply of electricity, gas, and water |
|---|---|---|---|---|---|
| Mulao | 12.9 | 0.5 | 0.3 | 2.8 | 0.4 |
| Naxi | 17.4 | 1.1 | 1.1 | 3.2 | 0.5 |
| Nu | 1.6 | 0.1 | 0.1 | 0.3 | 0.0 |
| Oroqen | 0.9 | 0.1 | 0.1 | 0.2 | 0.0 |
| Pumi | 1.9 | 0.1 | 0.1 | 0.4 | 0.1 |
| Qiang | 18.5 | 0.4 | 0.4 | 4.3 | 0.6 |
| Russian | 1.9 | 0.4 | 0.3 | 0.3 | 0.1 |
| Salar | 9.0 | 0.6 | 0.5 | 1.5 | 0.4 |
| She | 73.4 | 1.2 | 0.9 | 32.4 | 1.6 |
| Shui | 23.7 | 0.4 | 1.2 | 4.9 | 0.7 |
| Tajik | 5.2 | 1.3 | 1.3 | 0.6 | 0.1 |
| Tatar | 0.6 | 0.2 | 0.2 | 0.1 | 0.0 |
| Tibetan | 366.1 | 11.6 | 10.4 | 50.2 | 14.6 |
| Tu | 20.3 | 1.1 | 0.9 | 3.6 | 0.8 |
| Tujia | 541.8 | 16.7 | 17.8 | 130.8 | 14.8 |
| Uygur | 1,080.6 | 275.9 | 276.0 | 111.5 | 25.5 |
| Uzbek | 1.6 | 0.4 | 0.4 | 0.2 | 0.0 |
| Va | 22.5 | 1.4 | 1.4 | 4.3 | 0.6 |
| Xibe | 22.2 | 2.3 | 2.3 | 5.7 | 0.7 |
| Yao | 169.3 | 6.3 | 3.8 | 38.6 | 4.6 |
| Yi | 445.6 | 19.8 | 21.7 | 90.1 | 13.0 |
| Yugur | 1.1 | 0.1 | 0.1 | 0.2 | 0.0 |
| Zhuang | 1,016.4 | 47.4 | 21.2 | 217.9 | 28.6 |

| Ethnic group | Construction | Transport, storage, and post | Information transmission, computer service and software | Wholesale and retail trade | Hotels and catering services |
|---|---|---|---|---|---|
| *National total* | *8,543.2* | *5,791.6* | *1,167.6* | *5,083.1* | *1,665.0* |
| Achang | 0.1 | 0.1 | 0.0 | 0.1 | 0.0 |
| Bai | 8.5 | 5.3 | 1.1 | 4.9 | 1.7 |
| Baonan | 0.1 | 0.1 | 0.0 | 0.1 | 0.0 |
| Blang | 0.4 | 0.3 | 0.1 | 0.2 | 0.1 |
| Buyi | 18.4 | 7.2 | 1.4 | 9.9 | 2.3 |

Table 2.3  (cont.)

| Ethnic group | Construction | Transport, storage, and post | Information transmission, computer service and software | Wholesale and retail trade | Hotels and catering services |
|---|---|---|---|---|---|
| Dai | 4.8 | 3.3 | 0.7 | 3.0 | 1.0 |
| Daur | 0.9 | 0.9 | 0.2 | 0.6 | 0.2 |
| Deang | 0.1 | 0.1 | 0.0 | 0.0 | 0.0 |
| Derung | 0.0 | 0.0 | 0.0 | 0.0 | 0.0 |
| Dong | 18.6 | 8.6 | 1.6 | 8.9 | 2.7 |
| Dongxiang | 2.9 | 2.4 | 0.4 | 1.7 | 0.5 |
| Ewenki | 0.2 | 0.2 | 0.0 | 0.1 | 0.0 |
| Gaoshan | 0.0 | 0.0 | 0.0 | 0.0 | 0.0 |
| Gelao | 3.6 | 1.4 | 0.3 | 1.9 | 0.5 |
| *Han* | *7,899.5* | *5,328.9* | *1,078.6* | *4,727.0* | *1,541.4* |
| Hani | 5.9 | 4.1 | 0.9 | 3.7 | 1.3 |
| Hezhe | 0.0 | 0.0 | 0.0 | 0.0 | 0.0 |
| Hui | 65.2 | 53.0 | 11.4 | 42.9 | 14.4 |
| Jing | 0.1 | 0.1 | 0.0 | 0.1 | 0.0 |
| Jingpo | 0.5 | 0.4 | 0.1 | 0.3 | 0.1 |
| Jino | 0.1 | 0.1 | 0.0 | 0.1 | 0.0 |
| Kazak | 10.3 | 7.2 | 1.4 | 5.1 | 1.8 |
| Kirgiz | 1.3 | 0.9 | 0.2 | 0.7 | 0.2 |
| Korean | 12.2 | 13.5 | 2.4 | 8.2 | 2.5 |
| Lahu | 1.9 | 1.3 | 0.3 | 1.2 | 0.4 |
| Lhoba | 0.0 | 0.0 | 0.0 | 0.0 | 0.0 |
| Li | 8.1 | 6.6 | 1.4 | 4.5 | 4.8 |
| Lisu | 2.7 | 1.8 | 0.4 | 1.6 | 0.5 |
| Manchu | 71.9 | 74.8 | 14.0 | 48.3 | 16.2 |
| Maonan | 0.6 | 0.4 | 0.1 | 0.3 | 0.1 |
| Miao | 57.0 | 26.3 | 5.0 | 26.6 | 8.3 |
| Monba | 0.0 | 0.0 | 0.0 | 0.0 | 0.0 |
| Mongol | 34.4 | 38.5 | 6.5 | 20.5 | 7.1 |
| Mulao | 1.0 | 0.8 | 0.1 | 0.6 | 0.2 |
| Naxi | 1.3 | 0.9 | 0.2 | 0.8 | 0.3 |
| Nu | 0.1 | 0.1 | 0.0 | 0.1 | 0.0 |
| Oroqen | 0.1 | 0.1 | 0.0 | 0.0 | 0.0 |
| Pumi | 0.1 | 0.1 | 0.0 | 0.1 | 0.0 |
| Qiang | 2.7 | 0.8 | 0.2 | 0.7 | 0.2 |
| Russian | 0.1 | 0.1 | 0.0 | 0.1 | 0.0 |
| Salar | 0.6 | 0.7 | 0.1 | 0.3 | 0.1 |
| She | 7.0 | 2.8 | 0.6 | 2.4 | 1.0 |

*Table 2.3* (*cont.*)

| Ethnic group | Construction | Transport, storage, and post | Information transmission, computer service and software | Wholesale and retail trade | Hotels and catering services |
|---|---|---|---|---|---|
| Shui | 2.5 | 1.0 | 0.2 | 1.3 | 0.3 |
| Tajik | 0.3 | 0.2 | 0.0 | 0.2 | 0.1 |
| Tatar | 0.0 | 0.0 | 0.0 | 0.0 | 0.0 |
| Tibetan | 25.0 | 19.5 | 5.3 | 13.9 | 5.9 |
| Tu | 1.3 | 1.5 | 0.3 | 0.8 | 0.2 |
| Tujia | 58.8 | 29.8 | 5.2 | 24.8 | 8.0 |
| Uygur | 69.2 | 48.7 | 9.3 | 34.0 | 11.8 |
| Uzbek | 0.1 | 0.1 | 0.0 | 0.1 | 0.0 |
| Va | 1.7 | 1.1 | 0.2 | 1.0 | 0.3 |
| Xibe | 1.3 | 1.4 | 0.2 | 0.8 | 0.3 |
| Yao | 14.3 | 9.7 | 1.8 | 7.5 | 3.1 |
| Yi | 43.7 | 21.5 | 4.5 | 20.0 | 6.2 |
| Yugur | 0.1 | 0.1 | 0.0 | 0.0 | 0.0 |
| Zhuang | 77.0 | 61.1 | 10.4 | 48.5 | 18.1 |

| Ethnic group | Financial intermediation | Real estate | Leasing and business services | Scientific research, technical services, and geological prospecting | Management of water conservancy, environment, and public facilities |
|---|---|---|---|---|---|
| *National total* | *2,950.3* | *1,326.7* | *1,987.5* | *2,127.1* | *1,703.4* |
| Achang | 0.1 | 0.0 | 0.0 | 0.0 | 0.0 |
| Bai | 2.9 | 1.0 | 1.1 | 2.2 | 1.6 |
| Baonan | 0.0 | 0.0 | 0.0 | 0.0 | 0.0 |
| Blang | 0.1 | 0.0 | 0.1 | 0.1 | 0.1 |
| Buyi | 4.0 | 3.0 | 2.2 | 3.0 | 2.0 |
| Dai | 1.8 | 0.5 | 0.7 | 1.4 | 1.0 |
| Daur | 0.4 | 0.1 | 0.2 | 0.3 | 0.3 |
| Deang | 0.0 | 0.0 | 0.0 | 0.0 | 0.0 |
| Derung | 0.0 | 0.0 | 0.0 | 0.0 | 0.0 |
| Dong | 4.5 | 2.8 | 2.4 | 3.0 | 2.5 |
| Dongxiang | 1.2 | 0.2 | 0.5 | 1.0 | 0.8 |
| Ewenki | 0.1 | 0.0 | 0.0 | 0.1 | 0.1 |
| Gaoshan | 0.0 | 0.0 | 0.0 | 0.0 | 0.0 |
| Gelao | 0.8 | 0.6 | 0.4 | 0.6 | 0.4 |
| *Han* | *2,728.1* | *1,230.7* | *1,856.6* | *1,955.5* | *1,554.1* |

Table 2.3 (cont.)

| Ethnic group | Financial intermediation | Real estate | Leasing and business services | Scientific research, technical services, and geological prospecting | Management of water conservancy, environment, and public facilities |
|---|---|---|---|---|---|
| Hani | 2.3 | 0.7 | 0.8 | 1.7 | 1.3 |
| Hezhe | 0.0 | 0.0 | 0.0 | 0.0 | 0.0 |
| Hui | 25.8 | 11.2 | 18.3 | 22.6 | 18.6 |
| Jing | 0.0 | 0.0 | 0.0 | 0.0 | 0.0 |
| Jingpo | 0.2 | 0.1 | 0.1 | 0.2 | 0.1 |
| Jino | 0.0 | 0.0 | 0.0 | 0.0 | 0.0 |
| Kazak | 3.3 | 1.5 | 2.7 | 2.9 | 2.8 |
| Kirgiz | 0.4 | 0.2 | 0.3 | 0.4 | 0.4 |
| Korean | 6.0 | 2.4 | 3.0 | 4.5 | 4.6 |
| Lahu | 0.7 | 0.2 | 0.3 | 0.5 | 0.4 |
| Lhoba | 0.0 | 0.0 | 0.0 | 0.0 | 0.0 |
| Li | 2.8 | 2.2 | 2.1 | 2.3 | 3.2 |
| Lisu | 1.0 | 0.3 | 0.4 | 0.7 | 0.6 |
| Manchu | 33.0 | 14.8 | 21.7 | 24.8 | 23.8 |
| Maonan | 0.2 | 0.1 | 0.1 | 0.1 | 0.1 |
| Miao | 13.7 | 8.2 | 6.8 | 9.7 | 7.5 |
| Monba | 0.0 | 0.0 | 0.0 | 0.0 | 0.0 |
| Mongol | 17.3 | 4.8 | 8.1 | 11.2 | 13.7 |
| Mulao | 0.3 | 0.2 | 0.2 | 0.2 | 0.2 |
| Naxi | 0.5 | 0.1 | 0.2 | 0.4 | 0.3 |
| Nu | 0.0 | 0.0 | 0.0 | 0.0 | 0.0 |
| Oroqen | 0.0 | 0.0 | 0.0 | 0.0 | 0.0 |
| Pumi | 0.1 | 0.0 | 0.0 | 0.0 | 0.0 |
| Qiang | 0.5 | 0.2 | 0.2 | 0.4 | 0.3 |
| Russian | 0.0 | 0.0 | 0.0 | 0.0 | 0.0 |
| Salar | 0.3 | 0.1 | 0.1 | 0.4 | 0.1 |
| She | 1.8 | 0.9 | 1.2 | 0.9 | 0.8 |
| Shui | 0.5 | 0.4 | 0.3 | 0.4 | 0.3 |
| Tajik | 0.1 | 0.0 | 0.1 | 0.1 | 0.1 |
| Tatar | 0.0 | 0.0 | 0.0 | 0.0 | 0.0 |
| Tibetan | 11.8 | 1.4 | 3.2 | 11.7 | 5.0 |
| Tu | 0.6 | 0.1 | 0.3 | 0.8 | 0.3 |
| Tujia | 13.8 | 7.5 | 6.6 | 10.0 | 8.3 |
| Uygur | 22.0 | 10.0 | 18.0 | 19.4 | 19.1 |
| Uzbek | 0.0 | 0.0 | 0.0 | 0.0 | 0.0 |
| Va | 0.6 | 0.2 | 0.2 | 0.5 | 0.4 |
| Xibe | 0.6 | 0.3 | 0.4 | 0.4 | 0.5 |

*Table 2.3* (cont.)

| Ethnic group | Financial intermediation | Real estate | Leasing and business services | Scientific research, technical services, and geological prospecting | Management of water conservancy, environment, and public facilities |
|---|---|---|---|---|---|
| Yao | 4.7 | 2.3 | 2.9 | 3.0 | 2.8 |
| Yi | 12.2 | 4.1 | 4.9 | 9.3 | 6.5 |
| Yugur | 0.0 | 0.0 | 0.0 | 0.0 | 0.0 |
| Zhuang | 27.9 | 12.0 | 19.1 | 19.3 | 17.9 |

| Ethnic group | Services to households and other services | Education | Health, social securities, and social welfare | Culture, sports, and entertainment | Public management and social organization |
|---|---|---|---|---|---|
| National total | 471.5 | 14,447.3 | 4,913.7 | 1,170.2 | 12,134.9 |
| Achang | 0.0 | 0.4 | 0.1 | 0.0 | 0.3 |
| Bai | 0.2 | 19.9 | 5.4 | 1.4 | 16.7 |
| Baonan | 0.0 | 0.2 | 0.1 | 0.0 | 0.2 |
| Blang | 0.0 | 1.0 | 0.3 | 0.1 | 0.8 |
| Buyi | 0.7 | 31.1 | 7.5 | 1.7 | 26.8 |
| Dai | 0.1 | 12.5 | 3.3 | 0.9 | 10.3 |
| Daur | 0.1 | 1.8 | 0.6 | 0.2 | 1.6 |
| Deang | 0.0 | 0.2 | 0.1 | 0.0 | 0.2 |
| Derung | 0.0 | 0.1 | 0.0 | 0.0 | 0.1 |
| Dong | 0.6 | 31.3 | 9.0 | 1.8 | 27.1 |
| Dongxiang | 0.1 | 6.4 | 1.7 | 0.6 | 5.8 |
| Ewenki | 0.0 | 0.4 | 0.1 | 0.0 | 0.4 |
| Gaoshan | 0.0 | 0.1 | 0.0 | 0.0 | 0.0 |
| Gelao | 0.1 | 6.1 | 1.4 | 0.3 | 5.2 |
| Han | 443.3 | 13,177.4 | 4,505.1 | 1,068.0 | 11,022.9 |
| Hani | 0.2 | 15.5 | 4.1 | 1.1 | 12.8 |
| Hezhe | 0.0 | 0.1 | 0.0 | 0.0 | 0.1 |
| Hui | 3.9 | 126.2 | 42.2 | 12.5 | 115.7 |
| Jing | 0.0 | 0.3 | 0.1 | 0.0 | 0.2 |
| Jingpo | 0.0 | 1.4 | 0.4 | 0.1 | 1.2 |
| Jino | 0.0 | 0.2 | 0.1 | 0.0 | 0.2 |
| Kazak | 0.2 | 21.5 | 7.2 | 1.6 | 20.3 |
| Kirgiz | 0.0 | 2.8 | 0.9 | 0.2 | 2.6 |
| Korean | 1.3 | 25.1 | 9.8 | 2.6 | 20.7 |
| Lahu | 0.1 | 4.9 | 1.3 | 0.3 | 4.0 |
| Lhoba | 0.0 | 0.0 | 0.0 | 0.0 | 0.1 |

*Table 2.3* (*cont.*)

| Ethnic group | Services to households and other services | Education | Health, social securities, and social welfare | Culture, sports, and entertainment | Public management and social organization |
|---|---|---|---|---|---|
| Li | 0.1 | 14.3 | 4.7 | 1.9 | 13.4 |
| Lisu | 0.1 | 6.8 | 1.8 | 0.5 | 5.6 |
| Manchu | 7.0 | 134.8 | 51.1 | 13.9 | 118.5 |
| Maonan | 0.0 | 1.2 | 0.4 | 0.1 | 0.9 |
| Miao | 1.6 | 94.0 | 26.4 | 5.7 | 80.3 |
| Monba | 0.0 | 0.1 | 0.0 | 0.0 | 0.2 |
| Mongol | 2.4 | 79.1 | 26.4 | 7.6 | 73.4 |
| Mulao | 0.0 | 2.4 | 0.7 | 0.1 | 1.7 |
| Naxi | 0.0 | 3.3 | 0.9 | 0.2 | 2.8 |
| Nu | 0.0 | 0.3 | 0.1 | 0.0 | 0.3 |
| Oroqen | 0.0 | 0.1 | 0.0 | 0.0 | 0.1 |
| Pumi | 0.0 | 0.4 | 0.1 | 0.0 | 0.3 |
| Qiang | 0.1 | 2.9 | 0.9 | 0.2 | 2.3 |
| Russian | 0.0 | 0.2 | 0.1 | 0.0 | 0.2 |
| Salar | 0.0 | 1.3 | 0.5 | 0.1 | 1.4 |
| She | 0.2 | 8.2 | 2.7 | 0.6 | 6.2 |
| Shui | 0.1 | 4.3 | 1.0 | 0.2 | 3.6 |
| Tajik | 0.0 | 0.7 | 0.2 | 0.1 | 0.7 |
| Tatar | 0.0 | 0.1 | 0.0 | 0.0 | 0.1 |
| Tibetan | 0.9 | 60.3 | 20.9 | 7.8 | 87.5 |
| Tu | 0.1 | 3.0 | 1.1 | 0.3 | 3.2 |
| Tujia | 1.5 | 83.2 | 27.7 | 5.6 | 71.1 |
| Uygur | 1.4 | 144.3 | 48.6 | 11.0 | 136.1 |
| Uzbek | 0.0 | 0.2 | 0.1 | 0.0 | 0.2 |
| Va | 0.0 | 4.3 | 1.1 | 0.3 | 3.5 |
| Xibe | 0.1 | 2.5 | 1.0 | 0.2 | 2.3 |
| Yao | 0.4 | 29.7 | 9.7 | 1.9 | 22.6 |
| Yi | 1.1 | 80.7 | 22.4 | 5.4 | 66.0 |
| Yugur | 0.0 | 0.2 | 0.0 | 0.0 | 0.1 |
| Zhuang | 2.7 | 189.9 | 60.2 | 12.0 | 127.7 |

*Notes:* "Staff and workers" refers to persons working in, and receiving payment from units of state ownership, collective ownership, joint ownership, share-holding ownership, foreign ownership, and ownership by entrepreneurs from Hong Kong, Macau, and Taiwan, and other types of ownership and their affiliated units. It does not include: i) persons employed in township enterprises; ii) persons employed in private enterprises; iii) urban self-employed persons; iv) retirees; v) re-employed retirees; vi) teachers in the schools run by the local people; vii) foreigners and persons from Hong Kong, Macau, and Taiwan who work in urban units; and viii) other persons not to be included by relevant regulations. (Data of 1998 and afterward refer to fully employed staff and workers. Other related statistics such as total wage bill and average wage are adjusted since 1998 accordingly.)

*Table 2.4* Number of staff and workers in state-owned units at the year-end by sector (unit: 1,000 persons)

| Ethnic group | Total | Agriculture, forestry, animal husbandry, and fishing | Mining | Manufacturing | Production and supply of electricity, gas, and water |
|---|---|---|---|---|---|
| National total | 62,319.8 | 3,927.4 | 2,356.9 | 5,989.6 | 2,056.8 |
| Achang | 1.4 | 0.1 | 0.0 | 0.1 | 0.0 |
| Bai | 74.2 | 5.5 | 1.5 | 5.6 | 1.7 |
| Baonan | 1.0 | 0.1 | 0.0 | 0.2 | 0.0 |
| Blang | 3.7 | 0.3 | 0.1 | 0.3 | 0.1 |
| Buyi | 119.0 | 2.6 | 2.6 | 12.8 | 4.0 |
| Dai | 46.1 | 3.9 | 0.9 | 3.3 | 1.0 |
| Daur | 9.7 | 2.0 | 0.2 | 0.6 | 0.4 |
| Deang | 0.7 | 0.1 | 0.0 | 0.1 | 0.0 |
| Derung | 0.3 | 0.0 | 0.0 | 0.0 | 0.0 |
| Dong | 119.6 | 3.6 | 2.6 | 11.7 | 4.0 |
| Dongxiang | 33.7 | 3.3 | 1.4 | 5.3 | 1.2 |
| Ewenki | 2.1 | 0.4 | 0.1 | 0.1 | 0.1 |
| Gaoshan | 0.2 | 0.0 | 0.0 | 0.0 | 0.0 |
| Gelao | 23.2 | 0.5 | 0.5 | 2.5 | 0.8 |
| *Han* | *56,578.4* | *3,213.2* | *2,193.7* | *5,533.0* | *1,881.7* |
| Hani | 57.3 | 4.9 | 1.1 | 4.1 | 1.2 |
| Hezhe | 0.4 | 0.1 | 0.0 | 0.0 | 0.0 |
| Hui | 607.7 | 61.3 | 18.2 | 51.6 | 24.4 |
| Jing | 1.0 | 0.1 | 0.0 | 0.1 | 0.0 |
| Jingpo | 5.3 | 0.4 | 0.1 | 0.4 | 0.1 |
| Jino | 0.8 | 0.1 | 0.0 | 0.1 | 0.0 |
| Kazak | 123.0 | 40.7 | 4.8 | 3.4 | 1.6 |
| Kirgiz | 15.8 | 5.2 | 0.6 | 0.4 | 0.2 |
| Korean | 132.6 | 17.5 | 4.1 | 13.7 | 4.6 |
| Lahu | 18.1 | 1.5 | 0.3 | 1.3 | 0.4 |
| Lhoba | 0.2 | 0.0 | 0.0 | 0.0 | 0.0 |
| Li | 90.9 | 27.8 | 1.6 | 3.8 | 2.0 |
| Lisu | 25.2 | 2.1 | 0.5 | 1.8 | 0.5 |
| Manchu | 722.3 | 72.0 | 31.1 | 83.1 | 26.5 |
| Maonan | 4.5 | 0.2 | 0.1 | 0.5 | 0.2 |
| Miao | 361.7 | 13.8 | 8.2 | 35.7 | 11.4 |
| Monba | 0.5 | 0.0 | 0.0 | 0.0 | 0.0 |

Table 2.4 (cont.)

| Ethnic group | Total | Agriculture, forestry, animal husbandry, and fishing | Mining | Manufacturing | Production and supply of electricity, gas, and water |
|---|---|---|---|---|---|
| Mongol | 394.6 | 64.0 | 11.9 | 18.6 | 14.4 |
| Mulao | 8.9 | 0.5 | 0.1 | 0.9 | 0.3 |
| Naxi | 12.3 | 1.0 | 0.2 | 0.9 | 0.3 |
| Nu | 1.2 | 0.1 | 0.0 | 0.1 | 0.0 |
| Oroqen | 0.6 | 0.1 | 0.0 | 0.0 | 0.0 |
| Pumi | 1.3 | 0.1 | 0.0 | 0.1 | 0.0 |
| Qiang | 11.4 | 0.3 | 0.4 | 1.3 | 0.3 |
| Russian | 1.3 | 0.4 | 0.0 | 0.0 | 0.0 |
| Salar | 6.8 | 0.5 | 0.2 | 0.4 | 0.3 |
| She | 29.7 | 1.2 | 0.4 | 1.7 | 1.1 |
| Shui | 16.3 | 0.4 | 0.4 | 1.7 | 0.5 |
| Tajik | 4.0 | 1.3 | 0.2 | 0.1 | 0.1 |
| Tatar | 0.5 | 0.1 | 0.0 | 0.0 | 0.0 |
| Tibetan | 295.8 | 10.1 | 5.4 | 18.0 | 12.2 |
| Tu | 15.1 | 0.9 | 0.4 | 1.0 | 0.6 |
| Tujia | 342.9 | 15.8 | 8.6 | 38.0 | 10.8 |
| Uygur | 825.4 | 273.0 | 32.2 | 23.1 | 10.9 |
| Uzbek | 1.2 | 0.4 | 0.0 | 0.0 | 0.0 |
| Va | 15.8 | 1.3 | 0.3 | 1.1 | 0.3 |
| Xibe | 14.3 | 2.2 | 0.7 | 1.4 | 0.5 |
| Yao | 110.4 | 5.9 | 1.9 | 9.7 | 3.7 |
| Yi | 303.5 | 18.9 | 7.2 | 26.3 | 7.5 |
| Yugur | 0.9 | 0.1 | 0.0 | 0.1 | 0.0 |
| Zhuang | 695.5 | 44.9 | 10.7 | 66.3 | 23.5 |

| Ethnic group | Construction | Transport, storage, and post | Information transmission, computer service and software | Wholesale and retail trade | Hotels and catering services |
|---|---|---|---|---|---|
| National total | 2,502.6 | 4,218.3 | 592.8 | 2,043.6 | 633.4 |
| Achang | 0.1 | 0.1 | 0.0 | 0.0 | 0.0 |
| Bai | 3.2 | 4.4 | 0.7 | 2.0 | 0.6 |
| Baonan | 0.0 | 0.1 | 0.0 | 0.0 | 0.0 |
| Blang | 0.1 | 0.2 | 0.0 | 0.1 | 0.0 |

*Table 2.4* (*cont.*)

| Ethnic group | Construction | Transport, storage, and post | Information transmission, computer service and software | Wholesale and retail trade | Hotels and catering services |
|---|---|---|---|---|---|
| Buyi | 9.9 | 6.1 | 0.6 | 5.1 | 0.9 |
| Dai | 1.8 | 2.7 | 0.5 | 1.2 | 0.4 |
| Daur | 0.3 | 0.8 | 0.1 | 0.3 | 0.1 |
| Deang | 0.0 | 0.0 | 0.0 | 0.0 | 0.0 |
| Derung | 0.0 | 0.0 | 0.0 | 0.0 | 0.0 |
| Dong | 7.5 | 6.9 | 0.7 | 4.3 | 1.1 |
| Dongxiang | 1.4 | 2.2 | 0.4 | 0.9 | 0.3 |
| Ewenki | 0.1 | 0.2 | 0.0 | 0.1 | 0.0 |
| Gaoshan | 0.0 | 0.0 | 0.0 | 0.0 | 0.0 |
| Gelao | 1.9 | 1.2 | 0.1 | 1.0 | 0.2 |
| *Han* | *2,282.7* | *3,849.1* | *541.0* | *1,888.4* | *580.5* |
| Hani | 2.2 | 3.4 | 0.6 | 1.5 | 0.5 |
| Hezhe | 0.0 | 0.0 | 0.0 | 0.0 | 0.0 |
| Hui | 25.0 | 41.8 | 6.0 | 18.0 | 6.0 |
| Jing | 0.0 | 0.1 | 0.0 | 0.0 | 0.0 |
| Jingpo | 0.2 | 0.3 | 0.1 | 0.1 | 0.0 |
| Jino | 0.0 | 0.0 | 0.0 | 0.0 | 0.0 |
| Kazak | 3.4 | 6.0 | 0.8 | 1.6 | 1.0 |
| Kirgiz | 0.4 | 0.8 | 0.1 | 0.2 | 0.1 |
| Korean | 4.3 | 10.6 | 1.4 | 3.4 | 1.2 |
| Lahu | 0.7 | 1.1 | 0.2 | 0.5 | 0.1 |
| Lhoba | 0.0 | 0.0 | 0.0 | 0.0 | 0.0 |
| Li | 5.0 | 4.4 | 1.0 | 2.2 | 1.3 |
| Lisu | 1.0 | 1.5 | 0.3 | 0.7 | 0.2 |
| Manchu | 24.1 | 60.4 | 6.1 | 18.5 | 6.0 |
| Maonan | 0.2 | 0.3 | 0.0 | 0.2 | 0.0 |
| Miao | 22.2 | 21.3 | 2.6 | 12.5 | 3.1 |
| Monba | 0.0 | 0.0 | 0.0 | 0.0 | 0.0 |
| Mongol | 10.6 | 33.0 | 4.8 | 9.7 | 3.3 |
| Mulao | 0.3 | 0.5 | 0.1 | 0.3 | 0.1 |
| Naxi | 0.5 | 0.7 | 0.1 | 0.3 | 0.1 |
| Nu | 0.0 | 0.1 | 0.0 | 0.0 | 0.0 |
| Oroqen | 0.0 | 0.1 | 0.0 | 0.0 | 0.0 |
| Pumi | 0.1 | 0.1 | 0.0 | 0.0 | 0.0 |
| Qiang | 0.7 | 0.6 | 0.1 | 0.3 | 0.1 |
| Russian | 0.0 | 0.1 | 0.0 | 0.0 | 0.0 |
| Salar | 0.4 | 0.6 | 0.1 | 0.2 | 0.1 |

*Table 2.4* (*cont.*)

| Ethnic group | Construction | Transport, storage, and post | Information transmission, computer service and software | Wholesale and retail trade | Hotels and catering services |
|---|---|---|---|---|---|
| She | 1.5 | 2.0 | 0.3 | 0.9 | 0.3 |
| Shui | 1.3 | 0.8 | 0.1 | 0.7 | 0.1 |
| Tajik | 0.1 | 0.2 | 0.0 | 0.1 | 0.0 |
| Tatar | 0.0 | 0.0 | 0.0 | 0.0 | 0.0 |
| Tibetan | 10.7 | 16.7 | 4.7 | 8.8 | 4.6 |
| Tu | 0.8 | 1.3 | 0.2 | 0.5 | 0.1 |
| Tujia | 16.7 | 23.7 | 3.4 | 10.9 | 2.8 |
| Uygur | 22.5 | 40.5 | 5.2 | 10.5 | 6.4 |
| Uzbek | 0.0 | 0.1 | 0.0 | 0.0 | 0.0 |
| Va | 0.6 | 0.9 | 0.2 | 0.4 | 0.1 |
| Xibe | 0.4 | 1.1 | 0.1 | 0.3 | 0.1 |
| Yao | 3.3 | 7.0 | 0.9 | 3.4 | 1.2 |
| Yi | 15.2 | 17.2 | 3.0 | 8.5 | 2.2 |
| Yugur | 0.0 | 0.1 | 0.0 | 0.0 | 0.0 |
| Zhuang | 16.8 | 43.5 | 6.0 | 23.6 | 7.8 |

| Ethnic group | Financial intermediation | Real estate | Leasing and business services | Scientific research, technical services, and geological prospecting | Management of water conservancy, environment, and public facilities |
|---|---|---|---|---|---|
| National total | 1,549.0 | 439.0 | 1,047.5 | 1,797.4 | 1,525.2 |
| Achang | 0.0 | 0.0 | 0.0 | 0.0 | 0.0 |
| Bai | 1.8 | 0.2 | 0.6 | 1.9 | 1.4 |
| Baonan | 0.0 | 0.0 | 0.0 | 0.0 | 0.0 |
| Blang | 0.1 | 0.0 | 0.0 | 0.1 | 0.1 |
| Buyi | 2.0 | 0.5 | 1.2 | 2.6 | 1.8 |
| Dai | 1.2 | 0.1 | 0.3 | 1.2 | 0.9 |
| Daur | 0.2 | 0.1 | 0.1 | 0.3 | 0.3 |
| Deang | 0.0 | 0.0 | 0.0 | 0.0 | 0.0 |
| Derung | 0.0 | 0.0 | 0.0 | 0.0 | 0.0 |
| Dong | 2.2 | 0.6 | 1.4 | 2.7 | 2.2 |
| Dongxiang | 0.8 | 0.1 | 0.3 | 0.9 | 0.8 |
| Ewenki | 0.1 | 0.0 | 0.0 | 0.1 | 0.1 |

*Table 2.4  (cont.)*

| Ethnic group | Financial intermediation | Real estate | Leasing and business services | Scientific research, technical services, and geological prospecting | Management of water conservancy, environment, and public facilities |
|---|---|---|---|---|---|
| Gaoshan | 0.0 | 0.0 | 0.0 | 0.0 | 0.0 |
| Gelao | 0.4 | 0.1 | 0.2 | 0.5 | 0.3 |
| *Han* | *1,417.3* | *406.9* | *974.4* | *1,645.8* | *1,386.2* |
| Hani | 1.4 | 0.1 | 0.4 | 1.5 | 1.1 |
| Hezhe | 0.0 | 0.0 | 0.0 | 0.0 | 0.0 |
| Hui | 15.5 | 3.2 | 9.8 | 19.3 | 17.5 |
| Jing | 0.0 | 0.0 | 0.0 | 0.0 | 0.0 |
| Jingpo | 0.1 | 0.0 | 0.0 | 0.1 | 0.1 |
| Jino | 0.0 | 0.0 | 0.0 | 0.0 | 0.0 |
| Kazak | 2.1 | 0.5 | 1.3 | 2.6 | 2.7 |
| Kirgiz | 0.3 | 0.1 | 0.2 | 0.3 | 0.4 |
| Korean | 3.2 | 1.1 | 1.7 | 4.0 | 4.2 |
| Lahu | 0.5 | 0.0 | 0.1 | 0.5 | 0.4 |
| Lhoba | 0.0 | 0.0 | 0.0 | 0.0 | 0.0 |
| Li | 2.1 | 0.8 | 1.2 | 2.0 | 2.9 |
| Lisu | 0.6 | 0.1 | 0.2 | 0.7 | 0.5 |
| Manchu | 17.7 | 6.6 | 12.4 | 20.7 | 22.1 |
| Maonan | 0.1 | 0.0 | 0.1 | 0.1 | 0.1 |
| Miao | 6.9 | 1.8 | 3.8 | 8.2 | 6.8 |
| Monba | 0.0 | 0.0 | 0.0 | 0.0 | 0.0 |
| Mongol | 10.5 | 2.4 | 5.1 | 10.2 | 12.8 |
| Mulao | 0.2 | 0.1 | 0.1 | 0.2 | 0.2 |
| Naxi | 0.3 | 0.0 | 0.1 | 0.3 | 0.2 |
| Nu | 0.0 | 0.0 | 0.0 | 0.0 | 0.0 |
| Oroqen | 0.0 | 0.0 | 0.0 | 0.0 | 0.0 |
| Pumi | 0.0 | 0.0 | 0.0 | 0.0 | 0.0 |
| Qiang | 0.3 | 0.0 | 0.2 | 0.4 | 0.2 |
| Russian | 0.0 | 0.0 | 0.0 | 0.0 | 0.0 |
| Salar | 0.2 | 0.0 | 0.1 | 0.4 | 0.1 |
| She | 1.0 | 0.3 | 0.6 | 0.7 | 0.6 |
| Shui | 0.3 | 0.1 | 0.2 | 0.4 | 0.3 |
| Tajik | 0.1 | 0.0 | 0.0 | 0.1 | 0.1 |
| Tatar | 0.0 | 0.0 | 0.0 | 0.0 | 0.0 |
| Tibetan | 9.6 | 0.5 | 1.6 | 11.5 | 4.8 |
| Tu | 0.4 | 0.0 | 0.1 | 0.8 | 0.3 |
| Tujia | 7.1 | 2.2 | 3.7 | 8.1 | 7.5 |

Table 2.4  (cont.)

| Ethnic group | Financial intermediation | Real estate | Leasing and business services | Scientific research, technical services, and geological prospecting | Management of water conservancy, environment, and public facilities |
|---|---|---|---|---|---|
| Uygur | 14.4 | 3.3 | 8.9 | 17.7 | 18.3 |
| Uzbek | 0.0 | 0.0 | 0.0 | 0.0 | 0.0 |
| Va | 0.4 | 0.0 | 0.1 | 0.4 | 0.3 |
| Xibe | 0.3 | 0.1 | 0.2 | 0.4 | 0.4 |
| Yao | 2.6 | 0.8 | 1.8 | 2.7 | 2.6 |
| Yi | 7.3 | 0.9 | 2.8 | 8.4 | 5.8 |
| Yugur | 0.0 | 0.0 | 0.0 | 0.0 | 0.0 |
| Zhuang | 16.7 | 4.9 | 11.3 | 17.7 | 16.8 |

| Ethnic group | Services to households and other services | Education | Health, social securities, and social welfare | Culture, sports, and entertainment | Public management and social organization |
|---|---|---|---|---|---|
| *National total* | 210.3 | 13,907.7 | 4,377.8 | 1,061.5 | 12,083.1 |
| Achang | 0.0 | 0.4 | 0.1 | 0.0 | 0.3 |
| Bai | 0.1 | 19.8 | 5.3 | 1.3 | 16.6 |
| Baonan | 0.0 | 0.2 | 0.1 | 0.0 | 0.2 |
| Blang | 0.0 | 1.0 | 0.3 | 0.1 | 0.8 |
| Buyi | 0.2 | 30.7 | 7.3 | 1.6 | 26.7 |
| Dai | 0.0 | 12.5 | 3.3 | 0.8 | 10.3 |
| Daur | 0.1 | 1.7 | 0.5 | 0.2 | 1.6 |
| Deang | 0.0 | 0.2 | 0.1 | 0.0 | 0.2 |
| Derung | 0.0 | 0.1 | 0.0 | 0.0 | 0.1 |
| Dong | 0.2 | 30.8 | 8.5 | 1.6 | 27.0 |
| Dongxiang | 0.1 | 6.4 | 1.6 | 0.6 | 5.8 |
| Ewenki | 0.0 | 0.4 | 0.1 | 0.0 | 0.4 |
| Gaoshan | 0.0 | 0.0 | 0.0 | 0.0 | 0.0 |
| Gelao | 0.0 | 6.0 | 1.4 | 0.3 | 5.2 |
| *Han* | 197.0 | 12,654.8 | 3,991.2 | 966.3 | 10,974.2 |
| Hani | 0.1 | 15.5 | 4.1 | 1.0 | 12.7 |
| Hezhe | 0.0 | 0.1 | 0.0 | 0.0 | 0.1 |
| Hui | 1.7 | 121.4 | 39.7 | 11.7 | 115.4 |
| Jing | 0.0 | 0.3 | 0.1 | 0.0 | 0.2 |
| Jingpo | 0.0 | 1.4 | 0.4 | 0.1 | 1.2 |

*Table 2.4* (*cont.*)

| Ethnic group | Services to households and other services | Education | Health, social securities, and social welfare | Culture, sports, and entertainment | Public management and social organization |
|---|---|---|---|---|---|
| Jino | 0.0 | 0.2 | 0.1 | 0.0 | 0.2 |
| Kazak | 0.1 | 21.3 | 7.1 | 1.6 | 20.3 |
| Kirgiz | 0.0 | 2.7 | 0.9 | 0.2 | 2.6 |
| Korean | 0.7 | 24.9 | 9.0 | 2.4 | 20.7 |
| Lahu | 0.0 | 4.9 | 1.3 | 0.3 | 4.0 |
| Lhoba | 0.0 | 0.0 | 0.0 | 0.0 | 0.1 |
| Li | 0.0 | 13.8 | 4.1 | 1.5 | 13.4 |
| Lisu | 0.0 | 6.8 | 1.8 | 0.4 | 5.6 |
| Manchu | 3.5 | 133.2 | 47.2 | 12.7 | 118.1 |
| Maonan | 0.0 | 1.2 | 0.4 | 0.1 | 0.9 |
| Miao | 0.6 | 92.7 | 24.9 | 5.2 | 80.1 |
| Monba | 0.0 | 0.1 | 0.0 | 0.0 | 0.2 |
| Mongol | 1.3 | 78.0 | 23.4 | 7.4 | 73.3 |
| Mulao | 0.0 | 2.4 | 0.7 | 0.1 | 1.6 |
| Naxi | 0.0 | 3.3 | 0.9 | 0.2 | 2.7 |
| Nu | 0.0 | 0.3 | 0.1 | 0.0 | 0.3 |
| Oroqen | 0.0 | 0.1 | 0.0 | 0.0 | 0.1 |
| Pumi | 0.0 | 0.4 | 0.1 | 0.0 | 0.3 |
| Qiang | 0.0 | 2.9 | 0.8 | 0.2 | 2.3 |
| Russian | 0.0 | 0.2 | 0.1 | 0.0 | 0.2 |
| Salar | 0.0 | 1.3 | 0.5 | 0.1 | 1.4 |
| She | 0.1 | 8.1 | 2.3 | 0.6 | 6.1 |
| Shui | 0.0 | 4.2 | 1.0 | 0.2 | 3.6 |
| Tajik | 0.0 | 0.7 | 0.2 | 0.1 | 0.7 |
| Tatar | 0.0 | 0.1 | 0.0 | 0.0 | 0.1 |
| Tibetan | 0.7 | 60.2 | 19.9 | 7.7 | 87.4 |
| Tu | 0.1 | 3.0 | 1.1 | 0.3 | 3.2 |
| Tujia | 0.7 | 81.7 | 25.4 | 5.1 | 70.5 |
| Uygur | 0.8 | 143.3 | 47.8 | 10.7 | 136.0 |
| Uzbek | 0.0 | 0.2 | 0.1 | 0.0 | 0.2 |
| Va | 0.0 | 4.3 | 1.1 | 0.3 | 3.5 |
| Xibe | 0.0 | 2.5 | 0.9 | 0.2 | 2.3 |
| Yao | 0.1 | 29.3 | 9.3 | 1.7 | 22.5 |
| Yi | 0.5 | 80.1 | 21.0 | 5.0 | 65.8 |
| Yugur | 0.0 | 0.2 | 0.0 | 0.0 | 0.1 |
| Zhuang | 0.7 | 188.0 | 58.5 | 10.9 | 126.9 |

*Table 2.4 (cont.)*

*Notes:* (1) "Staff and workers" refers to persons working in, and receiving payment from units of state ownership, collective ownership, joint ownership, share-holding ownership, foreign ownership, and ownership by entrepreneurs from Hong Kong, Macau, and Taiwan, and other types of ownership and their affiliated units. It does not include: i) persons employed in township enterprises; ii) persons employed in private enterprises; iii) urban self-employed persons; iv) retirees; v) re-employed retirees; vi) teachers in the schools run by the local people; vii) foreigners and persons from Hong Kong, Macau, and Taiwan who work in urban units; and viii) other persons not to be included by relevant regulations. (Data of 1998 and afterward refer to fully employed staff and workers. Other related statistics such as total wage bill and average wage are adjusted since 1998 accordingly.) (2) "State-owned units" refers to economic units whose assets are owned by the state. Included are non-corporation units registered according to *Regulation of the People's Republic of China on the Registration of Enterprises and Corporations*, state organs, institutions, and social organizations at the central and local levels.

*Table 2.5* Number of scientific and technical personnel in urban collective-owned units at the year-end by sector (unit: 1,000 persons)

| Ethnic group | Total | Agriculture, forestry, animal husbandry, and fishing | Mining | Manufacturing | Production and supply of electricity, gas, and water |
|---|---|---|---|---|---|
| National total | 32,010.30 | 705.26 | 650.12 | 4,494.68 | 683.44 |
| Achang | 0.69 | 0.03 | 0.01 | 0.06 | 0.01 |
| Bai | 37.61 | 1.65 | 0.37 | 3.61 | 0.80 |
| Baonan | 0.37 | 0.01 | 0.01 | 0.04 | 0.01 |
| Blang | 1.86 | 0.09 | 0.02 | 0.17 | 0.04 |
| Buyi | 57.96 | 0.96 | 1.34 | 6.29 | 1.28 |
| Dai | 23.46 | 1.19 | 0.19 | 2.17 | 0.50 |
| Daur | 4.15 | 0.34 | 0.13 | 0.43 | 0.12 |
| Deang | 0.36 | 0.02 | 0.00 | 0.03 | 0.01 |
| Derung | 0.16 | 0.01 | 0.00 | 0.02 | 0.00 |
| Dong | 59.71 | 0.86 | 0.99 | 6.57 | 1.24 |
| Dongxiang | 11.94 | 0.54 | 0.22 | 1.22 | 0.26 |
| Ewenki | 0.96 | 0.08 | 0.03 | 0.10 | 0.03 |
| Gaoshan | 0.12 | 0.00 | 0.00 | 0.02 | 0.00 |
| Gelao | 11.26 | 0.18 | 0.26 | 1.22 | 0.25 |
| *Han* | *29,360.38* | *590.63* | *593.79* | *4,226.82* | *623.79* |
| Hani | 29.14 | 1.48 | 0.24 | 2.69 | 0.62 |
| Hezhe | 0.14 | 0.01 | 0.01 | 0.02 | 0.00 |
| Hui | 289.86 | 10.33 | 8.04 | 31.90 | 7.45 |

*Table 2.5* (*cont.*)

| Ethnic group | Total | Agriculture, forestry, animal husbandry, and fishing | Mining | Manufacturing | Production and supply of electricity, gas, and water |
|---|---|---|---|---|---|
| Jing | 0.49 | 0.01 | 0.00 | 0.04 | 0.01 |
| Jingpo | 2.68 | 0.14 | 0.02 | 0.25 | 0.06 |
| Jino | 0.42 | 0.02 | 0.00 | 0.04 | 0.01 |
| Kazak | 47.35 | 4.82 | 2.06 | 2.41 | 0.81 |
| Kirgiz | 6.08 | 0.62 | 0.26 | 0.31 | 0.10 |
| Korean | 61.00 | 3.26 | 1.56 | 7.33 | 1.49 |
| Lahu | 9.18 | 0.46 | 0.08 | 0.85 | 0.20 |
| Lhoba | 0.05 | 0.00 | 0.00 | 0.00 | 0.00 |
| Li | 30.83 | 3.84 | 0.28 | 1.82 | 0.46 |
| Lisu | 12.84 | 0.64 | 0.11 | 1.20 | 0.28 |
| Manchu | 337.45 | 9.76 | 8.31 | 46.47 | 8.53 |
| Maonan | 2.25 | 0.05 | 0.03 | 0.21 | 0.05 |
| Miao | 180.39 | 3.56 | 2.92 | 19.99 | 3.78 |
| Monba | 0.14 | 0.00 | 0.00 | 0.00 | 0.00 |
| Mongol | 181.58 | 12.21 | 4.62 | 19.75 | 5.22 |
| Mulao | 4.46 | 0.11 | 0.05 | 0.41 | 0.09 |
| Naxi | 6.26 | 0.31 | 0.05 | 0.58 | 0.13 |
| Nu | 0.58 | 0.03 | 0.00 | 0.05 | 0.01 |
| Oroqen | 0.25 | 0.02 | 0.01 | 0.03 | 0.01 |
| Pumi | 0.68 | 0.03 | 0.01 | 0.06 | 0.01 |
| Qiang | 5.96 | 0.14 | 0.09 | 0.75 | 0.15 |
| Russian | 0.56 | 0.05 | 0.02 | 0.04 | 0.01 |
| Salar | 3.03 | 0.15 | 0.04 | 0.22 | 0.09 |
| She | 19.21 | 0.23 | 0.10 | 3.61 | 0.40 |
| Shui | 7.94 | 0.14 | 0.18 | 0.85 | 0.17 |
| Tajik | 1.54 | 0.15 | 0.07 | 0.08 | 0.03 |
| Tatar | 0.18 | 0.02 | 0.01 | 0.01 | 0.00 |
| Tibetan | 106.48 | 2.68 | 0.97 | 7.64 | 3.02 |
| Tu | 6.79 | 0.32 | 0.09 | 0.54 | 0.20 |
| Tujia | 173.59 | 2.64 | 2.17 | 22.64 | 3.64 |
| Uygur | 317.93 | 32.29 | 13.83 | 16.23 | 5.43 |
| Uzbek | 0.47 | 0.05 | 0.02 | 0.02 | 0.01 |
| Va | 8.06 | 0.40 | 0.07 | 0.76 | 0.17 |
| Xibe | 6.26 | 0.25 | 0.18 | 0.83 | 0.16 |
| Yao | 56.58 | 1.19 | 0.49 | 5.80 | 1.14 |
| Yi | 154.76 | 6.13 | 1.81 | 15.93 | 3.46 |

Table 2.5  (cont.)

| Ethnic group | Total | Agriculture, forestry, animal husbandry, and fishing | Mining | Manufacturing | Production and supply of electricity, gas, and water |
|---|---|---|---|---|---|
| Yugur | 0.30 | 0.01 | 0.00 | 0.03 | 0.01 |
| Zhuang | 351.31 | 9.37 | 3.29 | 31.98 | 7.37 |

| Ethnic group | Construction | Transport, storage, and post | Information transmission, computer service and software | Wholesale and retail trade | Hotels and catering services |
|---|---|---|---|---|---|
| *National total* | 1,784.03 | 818.92 | 467.83 | 860.25 | 193.26 |
| Achang | 0.03 | 0.02 | 0.01 | 0.02 | 0.00 |
| Bai | 1.56 | 0.81 | 0.46 | 0.92 | 0.19 |
| Baonan | 0.02 | 0.01 | 0.00 | 0.01 | 0.00 |
| Blang | 0.07 | 0.04 | 0.02 | 0.05 | 0.01 |
| Buyi | 2.83 | 0.89 | 0.43 | 1.45 | 0.18 |
| Dai | 0.89 | 0.53 | 0.29 | 0.58 | 0.12 |
| Daur | 0.17 | 0.11 | 0.06 | 0.08 | 0.02 |
| Deang | 0.01 | 0.01 | 0.00 | 0.01 | 0.00 |
| Derung | 0.01 | 0.00 | 0.00 | 0.00 | 0.00 |
| Dong | 3.28 | 1.09 | 0.55 | 1.41 | 0.29 |
| Dongxiang | 0.50 | 0.32 | 0.15 | 0.22 | 0.06 |
| Ewenki | 0.04 | 0.02 | 0.01 | 0.02 | 0.00 |
| Gaoshan | 0.01 | 0.00 | 0.00 | 0.00 | 0.00 |
| Gelao | 0.55 | 0.17 | 0.08 | 0.28 | 0.03 |
| *Han* | 1,654.28 | 752.54 | 432.39 | 797.33 | 178.34 |
| Hani | 1.10 | 0.65 | 0.36 | 0.72 | 0.15 |
| Hezhe | 0.01 | 0.00 | 0.00 | 0.00 | 0.00 |
| Hui | 15.62 | 7.15 | 5.12 | 7.52 | 1.77 |
| Jing | 0.02 | 0.01 | 0.01 | 0.01 | 0.00 |
| Jingpo | 0.10 | 0.06 | 0.03 | 0.07 | 0.01 |
| Jino | 0.02 | 0.01 | 0.01 | 0.01 | 0.00 |
| Kazak | 2.38 | 1.15 | 0.52 | 1.13 | 0.30 |
| Kirgiz | 0.31 | 0.15 | 0.07 | 0.15 | 0.04 |
| Korean | 2.54 | 1.73 | 0.95 | 1.41 | 0.24 |
| Lahu | 0.35 | 0.21 | 0.11 | 0.23 | 0.05 |
| Lhoba | 0.00 | 0.00 | 0.00 | 0.00 | 0.00 |
| Li | 1.06 | 1.45 | 0.62 | 0.60 | 0.46 |

*Table 2.5* (cont.)

| Ethnic group | Construction | Transport, storage, and post | Information transmission, computer service and software | Wholesale and retail trade | Hotels and catering services |
|---|---|---|---|---|---|
| Lisu | 0.50 | 0.29 | 0.16 | 0.32 | 0.06 |
| Manchu | 15.96 | 10.23 | 6.30 | 8.97 | 2.13 |
| Maonan | 0.10 | 0.05 | 0.02 | 0.06 | 0.01 |
| Miao | 10.07 | 3.46 | 1.70 | 4.25 | 0.88 |
| Monba | 0.00 | 0.01 | 0.00 | 0.00 | 0.00 |
| Mongol | 7.43 | 4.78 | 2.54 | 3.32 | 0.86 |
| Mulao | 0.19 | 0.11 | 0.05 | 0.11 | 0.02 |
| Naxi | 0.24 | 0.14 | 0.08 | 0.15 | 0.03 |
| Nu | 0.02 | 0.01 | 0.01 | 0.01 | 0.00 |
| Oroqen | 0.01 | 0.01 | 0.00 | 0.01 | 0.00 |
| Pumi | 0.03 | 0.02 | 0.01 | 0.02 | 0.00 |
| Qiang | 0.47 | 0.12 | 0.06 | 0.11 | 0.02 |
| Russian | 0.03 | 0.01 | 0.01 | 0.01 | 0.00 |
| Salar | 0.17 | 0.10 | 0.06 | 0.06 | 0.01 |
| She | 1.41 | 0.42 | 0.25 | 0.48 | 0.11 |
| Shui | 0.38 | 0.13 | 0.06 | 0.20 | 0.03 |
| Tajik | 0.08 | 0.04 | 0.02 | 0.04 | 0.01 |
| Tatar | 0.01 | 0.00 | 0.00 | 0.00 | 0.00 |
| Tibetan | 5.02 | 3.28 | 2.22 | 1.28 | 0.30 |
| Tu | 0.39 | 0.22 | 0.12 | 0.13 | 0.03 |
| Tujia | 11.64 | 4.16 | 1.83 | 4.01 | 0.99 |
| Uygur | 15.97 | 7.71 | 3.50 | 7.60 | 2.02 |
| Uzbek | 0.02 | 0.01 | 0.01 | 0.01 | 0.00 |
| Va | 0.31 | 0.18 | 0.10 | 0.20 | 0.04 |
| Xibe | 0.29 | 0.20 | 0.10 | 0.16 | 0.04 |
| Yao | 2.79 | 1.38 | 0.67 | 1.38 | 0.36 |
| Yi | 7.71 | 3.25 | 1.74 | 3.54 | 0.68 |
| Yugur | 0.01 | 0.01 | 0.00 | 0.01 | 0.00 |
| Zhuang | 14.37 | 9.26 | 3.84 | 8.91 | 2.05 |

| Ethnic group | Financial intermediation | Real estate | Leasing and business services | Scientific research, technical services, and geological prospecting | Management of water conservancy, environment, and public facilities |
|---|---|---|---|---|---|
| *National total* | *1,562.39* | *334.90* | *382.64* | *1,135.00* | *276.68* |
| Achang | 0.03 | 0.00 | 0.00 | 0.03 | 0.01 |

Table 2.5 (cont.)

| Ethnic group | Financial intermediation | Real estate | Leasing and business services | Scientific research, technical services, and geological prospecting | Management of water conservancy, environment, and public facilities |
|---|---|---|---|---|---|
| Bai | 1.82 | 0.26 | 0.26 | 1.33 | 0.34 |
| Baonan | 0.01 | 0.00 | 0.00 | 0.02 | 0.01 |
| Blang | 0.09 | 0.01 | 0.01 | 0.07 | 0.02 |
| Buyi | 2.20 | 0.85 | 0.43 | 1.70 | 0.31 |
| Dai | 1.19 | 0.13 | 0.15 | 0.86 | 0.22 |
| Daur | 0.20 | 0.03 | 0.04 | 0.13 | 0.05 |
| Deang | 0.02 | 0.00 | 0.00 | 0.01 | 0.00 |
| Derung | 0.01 | 0.00 | 0.00 | 0.01 | 0.00 |
| Dong | 2.36 | 0.78 | 0.47 | 1.67 | 0.38 |
| Dongxiang | 0.47 | 0.06 | 0.07 | 0.51 | 0.16 |
| Ewenki | 0.05 | 0.01 | 0.01 | 0.03 | 0.01 |
| Gaoshan | 0.01 | 0.00 | 0.00 | 0.00 | 0.00 |
| Gelao | 0.42 | 0.17 | 0.08 | 0.33 | 0.06 |
| *Han* | *1,438.19* | *309.68* | *355.81* | *1,039.36* | *249.90* |
| Hani | 1.47 | 0.16 | 0.19 | 1.07 | 0.28 |
| Hezhe | 0.01 | 0.00 | 0.00 | 0.01 | 0.00 |
| Hui | 14.52 | 2.86 | 3.62 | 12.43 | 3.53 |
| Jing | 0.02 | 0.00 | 0.01 | 0.02 | 0.00 |
| Jingpo | 0.14 | 0.01 | 0.02 | 0.10 | 0.03 |
| Jino | 0.02 | 0.00 | 0.00 | 0.02 | 0.00 |
| Kazak | 1.61 | 0.36 | 0.53 | 1.82 | 0.65 |
| Kirgiz | 0.21 | 0.05 | 0.07 | 0.23 | 0.08 |
| Korean | 3.39 | 0.58 | 0.78 | 2.52 | 0.73 |
| Lahu | 0.46 | 0.05 | 0.06 | 0.34 | 0.09 |
| Lhoba | 0.00 | 0.00 | 0.00 | 0.00 | 0.00 |
| Li | 1.41 | 0.46 | 0.45 | 0.84 | 0.17 |
| Lisu | 0.65 | 0.07 | 0.08 | 0.47 | 0.12 |
| Manchu | 19.81 | 3.86 | 4.77 | 13.97 | 3.81 |
| Maonan | 0.10 | 0.02 | 0.02 | 0.07 | 0.02 |
| Miao | 7.31 | 2.22 | 1.37 | 5.31 | 1.18 |
| Monba | 0.01 | 0.00 | 0.00 | 0.01 | 0.00 |
| Mongol | 9.01 | 1.16 | 1.80 | 6.13 | 2.45 |
| Mulao | 0.20 | 0.05 | 0.05 | 0.14 | 0.04 |
| Naxi | 0.32 | 0.03 | 0.04 | 0.23 | 0.06 |
| Nu | 0.03 | 0.00 | 0.00 | 0.02 | 0.01 |
| Oroqen | 0.01 | 0.00 | 0.00 | 0.01 | 0.00 |
| Pumi | 0.03 | 0.00 | 0.00 | 0.03 | 0.01 |

*Table 2.5* (*cont.*)

| Ethnic group | Financial intermediation | Real estate | Leasing and business services | Scientific research, technical services, and geological prospecting | Management of water conservancy, environment, and public facilities |
|---|---|---|---|---|---|
| Qiang | 0.26 | 0.04 | 0.04 | 0.23 | 0.03 |
| Russian | 0.02 | 0.00 | 0.01 | 0.02 | 0.01 |
| Salar | 0.16 | 0.00 | 0.02 | 0.18 | 0.05 |
| She | 1.03 | 0.24 | 0.27 | 0.53 | 0.11 |
| Shui | 0.30 | 0.11 | 0.06 | 0.23 | 0.04 |
| Tajik | 0.05 | 0.01 | 0.02 | 0.06 | 0.02 |
| Tatar | 0.01 | 0.00 | 0.00 | 0.01 | 0.00 |
| Tibetan | 7.44 | 0.24 | 0.46 | 4.95 | 0.81 |
| Tu | 0.36 | 0.01 | 0.05 | 0.40 | 0.10 |
| Tujia | 7.06 | 2.08 | 1.32 | 5.08 | 1.31 |
| Uygur | 10.82 | 2.45 | 3.54 | 12.18 | 4.36 |
| Uzbek | 0.02 | 0.00 | 0.01 | 0.02 | 0.01 |
| Va | 0.41 | 0.04 | 0.05 | 0.29 | 0.08 |
| Xibe | 0.36 | 0.07 | 0.08 | 0.25 | 0.08 |
| Yao | 2.54 | 0.59 | 0.56 | 1.67 | 0.46 |
| Yi | 7.28 | 1.04 | 1.01 | 5.62 | 1.22 |
| Yugur | 0.01 | 0.00 | 0.00 | 0.01 | 0.00 |
| Zhuang | 15.92 | 3.32 | 3.69 | 11.04 | 3.04 |

| Ethnic group | Services to households and other services | Education | Health, social securities, and social welfare | Culture, sports, and entertainment | Public management and social organization |
|---|---|---|---|---|---|
| *National total* | *64.92* | *12,008.58* | *3,640.61* | *544.24* | *1,402.53* |
| Achang | 0.00 | 0.31 | 0.08 | 0.01 | 0.03 |
| Bai | 0.04 | 16.80 | 4.13 | 0.68 | 1.60 |
| Baonan | 0.00 | 0.16 | 0.04 | 0.01 | 0.02 |
| Blang | 0.00 | 0.83 | 0.20 | 0.04 | 0.07 |
| Buyi | 0.08 | 26.80 | 5.59 | 0.77 | 3.59 |
| Dai | 0.02 | 10.53 | 2.57 | 0.45 | 0.89 |
| Daur | 0.01 | 1.49 | 0.45 | 0.09 | 0.19 |
| Deang | 0.00 | 0.16 | 0.04 | 0.01 | 0.01 |
| Derung | 0.00 | 0.07 | 0.02 | 0.00 | 0.01 |
| Dong | 0.09 | 26.51 | 6.67 | 0.78 | 3.70 |

Table 2.5 (cont.)

| Ethnic group | Services to households and other services | Education | Health, social securities, and social welfare | Culture, sports, and entertainment | Public management and social organization |
|---|---|---|---|---|---|
| Dongxiang | 0.00 | 5.12 | 1.22 | 0.23 | 0.62 |
| Ewenki | 0.00 | 0.36 | 0.10 | 0.02 | 0.05 |
| Gaoshan | 0.00 | 0.04 | 0.01 | 0.00 | 0.01 |
| Gelao | 0.02 | 5.22 | 1.08 | 0.15 | 0.71 |
| *Han* | *59.97* | *10,953.44* | *3,337.90* | *493.95* | *1,271.17* |
| Hani | 0.02 | 13.08 | 3.19 | 0.56 | 1.10 |
| Hezhe | 0.00 | 0.05 | 0.02 | 0.00 | 0.01 |
| Hui | 0.64 | 104.87 | 31.60 | 6.39 | 14.35 |
| Jing | 0.00 | 0.22 | 0.06 | 0.01 | 0.02 |
| Jingpo | 0.00 | 1.20 | 0.29 | 0.05 | 0.10 |
| Jino | 0.00 | 0.19 | 0.05 | 0.01 | 0.02 |
| Kazak | 0.05 | 17.24 | 5.59 | 0.98 | 2.96 |
| Kirgiz | 0.01 | 2.21 | 0.72 | 0.13 | 0.38 |
| Korean | 0.13 | 21.22 | 7.25 | 1.27 | 2.62 |
| Lahu | 0.01 | 4.12 | 1.00 | 0.18 | 0.35 |
| Lhoba | 0.00 | 0.02 | 0.01 | 0.00 | 0.00 |
| Li | 0.00 | 12.08 | 3.37 | 0.77 | 0.67 |
| Lisu | 0.01 | 5.75 | 1.41 | 0.24 | 0.49 |
| Manchu | 1.09 | 114.91 | 38.28 | 7.12 | 13.17 |
| Maonan | 0.00 | 1.03 | 0.26 | 0.03 | 0.12 |
| Miao | 0.25 | 79.62 | 19.78 | 2.50 | 10.24 |
| Monba | 0.00 | 0.06 | 0.02 | 0.01 | 0.01 |
| Mongol | 0.36 | 67.39 | 19.84 | 4.15 | 8.54 |
| Mulao | 0.00 | 2.01 | 0.54 | 0.07 | 0.23 |
| Naxi | 0.01 | 2.80 | 0.69 | 0.12 | 0.24 |
| Nu | 0.00 | 0.26 | 0.06 | 0.01 | 0.02 |
| Oroqen | 0.00 | 0.09 | 0.03 | 0.01 | 0.01 |
| Pumi | 0.00 | 0.31 | 0.07 | 0.01 | 0.03 |
| Qiang | 0.01 | 2.45 | 0.69 | 0.08 | 0.25 |
| Russian | 0.00 | 0.20 | 0.06 | 0.01 | 0.03 |
| Salar | 0.01 | 1.13 | 0.36 | 0.08 | 0.12 |
| She | 0.03 | 7.15 | 1.96 | 0.28 | 0.58 |
| Shui | 0.01 | 3.68 | 0.77 | 0.11 | 0.49 |
| Tajik | 0.00 | 0.56 | 0.18 | 0.03 | 0.10 |
| Tatar | 0.00 | 0.07 | 0.02 | 0.00 | 0.01 |
| Tibetan | 0.16 | 43.64 | 12.42 | 3.30 | 5.20 |

*Table 2.5* (*cont.*)

| Ethnic group | Services to households and other services | Education | Health, social securities, and social welfare | Culture, sports, and entertainment | Public management and social organization |
|---|---|---|---|---|---|
| Tu | 0.02 | 2.55 | 0.80 | 0.17 | 0.26 |
| Tujia | 0.25 | 69.80 | 21.03 | 2.41 | 9.53 |
| Uygur | 0.33 | 115.75 | 37.52 | 6.56 | 19.86 |
| Uzbek | 0.00 | 0.17 | 0.06 | 0.01 | 0.03 |
| Va | 0.01 | 3.61 | 0.88 | 0.15 | 0.31 |
| Xibe | 0.01 | 2.07 | 0.74 | 0.13 | 0.25 |
| Yao | 0.07 | 24.66 | 7.10 | 0.81 | 2.90 |
| Yi | 0.16 | 68.13 | 16.97 | 2.64 | 6.44 |
| Yugur | 0.00 | 0.13 | 0.03 | 0.01 | 0.02 |
| Zhuang | 0.35 | 157.64 | 43.45 | 5.50 | 16.92 |

*Notes:* "Collective-owned units" refers to economic units registered according to *Regulation of the People's Republic of China on the Registration of Enterprises and Corporations* where the means of production are collectively owned.

*Table 2.6* Number of employed persons in private enterprises and self-employed individuals at the year-end by sector (1,000 persons)

| Ethnic group | Total | Manufacturing | Construction | Transport, storage, and post |
|---|---|---|---|---|
| *National total* | *107,246.07* | *29,880.84* | *3,796.23* | *3,988.59* |
| Achang | 2.06 | 0.34 | 0.21 | 0.08 |
| Bai | 108.29 | 18.18 | 9.99 | 4.18 |
| Baonan | 0.76 | 0.12 | 0.03 | 0.02 |
| Blang | 5.58 | 0.92 | 0.58 | 0.22 |
| Buyi | 103.61 | 19.60 | 2.49 | 4.13 |
| Dai | 70.19 | 11.43 | 7.31 | 2.74 |
| Daur | 9.19 | 1.58 | 0.29 | 0.54 |
| Deang | 1.08 | 0.17 | 0.11 | 0.04 |
| Derung | 0.48 | 0.09 | 0.04 | 0.02 |
| Dong | 139.61 | 27.67 | 2.94 | 5.45 |
| Dongxiang | 23.65 | 3.77 | 1.01 | 0.60 |
| Ewenki | 2.07 | 0.36 | 0.07 | 0.12 |
| Gaoshan | 0.35 | 0.09 | 0.01 | 0.02 |
| Gelao | 19.53 | 3.54 | 0.42 | 0.78 |
| *Han* | *100,114.01* | *28,532.27* | *3,508.37* | *3,626.77* |
| Hani | 87.28 | 14.25 | 9.11 | 3.41 |
| Hezhe | 0.35 | 0.06 | 0.01 | 0.02 |

*Table 2.6* (*cont.*)

| Ethnic group | Total | Manufacturing | Construction | Transport, storage, and post |
|---|---|---|---|---|
| Hui | 784.43 | 162.77 | 34.68 | 28.82 |
| Jing | 1.31 | 0.24 | 0.02 | 0.08 |
| Jingpo | 7.99 | 1.30 | 0.83 | 0.31 |
| Jino | 1.26 | 0.20 | 0.13 | 0.05 |
| Kazak | 96.86 | 14.08 | 2.36 | 5.34 |
| Kirgiz | 12.46 | 1.82 | 0.30 | 0.69 |
| Korean | 151.09 | 31.14 | 4.60 | 9.40 |
| Lahu | 27.48 | 4.50 | 2.86 | 1.07 |
| Lhoba | 0.19 | 0.01 | 0.02 | 0.01 |
| Li | 93.96 | 7.97 | 4.77 | 5.37 |
| Lisu | 38.46 | 6.34 | 3.93 | 1.50 |
| Manchu | 1,123.64 | 259.71 | 41.68 | 86.53 |
| Maonan | 5.39 | 0.96 | 0.08 | 0.31 |
| Miao | 439.05 | 84.92 | 15.89 | 16.72 |
| Monba | 0.59 | 0.04 | 0.06 | 0.02 |
| Mongol | 437.23 | 82.58 | 15.16 | 26.72 |
| Mulao | 11.49 | 2.11 | 0.18 | 0.67 |
| Naxi | 18.78 | 3.09 | 1.92 | 0.73 |
| Nu | 1.76 | 0.29 | 0.18 | 0.07 |
| Oroqen | 0.59 | 0.10 | 0.02 | 0.04 |
| Pumi | 2.04 | 0.34 | 0.21 | 0.08 |
| Qiang | 18.26 | 3.59 | 0.57 | 0.70 |
| Russian | 1.22 | 0.20 | 0.04 | 0.06 |
| Salar | 11.51 | 1.87 | 0.53 | 0.30 |
| She | 68.34 | 26.19 | 1.50 | 1.62 |
| Shui | 14.38 | 2.67 | 0.37 | 0.59 |
| Tajik | 3.18 | 0.47 | 0.08 | 0.17 |
| Tatar | 0.38 | 0.06 | 0.01 | 0.02 |
| Tibetan | 392.16 | 50.04 | 26.39 | 13.16 |
| Tu | 25.89 | 4.37 | 1.19 | 0.66 |
| Tujia | 472.87 | 100.74 | 14.16 | 17.75 |
| Uygur | 651.59 | 95.05 | 15.88 | 35.90 |
| Uzbek | 0.96 | 0.14 | 0.02 | 0.05 |
| Va | 24.16 | 4.02 | 2.47 | 0.94 |
| Xibe | 21.53 | 4.62 | 0.78 | 1.84 |
| Yao | 166.63 | 32.12 | 3.82 | 7.64 |
| Yi | 444.53 | 77.22 | 34.63 | 17.32 |
| Yugur | 0.61 | 0.10 | 0.03 | 0.01 |
| Zhuang | 959.15 | 173.98 | 20.31 | 55.18 |

*Table 2.6* (cont.)

| Ethnic group | Wholesale and retail trade | Hotels and catering services | Leasing and business services | Services to households and other services |
|---|---|---|---|---|
| *National total* | 40,658.30 | 7,203.38 | 3,859.10 | 6,496.40 |
| Achang | 0.80 | 0.22 | 0.04 | 0.11 |
| Bai | 42.44 | 11.02 | 3.20 | 5.93 |
| Baonan | 0.34 | 0.10 | 0.02 | 0.05 |
| Blang | 2.18 | 0.60 | 0.10 | 0.30 |
| Buyi | 41.15 | 7.84 | 1.93 | 6.63 |
| Dai | 27.46 | 7.60 | 1.30 | 3.83 |
| Daur | 3.69 | 1.01 | 0.21 | 0.74 |
| Deang | 0.42 | 0.12 | 0.02 | 0.06 |
| Derung | 0.19 | 0.05 | 0.01 | 0.03 |
| Dong | 56.58 | 9.29 | 10.74 | 8.09 |
| Dongxiang | 10.61 | 3.01 | 0.54 | 1.74 |
| Ewenki | 0.83 | 0.22 | 0.05 | 0.17 |
| Gaoshan | 0.13 | 0.02 | 0.01 | 0.02 |
| Gelao | 7.83 | 1.48 | 0.36 | 1.26 |
| *Han* | 37,796.34 | 6,551.48 | 3,615.43 | 6,039.36 |
| Hani | 34.12 | 9.44 | 1.61 | 4.76 |
| Hezhe | 0.14 | 0.04 | 0.01 | 0.02 |
| Hui | 308.52 | 70.51 | 25.64 | 52.27 |
| Jing | 0.59 | 0.10 | 0.04 | 0.08 |
| Jingpo | 3.13 | 0.87 | 0.15 | 0.44 |
| Jino | 0.50 | 0.14 | 0.02 | 0.07 |
| Kazak | 39.45 | 13.17 | 2.71 | 7.00 |
| Kirgiz | 5.07 | 1.69 | 0.35 | 0.90 |
| Korean | 63.54 | 12.20 | 4.36 | 8.77 |
| Lahu | 10.75 | 2.97 | 0.50 | 1.50 |
| Lhoba | 0.07 | 0.03 | 0.00 | 0.02 |
| Li | 37.36 | 6.80 | 4.38 | 6.13 |
| Lisu | 15.05 | 4.15 | 0.72 | 2.12 |
| Manchu | 415.77 | 83.39 | 32.89 | 62.66 |
| Maonan | 2.41 | 0.42 | 0.14 | 0.34 |
| Miao | 176.11 | 32.18 | 27.63 | 25.81 |
| Monba | 0.22 | 0.09 | 0.01 | 0.07 |
| Mongol | 171.55 | 42.89 | 10.42 | 33.20 |
| Mulao | 5.17 | 0.90 | 0.31 | 0.73 |
| Naxi | 7.34 | 2.03 | 0.36 | 1.04 |
| Nu | 0.68 | 0.19 | 0.03 | 0.10 |
| Oroqen | 0.23 | 0.06 | 0.01 | 0.04 |

*Table 2.6* (cont.)

| Ethnic group | Wholesale and retail trade | Hotels and catering services | Leasing and business services | Services to households and other services |
|---|---|---|---|---|
| Pumi | 0.80 | 0.22 | 0.04 | 0.11 |
| Qiang | 7.35 | 1.78 | 0.62 | 1.37 |
| Russian | 0.48 | 0.14 | 0.04 | 0.09 |
| Salar | 4.40 | 1.40 | 0.10 | 0.59 |
| She | 23.14 | 3.41 | 2.01 | 4.14 |
| Shui | 5.75 | 1.10 | 0.27 | 0.92 |
| Tajik | 1.29 | 0.43 | 0.09 | 0.23 |
| Tatar | 0.15 | 0.05 | 0.01 | 0.03 |
| Tibetan | 150.47 | 52.05 | 6.06 | 33.67 |
| Tu | 9.93 | 3.08 | 0.23 | 1.34 |
| Tujia | 192.19 | 31.70 | 37.10 | 29.12 |
| Uygur | 265.26 | 88.39 | 18.34 | 47.08 |
| Uzbek | 0.39 | 0.13 | 0.03 | 0.07 |
| Va | 9.45 | 2.59 | 0.46 | 1.32 |
| Xibe | 7.92 | 1.73 | 0.62 | 1.26 |
| Yao | 71.99 | 11.94 | 10.61 | 9.67 |
| Yi | 175.63 | 45.86 | 10.14 | 27.19 |
| Yugur | 0.28 | 0.08 | 0.01 | 0.04 |
| Zhuang | 432.84 | 77.08 | 25.64 | 60.13 |

*Table 2.7* Number of employed persons in private enterprises and self-employed individuals in urban areas at the year-end by sector (1,000 persons)

| Ethnic group | Total | Manufacturing | Construction | Transport, storage, and post |
|---|---|---|---|---|
| *National total* | *62,361.45* | *13,296.35* | *2,426.54* | *2,265.23* |
| Achang | 1.32 | 0.17 | 0.18 | 0.05 |
| Bai | 69.64 | 9.36 | 8.50 | 2.73 |
| Baonan | 0.51 | 0.06 | 0.03 | 0.01 |
| Blang | 3.57 | 0.47 | 0.50 | 0.14 |
| Buyi | 65.68 | 10.17 | 2.05 | 2.65 |
| Dai | 44.87 | 5.84 | 6.25 | 1.81 |
| Daur | 6.60 | 0.98 | 0.23 | 0.41 |
| Deang | 0.69 | 0.09 | 0.10 | 0.03 |
| Derung | 0.30 | 0.04 | 0.04 | 0.01 |
| Dong | 91.10 | 14.61 | 2.24 | 3.31 |

*Table 2.7* (*cont.*)

| Ethnic group | Total | Manufacturing | Construction | Transport, storage, and post |
|---|---|---|---|---|
| Dongxiang | 16.31 | 1.87 | 0.81 | 0.48 |
| Ewenki | 1.46 | 0.21 | 0.05 | 0.09 |
| Gaoshan | 0.21 | 0.04 | 0.01 | 0.01 |
| Gelao | 12.50 | 1.89 | 0.35 | 0.50 |
| *Han* | *57,627.48* | *12,570.33* | *2,199.77* | *2,031.82* |
| Hani | 55.79 | 7.29 | 7.79 | 2.25 |
| Hezhe | 0.25 | 0.04 | 0.01 | 0.02 |
| Hui | 485.99 | 74.40 | 24.13 | 17.04 |
| Jing | 0.77 | 0.12 | 0.02 | 0.04 |
| Jingpo | 5.11 | 0.67 | 0.71 | 0.21 |
| Jino | 0.81 | 0.11 | 0.11 | 0.03 |
| Kazak | 78.28 | 9.57 | 2.19 | 4.56 |
| Kirgiz | 10.06 | 1.23 | 0.28 | 0.59 |
| Korean | 116.57 | 22.15 | 3.52 | 6.92 |
| Lahu | 17.56 | 2.30 | 2.45 | 0.71 |
| Lhoba | 0.15 | 0.01 | 0.01 | 0.01 |
| Li | 75.23 | 5.71 | 4.47 | 3.55 |
| Lisu | 24.50 | 3.21 | 3.36 | 0.99 |
| Manchu | 720.41 | 140.82 | 28.72 | 50.81 |
| Maonan | 3.21 | 0.50 | 0.07 | 0.18 |
| Miao | 287.71 | 44.94 | 12.80 | 10.47 |
| Monba | 0.47 | 0.03 | 0.04 | 0.02 |
| Mongol | 302.44 | 47.75 | 11.72 | 18.41 |
| Mulao | 6.81 | 1.07 | 0.14 | 0.39 |
| Naxi | 11.98 | 1.56 | 1.63 | 0.48 |
| Nu | 1.12 | 0.15 | 0.15 | 0.05 |
| Oroqen | 0.42 | 0.06 | 0.01 | 0.03 |
| Pumi | 1.31 | 0.17 | 0.18 | 0.05 |
| Qiang | 10.83 | 1.53 | 0.42 | 0.44 |
| Russian | 0.91 | 0.12 | 0.03 | 0.05 |
| Salar | 7.73 | 1.05 | 0.45 | 0.13 |
| She | 38.69 | 10.49 | 0.98 | 0.84 |
| Shui | 9.10 | 1.41 | 0.31 | 0.38 |
| Tajik | 2.55 | 0.32 | 0.07 | 0.15 |
| Tatar | 0.30 | 0.04 | 0.01 | 0.02 |
| Tibetan | 277.15 | 28.27 | 20.29 | 9.09 |
| Tu | 17.27 | 2.41 | 1.01 | 0.29 |
| Tujia | 318.89 | 55.31 | 10.81 | 10.94 |
| Uygur | 526.06 | 64.44 | 14.71 | 30.62 |

*Table 2.7* (*cont.*)

| Ethnic group | Total | Manufacturing | Construction | Transport, storage, and post |
|---|---|---|---|---|
| Uzbek | 0.78 | 0.10 | 0.02 | 0.04 |
| Va | 15.40 | 2.05 | 2.11 | 0.62 |
| Xibe | 15.10 | 2.83 | 0.61 | 1.14 |
| Yao | 105.76 | 16.95 | 2.99 | 4.51 |
| Yi | 278.19 | 37.50 | 29.16 | 11.26 |
| Yugur | 0.41 | 0.05 | 0.02 | 0.01 |
| Zhuang | 571.41 | 89.12 | 16.44 | 32.18 |

| Ethnic group | Wholesale and retail trade | Hotels and catering services | Leasing and business services | Services to households and other services |
|---|---|---|---|---|
| National total | 25,347.97 | 4,656.22 | 3,026.11 | 4,278.45 |
| Achang | 0.51 | 0.15 | 0.03 | 0.08 |
| Bai | 26.90 | 7.55 | 2.96 | 4.16 |
| Baonan | 0.25 | 0.07 | 0.01 | 0.04 |
| Blang | 1.38 | 0.41 | 0.09 | 0.21 |
| Buyi | 25.09 | 5.05 | 1.65 | 4.47 |
| Dai | 17.35 | 5.22 | 1.17 | 2.69 |
| Daur | 2.81 | 0.75 | 0.17 | 0.56 |
| Deang | 0.27 | 0.08 | 0.02 | 0.04 |
| Derung | 0.12 | 0.03 | 0.01 | 0.02 |
| Dong | 35.87 | 6.16 | 10.08 | 5.59 |
| Dongxiang | 7.81 | 2.15 | 0.46 | 1.20 |
| Ewenki | 0.62 | 0.17 | 0.04 | 0.13 |
| Gaoshan | 0.09 | 0.02 | 0.01 | 0.01 |
| Gelao | 4.78 | 0.95 | 0.31 | 0.85 |
| Han | 23,385.70 | 4,196.69 | 2,811.87 | 3,954.04 |
| Hani | 21.55 | 6.48 | 1.46 | 3.34 |
| Hezhe | 0.11 | 0.03 | 0.01 | 0.02 |
| Hui | 207.54 | 48.80 | 20.02 | 34.07 |
| Jing | 0.34 | 0.07 | 0.03 | 0.06 |
| Jingpo | 1.98 | 0.59 | 0.13 | 0.31 |
| Jino | 0.31 | 0.09 | 0.02 | 0.05 |
| Kazak | 33.44 | 10.50 | 2.58 | 5.59 |
| Kirgiz | 4.30 | 1.35 | 0.33 | 0.72 |
| Korean | 52.37 | 9.21 | 3.85 | 6.94 |
| Lahu | 6.79 | 2.04 | 0.46 | 1.05 |
| Lhoba | 0.05 | 0.02 | 0.00 | 0.02 |

*Table 2.7 (cont.)*

| Ethnic group | Wholesale and retail trade | Hotels and catering services | Leasing and business services | Services to households and other services |
|---|---|---|---|---|
| Li | 30.77 | 4.80 | 4.12 | 4.54 |
| Lisu | 9.50 | 2.84 | 0.65 | 1.48 |
| Manchu | 287.15 | 55.94 | 27.43 | 43.07 |
| Maonan | 1.41 | 0.28 | 0.11 | 0.24 |
| Miao | 113.48 | 21.55 | 25.82 | 17.88 |
| Monba | 0.17 | 0.07 | 0.01 | 0.06 |
| Mongol | 126.47 | 31.59 | 8.51 | 24.42 |
| Mulao | 3.02 | 0.59 | 0.25 | 0.50 |
| Naxi | 4.64 | 1.39 | 0.32 | 0.73 |
| Nu | 0.43 | 0.13 | 0.03 | 0.07 |
| Oroqen | 0.18 | 0.05 | 0.01 | 0.03 |
| Pumi | 0.50 | 0.15 | 0.03 | 0.08 |
| Qiang | 4.75 | 1.04 | 0.49 | 0.80 |
| Russian | 0.38 | 0.11 | 0.03 | 0.07 |
| Salar | 3.28 | 1.01 | 0.09 | 0.45 |
| She | 15.66 | 2.23 | 1.70 | 2.85 |
| Shui | 3.49 | 0.71 | 0.23 | 0.63 |
| Tajik | 1.09 | 0.34 | 0.09 | 0.18 |
| Tatar | 0.13 | 0.04 | 0.01 | 0.02 |
| Tibetan | 110.83 | 38.70 | 5.24 | 26.01 |
| Tu | 7.33 | 2.20 | 0.21 | 1.00 |
| Tujia | 130.71 | 21.70 | 34.98 | 20.47 |
| Uygur | 224.62 | 70.42 | 17.46 | 37.54 |
| Uzbek | 0.33 | 0.10 | 0.03 | 0.06 |
| Va | 5.97 | 1.77 | 0.41 | 0.92 |
| Xibe | 6.01 | 1.26 | 0.55 | 0.90 |
| Yao | 44.91 | 8.04 | 9.72 | 6.77 |
| Yi | 111.41 | 30.13 | 8.66 | 17.92 |
| Yugur | 0.20 | 0.05 | 0.01 | 0.03 |
| Zhuang | 254.85 | 51.13 | 20.74 | 41.41 |

*Notes:* "Employed persons in private enterprises" refers to the persons employed in the private enterprises that have been registered at the departments of industrial and commercial administration and are situated in a county town (i.e. a town where the county government is located) for business operation or in urban areas with a higher level than a county town. "Self-employed individuals in urban areas" refers to persons who hold certificates of residence in urban areas or have resided in the urban areas for a long time and have been registered at the departments of industrial and commercial administration and approved to be engaged in individual industrial or commercial business, including self-employed persons as well as helpers and hired laborers who work in the individual households engaged in industrial or commercial business.

*Table 2.8* Number of employed persons in private enterprises at the year-end (unit: 1,000 persons)

| Ethnic group | Number of enterprises | Number of employed persons | Number of employed persons in urban areas | Number of employed persons in rural areas |
|---|---|---|---|---|
| National total | 4,300.92 | 58,240.66 | 34,584.31 | 23,656.35 |
| Achang | 0.05 | 0.89 | 0.62 | 0.27 |
| Bai | 2.91 | 47.70 | 33.35 | 14.34 |
| Baonan | 0.03 | 0.35 | 0.25 | 0.10 |
| Blang | 0.15 | 2.41 | 1.67 | 0.74 |
| Buyi | 3.90 | 48.80 | 34.73 | 14.08 |
| Dai | 1.84 | 30.26 | 21.00 | 9.26 |
| Daur | 0.30 | 4.08 | 2.95 | 1.13 |
| Deang | 0.03 | 0.47 | 0.32 | 0.14 |
| Derung | 0.01 | 0.22 | 0.15 | 0.07 |
| Dong | 4.22 | 65.83 | 47.38 | 18.45 |
| Dongxiang | 0.86 | 11.00 | 8.15 | 2.85 |
| Ewenki | 0.07 | 0.96 | 0.66 | 0.29 |
| Gaoshan | 0.01 | 0.19 | 0.12 | 0.07 |
| Gelao | 0.74 | 9.14 | 6.62 | 2.52 |
| *Han* | *4,074.94* | *54,949.97* | *32,256.04* | *22,693.94* |
| Hani | 2.29 | 37.64 | 26.11 | 11.53 |
| Hezhe | 0.01 | 0.15 | 0.11 | 0.04 |
| Hui | 30.55 | 415.89 | 258.36 | 157.53 |
| Jing | 0.03 | 0.47 | 0.31 | 0.16 |
| Jingpo | 0.21 | 3.44 | 2.39 | 1.05 |
| Jino | 0.03 | 0.55 | 0.38 | 0.17 |
| Kazak | 3.51 | 45.50 | 39.65 | 5.85 |
| Kirgiz | 0.45 | 5.85 | 5.09 | 0.76 |
| Korean | 5.21 | 73.98 | 58.95 | 15.03 |
| Lahu | 0.72 | 11.84 | 8.21 | 3.63 |
| Lhoba | 0.00 | 0.06 | 0.05 | 0.01 |
| Li | 5.15 | 57.85 | 50.66 | 7.19 |
| Lisu | 1.02 | 16.63 | 11.49 | 5.14 |
| Manchu | 36.89 | 549.62 | 370.97 | 178.65 |
| Maonan | 0.14 | 2.00 | 1.34 | 0.66 |
| Miao | 13.77 | 208.91 | 150.16 | 58.75 |
| Monba | 0.01 | 0.20 | 0.16 | 0.04 |
| Mongol | 14.36 | 205.71 | 142.47 | 63.24 |
| Mulao | 0.28 | 4.22 | 2.78 | 1.44 |
| Naxi | 0.50 | 8.14 | 5.62 | 2.52 |

*Table 2.8 (cont.)*

| Ethnic group | Number of enterprises | Number of employed persons | Number of employed persons in urban areas | Number of employed persons in rural areas |
|---|---|---|---|---|
| Nu | 0.05 | 0.76 | 0.52 | 0.23 |
| Oroqen | 0.02 | 0.26 | 0.19 | 0.07 |
| Pumi | 0.05 | 0.88 | 0.61 | 0.27 |
| Qiang | 0.67 | 8.92 | 5.74 | 3.18 |
| Russian | 0.05 | 0.60 | 0.46 | 0.14 |
| Salar | 0.24 | 5.54 | 3.84 | 1.71 |
| She | 3.14 | 40.46 | 23.20 | 17.27 |
| Shui | 0.53 | 6.67 | 4.74 | 1.92 |
| Tajik | 0.12 | 1.50 | 1.29 | 0.21 |
| Tatar | 0.01 | 0.18 | 0.15 | 0.03 |
| Tibetan | 8.81 | 161.07 | 115.86 | 45.20 |
| Tu | 0.56 | 12.52 | 8.61 | 3.91 |
| Tujia | 15.41 | 222.94 | 162.57 | 60.37 |
| Uygur | 23.61 | 306.40 | 266.58 | 39.82 |
| Uzbek | 0.04 | 0.46 | 0.39 | 0.06 |
| Va | 0.64 | 10.46 | 7.24 | 3.23 |
| Xibe | 0.70 | 10.27 | 7.78 | 2.49 |
| Yao | 4.23 | 69.98 | 49.44 | 20.53 |
| Yi | 13.30 | 199.85 | 135.91 | 63.94 |
| Yugur | 0.02 | 0.29 | 0.21 | 0.08 |
| Zhuang | 22.60 | 348.30 | 231.42 | 116.89 |

*Note:* "Persons employed in private enterprises" refers to the persons employed in the private enterprises that have been registered at the departments of industrial and commercial administration and are situated in a county town (i.e. a town where the county government is located) for business operation or in urban areas with a higher level than a county town.

*Table 2.9* Number of self-employed individuals at the year-end (unit: 1,000 persons)

| Ethnic group | Number of enterprises | Number of employed persons | Urban employed persons | Rural employed persons |
|---|---|---|---|---|
| *National total* | *24,638.93* | *49,005.41* | *27,777.14* | *21,228.28* |
| Achang | 0.59 | 1.17 | 0.70 | 0.47 |
| Bai | 31.04 | 60.60 | 36.29 | 24.31 |
| Baonan | 0.22 | 0.41 | 0.26 | 0.15 |
| Blang | 1.59 | 3.17 | 1.89 | 1.27 |

Table 2.9  (cont.)

| Ethnic group | Number of enterprises | Number of employed persons | Urban employed persons | Rural employed persons |
|---|---|---|---|---|
| Buyi | 38.13 | 54.80 | 30.95 | 23.85 |
| Dai | 20.01 | 39.94 | 23.87 | 16.06 |
| Daur | 2.70 | 5.10 | 3.64 | 1.46 |
| Deang | 0.31 | 0.62 | 0.37 | 0.25 |
| Derung | 0.13 | 0.26 | 0.16 | 0.11 |
| Dong | 44.15 | 73.78 | 43.72 | 30.06 |
| Dongxiang | 7.17 | 12.65 | 8.16 | 4.49 |
| Ewenki | 0.62 | 1.11 | 0.80 | 0.31 |
| Gaoshan | 0.09 | 0.17 | 0.10 | 0.07 |
| Gelao | 7.33 | 10.39 | 5.88 | 4.51 |
| *Han* | *22,533.37* | *45,164.03* | *25,371.44* | *19,792.59* |
| Hani | 24.84 | 49.64 | 29.68 | 19.96 |
| Hezhe | 0.09 | 0.20 | 0.14 | 0.06 |
| Hui | 195.87 | 368.55 | 227.63 | 140.92 |
| Jing | 0.51 | 0.83 | 0.46 | 0.37 |
| Jingpo | 2.28 | 4.55 | 2.72 | 1.83 |
| Jino | 0.36 | 0.72 | 0.43 | 0.29 |
| Kazak | 32.28 | 51.36 | 38.64 | 12.73 |
| Kirgiz | 4.15 | 6.62 | 4.97 | 1.64 |
| Korean | 37.58 | 77.10 | 57.62 | 19.48 |
| Lahu | 7.83 | 15.64 | 9.35 | 6.30 |
| Lhoba | 0.07 | 0.13 | 0.10 | 0.03 |
| Li | 19.40 | 36.11 | 24.57 | 11.54 |
| Lisu | 10.98 | 21.83 | 13.01 | 8.83 |
| Manchu | 264.97 | 574.02 | 349.44 | 224.58 |
| Maonan | 2.14 | 3.39 | 1.88 | 1.52 |
| Miao | 133.17 | 230.14 | 137.54 | 92.59 |
| Monba | 0.21 | 0.39 | 0.31 | 0.08 |
| Mongol | 123.86 | 231.52 | 159.97 | 71.55 |
| Mulao | 4.51 | 7.28 | 4.02 | 3.25 |
| Naxi | 5.36 | 10.64 | 6.36 | 4.28 |
| Nu | 0.50 | 1.00 | 0.60 | 0.40 |
| Oroqen | 0.17 | 0.33 | 0.23 | 0.10 |
| Pumi | 0.58 | 1.16 | 0.69 | 0.47 |
| Qiang | 5.69 | 9.34 | 5.08 | 4.25 |
| Russian | 0.37 | 0.62 | 0.45 | 0.17 |
| Salar | 2.91 | 5.96 | 3.89 | 2.07 |
| She | 14.71 | 27.88 | 15.50 | 12.38 |

*Table 2.9 (cont.)*

| Ethnic group | Number of enterprises | Number of employed persons | Urban employed persons | Rural employed persons |
|---|---|---|---|---|
| Shui | 5.33 | 7.71 | 4.36 | 3.35 |
| Tajik | 1.05 | 1.68 | 1.26 | 0.43 |
| Tatar | 0.12 | 0.20 | 0.15 | 0.05 |
| Tibetan | 122.69 | 231.10 | 161.29 | 69.81 |
| Tu | 6.51 | 13.37 | 8.66 | 4.71 |
| Tujia | 125.34 | 249.93 | 156.32 | 93.62 |
| Uygur | 216.79 | 345.19 | 259.49 | 85.71 |
| Uzbek | 0.32 | 0.51 | 0.38 | 0.13 |
| Va | 6.85 | 13.69 | 8.16 | 5.53 |
| Xibe | 5.39 | 11.26 | 7.32 | 3.94 |
| Yao | 54.67 | 96.65 | 56.32 | 40.34 |
| Yi | 132.79 | 244.68 | 142.28 | 102.40 |
| Yugur | 0.18 | 0.32 | 0.20 | 0.12 |
| Zhuang | 368.82 | 610.85 | 340.00 | 270.85 |

*Note:* "Self-employed individuals" refers to persons who hold certificates of residence in urban areas or have resided in urban areas for a long time and have been registered at the departments of industrial and commercial administration and approved to be engaged in individual industrial or commercial business, including self-employed persons as well as helpers and hired laborers who work in the individual households engaged in industrial or commercial business.

*Table 2.10* Total wages bill of staff and workers by sector (unit: million yuan)

| Ethnic group | Total | Agriculture, forestry, animal husbandry, and fishing | Mining | Manufacturing | Production and supply of electricity, gas, and water |
|---|---|---|---|---|---|
| National total | 1,978,985.50 | 34,669.18 | 101,631.89 | 482,173.76 | 73,565.18 |
| Achang | 30.54 | 1.34 | 0.72 | 6.06 | 1.44 |
| Bai | 1,687.17 | 63.17 | 45.89 | 334.45 | 78.73 |
| Baonan | 19.40 | 0.73 | 1.11 | 4.10 | 0.98 |
| Blang | 82.78 | 3.60 | 1.98 | 16.47 | 3.90 |
| Buyi | 2,527.68 | 28.83 | 150.25 | 498.10 | 142.13 |
| Dai | 1,042.33 | 45.50 | 24.64 | 206.90 | 49.12 |
| Daur | 237.82 | 15.50 | 20.08 | 41.86 | 13.67 |

*Table 2.10* (cont.)

| Ethnic group | Total | Agriculture, forestry, animal husbandry, and fishing | Mining | Manufacturing | Production and supply of electricity, gas, and water |
|---|---|---|---|---|---|
| Deang | 16.08 | 0.71 | 0.38 | 3.18 | 0.76 |
| Derung | 7.73 | 0.30 | 0.31 | 1.61 | 0.35 |
| Dong | 2,734.45 | 32.99 | 114.83 | 551.58 | 126.10 |
| Dongxiang | 631.87 | 34.58 | 39.20 | 126.24 | 30.40 |
| Ewenki | 53.07 | 3.25 | 3.79 | 9.15 | 3.44 |
| Gaoshan | 7.25 | 0.13 | 0.33 | 1.74 | 0.27 |
| Gelao | 488.43 | 5.26 | 29.39 | 95.89 | 27.66 |
| Han | 1,837,971.82 | 27,675.34 | 94,257.26 | 456,165.31 | 67,388.81 |
| Hani | 1,293.69 | 56.66 | 30.62 | 257.00 | 61.05 |
| Hezhe | 9.06 | 0.48 | 0.91 | 1.80 | 0.39 |
| Hui | 17,279.54 | 638.26 | 1,213.29 | 3,268.90 | 864.93 |
| Jing | 22.00 | 0.58 | 0.45 | 4.35 | 0.93 |
| Jingpo | 119.07 | 5.20 | 2.85 | 23.64 | 5.61 |
| Jino | 18.80 | 0.82 | 0.44 | 3.73 | 0.89 |
| Kazak | 2,623.86 | 438.62 | 225.29 | 244.89 | 81.01 |
| Kirgiz | 337.27 | 56.11 | 29.05 | 31.77 | 10.46 |
| Korean | 3,266.96 | 115.67 | 244.34 | 750.40 | 136.92 |
| Lahu | 407.60 | 17.80 | 9.81 | 81.00 | 19.23 |
| Lhoba | 5.22 | 0.08 | 0.03 | 0.21 | 0.20 |
| Li | 1,699.13 | 181.47 | 29.57 | 153.85 | 58.51 |
| Lisu | 570.94 | 24.46 | 14.05 | 113.62 | 26.82 |
| Manchu | 20,587.44 | 484.92 | 1,398.89 | 4,968.99 | 921.69 |
| Maonan | 99.24 | 2.18 | 3.00 | 19.49 | 4.58 |
| Miao | 8,349.75 | 133.98 | 343.33 | 1,695.39 | 382.92 |
| Monba | 16.14 | 0.23 | 0.06 | 0.63 | 0.60 |
| Mongol | 10,047.23 | 557.33 | 691.44 | 1,852.08 | 610.92 |
| Mulao | 202.28 | 4.71 | 4.74 | 40.40 | 8.78 |
| Naxi | 281.70 | 11.91 | 6.72 | 55.56 | 13.13 |
| Nu | 26.48 | 1.12 | 0.62 | 5.16 | 1.24 |
| Oroqen | 14.95 | 0.85 | 1.33 | 2.81 | 0.81 |
| Pumi | 30.41 | 1.32 | 0.74 | 6.04 | 1.43 |
| Qiang | 291.39 | 3.60 | 12.45 | 61.87 | 10.98 |
| Russian | 32.19 | 3.76 | 2.37 | 4.17 | 1.32 |
| Salar | 168.69 | 6.43 | 6.96 | 22.09 | 8.87 |
| She | 1,395.06 | 12.33 | 14.30 | 468.03 | 48.08 |

*Table 2.10* (*cont.*)

| Ethnic group | Total | Agriculture, forestry, animal husbandry, and fishing | Mining | Manufacturing | Production and supply of electricity, gas, and water |
|---|---|---|---|---|---|
| Shui | 342.79 | 4.33 | 20.03 | 67.19 | 19.25 |
| Tajik | 85.31 | 13.95 | 7.28 | 8.27 | 2.65 |
| Tatar | 10.28 | 1.60 | 0.84 | 1.05 | 0.32 |
| Tibetan | 7,983.62 | 156.84 | 166.48 | 727.13 | 338.82 |
| Tu | 379.35 | 12.52 | 15.05 | 54.25 | 19.98 |
| Tujia | 8,463.09 | 121.47 | 271.76 | 1,899.68 | 317.19 |
| Uygur | 17,627.74 | 2,940.24 | 1,511.72 | 1,652.26 | 543.99 |
| Uzbek | 26.05 | 4.27 | 2.20 | 2.50 | 0.80 |
| Va | 360.83 | 15.37 | 9.29 | 72.45 | 16.87 |
| Xibe | 385.89 | 19.36 | 28.38 | 90.66 | 16.83 |
| Yao | 2,786.69 | 55.07 | 52.33 | 590.28 | 107.65 |
| Yi | 7,028.85 | 220.02 | 233.41 | 1,420.93 | 319.55 |
| Yugur | 16.30 | 0.55 | 0.91 | 3.52 | 0.81 |
| Zhuang | 16,139.11 | 424.61 | 297.10 | 3,264.40 | 675.33 |

| Ethnic group | Construction | Transport, storage, and post | Information transmission, computer service and software | Wholesale and retail trade | Hotels and catering services |
|---|---|---|---|---|---|
| *National total* | *123,790.25* | *123,065.80* | *46,132.24* | *77,653.48* | *22,881.59* |
| Achang | 1.75 | 1.86 | 0.55 | 1.40 | 0.31 |
| Bai | 102.67 | 101.32 | 30.73 | 75.56 | 17.61 |
| Baonan | 1.00 | 1.37 | 0.24 | 0.51 | 0.14 |
| Blang | 4.75 | 5.04 | 1.49 | 3.80 | 0.83 |
| Buyi | 186.52 | 132.39 | 35.16 | 104.93 | 23.67 |
| Dai | 59.79 | 63.47 | 18.89 | 47.98 | 10.53 |
| Daur | 14.21 | 17.28 | 4.51 | 7.17 | 2.16 |
| Deang | 0.92 | 0.98 | 0.29 | 0.74 | 0.16 |
| Derung | 0.45 | 0.48 | 0.14 | 0.33 | 0.08 |
| Dong | 205.16 | 157.84 | 45.26 | 105.29 | 30.76 |
| Dongxiang | 35.13 | 43.66 | 7.62 | 16.68 | 4.75 |
| Ewenki | 2.81 | 3.98 | 0.96 | 1.38 | 0.53 |
| Gaoshan | 0.45 | 0.45 | 0.20 | 0.30 | 0.09 |

*Table 2.10 (cont.)*

| Ethnic group | Construction | Transport, storage, and post | Information transmission, computer service and software | Wholesale and retail trade | Hotels and catering services |
|---|---|---|---|---|---|
| Gelao | 36.01 | 25.61 | 6.81 | 20.37 | 4.59 |
| *Han* | *114,619.46* | *113,897.68* | *43,194.05* | *72,736.08* | *21,391.56* |
| Hani | 73.93 | 78.81 | 23.31 | 59.56 | 13.04 |
| Hezhe | 0.62 | 0.62 | 0.23 | 0.37 | 0.08 |
| Hui | 1,038.18 | 1,094.62 | 453.20 | 651.89 | 193.15 |
| Jing | 1.44 | 1.54 | 0.42 | 0.81 | 0.25 |
| Jingpo | 6.80 | 7.25 | 2.16 | 5.48 | 1.21 |
| Jino | 1.08 | 1.15 | 0.34 | 0.87 | 0.19 |
| Kazak | 216.83 | 171.77 | 37.91 | 76.40 | 22.07 |
| Kirgiz | 27.85 | 22.09 | 4.88 | 9.84 | 2.83 |
| Korean | 167.94 | 232.68 | 77.91 | 108.85 | 30.50 |
| Lahu | 23.35 | 24.79 | 7.31 | 18.74 | 4.10 |
| Lhoba | 0.14 | 0.21 | 0.14 | 0.12 | 0.06 |
| Li | 92.23 | 142.77 | 66.20 | 51.34 | 51.88 |
| Lisu | 33.40 | 34.54 | 10.25 | 26.03 | 5.69 |
| Manchu | 1,067.40 | 1,445.62 | 574.96 | 729.12 | 220.29 |
| Maonan | 6.72 | 6.56 | 1.73 | 3.75 | 1.08 |
| Miao | 641.81 | 483.79 | 141.69 | 327.26 | 91.74 |
| Monba | 0.41 | 0.67 | 0.45 | 0.37 | 0.19 |
| Mongol | 528.73 | 744.69 | 191.43 | 269.00 | 99.69 |
| Mulao | 13.40 | 13.88 | 3.85 | 7.59 | 2.32 |
| Naxi | 16.45 | 17.02 | 5.24 | 12.87 | 2.86 |
| Nu | 1.50 | 1.59 | 0.49 | 1.20 | 0.27 |
| Oroqen | 0.92 | 1.07 | 0.31 | 0.50 | 0.13 |
| Pumi | 1.74 | 1.85 | 0.56 | 1.40 | 0.31 |
| Qiang | 29.52 | 14.68 | 5.43 | 9.99 | 2.20 |
| Russian | 2.26 | 2.20 | 0.64 | 1.00 | 0.33 |
| Salar | 9.85 | 14.42 | 4.32 | 4.49 | 1.39 |
| She | 111.01 | 67.78 | 26.10 | 44.61 | 14.31 |
| Shui | 24.96 | 18.20 | 4.74 | 14.20 | 3.19 |
| Tajik | 7.01 | 5.59 | 1.25 | 2.50 | 0.72 |
| Tatar | 0.83 | 0.67 | 0.17 | 0.31 | 0.09 |
| Tibetan | 361.43 | 432.38 | 197.06 | 199.31 | 79.16 |
| Tu | 21.86 | 32.12 | 9.38 | 10.20 | 3.15 |
| Tujia | 720.98 | 529.64 | 151.52 | 304.22 | 91.67 |
| Uygur | 1,456.05 | 1,153.87 | 255.37 | 514.09 | 148.57 |
| Uzbek | 2.14 | 1.71 | 0.39 | 0.77 | 0.23 |

*Table 2.10* (*cont.*)

| Ethnic group | Construction | Transport, storage, and post | Information transmission, computer service and software | Wholesale and retail trade | Hotels and catering services |
|---|---|---|---|---|---|
| Va | 20.84 | 21.87 | 6.46 | 16.46 | 3.64 |
| Xibe | 21.31 | 27.96 | 8.59 | 11.82 | 3.62 |
| Yao | 185.12 | 188.50 | 57.82 | 105.18 | 36.35 |
| Yi | 504.05 | 400.43 | 124.56 | 296.20 | 64.92 |
| Yugur | 0.83 | 1.13 | 0.23 | 0.45 | 0.13 |
| Zhuang | 1,031.00 | 1,137.78 | 318.00 | 606.37 | 190.52 |

| Ethnic group | Financial intermediation | Real estate | Leasing and business services | Scientific research, technical services, and geological prospecting | Management of water conservancy, environment, and public facilities |
|---|---|---|---|---|---|
| *National total* | *94,757.58* | *26,947.26* | *40,360.24* | *57,967.32* | *24,953.34* |
| Achang | 1.29 | 0.21 | 0.36 | 0.75 | 0.35 |
| Bai | 71.70 | 13.89 | 20.93 | 40.96 | 19.24 |
| Baonan | 0.70 | 0.08 | 0.17 | 0.63 | 0.33 |
| Blang | 3.51 | 0.57 | 0.97 | 2.02 | 0.95 |
| Buyi | 105.43 | 31.41 | 30.84 | 56.93 | 24.37 |
| Dai | 44.28 | 7.17 | 12.38 | 25.62 | 11.91 |
| Daur | 9.13 | 1.90 | 3.15 | 6.05 | 3.83 |
| Deang | 0.68 | 0.11 | 0.19 | 0.39 | 0.18 |
| Derung | 0.33 | 0.06 | 0.10 | 0.19 | 0.09 |
| Dong | 115.24 | 36.16 | 35.62 | 58.71 | 31.09 |
| Dongxiang | 22.22 | 3.03 | 5.81 | 18.33 | 10.87 |
| Ewenki | 2.08 | 0.36 | 0.73 | 1.22 | 0.96 |
| Gaoshan | 0.35 | 0.11 | 0.18 | 0.24 | 0.09 |
| Gelao | 20.30 | 6.19 | 5.99 | 11.05 | 4.67 |
| *Han* | *88,691.39* | *25,442.75* | *38,132.96* | *54,055.22* | *23,013.62* |
| Hani | 54.88 | 8.83 | 15.21 | 31.63 | 14.80 |
| Hezhe | 0.37 | 0.11 | 0.15 | 0.30 | 0.11 |
| Hui | 797.66 | 217.70 | 380.99 | 614.63 | 266.97 |
| Jing | 0.95 | 0.25 | 0.38 | 0.54 | 0.30 |
| Jingpo | 5.05 | 0.83 | 1.42 | 2.92 | 1.36 |
| Jino | 0.80 | 0.13 | 0.22 | 0.46 | 0.22 |

*Table 2.10 (cont.)*

| Ethnic group | Financial intermediation | Real estate | Leasing and business services | Scientific research, technical services, and geological prospecting | Management of water conservancy, environment, and public facilities |
|---|---|---|---|---|---|
| Kazak | 82.24 | 21.75 | 36.33 | 55.33 | 39.25 |
| Kirgiz | 10.59 | 2.80 | 4.65 | 7.12 | 5.04 |
| Korean | 149.29 | 38.65 | 57.71 | 101.41 | 51.38 |
| Lahu | 17.27 | 2.77 | 4.76 | 9.93 | 4.66 |
| Lhoba | 0.33 | 0.01 | 0.02 | 0.20 | 0.03 |
| Li | 79.48 | 34.45 | 31.80 | 35.50 | 37.81 |
| Lisu | 24.27 | 3.87 | 6.70 | 14.09 | 6.51 |
| Manchu | 989.71 | 276.92 | 440.03 | 668.30 | 309.22 |
| Maonan | 4.22 | 1.13 | 1.56 | 2.34 | 1.25 |
| Miao | 355.90 | 104.25 | 104.60 | 190.42 | 94.28 |
| Monba | 1.05 | 0.04 | 0.08 | 0.62 | 0.10 |
| Mongol | 408.95 | 76.84 | 146.50 | 246.75 | 177.57 |
| Mulao | 8.80 | 2.37 | 3.48 | 4.89 | 2.65 |
| Naxi | 12.11 | 1.99 | 3.49 | 7.13 | 3.20 |
| Nu | 1.14 | 0.18 | 0.31 | 0.66 | 0.30 |
| Oroqen | 0.59 | 0.14 | 0.21 | 0.41 | 0.22 |
| Pumi | 1.29 | 0.21 | 0.37 | 0.75 | 0.35 |
| Qiang | 13.92 | 2.31 | 4.19 | 10.21 | 2.99 |
| Russian | 1.19 | 0.32 | 0.60 | 0.84 | 0.51 |
| Salar | 6.46 | 0.70 | 1.81 | 11.22 | 2.04 |
| She | 71.50 | 18.41 | 23.31 | 24.36 | 13.41 |
| Shui | 14.18 | 4.17 | 4.12 | 7.72 | 3.36 |
| Tajik | 2.71 | 0.72 | 1.19 | 1.82 | 1.27 |
| Tatar | 0.34 | 0.09 | 0.16 | 0.24 | 0.15 |
| Tibetan | 431.97 | 25.24 | 50.40 | 355.18 | 67.80 |
| Tu | 14.78 | 1.68 | 3.83 | 24.31 | 4.58 |
| Tujia | 352.06 | 114.57 | 102.65 | 207.98 | 107.24 |
| Uygur | 553.56 | 146.61 | 244.76 | 372.01 | 263.48 |
| Uzbek | 0.83 | 0.22 | 0.38 | 0.56 | 0.39 |
| Va | 15.28 | 2.51 | 4.25 | 8.76 | 4.13 |
| Xibe | 17.25 | 4.41 | 6.03 | 10.34 | 5.95 |
| Yao | 124.68 | 37.83 | 46.33 | 62.17 | 36.21 |
| Yi | 308.11 | 54.02 | 87.86 | 192.11 | 76.66 |
| Yugur | 0.60 | 0.09 | 0.18 | 0.53 | 0.28 |
| Zhuang | 707.11 | 185.64 | 279.68 | 388.50 | 216.91 |

*Table 2.10* (*cont.*)

| Ethnic group | Services to households and other services | Education | Health, social securities, and social welfare | Culture, sports, and entertainment | Public management and social organization |
|---|---|---|---|---|---|
| *National total* | *7,849.99* | *265,062.34* | *102,367.58* | *26,581.39* | *246,575.12* |
| Achang | 0.05 | 5.56 | 1.63 | 0.39 | 4.52 |
| Bai | 2.90 | 303.32 | 90.83 | 21.03 | 252.22 |
| Baonan | 0.03 | 3.19 | 0.83 | 0.27 | 2.98 |
| Blang | 0.13 | 15.06 | 4.42 | 1.04 | 12.25 |
| Buyi | 6.29 | 441.44 | 113.82 | 24.34 | 390.84 |
| Dai | 1.60 | 189.64 | 55.63 | 13.16 | 154.11 |
| Daur | 1.18 | 31.67 | 10.72 | 3.27 | 30.46 |
| Deang | 0.02 | 2.93 | 0.86 | 0.20 | 2.38 |
| Derung | 0.02 | 1.29 | 0.40 | 0.10 | 1.09 |
| Dong | 6.23 | 472.79 | 154.30 | 29.93 | 424.57 |
| Dongxiang | 0.80 | 102.30 | 26.88 | 8.54 | 94.82 |
| Ewenki | 0.17 | 7.62 | 2.46 | 0.82 | 7.36 |
| Gaoshan | 0.03 | 0.95 | 0.36 | 0.11 | 0.86 |
| Gelao | 1.23 | 85.39 | 21.76 | 4.68 | 75.60 |
| *Han* | *7,447.12* | *243,906.56* | *94,962.51* | *24,620.98* | *226,373.08* |
| Hani | 1.96 | 235.69 | 69.02 | 16.30 | 191.40 |
| Hezhe | 0.08 | 1.00 | 0.39 | 0.11 | 0.95 |
| Hui | 72.41 | 2,268.18 | 817.94 | 272.20 | 2,154.45 |
| Jing | 0.05 | 3.89 | 1.48 | 0.29 | 3.10 |
| Jingpo | 0.18 | 21.65 | 6.34 | 1.50 | 17.60 |
| Jino | 0.03 | 3.42 | 1.00 | 0.24 | 2.78 |
| Kazak | 2.41 | 365.72 | 123.68 | 28.03 | 354.32 |
| Kirgiz | 0.33 | 46.92 | 15.89 | 3.60 | 45.46 |
| Korean | 16.80 | 424.37 | 157.09 | 45.37 | 359.68 |
| Lahu | 0.62 | 74.26 | 21.75 | 5.12 | 60.34 |
| Lhoba | 0.00 | 0.94 | 0.32 | 0.18 | 1.98 |
| Li | 1.85 | 261.21 | 91.24 | 34.97 | 263.03 |
| Lisu | 0.90 | 103.55 | 30.58 | 7.16 | 84.43 |
| Manchu | 103.37 | 2,439.93 | 945.63 | 308.50 | 2,293.96 |
| Maonan | 0.22 | 17.65 | 6.18 | 1.20 | 14.39 |
| Miao | 18.50 | 1,429.39 | 454.38 | 92.81 | 1,263.32 |
| Monba | 0.01 | 2.89 | 1.01 | 0.56 | 6.19 |
| Mongol | 30.43 | 1,422.67 | 472.28 | 153.13 | 1,366.81 |
| Mulao | 0.46 | 35.44 | 13.21 | 2.59 | 28.72 |
| Naxi | 0.46 | 50.80 | 15.09 | 3.64 | 42.02 |

Table 2.10 (cont.)

| Ethnic group | Services to households and other services | Education | Health, social securities, and social welfare | Culture, sports, and entertainment | Public management and social organization |
|---|---|---|---|---|---|
| Nu | 0.04 | 4.80 | 1.42 | 0.35 | 4.09 |
| Oroqen | 0.09 | 1.89 | 0.66 | 0.20 | 1.81 |
| Pumi | 0.05 | 5.52 | 1.62 | 0.39 | 4.49 |
| Qiang | 1.05 | 43.79 | 17.75 | 3.39 | 41.08 |
| Russian | 0.07 | 4.40 | 1.51 | 0.45 | 4.26 |
| Salar | 1.45 | 25.49 | 9.87 | 2.74 | 28.11 |
| She | 3.38 | 183.84 | 71.55 | 15.64 | 163.12 |
| Shui | 0.83 | 60.36 | 15.66 | 3.32 | 52.98 |
| Tajik | 0.09 | 11.88 | 4.03 | 0.92 | 11.49 |
| Tatar | 0.01 | 1.42 | 0.48 | 0.12 | 1.37 |
| Tibetan | 22.89 | 1,360.15 | 485.70 | 205.93 | 2,318.70 |
| Tu | 3.15 | 57.49 | 22.17 | 5.99 | 62.86 |
| Tujia | 19.96 | 1,341.57 | 497.40 | 100.25 | 1,211.28 |
| Uygur | 16.37 | 2,455.78 | 831.36 | 188.43 | 2,379.22 |
| Uzbek | 0.03 | 3.62 | 1.23 | 0.28 | 3.50 |
| Va | 0.58 | 65.18 | 19.22 | 4.51 | 53.16 |
| Xibe | 1.30 | 45.32 | 17.81 | 4.94 | 44.03 |
| Yao | 6.29 | 468.90 | 184.15 | 35.44 | 406.37 |
| Yi | 15.65 | 1,211.11 | 384.00 | 84.29 | 1,030.97 |
| Yugur | 0.03 | 2.65 | 0.68 | 0.24 | 2.45 |
| Zhuang | 35.19 | 2,819.44 | 1,079.96 | 211.26 | 2,270.32 |

*Notes:* "Total wages bill" refers to the total remuneration payment to staff and workers in various units during a certain period of time. The calculation of total wages is based on the total remuneration payment to the staff and workers. Therefore, all the wages and salaries and other payments to staff and workers are included in the total wages regardless of their sources, category, and forms (in kind or cash). (Total wages of staff and workers in this book include only total wages of fully employed staff and workers, excluding the living allowances distributed to those who have left their working units while keeping their labor contract/ employment relation unchanged.)

*Table 2.11* Average wage of staff and workers by sector (unit: yuan)

| Ethnic group | Total | Agriculture, forestry, animal husbandry, and fishing | Mining | Manufacturing | Production and supply of electricity, gas, and water |
|---|---|---|---|---|---|
| National total | 18,364 | 8,309 | 20,626 | 15,757 | 25,073 |
| Achang | 16,161 | 11,225 | 15,813 | 17,135 | 26,730 |
| Bai | 15,987 | 10,922 | 15,853 | 16,577 | 26,128 |
| Baonan | 15,158 | 10,015 | 17,896 | 14,918 | 21,595 |
| Blang | 16,171 | 11,228 | 15,829 | 17,130 | 26,716 |
| Buyi | 14,597 | 11,039 | 17,257 | 13,630 | 26,476 |
| Dai | 16,161 | 11,224 | 15,819 | 17,134 | 26,704 |
| Daur | 15,646 | 7,928 | 17,515 | 14,174 | 26,823 |
| Deang | 16,148 | 11,222 | 15,793 | 17,148 | 26,719 |
| Derung | 16,287 | 10,871 | 16,634 | 16,669 | 26,231 |
| Dong | 15,148 | 9,611 | 16,207 | 14,021 | 23,775 |
| Dongxiang | 15,048 | 9,940 | 18,316 | 14,918 | 21,514 |
| Ewenki | 16,072 | 8,470 | 16,718 | 14,501 | 29,682 |
| Gaoshan | 16,688 | 9,150 | 19,730 | 14,633 | 24,277 |
| Gelao | 14,538 | 11,009 | 172,61 | 135,77 | 26,445 |
| *Han* | *17,366* | *9,893* | *20,385* | *14,852* | *24,767* |
| Hani | 16,163 | 11,231 | 15,821 | 17,147 | 26,738 |
| Hezhe | 15,113 | 6,729 | 18,820 | 13,619 | 21,420 |
| Hui | 16,844 | 9,905 | 21,582 | 14,704 | 24,539 |
| Jing | 15,596 | 8,875 | 16,121 | 14,667 | 22,894 |
| Jingpo | 16,158 | 11,221 | 15,825 | 17,129 | 26,725 |
| Jino | 16,161 | 11,227 | 15,812 | 17,151 | 26,723 |
| Kazak | 15,566 | 9,899 | 23,318 | 14,875 | 21,933 |
| Kirgiz | 15,559 | 9,865 | 23,277 | 14,859 | 21,935 |
| Korean | 15,257 | 6,749 | 19,372 | 14,620 | 21,181 |
| Lahu | 16,157 | 11,224 | 15,832 | 17,130 | 26,709 |
| Lhoba | 27,835 | 19,449 | 16,052 | 13,679 | 26,296 |
| Li | 14,500 | 6,617 | 15,492 | 12,916 | 19,334 |
| Lisu | 16,146 | 11,194 | 15,854 | 17,053 | 26,521 |
| Manchu | 16,616 | 6,686 | 19,988 | 15,246 | 24,076 |
| Maonan | 15,269 | 9,436 | 16,426 | 14,339 | 23,823 |
| Miao | 15,302 | 9,959 | 16,197 | 14,414 | 24,074 |
| Monba | 28,554 | 20,028 | 16,304 | 13,775 | 26,459 |
| Mongol | 16,211 | 8,344 | 17,444 | 14,713 | 28,454 |

Table 2.11 (cont.)

| Ethnic group | Total | Agriculture, forestry, animal husbandry, and fishing | Mining | Manufacturing | Production and supply of electricity, gas, and water |
|---|---|---|---|---|---|
| Mulao | 15,578 | 9,138 | 16,352 | 14,568 | 23,422 |
| Naxi | 16,221 | 11,251 | 15,852 | 17,055 | 26,570 |
| Nu | 16,370 | 11,370 | 15,851 | 17,067 | 26,750 |
| Oroqen | 15,518 | 7,512 | 17,766 | 14,013 | 25,432 |
| Pumi | 16,173 | 11,215 | 15,849 | 17,119 | 26,693 |
| Qiang | 15,851 | 10,161 | 16,864 | 14,291 | 19,584 |
| Russian | 16,157 | 9,554 | 20,968 | 14,945 | 25,428 |
| Salar | 18,547 | 11,531 | 18,577 | 14,722 | 24,697 |
| She | 18,982 | 13,234 | 17,237 | 14,643 | 30,607 |
| Shui | 14,593 | 10,929 | 17,181 | 13,696 | 26,335 |
| Tajik | 15,613 | 9,884 | 23,201 | 14,874 | 21,977 |
| Tatar | 15,731 | 9,940 | 23,044 | 14,960 | 22,216 |
| Tibetan | 22,325 | 15,073 | 16,740 | 14,161 | 24,112 |
| Tu | 18,503 | 11,475 | 18,524 | 14,786 | 24,916 |
| Tujia | 15,523 | 8,472 | 15,311 | 14,363 | 21,193 |
| Uygur | 15,576 | 9,897 | 23,320 | 14,876 | 21,943 |
| Uzbek | 15,640 | 9,907 | 23,262 | 14,900 | 22,050 |
| Va | 16,165 | 11,218 | 15,938 | 17,064 | 26,609 |
| Xibe | 16,945 | 7,087 | 20,326 | 15,830 | 23,757 |
| Yao | 16,219 | 8,647 | 15,989 | 15,014 | 22,671 |
| Yi | 15,885 | 10,901 | 16,265 | 15,953 | 24,704 |
| Yugur | 15,103 | 9,964 | 17,871 | 14,956 | 21,619 |
| Zhuang | 15,832 | 8,975 | 16,245 | 14,923 | 23,264 |

| Ethnic group | Construction | Transport, storage, and post | Information transmission, computer service and software | Wholesale and retail trade | Hotels and catering services |
|---|---|---|---|---|---|
| National total | 14,338 | 21,352 | 40,558 | 15,241 | 13,857 |
| Achang | 13,322 | 19,127 | 26,562 | 15,747 | 10,338 |
| Bai | 13,045 | 18,915 | 26,567 | 15,129 | 10,479 |
| Baonan | 10,156 | 17,852 | 17,179 | 9,173 | 8,821 |
| Blang | 13,327 | 19,121 | 26,576 | 15,745 | 10,347 |
| Buyi | 11,363 | 18,064 | 23,943 | 10,606 | 10,129 |

*Table 2.11 (cont.)*

| Ethnic group | Construction | Transport, storage, and post | Information transmission, computer service and software | Wholesale and retail trade | Hotels and catering services |
|---|---|---|---|---|---|
| Dai | 13,317 | 19,113 | 26,562 | 15,749 | 10,339 |
| Daur | 12,479 | 18,516 | 27,632 | 12,061 | 13,232 |
| Deang | 13,318 | 19,105 | 26,474 | 15,748 | 10,324 |
| Derung | 13,305 | 19,196 | 27,378 | 15,208 | 10,687 |
| Dong | 11,985 | 18,091 | 26,552 | 11,998 | 10,899 |
| Dongxiang | 10,253 | 18,172 | 17,542 | 9,486 | 8,888 |
| Ewenki | 11,967 | 19,097 | 26,016 | 11,918 | 13,963 |
| Gaoshan | 13,715 | 19,569 | 31,529 | 13,286 | 11,739 |
| Gelao | 11,309 | 18,029 | 23,779 | 10,490 | 10,108 |
| *Han* | *13,792* | *20,184* | *32,943* | *13,943* | *12,114* |
| Hani | 13,327 | 19,117 | 26,534 | 15,755 | 10,337 |
| Hezhe | 13,564 | 16,958 | 32,066 | 12,390 | 11,774 |
| Hui | 13,101 | 19,476 | 29,317 | 12,825 | 11,356 |
| Jing | 13,946 | 18,245 | 28,845 | 11,697 | 10,110 |
| Jingpo | 13,319 | 19,127 | 26,535 | 15,737 | 10,338 |
| Jino | 13,325 | 19,109 | 26,526 | 15,757 | 10,334 |
| Kazak | 13,998 | 23,615 | 27,538 | 15,115 | 12,410 |
| Kirgiz | 14,001 | 23,559 | 27,607 | 15,099 | 12,413 |
| Korean | 11,888 | 16,753 | 29,460 | 11,514 | 11,007 |
| Lahu | 13,321 | 19,113 | 26,528 | 15,737 | 10,337 |
| Lhoba | 19,391 | 27,359 | 46,336 | 16,544 | 14,311 |
| Li | 12,093 | 21,384 | 43,928 | 11,263 | 10,876 |
| Lisu | 13,259 | 19,068 | 26,701 | 15,688 | 10,351 |
| Manchu | 12,722 | 18,437 | 34,139 | 12,774 | 11,734 |
| Maonan | 13,241 | 18,126 | 27,351 | 11,234 | 10,060 |
| Miao | 12,092 | 18,120 | 26,766 | 12,463 | 10,824 |
| Monba | 19,839 | 27,826 | 47,487 | 16,878 | 14,568 |
| Mongol | 12,058 | 19,145 | 27,215 | 12,118 | 13,490 |
| Mulao | 13,736 | 18,348 | 28,524 | 11,620 | 10,172 |
| Naxi | 13,306 | 19,123 | 26,833 | 15,728 | 10,380 |
| Nu | 13,433 | 19,278 | 26,946 | 15,769 | 10,421 |
| Oroqen | 12,728 | 17,946 | 28,982 | 12,070 | 12,839 |
| Pumi | 13,322 | 19,116 | 26,595 | 15,732 | 10,350 |
| Qiang | 11,276 | 17,718 | 32,800 | 14,138 | 11,086 |
| Russian | 13,428 | 21,932 | 27,840 | 14,126 | 13,115 |
| Salar | 15,066 | 20,847 | 28,245 | 12,814 | 14,069 |
| She | 15,964 | 23,721 | 40,853 | 18,031 | 13,107 |

Table 2.11 (cont.)

| Ethnic group | Construction | Transport, storage, and post | Information transmission, computer service and software | Wholesale and retail trade | Hotels and catering services |
|---|---|---|---|---|---|
| Shui | 11,440 | 18,010 | 23,959 | 10,616 | 10,097 |
| Tajik | 13,992 | 23,478 | 27,682 | 15,061 | 12,394 |
| Tatar | 13,929 | 23,324 | 27,609 | 14,969 | 12,326 |
| Tibetan | 16,027 | 23,096 | 37,407 | 14,741 | 13,181 |
| Tu | 14,925 | 20,851 | 28,415 | 12,907 | 13,901 |
| Tujia | 12,571 | 17,541 | 27,941 | 12,520 | 11,167 |
| Uygur | 14,008 | 23,614 | 27,589 | 15,126 | 12,419 |
| Uzbek | 14,032 | 23,611 | 27,784 | 15,155 | 12,433 |
| Va | 13,313 | 19,129 | 26,649 | 15,676 | 10,368 |
| Xibe | 13,088 | 20,153 | 35,675 | 14,284 | 12,377 |
| Yao | 13,673 | 19,061 | 30,349 | 13,542 | 11,238 |
| Yi | 12,527 | 18,591 | 27,935 | 14,705 | 10,510 |
| Yugur | 10,015 | 17,715 | 17,006 | 9,084 | 8,658 |
| Zhuang | 14,092 | 18,595 | 29,272 | 12,172 | 10,252 |

| Ethnic group | Financial intermediation | Real estate | Leasing and business services | Scientific research, technical services, and geological prospecting | Management of water conservancy, environment, and public facilities |
|---|---|---|---|---|---|
| *National total* | *32,228* | *20,581* | *20,992* | *27,434* | *14,753* |
| Achang | 23,991 | 13,357 | 19,200 | 18,976 | 11,914 |
| Bai | 24,151 | 13,211 | 18,319 | 18,949 | 12,047 |
| Baonan | 18,562 | 11,457 | 11,342 | 19,060 | 13,301 |
| Blang | 24,021 | 13,374 | 19,190 | 19,011 | 11,930 |
| Buyi | 25,432 | 10,264 | 13,979 | 18,533 | 12,226 |
| Dai | 23,999 | 13,357 | 19,212 | 19,004 | 11,910 |
| Daur | 22,832 | 13,923 | 15,363 | 20,067 | 12,413 |
| Deang | 23,936 | 13,321 | 19,201 | 18,940 | 11,891 |
| Derung | 24,583 | 13,748 | 18,457 | 19,637 | 12,260 |
| Dong | 24,784 | 12,552 | 14,139 | 18,860 | 12,582 |
| Dongxiang | 18,858 | 11,665 | 11,506 | 18,638 | 13,267 |
| Ewenki | 21,987 | 13,787 | 16,499 | 19,767 | 13,022 |
| Gaoshan | 28,094 | 16,033 | 15,616 | 22,719 | 13,803 |
| Gelao | 25,402 | 10,130 | 13,879 | 18,464 | 12,192 |
| *Han* | *28,790* | *17,088* | *16,336* | *24,308* | *14,383* |

*Table 2.11* (*cont.*)

| Ethnic group | Financial intermediation | Real estate | Leasing and business services | Scientific research, technical services, and geological prospecting | Management of water conservancy, environment, and public facilities |
|---|---|---|---|---|---|
| Hani | 23,979 | 13,355 | 19,209 | 18,974 | 11,914 |
| Hezhe | 25,527 | 14,592 | 13,492 | 21,506 | 11,277 |
| Hui | 26,722 | 14,628 | 14,286 | 21,827 | 13,726 |
| Jing | 24,076 | 14,627 | 13,731 | 19,476 | 12,163 |
| Jingpo | 23,990 | 13,344 | 19,187 | 18,979 | 11,912 |
| Jino | 23,983 | 13,345 | 19,215 | 18,974 | 11,905 |
| Kazak | 25,156 | 14,515 | 14,176 | 19,093 | 13,423 |
| Kirgiz | 25,166 | 14,524 | 14,176 | 19,115 | 13,401 |
| Korean | 23,538 | 14,168 | 15,850 | 20,259 | 10,957 |
| Lahu | 23,975 | 13,355 | 19,191 | 18,979 | 11,914 |
| Lhoba | 48,003 | 21,124 | 18,001 | 32,558 | 14,232 |
| Li | 28,065 | 15,434 | 15,144 | 15,528 | 11,993 |
| Lisu | 24,063 | 13,383 | 19,196 | 19,154 | 11,911 |
| Manchu | 27,186 | 15,106 | 14,908 | 23,042 | 12,529 |
| Maonan | 24,319 | 13,334 | 13,624 | 19,139 | 12,131 |
| Miao | 25,243 | 12,640 | 14,897 | 19,125 | 12,595 |
| Monba | 49,193 | 21,691 | 18,330 | 33,338 | 14,401 |
| Mongol | 22,831 | 13,906 | 16,240 | 20,356 | 12,996 |
| Mulao | 24,437 | 14,250 | 13,748 | 19,610 | 12,251 |
| Naxi | 24,243 | 13,441 | 19,212 | 19,235 | 11,940 |
| Nu | 24,440 | 13,532 | 19,169 | 19,264 | 11,991 |
| Oroqen | 23,562 | 14,134 | 14,895 | 20,544 | 12,091 |
| Pumi | 24,025 | 13,379 | 19,188 | 19,034 | 11,924 |
| Qiang | 27,562 | 14,627 | 19,345 | 25,265 | 12,000 |
| Russian | 25,025 | 14,626 | 15,397 | 19,989 | 13,562 |
| Salar | 23,688 | 11,875 | 12,265 | 29,282 | 14,443 |
| She | 36,971 | 20,385 | 17,935 | 26,794 | 17,562 |
| Shui | 25,237 | 10,354 | 13,974 | 18,459 | 12,174 |
| Tajik | 25,256 | 14,574 | 14,225 | 19,223 | 13,439 |
| Tatar | 25,419 | 14,587 | 14,247 | 19,424 | 13,536 |
| Tibetan | 36,007 | 16,930 | 16,715 | 29,476 | 13,647 |
| Tu | 23,960 | 12,187 | 12,604 | 29,061 | 14,474 |
| Tujia | 24,917 | 14,850 | 14,434 | 20,011 | 13,022 |
| Uygur | 25,190 | 14,537 | 14,193 | 19,114 | 13,429 |
| Uzbek | 25,369 | 14,612 | 14,259 | 19,234 | 13,470 |
| Va | 24,061 | 13,404 | 19,122 | 19,067 | 11,962 |

*Table 2.11  (cont.)*

| Ethnic group | Financial intermediation | Real estate | Leasing and business services | Scientific research, technical services, and geological prospecting | Management of water conservancy, environment, and public facilities |
|---|---|---|---|---|---|
| Xibe | 27,957 | 15,233 | 15,058 | 22,815 | 12,856 |
| Yao | 25,087 | 15,456 | 14,939 | 20,477 | 12,855 |
| Yi | 25,100 | 13,335 | 18,642 | 20,641 | 11,956 |
| Yugur | 18,619 | 11,512 | 11,372 | 18,800 | 13,304 |
| Zhuang | 24,404 | 14,877 | 14,210 | 19,911 | 12,275 |

| Ethnic group | Total | Services to households and other services | Education | Health, social securities, and social welfare | Culture, sports, and entertainment | Public management and social organization |
|---|---|---|---|---|---|---|
| National total | *18,364* | *16,642* | *18,470* | *21,048* | *22,885* | *20,505* |
| Achang | 16,161 | 11,605 | 15,292 | 16,795 | 14,666 | 15,134 |
| Bai | 15,987 | 11,601 | 15,310 | 16,807 | 14,860 | 15,221 |
| Baonan | 15,158 | 11,672 | 16,212 | 15,806 | 15,457 | 16,462 |
| Blang | 16,171 | 11,632 | 15,303 | 16,811 | 14,700 | 15,161 |
| Buyi | 14,597 | 9,451 | 14,304 | 15,040 | 13,500 | 14,723 |
| Dai | 16,161 | 11,614 | 15,280 | 16,794 | 14,671 | 15,132 |
| Daur | 15,646 | 11,529 | 17,900 | 17,494 | 18,519 | 18,466 |
| Deang | 16,148 | 11,565 | 15,260 | 16,755 | 14,613 | 15,078 |
| Derung | 16,287 | 12,118 | 15,762 | 17,154 | 15,587 | 15,949 |
| Dong | 15,148 | 11,402 | 15,225 | 16,788 | 15,670 | 15,795 |
| Dongxiang | 15,048 | 11,044 | 16,153 | 15,745 | 15,392 | 16,399 |
| Ewenki | 16,072 | 10,838 | 18,153 | 17,852 | 19,371 | 18,732 |
| Gaoshan | 16,688 | 14,035 | 17,405 | 18,864 | 18,740 | 19,090 |
| Gelao | 14,538 | 9,320 | 14,208 | 14,927 | 13,391 | 14,608 |
| *Han* | *17,366* | *16,056* | *18,373* | *20,101* | *20,367* | *20,720* |
| Hani | 16,163 | 11,592 | 15,285 | 16,786 | 14,656 | 15,122 |
| Hezhe | 15,113 | 13,363 | 17,719 | 17,249 | 17,347 | 18,562 |
| Hui | 16,844 | 15,232 | 17,620 | 18,195 | 17,657 | 18,265 |
| Jing | 15,596 | 12,143 | 14,810 | 17,937 | 17,163 | 17,577 |
| Jingpo | 16,158 | 11,587 | 15,283 | 16,784 | 14,657 | 15,121 |
| Jino | 16,161 | 11,577 | 15,275 | 16,778 | 14,646 | 15,109 |
| Kazak | 15,566 | 12,167 | 17,188 | 17,304 | 16,979 | 17,669 |
| Kirgiz | 15,559 | 12,177 | 17,196 | 17,307 | 16,988 | 17,682 |
| Korean | 15,257 | 12,445 | 16,839 | 15,874 | 16,260 | 17,257 |

*Table 2.11* (*cont.*)

| Ethnic group | Total | Services to households and other services | Education | Health, social securities, and social welfare | Culture, sports, and enter- tainment | Public management and social organization |
|---|---|---|---|---|---|---|
| Lahu | 16,157 | 11,606 | 15,284 | 16,784 | 14,661 | 15,122 |
| Lhoba | 27,835 | 25,407 | 28,699 | 27,415 | 29,873 | 30,436 |
| Li | 14,500 | 15,771 | 18,493 | 19,493 | 17,963 | 19,695 |
| Lisu | 16,146 | 11,805 | 15,277 | 16,837 | 14,768 | 15,196 |
| Manchu | 16,616 | 14,221 | 17,772 | 17,641 | 18,459 | 18,930 |
| Maonan | 15,269 | 11,302 | 14,537 | 17,054 | 16,073 | 16,708 |
| Miao | 15,302 | 11,557 | 15,305 | 16,825 | 15,745 | 15,906 |
| Monba | 28,554 | 26,114 | 29,392 | 28,039 | 30,693 | 31,200 |
| Mongol | 16,211 | 11,632 | 17,957 | 17,735 | 19,075 | 18,603 |
| Mulao | 15,578 | 11,902 | 14,814 | 17,768 | 16,952 | 17,458 |
| Naxi | 16,221 | 11,837 | 15,369 | 16,919 | 14,863 | 15,307 |
| Nu | 16,370 | 11,881 | 15,554 | 17,024 | 14,984 | 15,461 |
| Oroqen | 15,518 | 12,078 | 17,853 | 17,440 | 18,265 | 18,524 |
| Pumi | 16,173 | 11,652 | 15,306 | 16,812 | 14,706 | 15,171 |
| Qiang | 15,851 | 18,228 | 15,197 | 18,879 | 18,871 | 18,041 |
| Russian | 16,157 | 11,989 | 17,880 | 17,975 | 18,391 | 18,583 |
| Salar | 18,547 | 28,436 | 19,423 | 20,053 | 19,562 | 20,015 |
| She | 18,982 | 16,718 | 22,752 | 25,372 | 24,355 | 26,300 |
| Shui | 14,593 | 9,486 | 14,230 | 15,034 | 13,509 | 14,699 |
| Tajik | 15,613 | 12,260 | 17,201 | 17,373 | 17,075 | 17,738 |
| Tatar | 15,731 | 12,315 | 17,312 | 17,495 | 17,191 | 17,899 |
| Tibetan | 22,325 | 23,901 | 22,796 | 23,139 | 24,180 | 24,402 |
| Tu | 18,503 | 27,526 | 19,354 | 20,104 | 19,638 | 20,108 |
| Tujia | 15,523 | 13,692 | 16,178 | 17,865 | 17,727 | 17,271 |
| Uygur | 15,576 | 12,180 | 17,196 | 17,321 | 17,000 | 17,685 |
| Uzbek | 15,640 | 12,233 | 17,256 | 17,428 | 17,110 | 17,799 |
| Va | 16,165 | 11,751 | 15,329 | 16,843 | 14,780 | 15,201 |
| Xibe | 16,945 | 13,107 | 18,340 | 18,042 | 19,195 | 19,620 |
| Yao | 16,219 | 13,184 | 15,947 | 19,043 | 18,411 | 18,070 |
| Yi | 15,885 | 13,166 | 15,127 | 17,140 | 15,661 | 15,853 |
| Yugur | 15,103 | 11,101 | 16,155 | 15,749 | 15,407 | 16,437 |
| Zhuang | 15,832 | 12,315 | 14,988 | 18,206 | 17,437 | 17,824 |

*Note:* "Average wage" refers to the average wage in money terms per person during a certain period of time for staff and workers in enterprises, institutions, and government agencies, which reflects the general level of wage income during a certain period of time and is calculated as follows:

Average wage = "Total wages of staff and workers at reference time" ÷ "Average number of staff and workers at reference time."

*Table 2.12* Average wage of staff and workers in state-owned units by sector (unit: yuan)

| Ethnic group | Total | Agriculture, forestry, animal husbandry, and fishing | Mining | Manufacturing | Production and supply of electricity, gas, and water |
|---|---|---|---|---|---|
| National total | 19,313 | 8,230 | 20,992 | 16,963 | 24,378 |
| Achang | 16,946 | 11,269 | 16,836 | 26,040 | 26,656 |
| Bai | 16,769 | 10,948 | 16,620 | 24,243 | 25,844 |
| Baonan | 16,071 | 10,014 | 19,725 | 16,521 | 21,533 |
| Blang | 16,964 | 11,273 | 16,856 | 26,016 | 26,654 |
| Buyi | 15,098 | 11,060 | 16,215 | 14,592 | 24,563 |
| Dai | 16,947 | 11,268 | 16,856 | 26,033 | 26,647 |
| Daur | 16,072 | 8,022 | 14,664 | 13,850 | 24,486 |
| Deang | 16,916 | 11,266 | 16,821 | 26,084 | 26,647 |
| Derung | 17,181 | 10,926 | 17,389 | 24,106 | 26,104 |
| Dong | 15,911 | 9,536 | 15,623 | 15,902 | 22,457 |
| Dongxiang | 15,836 | 9,870 | 19,716 | 16,301 | 21,450 |
| Ewenki | 16,715 | 8,562 | 15,246 | 13,878 | 26,233 |
| Gaoshan | 18,253 | 9,295 | 18,864 | 16,958 | 24,274 |
| Gelao | 14,990 | 11,027 | 16,200 | 14,398 | 24,461 |
| Han | 19,483 | 10,009 | 20,062 | 17,406 | 25,074 |
| Hani | 16,945 | 11,275 | 16,844 | 26,069 | 26,667 |
| Hezhe | 15,345 | 6,888 | 12,997 | 14,201 | 21,416 |
| Hui | 17,869 | 10,297 | 19,992 | 16,738 | 24,836 |
| Jing | 16,349 | 8,819 | 15,109 | 16,795 | 22,403 |
| Jingpo | 16,939 | 11,264 | 16,840 | 26,014 | 26,646 |
| Jino | 16,937 | 11,271 | 16,836 | 26,072 | 26,659 |
| Kazak | 15,378 | 9,903 | 21,712 | 14,911 | 22,437 |
| Kirgiz | 15,376 | 9,868 | 21,617 | 14,897 | 22,431 |
| Korean | 15,659 | 6,799 | 14,480 | 16,196 | 21,387 |
| Lahu | 16,943 | 11,269 | 16,855 | 26,029 | 26,642 |
| Lhoba | 28,601 | 20,199 | 16,124 | 14,214 | 26,296 |
| Li | 14,580 | 6,589 | 15,690 | 11,856 | 16,612 |
| Lisu | 16,966 | 11,245 | 16,962 | 25,815 | 26,530 |
| Manchu | 17,461 | 6,739 | 18,765 | 17,535 | 23,563 |
| Maonan | 15,907 | 9,394 | 15,342 | 15,988 | 22,891 |
| Miao | 16,145 | 9,940 | 15,976 | 17,118 | 23,097 |
| Monba | 29,322 | 20,814 | 16,501 | 14,253 | 26,485 |
| Mongol | 16,929 | 8,441 | 16,519 | 14,835 | 25,689 |

*Table 2.12* (cont.)

| Ethnic group | Total | Agriculture, forestry, animal husbandry, and fishing | Mining | Manufacturing | Production and supply of electricity, gas, and water |
|---|---|---|---|---|---|
| Mulao | 16,345 | 9,075 | 15,264 | 16,472 | 22,762 |
| Naxi | 17,051 | 11,307 | 16,939 | 25,789 | 26,592 |
| Nu | 17,187 | 11,426 | 16,842 | 25,806 | 26,697 |
| Oroqen | 15,926 | 7,619 | 14,099 | 13,987 | 23,662 |
| Pumi | 16,963 | 11,262 | 16,873 | 25,977 | 26,637 |
| Qiang | 17,916 | 10,402 | 20,793 | 17,966 | 22,340 |
| Russian | 16,434 | 9,692 | 19,605 | 14,875 | 24,516 |
| Salar | 20,412 | 13,262 | 23,742 | 18,855 | 25,817 |
| She | 24,436 | 13,216 | 14,232 | 20,099 | 32,845 |
| Shui | 15,051 | 10,947 | 16,176 | 14,764 | 24,441 |
| Tajik | 15,482 | 9,891 | 21,639 | 14,970 | 22,468 |
| Tatar | 15,674 | 9,988 | 21,622 | 15,141 | 22,719 |
| Tibetan | 23,650 | 15,898 | 19,122 | 16,494 | 25,020 |
| Tu | 20,445 | 13,054 | 23,377 | 18,973 | 25,924 |
| Tujia | 16,792 | 8,461 | 16,328 | 17,374 | 20,920 |
| Uygur | 15,395 | 9,901 | 21,710 | 14,918 | 22,446 |
| Uzbek | 15,500 | 9,919 | 21,669 | 14,977 | 22,550 |
| Va | 16,982 | 11,273 | 16,976 | 25,817 | 26,550 |
| Xibe | 17,725 | 6,977 | 20,434 | 18,375 | 23,663 |
| Yao | 17,302 | 8,468 | 15,450 | 18,148 | 22,207 |
| Yi | 16,979 | 10,996 | 17,857 | 22,513 | 25,204 |
| Yugur | 16,008 | 9,927 | 19,556 | 16,487 | 21,526 |
| Zhuang | 16,660 | 8,889 | 15,311 | 17,498 | 22,821 |

| Ethnic group | Construction | Transport, storage, and post | Information transmission, computer service and software | Wholesale and retail trade | Hotels and catering services |
|---|---|---|---|---|---|
| *National total* | *16,361* | *21,160* | *31,654* | *15,729* | *13,453* |
| Achang | 14,739 | 20,501 | 26,057 | 21,752 | 10,734 |
| Bai | 14,398 | 20,200 | 25,645 | 20,418 | 10,725 |
| Baonan | 11,363 | 18,874 | 17,176 | 10,152 | 9,427 |
| Blang | 14,750 | 20,498 | 26,068 | 21,743 | 10,743 |

Table 2.12 (cont.)

| Ethnic group | Construction | Transport, storage, and post | Information transmission, computer service and software | Wholesale and retail trade | Hotels and catering services |
|---|---|---|---|---|---|
| Buyi | 12,143 | 19,206 | 22,004 | 11,365 | 9,356 |
| Dai | 14,738 | 20,488 | 26,064 | 21,750 | 10,743 |
| Daur | 14,296 | 19,345 | 26,172 | 13,224 | 14,836 |
| Deang | 14,722 | 20,484 | 25,971 | 21,764 | 10,723 |
| Derung | 14,886 | 20,470 | 26,698 | 20,447 | 11,122 |
| Dong | 12,805 | 19,073 | 24,431 | 13,686 | 10,506 |
| Dongxiang | 11,374 | 19,180 | 17,504 | 10,646 | 9,472 |
| Ewenki | 13,752 | 19,991 | 24,908 | 13,003 | 16,607 |
| Gaoshan | 15,749 | 20,488 | 29,220 | 15,627 | 11,853 |
| Gelao | 12,044 | 19,161 | 21,800 | 11,108 | 9,301 |
| *Han* | *16,683* | *21,104* | *30,971* | *16,594* | *12,302* |
| Hani | 14,742 | 20,496 | 26,026 | 21,769 | 10,734 |
| Hezhe | 15,678 | 17,578 | 29,613 | 13,556 | 11,138 |
| Hui | 15,008 | 20,510 | 27,986 | 14,997 | 11,612 |
| Jing | 13,105 | 19,871 | 31,214 | 12,728 | 10,737 |
| Jingpo | 14,729 | 20,500 | 26,021 | 21,722 | 10,732 |
| Jino | 14,734 | 20,485 | 26,026 | 21,771 | 10,734 |
| Kazak | 14,917 | 24,987 | 27,251 | 19,009 | 13,174 |
| Kirgiz | 14,932 | 24,924 | 27,298 | 18,971 | 13,164 |
| Korean | 14,007 | 17,853 | 28,083 | 12,664 | 10,833 |
| Lahu | 14,738 | 20,492 | 26,013 | 21,739 | 10,732 |
| Lhoba | 17,836 | 27,928 | 46,143 | 17,492 | 14,533 |
| Li | 14,185 | 19,338 | 46,438 | 12,972 | 10,316 |
| Lisu | 14,738 | 20,433 | 26,244 | 21,625 | 10,788 |
| Manchu | 15,771 | 19,036 | 31,846 | 14,475 | 12,057 |
| Maonan | 12,691 | 19,647 | 28,689 | 12,019 | 10,308 |
| Miao | 13,126 | 19,126 | 24,941 | 14,819 | 10,530 |
| Monba | 18,140 | 28,374 | 47,418 | 17,794 | 14,847 |
| Mongol | 14,042 | 20,069 | 25,968 | 13,441 | 15,741 |
| Mulao | 13,000 | 19,921 | 30,489 | 12,517 | 10,656 |
| Naxi | 14,768 | 20,484 | 26,360 | 21,668 | 10,816 |
| Nu | 14,824 | 20,643 | 26,443 | 21,694 | 10,819 |
| Oroqen | 14,680 | 18,702 | 27,200 | 13,133 | 13,832 |
| Pumi | 14,753 | 20,491 | 26,083 | 21,709 | 10,752 |
| Qiang | 14,660 | 18,611 | 33,703 | 17,682 | 12,851 |
| Russian | 14,815 | 23,100 | 26,992 | 17,031 | 14,567 |
| Salar | 17,874 | 22,933 | 28,684 | 14,861 | 15,467 |

*Table 2.12* (*cont.*)

| Ethnic group | Construction | Transport, storage, and post | Information transmission, computer service and software | Wholesale and retail trade | Hotels and catering services |
|---|---|---|---|---|---|
| She | 19,157 | 24,670 | 39,265 | 24,378 | 13,301 |
| Shui | 12,151 | 19,182 | 22,162 | 11,378 | 9,365 |
| Tajik | 14,950 | 24,832 | 27,362 | 18,902 | 13,140 |
| Tatar | 14,947 | 24,651 | 27,188 | 18,761 | 13,062 |
| Tibetan | 16,747 | 24,124 | 37,718 | 16,577 | 14,087 |
| Tu | 17,722 | 22,831 | 28,726 | 14,938 | 15,211 |
| Tujia | 14,297 | 18,420 | 26,165 | 15,060 | 10,962 |
| Uygur | 14,932 | 24,984 | 27,290 | 19,021 | 13,181 |
| Uzbek | 14,976 | 24,962 | 27,457 | 19,038 | 13,188 |
| Va | 14,755 | 20,503 | 26,129 | 21,609 | 10,762 |
| Xibe | 15,773 | 20,869 | 33,105 | 16,501 | 12,884 |
| Yao | 13,784 | 20,199 | 30,429 | 15,647 | 11,671 |
| Yi | 14,409 | 19,808 | 27,658 | 19,429 | 11,153 |
| Yugur | 11,192 | 18,692 | 16,917 | 10,030 | 9,229 |
| Zhuang | 13,322 | 20,183 | 31,609 | 13,422 | 10,916 |

| Ethnic group | Financial intermediation | Real estate | Leasing and business services | Scientific research, technical services, and geological prospecting | Management of water conservancy, environment, and public facilities |
|---|---|---|---|---|---|
| National total | 32,849 | 20,077 | 19,972 | 26,309 | 14,700 |
| Achang | 27,382 | 14,838 | 19,865 | 18,057 | 18,057 |
| Bai | 27,083 | 14,831 | 19,105 | 18,221 | 18,221 |
| Baonan | 19,888 | 12,771 | 12,433 | 19,149 | 19,149 |
| Blang | 27,398 | 14,856 | 19,860 | 18,105 | 18,105 |
| Buyi | 26,587 | 12,484 | 16,002 | 18,815 | 18,815 |
| Dai | 27,390 | 14,849 | 19,883 | 18,086 | 18,086 |
| Daur | 25,002 | 15,113 | 17,265 | 20,353 | 20,353 |
| Deang | 27,334 | 14,808 | 19,863 | 18,014 | 18,014 |
| Derung | 27,654 | 15,152 | 19,190 | 18,950 | 18,950 |
| Dong | 25,722 | 14,578 | 15,613 | 19,014 | 19,014 |
| Dongxiang | 20,226 | 13,101 | 12,474 | 18,714 | 18,714 |
| Ewenki | 23,858 | 15,139 | 18,641 | 20,024 | 20,024 |
| Gaoshan | 30,042 | 17,397 | 16,288 | 22,778 | 22,778 |
| Gelao | 26,535 | 12,334 | 15,913 | 18,763 | 18,763 |

Table 2.12  (cont.)

| Ethnic group | Financial intermediation | Real estate | Leasing and business services | Scientific research, technical services, and geological prospecting | Management of water conservancy, environment, and public facilities |
|---|---|---|---|---|---|
| Han | 30,544 | 18,289 | 17,175 | 24,481 | 24,481 |
| Hani | 27,374 | 14,840 | 19,873 | 18,052 | 18,052 |
| Hezhe | 28,403 | 15,077 | 14,868 | 21,903 | 21,903 |
| Hui | 28,564 | 16,598 | 15,027 | 21,699 | 21,699 |
| Jing | 25,393 | 15,456 | 15,612 | 19,553 | 19,553 |
| Jingpo | 27,381 | 14,824 | 19,851 | 18,062 | 18,062 |
| Jino | 27,383 | 14,832 | 19,878 | 18,054 | 18,054 |
| Kazak | 27,092 | 18,057 | 14,823 | 19,082 | 19,082 |
| Kirgiz | 27,112 | 18,039 | 14,832 | 19,107 | 19,107 |
| Korean | 26,624 | 14,058 | 16,419 | 20,242 | 20,242 |
| Lahu | 27,364 | 14,839 | 19,855 | 18,064 | 18,064 |
| Lhoba | 48,609 | 22,571 | 17,905 | 32,586 | 32,586 |
| Li | 31,457 | 14,617 | 15,088 | 15,486 | 15,486 |
| Lisu | 27,406 | 14,911 | 19,913 | 18,266 | 18,266 |
| Manchu | 29,670 | 15,647 | 15,653 | 22,439 | 22,439 |
| Maonan | 25,570 | 14,523 | 15,598 | 19,291 | 19,291 |
| Miao | 26,413 | 14,557 | 16,310 | 19,401 | 19,401 |
| Monba | 49,924 | 23,137 | 18,154 | 33,307 | 33,307 |
| Mongol | 24,753 | 15,234 | 18,100 | 20,394 | 20,394 |
| Mulao | 25,761 | 15,203 | 15,672 | 19,734 | 19,734 |
| Naxi | 27,575 | 14,981 | 19,922 | 18,353 | 18,353 |
| Nu | 27,765 | 15,030 | 19,836 | 18,371 | 18,371 |
| Oroqen | 25,935 | 15,034 | 16,672 | 20,853 | 20,853 |
| Pumi | 27,401 | 14,865 | 19,859 | 18,121 | 18,121 |
| Qiang | 29,307 | 17,597 | 21,696 | 25,437 | 25,437 |
| Russian | 26,927 | 17,273 | 16,526 | 20,078 | 20,078 |
| Salar | 25,125 | 14,740 | 15,675 | 29,451 | 29,451 |
| She | 37,681 | 24,227 | 19,723 | 27,443 | 27,443 |
| Shui | 26,400 | 12,502 | 15,984 | 18,708 | 18,708 |
| Tajik | 27,185 | 18,026 | 14,875 | 19,228 | 19,228 |
| Tatar | 27,328 | 17,960 | 14,875 | 19,427 | 19,427 |
| Tibetan | 37,147 | 19,025 | 18,070 | 29,537 | 29,537 |
| Tu | 25,479 | 14,873 | 15,860 | 29,208 | 29,208 |
| Tujia | 25,318 | 16,156 | 15,297 | 20,872 | 20,872 |
| Uygur | 27,127 | 18,074 | 14,837 | 19,102 | 19,102 |
| Uzbek | 27,311 | 18,105 | 14,895 | 19,226 | 19,226 |

*Table 2.12  (cont.)*

| Ethnic group | Financial intermediation | Real estate | Leasing and business services | Scientific research, technical services, and geological prospecting | Management of water conservancy, environment, and public facilities |
|---|---|---|---|---|---|
| Va | 27,418 | 14,871 | 19,793 | 18,191 | 18,191 |
| Xibe | 30,454 | 16,136 | 15,760 | 21,702 | 21,702 |
| Yao | 26,560 | 16,526 | 16,171 | 20,422 | 20,422 |
| Yi | 27,785 | 15,314 | 19,927 | 20,156 | 20,156 |
| Yugur | 19,930 | 12,748 | 12,372 | 18,897 | 18,897 |
| Zhuang | 25,959 | 15,618 | 15,992 | 19,925 | 19,925 |

| Ethnic group | Services to households and other services | Education | Health, social securities, and social welfare | Culture, sports, and entertainment | Public management and social organization |
|---|---|---|---|---|---|
| National total | 19,108 | 18,622 | 21,760 | 23,342 | 20,531 |
| Achang | 14,712 | 15,247 | 16,855 | 15,069 | 15,138 |
| Bai | 14,535 | 15,275 | 16,921 | 15,199 | 15,227 |
| Baonan | 13,091 | 16,216 | 15,943 | 15,477 | 16,463 |
| Blang | 14,722 | 15,259 | 16,876 | 15,100 | 15,166 |
| Buyi | 12,454 | 14,344 | 15,161 | 14,057 | 14,735 |
| Dai | 14,735 | 15,235 | 16,857 | 15,071 | 15,136 |
| Daur | 14,324 | 17,964 | 18,254 | 18,633 | 18,468 |
| Deang | 14,681 | 15,215 | 16,807 | 15,010 | 15,082 |
| Derung | 14,925 | 15,742 | 17,382 | 15,998 | 15,957 |
| Dong | 14,241 | 15,241 | 17,083 | 15,868 | 15,811 |
| Dongxiang | 12,458 | 16,158 | 15,867 | 15,408 | 16,400 |
| Ewenki | 13,314 | 18,234 | 18,844 | 19,522 | 18,733 |
| Gaoshan | 16,803 | 17,651 | 19,570 | 19,377 | 19,122 |
| Gelao | 12,309 | 14,248 | 15,034 | 13,953 | 14,619 |
| *Han* | *17,865* | *18,508* | *21,024* | *21,035* | *20,758* |
| Hani | 14,698 | 15,240 | 16,845 | 15,055 | 15,127 |
| Hezhe | 17,038 | 17,763 | 17,620 | 17,513 | 18,571 |
| Hui | 17,192 | 17,767 | 18,641 | 18,014 | 18,281 |
| Jing | 19,899 | 14,827 | 18,067 | 17,836 | 17,634 |
| Jingpo | 14,693 | 15,238 | 16,841 | 15,061 | 15,125 |
| Jino | 14,697 | 15,230 | 16,835 | 15,045 | 15,114 |
| Kazak | 13,693 | 17,219 | 17,287 | 17,057 | 17,676 |
| Kirgiz | 13,727 | 17,227 | 17,294 | 17,066 | 17,689 |

*Table 2.12* (*cont.*)

| Ethnic group | Services to households and other services | Education | Health, social securities, and social welfare | Culture, sports, and entertainment | Public management and social organization |
|---|---|---|---|---|---|
| Korean | 14,751 | 16,871 | 16,320 | 16,452 | 17,275 |
| Lahu | 14,698 | 15,240 | 16,845 | 15,059 | 15,126 |
| Lhoba | 25,920 | 28,708 | 27,479 | 29,964 | 30,439 |
| Li | 20,267 | 18,576 | 20,396 | 19,837 | 19,695 |
| Lisu | 14,924 | 15,232 | 16,933 | 15,164 | 15,200 |
| Manchu | 16,790 | 17,838 | 18,293 | 18,894 | 18,956 |
| Maonan | 17,961 | 14,560 | 17,154 | 16,718 | 16,753 |
| Miao | 14,137 | 15,318 | 17,164 | 15,973 | 15,922 |
| Monba | 26,579 | 29,400 | 28,102 | 30,780 | 31,202 |
| Mongol | 13,966 | 18,042 | 18,650 | 19,265 | 18,609 |
| Mulao | 19,299 | 14,836 | 17,883 | 17,646 | 17,511 |
| Naxi | 14,977 | 15,326 | 17,015 | 15,262 | 15,312 |
| Nu | 14,948 | 15,511 | 17,094 | 15,384 | 15,466 |
| Oroqen | 15,104 | 17,911 | 18,122 | 18,404 | 18,528 |
| Pumi | 14,757 | 15,263 | 16,881 | 15,108 | 15,176 |
| Qiang | 22,048 | 15,162 | 20,219 | 19,172 | 18,044 |
| Russian | 13,947 | 17,951 | 18,412 | 18,578 | 18,592 |
| Salar | 30,381 | 19,439 | 20,196 | 19,773 | 20,018 |
| She | 19,906 | 22,837 | 26,721 | 25,408 | 26,382 |
| Shui | 12,639 | 14,267 | 15,150 | 14,060 | 14,711 |
| Tajik | 13,804 | 17,234 | 17,386 | 17,169 | 17,746 |
| Tatar | 13,912 | 17,353 | 17,529 | 17,312 | 17,908 |
| Tibetan | 25,573 | 22,790 | 23,504 | 24,331 | 24,404 |
| Tu | 29,526 | 19,370 | 20,277 | 19,910 | 20,112 |
| Tujia | 15,094 | 16,210 | 18,417 | 17,649 | 17,331 |
| Uygur | 13,708 | 17,228 | 17,308 | 17,080 | 17,692 |
| Uzbek | 13,816 | 17,290 | 17,427 | 17,215 | 17,807 |
| Va | 14,740 | 15,291 | 16,923 | 15,179 | 15,206 |
| Xibe | 15,383 | 18,390 | 18,633 | 19,510 | 19,648 |
| Yao | 18,577 | 15,944 | 19,320 | 18,843 | 18,105 |
| Yi | 16,464 | 15,094 | 17,559 | 16,048 | 15,857 |
| Yugur | 12,561 | 16,164 | 15,902 | 15,444 | 16,439 |
| Zhuang | 20,036 | 15,002 | 18,314 | 18,163 | 17,879 |

*Note:* "Average wage" refers to the average wage in money terms per person during a certain period of time for staff and workers in enterprises, institutions, and government agencies, which reflects the general level of wage income during a certain period of time and is calculated as follows:

Average wage = "Total wages of staff and workers at reference time" ÷ "Average number of staff and workers at reference time."

*Table 2.13* Employed persons at the year-end and earnings in state-owned and state-share-holding enterprises

| Ethnic group | Number of employed persons (1,000 persons) | Female | Staff and workers (1,000 persons) | Technical personnel | Earnings of employed persons (million yuan) | Average wage of staff and workers (yuan) |
|---|---|---|---|---|---|---|
| National total | 42,883.00 | 1,435.10 | 40,364.00 | 931.10 | 845,510.00 | 20,079 |
| Achang | 0.71 | 0.02 | 0.67 | 0.02 | 13.11 | 19,031 |
| Bai | 39.74 | 1.33 | 37.36 | 0.93 | 724.48 | 18,854 |
| Baonan | 0.64 | 0.02 | 0.62 | 0.01 | 10.65 | 16,829 |
| Blang | 1.93 | 0.07 | 1.82 | 0.05 | 35.50 | 19,043 |
| Buyi | 69.69 | 2.06 | 66.09 | 1.36 | 1,217.51 | 18,318 |
| Dai | 24.36 | 0.83 | 22.95 | 0.59 | 447.90 | 19,034 |
| Daur | 7.16 | 0.23 | 6.70 | 0.12 | 110.50 | 15,630 |
| Deang | 0.38 | 0.01 | 0.36 | 0.01 | 6.92 | 19,017 |
| Derung | 0.19 | 0.01 | 0.18 | 0.00 | 3.47 | 18,989 |
| Dong | 68.16 | 2.12 | 63.76 | 1.37 | 1,177.27 | 17,987 |
| Dongxiang | 21.28 | 0.75 | 20.60 | 0.41 | 349.86 | 16,512 |
| Ewenki | 1.42 | 0.05 | 1.37 | 0.03 | 23.00 | 16,071 |
| Gaoshan | 0.16 | 0.01 | 0.15 | 0.00 | 3.18 | 19,116 |
| Gelao | 13.58 | 0.40 | 12.88 | 0.26 | 236.94 | 18,281 |
| *Han* | *39,015.12* | *1,300.20* | *36,696.52* | *847.40* | *776,898.75* | *19,901* |
| Hani | 30.24 | 1.03 | 28.50 | 0.74 | 556.00 | 19,038 |
| Hezhe | 0.31 | 0.01 | 0.28 | 0.00 | 4.60 | 15,383 |
| Hui | 421.54 | 14.30 | 397.37 | 8.88 | 8,314.17 | 18,960 |
| Jing | 0.56 | 0.02 | 0.52 | 0.01 | 9.33 | 17,217 |
| Jingpo | 2.78 | 0.09 | 2.62 | 0.07 | 51.17 | 19,036 |
| Jino | 0.44 | 0.01 | 0.41 | 0.01 | 8.09 | 19,034 |
| Kazak | 87.72 | 3.52 | 84.07 | 1.49 | 1,416.97 | 15,248 |
| Kirgiz | 11.29 | 0.45 | 10.81 | 0.19 | 182.02 | 15,242 |
| Korean | 100.92 | 3.21 | 95.58 | 2.14 | 1,715.68 | 16,689 |
| Lahu | 9.53 | 0.32 | 8.98 | 0.23 | 174.94 | 19,032 |
| Lhoba | 0.09 | 0.00 | 0.08 | 0.00 | 2.22 | 26,987 |
| Li | 59.13 | 2.25 | 57.79 | 0.99 | 720.35 | 12,360 |
| Lisu | 13.35 | 0.45 | 12.58 | 0.32 | 244.92 | 19,008 |
| Manchu | 714.51 | 24.84 | 681.91 | 18.98 | 1,3298.50 | 18,077 |
| Maonan | 2.60 | 0.09 | 2.44 | 0.06 | 43.73 | 17,477 |
| Miao | 204.44 | 6.42 | 192.00 | 4.16 | 3,563.04 | 18,167 |
| Monba | 0.28 | 0.01 | 0.24 | 0.01 | 6.91 | 27,557 |
| Mongol | 284.45 | 9.73 | 275.38 | 6.00 | 4,844.42 | 16,629 |

*Table 2.13* (cont.)

| Ethnic group | Number of employed persons (1,000 persons) | Female | Staff and workers (1,000 persons) | Technical personnel | Earnings of employed persons (million yuan) | Average wage of staff and workers (yuan) |
|---|---|---|---|---|---|---|
| Mulao | 5.09 | 0.17 | 4.78 | 0.11 | 86.37 | 17,505 |
| Naxi | 6.54 | 0.22 | 6.16 | 0.16 | 120.84 | 19,071 |
| Nu | 0.61 | 0.02 | 0.57 | 0.01 | 11.33 | 19,190 |
| Oroqen | 0.47 | 0.01 | 0.43 | 0.01 | 7.13 | 15,633 |
| Pumi | 0.71 | 0.02 | 0.67 | 0.02 | 13.08 | 19,037 |
| Qiang | 6.50 | 0.22 | 6.16 | 0.15 | 118.07 | 18,357 |
| Russian | 0.95 | 0.04 | 0.91 | 0.02 | 16.06 | 16,130 |
| Salar | 3.52 | 0.12 | 3.34 | 0.09 | 74.47 | 21,727 |
| She | 16.16 | 0.55 | 15.15 | 0.36 | 368.40 | 24,049 |
| Shui | 9.53 | 0.28 | 9.04 | 0.19 | 165.55 | 18,213 |
| Tajik | 2.83 | 0.11 | 2.71 | 0.05 | 45.87 | 15,378 |
| Tatar | 0.33 | 0.01 | 0.32 | 0.01 | 5.50 | 15,584 |
| Tibetan | 155.98 | 5.40 | 142.66 | 3.45 | 3,433.34 | 23,316 |
| Tu | 7.80 | 0.27 | 7.40 | 0.20 | 165.17 | 21,779 |
| Tujia | 202.19 | 6.72 | 189.51 | 4.30 | 3,345.18 | 17,310 |
| Uygur | 588.59 | 23.58 | 564.00 | 10.00 | 9,513.11 | 15,265 |
| Uzbek | 0.86 | 0.03 | 0.83 | 0.01 | 13.99 | 15,370 |
| Va | 8.39 | 0.28 | 7.91 | 0.20 | 154.35 | 19,041 |
| Xibe | 15.28 | 0.56 | 14.67 | 0.42 | 278.28 | 18,016 |
| Yao | 61.51 | 2.08 | 57.32 | 1.36 | 1,090.62 | 18,221 |
| Yi | 165.84 | 5.52 | 156.63 | 3.85 | 3,014.92 | 18,748 |
| Yugur | 0.53 | 0.02 | 0.52 | 0.01 | 8.96 | 16,748 |
| Zhuang | 395.89 | 13.61 | 371.42 | 9.06 | 6,743.78 | 17,585 |

*Table 2.14* Registered urban unemployed persons and unemployment rate

| Ethnic group | Unemployment (1,000 persons) | | Unemployment rate (%) | |
|---|---|---|---|---|
| | 1990 | 2005 | 1990 | 2005 |
| Achang | 79.24 | 131.81 | 2.50 | 4.16 |
| Bai | 88.71 | 152.85 | 2.67 | 4.17 |
| Baonan | 120.81 | 91.80 | 4.84 | 3.31 |
| Blang | 79.53 | 132.59 | 2.50 | 4.16 |
| Buyi | 108.64 | 128.03 | 4.01 | 4.18 |
| Dai | 80.47 | 132.46 | 2.51 | 4.17 |
| Daur | 166.20 | 225.64 | 3.16 | 4.28 |

*Table 2.14* (*cont.*)

| Ethnic group | Unemployment (1,000 persons) | | Unemployment rate (%) | |
| --- | --- | --- | --- | --- |
| | 1990 | 2005 | 1990 | 2005 |
| Deang | 78.65 | 130.74 | 2.50 | 4.17 |
| Derung | 92.68 | 160.74 | 2.51 | 4.13 |
| Dong | 127.65 | 229.20 | 3.55 | 4.18 |
| Dongxiang | 121.07 | 94.41 | 4.69 | 3.34 |
| Ewenki | 155.96 | 195.64 | 3.58 | 4.24 |
| Gaoshan | 160.59 | 278.24 | 2.81 | 3.87 |
| Gelao | 108.15 | 126.16 | 4.04 | 4.18 |
| *Han* | *168.49* | *307.84* | *2.56* | *3.79* |
| Hani | 79.10 | 131.78 | 2.50 | 4.16 |
| Hezhe | 192.01 | 306.81 | 2.22 | 4.33 |
| Hui | 118.17 | 180.74 | 3.65 | 3.91 |
| Jing | 136.77 | 186.80 | 3.79 | 4.11 |
| Jingpo | 79.34 | 131.91 | 2.51 | 4.16 |
| Jino | 79.00 | 131.29 | 2.50 | 4.17 |
| Kazak | 96.09 | 111.43 | 3.00 | 3.92 |
| Kirgiz | 97.15 | 113.62 | 2.99 | 3.92 |
| Korean | 144.61 | 323.56 | 2.04 | 4.36 |
| Lahu | 79.73 | 132.55 | 2.50 | 4.16 |
| Lhoba | 11.34 | 20.27 | 0.26 | 0.37 |
| Li | 40.14 | 57.82 | 3.04 | 3.58 |
| Lisu | 87.82 | 138.08 | 2.53 | 4.18 |
| Manchu | 177.41 | 435.33 | 2.02 | 4.82 |
| Maonan | 130.13 | 168.93 | 3.93 | 4.14 |
| Miao | 116.55 | 210.89 | 3.24 | 4.18 |
| Monba | 8.68 | 12.85 | 0.13 | 0.16 |
| Mongol | 157.57 | 237.60 | 3.38 | 4.35 |
| Mulao | 135.58 | 181.98 | 3.86 | 4.11 |
| Naxi | 86.79 | 136.87 | 2.52 | 4.16 |
| Nu | 79.00 | 131.53 | 2.47 | 4.10 |
| Oroqen | 175.97 | 255.59 | 2.89 | 4.31 |
| Pumi | 80.79 | 133.46 | 2.51 | 4.16 |
| Qiang | 375.27 | 340.59 | 3.68 | 4.60 |
| Russian | 118.79 | 149.91 | 3.18 | 4.00 |
| Salar | 54.58 | 48.81 | 5.36 | 3.84 |
| She | 102.69 | 200.85 | 2.56 | 3.80 |
| Shui | 108.78 | 128.65 | 4.00 | 4.18 |
| Tajik | 97.61 | 116.90 | 2.98 | 3.91 |
| Tatar | 98.51 | 116.33 | 3.05 | 3.88 |
| Tibetan | 111.11 | 101.36 | 2.48 | 2.28 |

*Table 2.14* (cont.)

| Ethnic group | Unemployment (1,000 persons) | | Unemployment rate (%) | |
|---|---|---|---|---|
| | 1990 | 2005 | 1990 | 2005 |
| Tu | 61.23 | 62.23 | 5.23 | 3.82 |
| Tujia | 113.62 | 344.93 | 2.19 | 4.21 |
| Uygur | 96.36 | 112.47 | 3.00 | 3.92 |
| Uzbek | 96.69 | 113.70 | 3.00 | 3.91 |
| Va | 82.52 | 136.90 | 2.51 | 4.15 |
| Xibe | 201.63 | 474.41 | 2.37 | 5.13 |
| Yao | 143.13 | 254.88 | 3.34 | 4.06 |
| Yi | 164.56 | 189.00 | 3.00 | 4.29 |
| Yugur | 123.18 | 94.68 | 4.82 | 3.29 |
| Zhuang | 136.11 | 187.21 | 3.72 | 4.09 |

*Notes:* (1) "Registered urban unemployed persons" refers to the persons with non-agricultural household registration at certain working ages (16–50 years for males and 16–45 years for females), who are capable of work, unemployed and willing to work, and have been registered at the local employment service agencies to apply for a job. (2) "Registered urban unemployment rate" refers to the ratio of the number of registered unemployed persons to the sum of the number of persons employed in various units (minus the rural labor force, retirees, and Hong Kong, Macau, Taiwan, or foreign employees they employ), laid-off workers in urban units, owners and employees in urban private enterprises, urban self-employed individuals, and the registered urban unemployed persons. The formula is as follows:

"Registered urban unemployment rate" = "number of registered urban unemployed persons" ÷ ("number of persons employed in urban units" – "rural labor force employed and retirees employed" – "Hong Kong, Macau, Taiwan, or foreign employees they employ" + "laid-off workers" + "owners and employees in urban private enterprises" + "self-employed individuals in urban areas" + "registered urban unemployed persons") × 100%.

# 3 People's livelihood

Statistics on the consumer price indices of residents are organized by the Department of Urban Socio-economic Surveys at the National Bureau of Statistics (NBS). The urban socioeconomic survey organizations of the provinces, autonomous regions, and municipalities, and of the selected cities and counties, collect data from the grassroots units in accordance with the scheme of price survey stipulated by the NBS, tabulate them, and report them to the higher agencies.

Data for calculation of the consumer price indices of residents are collected through a combination of sample surveys and surveys of key units. Areas distributed in different economic regions are selected as the sample areas and the representative commodities are selected as the sample commodities. Regular surveys are conducted to collect data on the market prices. Estimation of population is made on the basis of the sample. At present, 226 cities and counties have been selected for this purpose. Major steps in the process of calculation of the price indices are as follows:

(i)   The selection of the areas and places for survey: Based on such principles as regional economic features and reasonable geographic distribution, representative sample areas for the national survey are selected, which include large, medium, and small cities and counties. When the sample areas are selected, large-scale shops and markets (including fairs and service outlets) with great varieties of commodities are selected as the survey places.

(ii)  The selection of the representative commodities and their specifications or varieties: The representative commodities are the commodities consumed in large quantity and representative in price changes. The representative specifications or varieties are determined according to the data on the retail sales of commodities and the account data of the residents of close to 50,000 urban households and 68,000 rural households, following the related instructions for selection. In principle, only those specifications or varieties of the commodities can be selected: (a) They are closely related to people's livelihood; (b) They are sold in large quantities (or large values); (c) The market supply is stable; (d) The changes of their prices are representative in trend; (e) There is great difference among the specifications or varieties selected. At present, data are collected on about 600–700 specifications each month under 251 basic headings in 8 categories in the consumer price surveys.

(iii) Data collection: Enumerators are sent to the survey places to take the records of the prices. Nearly 10,000 assistant enumerators are invited to assist the survey work.

(iv) The weights for calculation of the consumer price indices are determined according to the composition of the consumption expenditures of close to 120,000 urban and rural households.

Data on the livelihood of the urban residents in this chapter come from the data collected through the samples survey on the urban households conducted by the Department of Urban Socio-economic Surveys at the NBS. The main content of the survey includes the population in the household and its composition, the cash income and expenditure of the household, the quantity of and the expenditure on major commodities purchased, the employment of the household members, the housing condition, and the possession of the durable consumer goods.

The survey on the urban households is organized by the Department of Urban Socio-economic Surveys at the NBS. The survey organizations of the provinces, autonomous regions, and municipalities directly under the central government as well as the survey organizations of the selected cities and counties collect the data in accordance with the survey scheme stipulated by the NBS and report them to the higher organization. The survey on the urban households is conducted in such a way that households selected by sampling method keep accounts for a successive three years and are interviewed by the enumerators. By a rotation sampling scheme, one-third of the old sample households should be replaced by the new sample households every year. The respondent households are selected by the two-stage stratified systematic random sampling scheme.

In the first stage, the cities and counties are first classified into five categories by their population size, namely the particularly large cities, large cities, medium-sized cities, small cities, and counties. Second, they are grouped into the six administrative regions (northeastern region, north region, eastern region, central region, northwestern region, and southwestern region). In each administrative region, the cities and counties are arranged in the order of the average wages of their staff and workers in the urban areas. Third, the numbers of the staff and workers of the cities are accumulated and the sample cities or counties are selected by a systematic sampling scheme; the sampling interval is one million staff and workers.

In the second stage, the sample households are selected by the multi-stage and two-phase sampling scheme. In large cities, the first-phase sample is selected by a three-stage sampling method: (i) the sample subdistricts are selected; (ii) the sample residents' committees are selected from the sample subdistricts; and (iii) the sample households are selected from the sample residents' committees. In medium-sized and small cities and counties, the first-phase sample is selected by a two-stage sampling method: (i) the sample residents' committees are directly selected; and (ii) the sample households are selected from the sample residents' committees. The second-phase sample is composed of the sample households, which are surveyed in a regular way and these households are selected with a stratified sampling method from the households in the first-phase sample.

In total, 25,000 households in 226 cities and counties are selected by the NBS in the above-mentioned approach. Additional local samples are selected by local statistical offices by the same sample design, making the total sample size reach over 50,000 households.

Data on the livelihood of the rural residents come from data collected through the sample survey on the rural households, which is organized by the Department of Rural Socio-economic Surveys at the NBS. The main content of the survey includes the basic condition of the rural households, consumption expenditure, consumption of major consumer goods, and the quantity of durable consumer goods owned.

The sample survey on the rural households is conducted by first selecting sample villages and then selecting households in the selected villages in each province, with all rural households in the province as the population. Various sampling approaches are used to identify a total of 68,000 households selected from 7,100 villages throughout the whole country.

It is required that the sampling error should not exceed ±3 percent, with confidence of probability as 95 percent. In order to ensure the accuracy of the data of the survey on the rural households, two accounts are designed for the respondent households by the Department of Rural Socio-economic Surveys at the NBS, the cash account and the account on goods in kind. Nearly 10,000 assistant enumerators have been invited to help the households to keep good accounts and check and tabulate the data of the survey.

In order to stop the respondent households getting bored, to solve the problem of aging samples, and to make the sample more representative of the population and able to reflect the rural social and economic situation more accurately and in a timely manner, a rotation sampling scheme has been implemented by the Department of Rural Socio-economic Surveys at the NBS in selecting the rural sample households, with the cycle of complete rotation being five years.

*Table 3.1* Consumer price indices by category (preceding year=100)

| Ethnic group | General index | Food | Grain | Oil or fat | Meat, poultry, and products |
|---|---|---|---|---|---|
| 2001 China | 100.73 | 100.01 | 99.34 | 91.73 | 101.63 |
| 2002 China | 99.25 | 99.40 | 98.33 | 98.71 | 99.55 |
| 2003 China | 101.17 | 103.43 | 102.30 | 112.62 | 103.31 |
| 2004 China | 103.88 | 109.87 | 126.42 | 118.17 | 117.57 |
| 2005 China | 101.81 | 102.91 | 101.43 | 94.25 | 102.49 |
| Achang | 101.43 | 100.81 | 103.56 | 97.85 | 98.64 |
| Bai | 101.46 | 101.03 | 102.95 | 96.76 | 99.00 |
| Baonan | 101.68 | 101.06 | 102.07 | 96.57 | 102.04 |
| Blang | 101.43 | 100.82 | 103.56 | 97.81 | 98.66 |
| Buyi | 101.05 | 101.34 | 100.51 | 89.08 | 100.86 |
| Dai | 101.43 | 100.82 | 103.57 | 97.84 | 98.65 |
| Daur | 101.91 | 101.81 | 102.53 | 94.75 | 100.80 |
| Deang | 101.43 | 100.80 | 103.58 | 97.87 | 98.62 |
| Derung | 101.48 | 101.09 | 103.24 | 96.80 | 99.24 |
| Dong | 101.61 | 102.05 | 100.31 | 91.50 | 100.97 |
| Dongxiang | 101.63 | 100.87 | 102.06 | 96.35 | 101.62 |
| Ewenki | 102.29 | 102.66 | 103.37 | 96.31 | 101.59 |
| Gaoshan | 101.86 | 102.78 | 101.54 | 93.45 | 102.43 |
| Gelao | 101.04 | 101.34 | 100.48 | 88.90 | 100.88 |
| *Han* | *101.80* | *102.74* | *101.26* | *94.02* | *102.37* |
| Hani | 101.43 | 100.81 | 103.57 | 97.85 | 98.64 |
| Hezhe | 101.25 | 100.51 | 100.83 | 91.75 | 99.89 |
| Hui | 101.52 | 101.80 | 102.36 | 94.75 | 101.65 |
| Jing | 102.35 | 102.64 | 101.60 | 92.46 | 102.90 |
| Jingpo | 101.43 | 100.82 | 103.56 | 97.84 | 98.65 |
| Jino | 101.43 | 100.81 | 103.58 | 97.85 | 98.64 |
| Kazak | 100.73 | 98.51 | 101.95 | 91.80 | 96.25 |
| Kirgiz | 100.74 | 98.52 | 101.94 | 91.79 | 96.28 |
| Korean | 101.44 | 101.57 | 103.22 | 91.54 | 101.03 |
| Lahu | 101.43 | 100.82 | 103.56 | 97.84 | 98.65 |
| Lhoba | 101.47 | 101.35 | 102.02 | 99.63 | 104.21 |
| Li | 101.45 | 101.68 | 100.75 | 94.97 | 100.83 |
| Lisu | 101.44 | 100.85 | 103.53 | 97.75 | 98.72 |
| Manchu | 101.51 | 101.92 | 103.41 | 90.50 | 101.06 |
| Maonan | 102.02 | 102.30 | 101.28 | 91.32 | 102.43 |
| Miao | 101.49 | 101.75 | 100.83 | 91.69 | 100.68 |
| Monba | 101.48 | 101.37 | 102.11 | 100.10 | 104.43 |
| Mongol | 102.11 | 102.52 | 103.45 | 95.03 | 101.45 |

*Table 3.1  (cont.)*

| Ethnic group | General index | Food | Grain | Oil or fat | Meat, poultry, and products |
|---|---|---|---|---|---|
| Mulao | 102.23 | 102.54 | 101.46 | 91.98 | 102.80 |
| Naxi | 101.44 | 100.85 | 103.52 | 97.76 | 98.75 |
| Nu | 101.43 | 100.84 | 103.52 | 97.86 | 98.76 |
| Oroqen | 101.77 | 101.58 | 102.09 | 93.98 | 100.72 |
| Pumi | 101.43 | 100.83 | 103.55 | 97.82 | 98.67 |
| Qiang | 101.66 | 102.12 | 102.12 | 94.21 | 101.40 |
| Russian | 101.36 | 100.33 | 102.55 | 93.65 | 98.62 |
| Salar | 100.89 | 100.93 | 102.02 | 92.88 | 101.32 |
| She | 101.87 | 103.33 | 99.54 | 95.76 | 103.30 |
| Shui | 101.10 | 101.36 | 100.58 | 89.22 | 100.88 |
| Tajik | 100.77 | 98.64 | 101.93 | 91.83 | 96.45 |
| Tatar | 100.80 | 98.77 | 101.95 | 92.08 | 96.70 |
| Tibetan | 101.40 | 101.41 | 102.12 | 96.93 | 102.80 |
| Tu | 100.97 | 101.10 | 101.98 | 93.15 | 101.52 |
| Tujia | 101.95 | 102.51 | 100.64 | 91.38 | 101.60 |
| Uygur | 100.74 | 98.52 | 101.95 | 91.80 | 96.26 |
| Uzbek | 100.76 | 98.59 | 101.94 | 91.87 | 96.37 |
| Va | 101.44 | 100.85 | 103.51 | 97.74 | 98.71 |
| Xibe | 101.26 | 101.19 | 103.41 | 88.22 | 99.75 |
| Yao | 102.29 | 102.74 | 101.18 | 94.19 | 102.04 |
| Yi | 101.45 | 101.23 | 102.83 | 95.85 | 99.65 |
| Yugur | 101.72 | 101.13 | 102.08 | 96.74 | 102.14 |
| Zhuang | 102.35 | 102.62 | 101.77 | 92.93 | 102.83 |

| Ethnic group | Eggs | Aquatic products | Vegetables | Dried and fresh melons and fruits | Eating outside the home |
|---|---|---|---|---|---|
| *2001 China* | *106.02* | *97.15* | *100.94* | *99.87* | *100.19* |
| *2002 China* | *102.63* | *96.67* | *98.20* | *103.12* | *99.93* |
| *2003 China* | *98.55* | *100.32* | *117.73* | *102.99* | *100.14* |
| *2004 China* | *120.15* | *112.74* | *95.10* | *104.00* | *104.06* |
| *2005 China* | *104.59* | *105.95* | *109.09* | *102.22* | *102.35* |
| Achang | 104.90 | 113.64 | 93.07 | 101.60 | 100.65 |
| Bai | 104.90 | 112.33 | 96.23 | 101.56 | 101.10 |
| Baonan | 104.67 | 103.13 | 100.55 | 102.30 | 101.05 |
| Blang | 104.90 | 113.60 | 93.12 | 101.59 | 100.66 |
| Buyi | 102.26 | 106.34 | 103.73 | 100.15 | 103.96 |
| Dai | 104.90 | 113.62 | 93.08 | 101.61 | 100.66 |

Table 3.1 (cont.)

| Ethnic group | Eggs | Aquatic products | Vegetables | Dried and fresh melons and fruits | Eating outside the home |
|---|---|---|---|---|---|
| Daur | 103.30 | 100.22 | 108.30 | 101.06 | 101.95 |
| Deang | 104.90 | 113.68 | 92.98 | 101.60 | 100.64 |
| Derung | 104.75 | 111.71 | 95.95 | 101.63 | 100.91 |
| Dong | 104.42 | 106.56 | 109.48 | 101.11 | 103.05 |
| Dongxiang | 104.39 | 103.32 | 99.93 | 102.13 | 101.04 |
| Ewenki | 103.65 | 100.18 | 108.25 | 103.38 | 102.46 |
| Gaoshan | 104.35 | 104.60 | 109.17 | 103.84 | 101.89 |
| Gelao | 102.19 | 106.26 | 103.81 | 100.11 | 104.03 |
| *Han* | *104.86* | *104.78* | *109.24* | *102.64* | *101.95* |
| Hani | 104.90 | 113.66 | 93.04 | 101.60 | 100.65 |
| Hezhe | 102.99 | 100.06 | 110.02 | 96.78 | 100.99 |
| Hui | 104.10 | 103.85 | 103.59 | 102.57 | 101.60 |
| Jing | 103.81 | 107.95 | 106.21 | 100.50 | 101.54 |
| Jingpo | 104.89 | 113.63 | 93.10 | 101.61 | 100.66 |
| Jino | 104.90 | 113.66 | 93.01 | 101.60 | 100.65 |
| Kazak | 100.79 | 105.96 | 93.87 | 98.09 | 100.86 |
| Kirgiz | 100.80 | 105.90 | 94.03 | 98.06 | 100.86 |
| Korean | 103.40 | 101.41 | 105.96 | 103.82 | 100.83 |
| Lahu | 104.90 | 113.62 | 93.10 | 101.62 | 100.65 |
| Lhoba | 106.64 | 96.83 | 101.70 | 93.08 | 101.34 |
| Li | 105.99 | 104.18 | 108.34 | 96.32 | 100.47 |
| Lisu | 104.92 | 113.38 | 93.36 | 101.66 | 100.71 |
| Manchu | 102.85 | 102.55 | 104.96 | 105.11 | 101.35 |
| Maonan | 103.28 | 107.48 | 105.59 | 100.37 | 102.25 |
| Miao | 104.40 | 107.13 | 106.60 | 100.87 | 102.76 |
| Monba | 106.85 | 96.49 | 101.48 | 92.73 | 101.31 |
| Mongol | 103.52 | 101.04 | 107.02 | 103.99 | 102.25 |
| Mulao | 103.57 | 107.76 | 106.09 | 100.43 | 101.86 |
| Naxi | 104.93 | 113.32 | 93.40 | 101.60 | 100.72 |
| Nu | 104.93 | 113.31 | 93.34 | 101.47 | 100.68 |
| Oroqen | 103.29 | 100.08 | 109.19 | 100.08 | 101.72 |
| Pumi | 104.90 | 113.56 | 93.18 | 101.61 | 100.67 |
| Qiang | 105.58 | 104.49 | 104.46 | 102.67 | 102.81 |
| Russian | 102.07 | 103.79 | 99.86 | 100.53 | 101.57 |
| Salar | 104.02 | 103.87 | 102.57 | 98.31 | 100.97 |
| She | 104.93 | 105.84 | 111.41 | 102.47 | 102.29 |
| Shui | 102.30 | 106.49 | 103.63 | 100.15 | 103.87 |
| Tajik | 100.92 | 105.91 | 94.38 | 98.19 | 100.89 |

*Table 3.1* (cont.)

| Ethnic group | Eggs | Aquatic products | Vegetables | Dried and fresh melons and fruits | Eating outside the home |
|---|---|---|---|---|---|
| Tatar | 101.09 | 105.79 | 94.71 | 98.44 | 100.92 |
| Tibetan | 105.79 | 100.64 | 102.20 | 96.97 | 101.52 |
| Tu | 104.13 | 104.09 | 102.96 | 98.59 | 101.07 |
| Tujia | 105.98 | 105.80 | 111.71 | 102.34 | 102.29 |
| Uygur | 100.80 | 105.96 | 93.93 | 98.10 | 100.86 |
| Uzbek | 100.86 | 105.96 | 94.17 | 98.15 | 100.88 |
| Va | 104.90 | 113.42 | 93.42 | 101.67 | 100.67 |
| Xibe | 102.29 | 103.24 | 103.31 | 103.25 | 101.32 |
| Yao | 105.27 | 108.12 | 109.63 | 101.14 | 101.62 |
| Yi | 104.79 | 110.29 | 97.41 | 101.74 | 101.63 |
| Yugur | 104.73 | 103.09 | 100.66 | 102.51 | 101.08 |
| Zhuang | 103.86 | 108.42 | 105.51 | 100.53 | 101.46 |

| Ethnic group | Tobacco, liquor, and articles | Clothing | Household facilities, articles, and services | Health care and personal articles | Transportation and communication |
|---|---|---|---|---|---|
| *2001 China* | *99.71* | *98.12* | *97.74* | *100.00* | *99.00* |
| *2002 China* | *99.93* | *97.64* | *97.45* | *98.84* | *98.09* |
| *2003 China* | *99.85* | *97.78* | *97.42* | *100.87* | *97.80* |
| *2004 China* | *101.23* | *98.48* | *98.64* | *99.69* | *98.52* |
| *2005 China* | *100.42* | *98.31* | *99.89* | *99.92* | *99.01* |
| Achang | 103.67 | 97.96 | 100.39 | 102.15 | 98.35 |
| Bai | 103.01 | 98.20 | 100.30 | 101.75 | 98.54 |
| Baonan | 98.01 | 97.17 | 99.44 | 103.40 | 97.23 |
| Blang | 103.66 | 97.95 | 100.39 | 102.15 | 98.35 |
| Buyi | 100.15 | 99.19 | 99.47 | 100.55 | 99.42 |
| Dai | 103.66 | 97.96 | 100.39 | 102.16 | 98.35 |
| Daur | 100.43 | 99.71 | 100.20 | 103.66 | 99.61 |
| Deang | 103.68 | 97.96 | 100.39 | 102.17 | 98.34 |
| Derung | 103.02 | 97.93 | 100.29 | 101.93 | 98.53 |
| Dong | 100.03 | 99.05 | 99.85 | 99.99 | 99.59 |
| Dongxiang | 98.04 | 97.27 | 99.39 | 103.88 | 97.58 |
| Ewenki | 100.14 | 99.96 | 100.29 | 104.86 | 99.72 |
| Gaoshan | 100.44 | 98.03 | 99.71 | 99.69 | 99.34 |
| Gelao | 100.10 | 99.22 | 99.45 | 100.53 | 99.44 |
| *Han* | *100.48* | *98.16* | *99.80* | *99.86* | *99.31* |
| Hani | 103.68 | 97.96 | 100.39 | 102.16 | 98.34 |

*Table 3.1* (*cont.*)

| Ethnic group | Tobacco, liquor, and articles | Clothing | Household facilities, articles, and services | Health care and personal articles | Transportation and communication |
|---|---|---|---|---|---|
| Hezhe | 101.19 | 99.25 | 100.09 | 100.02 | 99.21 |
| Hui | 99.92 | 99.12 | 99.50 | 100.82 | 98.67 |
| Jing | 100.02 | 97.26 | 99.88 | 100.26 | 100.89 |
| Jingpo | 103.66 | 97.97 | 100.39 | 102.15 | 98.35 |
| Jino | 103.68 | 97.96 | 100.39 | 102.16 | 98.34 |
| Kazak | 99.34 | 98.41 | 99.08 | 109.25 | 99.50 |
| Kirgiz | 99.36 | 98.42 | 99.09 | 109.16 | 99.50 |
| Korean | 101.05 | 99.64 | 99.49 | 99.10 | 97.38 |
| Lahu | 103.67 | 97.96 | 100.39 | 102.15 | 98.35 |
| Lhoba | 102.06 | 100.47 | 99.62 | 100.44 | 100.05 |
| Li | 101.12 | 97.10 | 100.66 | 99.77 | 100.47 |
| Lisu | 103.58 | 97.96 | 100.37 | 102.13 | 98.40 |
| Manchu | 100.64 | 98.13 | 99.44 | 99.58 | 98.63 |
| Maonan | 99.97 | 97.78 | 99.75 | 100.30 | 100.56 |
| Miao | 100.54 | 98.56 | 99.89 | 100.43 | 99.43 |
| Monba | 102.14 | 100.52 | 99.63 | 100.40 | 100.08 |
| Mongol | 100.18 | 99.50 | 100.08 | 104.00 | 99.38 |
| Mulao | 99.96 | 97.47 | 99.83 | 100.23 | 100.78 |
| Naxi | 103.57 | 97.96 | 100.36 | 102.12 | 98.40 |
| Nu | 103.62 | 98.00 | 100.37 | 102.12 | 98.38 |
| Oroqen | 100.67 | 99.60 | 100.19 | 102.42 | 99.49 |
| Pumi | 103.64 | 97.97 | 100.38 | 102.14 | 98.35 |
| Qiang | 100.40 | 97.64 | 99.67 | 101.26 | 100.21 |
| Russian | 99.67 | 98.96 | 99.55 | 107.09 | 99.51 |
| Salar | 99.76 | 97.37 | 99.72 | 102.39 | 92.87 |
| She | 99.98 | 97.33 | 99.74 | 99.63 | 98.36 |
| Shui | 100.18 | 99.13 | 99.49 | 100.57 | 99.46 |
| Tajik | 99.38 | 98.37 | 99.11 | 108.94 | 99.50 |
| Tatar | 99.33 | 98.35 | 99.13 | 108.65 | 99.39 |
| Tibetan | 101.02 | 98.92 | 99.67 | 101.20 | 98.22 |
| Tu | 99.82 | 97.40 | 99.75 | 102.12 | 93.24 |
| Tujia | 100.41 | 98.21 | 99.81 | 99.71 | 100.00 |
| Uygur | 99.35 | 98.41 | 99.08 | 109.22 | 99.50 |
| Uzbek | 99.36 | 98.40 | 99.10 | 109.07 | 99.50 |
| Va | 103.60 | 97.95 | 100.38 | 102.11 | 98.38 |
| Xibe | 100.57 | 97.49 | 99.57 | 101.25 | 98.84 |
| Yao | 100.26 | 97.92 | 100.17 | 99.97 | 100.21 |
| Yi | 102.37 | 98.01 | 100.08 | 101.73 | 98.98 |

*Table 3.1  (cont.)*

| Ethnic group | Tobacco, liquor, and articles | Clothing | Household facilities, articles, and services | Health care and personal articles | Transportation and communication |
|---|---|---|---|---|---|
| Yugur | 97.96 | 97.18 | 99.44 | 103.30 | 97.39 |
| Zhuang | 100.22 | 97.25 | 99.93 | 100.32 | 100.80 |

| Ethnic group | Recreation, education, and culture | Durable consumer goods and service for recreational use | Education | Tuition and child care | Cultural and recreational articles |
|---|---|---|---|---|---|
| *2001 China* | *106.62* | *91.17* | *113.63* | *114.15* | *101.74* |
| *2002 China* | *100.61* | *90.46* | *103.68* | *103.99* | *101.24* |
| *2003 China* | *101.33* | *92.67* | *104.33* | *104.51* | *101.26* |
| *2004 China* | *101.29* | *93.34* | *103.40* | *103.44* | *101.06* |
| *2005 China* | *102.22* | *93.84* | *105.07* | *105.41* | *101.16* |
| Achang | 102.27 | 88.75 | 113.89 | 115.37 | 99.54 |
| Bai | 102.00 | 89.96 | 111.94 | 113.20 | 99.82 |
| Baonan | 103.83 | 93.88 | 109.17 | 109.43 | 100.46 |
| Blang | 102.27 | 88.76 | 113.87 | 115.35 | 99.55 |
| Buyi | 99.21 | 94.08 | 101.73 | 102.02 | 100.66 |
| Dai | 102.28 | 88.76 | 113.87 | 115.35 | 99.55 |
| Daur | 100.38 | 94.91 | 101.69 | 101.75 | 100.37 |
| Deang | 102.27 | 88.72 | 113.94 | 115.43 | 99.54 |
| Derung | 102.39 | 89.74 | 112.38 | 113.67 | 99.78 |
| Dong | 101.12 | 94.99 | 103.70 | 104.02 | 101.08 |
| Dongxiang | 103.44 | 93.92 | 108.50 | 108.75 | 100.55 |
| Ewenki | 100.47 | 95.16 | 101.74 | 101.79 | 100.25 |
| Gaoshan | 102.94 | 93.82 | 106.30 | 106.82 | 100.88 |
| Gelao | 99.13 | 94.14 | 101.53 | 101.80 | 100.67 |
| *Han* | *102.56* | *93.93* | *105.44* | *105.81* | *100.98* |
| Hani | 102.27 | 88.73 | 113.91 | 115.39 | 99.54 |
| Hezhe | 100.60 | 94.23 | 102.14 | 102.25 | 100.60 |
| Hui | 101.87 | 92.80 | 105.30 | 105.62 | 101.20 |
| Jing | 106.00 | 92.56 | 110.82 | 111.60 | 101.63 |
| Jingpo | 102.26 | 88.76 | 113.86 | 115.34 | 99.55 |
| Jino | 102.27 | 88.73 | 113.92 | 115.41 | 99.54 |
| Kazak | 98.64 | 95.03 | 100.28 | 100.42 | 101.23 |
| Kirgiz | 98.65 | 95.03 | 100.28 | 100.41 | 101.22 |
| Korean | 102.73 | 93.42 | 106.27 | 106.73 | 101.09 |
| Lahu | 102.27 | 88.75 | 113.88 | 115.37 | 99.55 |

*Table 3.1* (cont.)

| Ethnic group | Recreation, education, and culture | Durable consumer goods and service for recreational use | Education | Tuition and child care | Cultural and recreational articles |
|---|---|---|---|---|---|
| Lhoba | 99.79 | 95.41 | 104.91 | 105.96 | 100.60 |
| Li | 101.05 | 93.83 | 104.14 | 103.99 | 99.73 |
| Lisu | 102.34 | 88.93 | 113.66 | 115.11 | 99.58 |
| Manchu | 104.53 | 92.35 | 109.06 | 109.84 | 100.26 |
| Maonan | 104.28 | 93.03 | 108.37 | 109.01 | 101.42 |
| Miao | 101.22 | 94.00 | 105.06 | 105.54 | 100.82 |
| Monba | 99.76 | 95.42 | 104.94 | 106.01 | 100.60 |
| Mongol | 101.39 | 94.57 | 103.50 | 103.74 | 100.27 |
| Mulao | 105.34 | 92.81 | 109.77 | 110.49 | 101.58 |
| Naxi | 102.31 | 88.95 | 113.61 | 115.06 | 99.59 |
| Nu | 102.23 | 88.90 | 113.68 | 115.15 | 99.57 |
| Oroqen | 100.58 | 94.67 | 101.99 | 102.08 | 100.42 |
| Pumi | 102.28 | 88.79 | 113.82 | 115.30 | 99.56 |
| Qiang | 104.40 | 95.36 | 105.15 | 105.51 | 101.02 |
| Russian | 99.54 | 94.97 | 101.12 | 101.25 | 100.88 |
| Salar | 103.41 | 94.50 | 108.09 | 108.45 | 100.01 |
| She | 102.53 | 94.72 | 105.79 | 106.23 | 101.19 |
| Shui | 99.45 | 93.95 | 102.18 | 102.49 | 100.68 |
| Tajik | 98.79 | 94.99 | 100.49 | 100.64 | 101.22 |
| Tatar | 98.96 | 94.94 | 100.79 | 100.94 | 101.19 |
| Tibetan | 102.00 | 95.00 | 106.26 | 106.98 | 100.51 |
| Tu | 103.40 | 94.37 | 108.14 | 108.50 | 100.04 |
| Tujia | 102.60 | 94.56 | 106.05 | 106.45 | 100.97 |
| Uygur | 98.65 | 95.03 | 100.28 | 100.42 | 101.23 |
| Uzbek | 98.71 | 95.01 | 100.36 | 100.50 | 101.23 |
| Va | 102.29 | 88.88 | 113.72 | 115.18 | 99.57 |
| Xibe | 104.29 | 91.96 | 109.29 | 110.24 | 100.21 |
| Yao | 104.69 | 93.74 | 109.08 | 109.72 | 101.48 |
| Yi | 102.51 | 91.17 | 110.11 | 111.15 | 100.08 |
| Yugur | 103.88 | 93.82 | 109.23 | 109.49 | 100.49 |
| Zhuang | 106.00 | 92.31 | 111.24 | 112.06 | 101.56 |

| Ethnic group | Residence | Building and decoration materials | Renting | Private housing | Water, electricity, and fuels |
|---|---|---|---|---|---|
| 2001 China | 101.15 | 98.80 | 108.64 | 100.01 | 102.49 |
| 2002 China | 99.94 | 98.36 | 104.41 | 95.38 | 102.89 |

*Table 3.1* (*cont.*)

| Ethnic group | Residence | Building and decoration materials | Renting | Private housing | Water, electricity, and fuels |
|---|---|---|---|---|---|
| *2003 China* | *102.09* | *99.51* | *103.53* | *99.05* | *105.72* |
| *2004 China* | *104.87* | *104.27* | *103.01* | *100.92* | *107.46* |
| *2005 China* | *105.44* | *102.63* | *101.86* | *105.57* | *108.56* |
| Achang | 105.89 | 105.26 | 103.61 | 103.44 | 107.46 |
| Bai | 106.03 | 104.84 | 104.12 | 103.78 | 108.10 |
| Baonan | 108.95 | 103.47 | 101.86 | 115.37 | 110.76 |
| Blang | 105.88 | 105.25 | 103.60 | 103.45 | 107.45 |
| Buyi | 106.36 | 101.77 | 109.60 | 105.48 | 110.79 |
| Dai | 105.88 | 105.25 | 103.60 | 103.43 | 107.45 |
| Daur | 107.67 | 103.37 | 102.37 | 106.22 | 111.65 |
| Deang | 105.90 | 105.28 | 103.63 | 103.44 | 107.46 |
| Derung | 105.83 | 104.72 | 103.37 | 103.84 | 107.67 |
| Dong | 106.36 | 102.78 | 106.01 | 105.20 | 110.56 |
| Dongxiang | 108.91 | 103.53 | 103.12 | 114.59 | 110.80 |
| Ewenki | 107.04 | 101.91 | 101.81 | 105.68 | 111.41 |
| Gaoshan | 105.87 | 102.61 | 101.64 | 105.59 | 109.37 |
| Gelao | 106.37 | 101.71 | 109.76 | 105.53 | 110.86 |
| *Han* | *105.56* | *102.59* | *101.96* | *105.43* | *108.64* |
| Hani | 105.89 | 105.27 | 103.62 | 103.44 | 107.46 |
| Hezhe | 108.87 | 106.05 | 101.56 | 107.97 | 112.08 |
| Hui | 106.55 | 103.07 | 104.78 | 106.68 | 109.60 |
| Jing | 104.16 | 102.85 | 99.37 | 103.53 | 107.06 |
| Jingpo | 105.90 | 105.25 | 103.63 | 103.45 | 107.48 |
| Jino | 105.89 | 105.26 | 103.61 | 103.44 | 107.45 |
| Kazak | 107.33 | 105.72 | 117.15 | 100.66 | 109.68 |
| Kirgiz | 107.34 | 105.73 | 117.02 | 100.70 | 109.70 |
| Korean | 107.44 | 103.01 | 100.66 | 106.07 | 110.82 |
| Lahu | 105.89 | 105.26 | 103.60 | 103.45 | 107.47 |
| Lhoba | 106.64 | 101.74 | 105.28 | 100.54 | 110.92 |
| Li | 105.95 | 105.04 | 101.34 | 105.16 | 106.88 |
| Lisu | 105.83 | 105.16 | 103.55 | 103.40 | 107.44 |
| Manchu | 105.65 | 102.88 | 102.15 | 104.98 | 108.19 |
| Maonan | 104.71 | 102.49 | 102.11 | 104.04 | 108.08 |
| Miao | 106.13 | 102.91 | 105.70 | 105.08 | 109.84 |
| Monba | 106.61 | 101.68 | 105.08 | 100.35 | 110.87 |
| Mongol | 106.58 | 101.99 | 102.21 | 105.33 | 110.51 |
| Mulao | 104.34 | 102.67 | 100.40 | 103.72 | 107.45 |
| Naxi | 105.84 | 105.15 | 103.56 | 103.40 | 107.45 |
| Nu | 105.90 | 105.19 | 103.63 | 103.40 | 107.52 |

*Table 3.1 (cont.)*

| Ethnic group | Residence | Building and decoration materials | Renting | Private housing | Water, electricity, and fuels |
|---|---|---|---|---|---|
| Oroqen | 107.95 | 103.99 | 101.69 | 106.83 | 111.76 |
| Pumi | 105.89 | 105.24 | 103.59 | 103.45 | 107.46 |
| Qiang | 103.86 | 101.79 | 101.26 | 102.32 | 106.69 |
| Russian | 107.07 | 104.09 | 110.64 | 102.76 | 110.19 |
| Salar | 106.63 | 106.49 | 100.81 | 106.45 | 107.48 |
| She | 105.94 | 101.98 | 101.67 | 104.85 | 110.07 |
| Shui | 106.29 | 101.86 | 109.26 | 105.39 | 110.65 |
| Tajik | 107.26 | 105.62 | 116.62 | 100.81 | 109.62 |
| Tatar | 107.33 | 105.54 | 115.96 | 101.41 | 109.68 |
| Tibetan | 106.11 | 102.98 | 102.88 | 103.14 | 109.08 |
| Tu | 106.58 | 106.18 | 100.61 | 106.68 | 107.56 |
| Tujia | 105.86 | 102.91 | 102.50 | 106.12 | 109.24 |
| Uygur | 107.32 | 105.72 | 117.12 | 100.64 | 109.67 |
| Uzbek | 107.29 | 105.67 | 116.85 | 100.73 | 109.65 |
| Va | 105.87 | 105.19 | 103.56 | 103.48 | 107.49 |
| Xibe | 105.35 | 103.55 | 104.39 | 104.97 | 107.04 |
| Yao | 105.10 | 103.47 | 100.27 | 104.01 | 108.26 |
| Yi | 105.38 | 103.91 | 103.64 | 103.36 | 107.63 |
| Yugur | 109.00 | 103.33 | 101.72 | 115.74 | 110.86 |
| Zhuang | 104.15 | 102.98 | 99.23 | 103.45 | 106.93 |

*Notes:* "Consumer price indices" reflect the trend and degree of changes in prices of consumer goods and services purchased by urban and rural households during a given period. The indices are obtained by combining consumer price indices of urban households and consumer price indices of rural households. The indices enable the observation and analysis of the degree of impact of the changes in the prices of retail goods and services on the actual living expenses of urban and rural residents.

*Table 3.2* Per capita annual income of urban households by sources (unit: yuan)

| Ethnic group | Disposable income | Total income | Income from wages and salaries | Income from properties | Income from transfers |
|---|---|---|---|---|---|
| National average | 10,493.03 | 11,320.77 | 7,797.54 | 192.91 | 2,650.70 |
| Achang | 9,283.77 | 10,013.90 | 6,195.27 | 425.48 | 2,795.63 |
| Bai | 9,208.28 | 9,881.64 | 6,195.00 | 374.02 | 2,676.56 |
| Baonan | 8,096.35 | 8,753.18 | 6,466.12 | 41.84 | 1,859.30 |
| Blang | 9,289.76 | 10,020.75 | 6,203.02 | 424.50 | 2,795.85 |

*Table 3.2* (*cont.*)

| Ethnic group | Disposable income | Total income | Income from wages and salaries | Income from properties | Income from transfers |
|---|---|---|---|---|---|
| Buyi | 8,324.93 | 8,600.57 | 5,669.77 | 104.71 | 2,032.75 |
| Dai | 9,278.51 | 10,008.28 | 6,190.30 | 424.99 | 2,796.49 |
| Daur | 8,894.47 | 9,363.34 | 6,338.77 | 127.44 | 2,066.60 |
| Deang | 9,270.22 | 9,999.24 | 6,180.45 | 426.07 | 2,797.04 |
| Derung | 9,364.28 | 10,089.72 | 6,395.55 | 372.94 | 2,715.13 |
| Dong | 8,888.14 | 9,322.58 | 6,258.14 | 140.57 | 2,135.94 |
| Dongxiang | 8,082.91 | 8,740.44 | 6,490.25 | 41.90 | 1,814.24 |
| Ewenki | 9,182.66 | 9,641.45 | 6,666.36 | 155.16 | 1,972.89 |
| Gaoshan | 9,953.57 | 10,671.48 | 7,194.94 | 182.60 | 2,606.68 |
| Gelao | 8,286.50 | 8,549.99 | 5,644.03 | 98.61 | 2,013.96 |
| *Han* | *10,290.42* | *11,080.44* | *7,628.75* | *195.89* | *2,554.51* |
| Hani | 9,283.90 | 10,014.20 | 6,192.77 | 425.88 | 2,798.26 |
| Hezhe | 8,620.52 | 9,124.85 | 5,818.52 | 84.25 | 2,399.27 |
| Hui | 9,025.49 | 9,718.31 | 6,636.38 | 120.12 | 2,323.86 |
| Jing | 9,351.15 | 10,080.60 | 6,992.35 | 182.79 | 2,361.26 |
| Jingpo | 9,282.29 | 10,011.45 | 6,196.05 | 424.61 | 2,793.41 |
| Jino | 9,279.43 | 10,009.31 | 6,188.36 | 425.80 | 2,798.97 |
| Kazak | 7,995.73 | 8,699.48 | 6,555.78 | 54.70 | 1,567.11 |
| Kirgiz | 8,002.28 | 8,703.81 | 6,547.94 | 55.23 | 1,574.61 |
| Korean | 8,893.07 | 9,406.85 | 6,075.82 | 89.38 | 2,533.77 |
| Lahu | 9,282.91 | 10,012.81 | 6,194.97 | 424.95 | 2,795.70 |
| Lhoba | 9,466.03 | 10,644.63 | 10,100.68 | 25.31 | 414.51 |
| Li | 8,186.67 | 8,727.02 | 6,096.38 | 195.00 | 1,765.06 |
| Lisu | 9,254.99 | 9,981.43 | 6,180.89 | 419.23 | 2,786.79 |
| Manchu | 9,226.00 | 9,871.14 | 6,324.19 | 104.03 | 2,851.19 |
| Maonan | 9,038.09 | 9,637.99 | 6,622.88 | 154.77 | 2,252.11 |
| Miao | 8,946.87 | 9,424.01 | 6,272.88 | 174.24 | 2,227.31 |
| Monba | 9,545.07 | 10,763.45 | 10,319.94 | 21.07 | 348.95 |
| Mongol | 9,142.02 | 9,645.59 | 6,594.59 | 145.08 | 2,132.61 |
| Mulao | 9,300.23 | 9,988.23 | 6,924.73 | 171.71 | 2,315.20 |
| Naxi | 9,268.11 | 9,998.18 | 6,205.70 | 418.08 | 2,780.66 |
| Nu | 9,307.20 | 10,046.64 | 6,276.41 | 418.08 | 2,759.65 |
| Oroqen | 8,869.90 | 9,346.91 | 6,209.53 | 118.61 | 2,184.84 |
| Pumi | 9,282.39 | 10,012.61 | 6,198.40 | 423.23 | 2,794.29 |
| Qiang | 8,413.40 | 9,032.54 | 5,863.60 | 211.03 | 2,439.13 |
| Russian | 8,673.47 | 9,309.03 | 6,747.16 | 99.39 | 1,822.41 |
| Salar | 8,123.25 | 8,831.35 | 5,808.37 | 61.40 | 2,462.76 |
| She | 12,669.81 | 13,759.93 | 9,178.09 | 404.33 | 3,109.57 |
| Shui | 8,330.15 | 8,618.34 | 5,679.48 | 108.75 | 2,050.00 |

*Table 3.2* (*cont.*)

| Ethnic group | Disposable income | Total income | Income from wages and salaries | Income from properties | Income from transfers |
|---|---|---|---|---|---|
| Tajik | 8,063.20 | 8,769.02 | 6,587.54 | 58.86 | 1,596.85 |
| Tatar | 8,127.61 | 8,838.63 | 6,620.50 | 59.58 | 1,636.88 |
| Tibetan | 8,810.68 | 9,728.27 | 7,924.33 | 82.11 | 1,426.29 |
| Tu | 8,318.28 | 9,035.67 | 5,964.65 | 77.49 | 2,473.14 |
| Tujia | 9,361.45 | 9,961.64 | 6,842.19 | 159.71 | 2,286.78 |
| Uygur | 8,006.39 | 8,710.66 | 6,561.56 | 55.32 | 1,570.72 |
| Uzbek | 8,060.32 | 8,769.12 | 6,596.42 | 58.29 | 1,588.53 |
| Va | 9,300.12 | 10,031.00 | 6,231.58 | 419.56 | 2,783.37 |
| Xibe | 8,953.17 | 9,665.40 | 6,259.80 | 90.55 | 2,793.32 |
| Yao | 9,760.75 | 10,504.43 | 7,259.91 | 216.92 | 2,361.49 |
| Yi | 8,923.62 | 9,570.10 | 6,032.56 | 329.60 | 2,611.17 |
| Yugur | 8,146.38 | 8,805.03 | 6,515.64 | 43.02 | 1,862.39 |
| Zhuang | 9,487.96 | 10,248.49 | 7,107.55 | 202.67 | 2,390.46 |

*Notes:* "Disposable income of urban households" refers to the actual income at the disposal of members of the households that can be used for final consumption, other non-compulsory expenditure, and savings. This equals total income minus income tax, personal contribution to social security, and sample household subsidy for keeping diaries. The following formula is used: Disposable income = total household income –
income tax – personal contribution to social security – sample household subsidy for keeping diaries. "Total income" refers to the sum of income earned from various sources by the urban households and their members during the reference period, and is classified as income from wages and salaries, income from household operations, income from properties, and income from transfers. "Income from wages and salaries" refers to income from labor earned by the members of urban households employed by other units or individuals. "Income from properties" refers to the income received as returns by owners of financial assets or tangible non-productive assets by providing capital or tangible non-productive assets to other institutional units. "Income from transfers" refers to the receipt by urban households and their members of goods, services, capital, or rights of assets without giving or repaying accordingly, excluding capital provided to them for the formation of fixed assets. In general, it refers to all income received by urban households through redistribution.

*Table 3.3* Per capita annual consumption expenditure of urban households (unit: yuan)

| Ethnic group | Consumption expenditure | Food | Clothing | Household appliances and services | Health care and medical services |
|---|---|---|---|---|---|
| National average | 7,942.88 | 2,914.39 | 800.51 | 446.52 | 600.85 |
| Achang | 7,009.02 | 2,996.37 | 645.52 | 293.41 | 661.79 |
| Bai | 6,978.55 | 2,924.77 | 663.20 | 310.57 | 631.20 |
| Baonan | 6,517.50 | 2,351.07 | 802.82 | 364.51 | 495.38 |

*Table 3.3* (cont.)

| Ethnic group | Consumption expenditure | Food | Clothing | Household appliances and services | Health care and medical services |
|---|---|---|---|---|---|
| Blang | 7,015.68 | 2,996.63 | 646.73 | 294.60 | 661.64 |
| Buyi | 6,294.20 | 2,504.48 | 705.57 | 341.62 | 416.70 |
| Dai | 7,008.92 | 2,996.07 | 645.35 | 293.74 | 661.16 |
| Daur | 6,720.15 | 2,184.07 | 972.97 | 357.47 | 568.22 |
| Deang | 7,000.30 | 2,994.78 | 645.10 | 292.33 | 662.31 |
| Derung | 7,087.65 | 2,937.11 | 681.46 | 317.06 | 643.65 |
| Dong | 6,816.69 | 2,626.89 | 715.51 | 386.79 | 479.36 |
| Dongxiang | 6,496.41 | 2,343.43 | 807.71 | 360.47 | 493.76 |
| Ewenki | 6,958.59 | 2,220.33 | 1,019.46 | 389.19 | 549.63 |
| Gaoshan | 7,408.97 | 2,755.66 | 762.04 | 419.78 | 557.21 |
| Gelao | 6,268.80 | 2,494.20 | 704.20 | 341.36 | 411.62 |
| *Han* | *7,748.97* | *2,844.97* | *794.89* | *442.23* | *575.90* |
| Hani | 7,009.70 | 2,997.01 | 645.84 | 293.25 | 662.25 |
| Hezhe | 6,466.42 | 2,189.22 | 874.93 | 305.76 | 627.48 |
| Hui | 6,871.89 | 2,485.67 | 792.23 | 393.85 | 569.17 |
| Jing | 7,079.54 | 2,910.16 | 538.51 | 418.43 | 472.75 |
| Jingpo | 7,008.85 | 2,995.09 | 645.87 | 293.49 | 661.47 |
| Jino | 7,009.55 | 2,997.14 | 645.41 | 293.15 | 662.40 |
| Kazak | 6,212.13 | 2,259.02 | 825.89 | 310.41 | 499.53 |
| Kirgiz | 6,213.90 | 2,257.87 | 826.63 | 310.22 | 500.75 |
| Korean | 6,892.35 | 2,413.62 | 830.94 | 302.29 | 674.94 |
| Lahu | 7,007.85 | 2,994.37 | 646.49 | 293.69 | 661.72 |
| Lhoba | 8,508.58 | 3,735.29 | 1,026.24 | 470.31 | 357.91 |
| Li | 5,992.12 | 2,813.49 | 334.01 | 308.53 | 357.91 |
| Lisu | 7,002.35 | 2,986.14 | 646.14 | 296.98 | 655.99 |
| Manchu | 7,192.18 | 2,625.77 | 797.15 | 343.96 | 706.11 |
| Maonan | 6,847.22 | 2,793.56 | 578.30 | 398.42 | 452.24 |
| Miao | 6,891.14 | 2,684.03 | 716.77 | 382.67 | 503.68 |
| Monba | 8,634.68 | 3,803.45 | 1,039.39 | 478.47 | 352.18 |
| Mongol | 6,983.55 | 2,315.50 | 964.25 | 380.32 | 571.82 |
| Mulao | 7,055.11 | 2,881.02 | 555.37 | 414.53 | 466.73 |
| Naxi | 7,019.69 | 2,993.38 | 648.25 | 297.98 | 655.50 |
| Nu | 7,047.04 | 3,009.18 | 653.67 | 297.94 | 656.71 |
| Oroqen | 6,683.47 | 2,195.51 | 946.93 | 345.81 | 587.24 |
| Pumi | 7,010.70 | 2,994.00 | 646.85 | 294.41 | 660.79 |
| Qiang | 6,903.33 | 2,712.32 | 643.18 | 422.72 | 444.84 |
| Russian | 6,662.36 | 2,304.92 | 899.48 | 353.59 | 532.62 |
| Salar | 6,326.18 | 2,294.97 | 712.17 | 359.13 | 547.84 |

*Table 3.3* (cont.)

| Ethnic group | Consumption expenditure | Food | Clothing | Household appliances and services | Health care and medical services |
|---|---|---|---|---|---|
| She | 9,268.70 | 3,548.55 | 835.83 | 487.50 | 553.17 |
| Shui | 6,293.23 | 2,514.07 | 697.25 | 342.16 | 419.12 |
| Tajik | 6,259.91 | 2,278.53 | 823.94 | 314.90 | 501.63 |
| Tatar | 6,314.68 | 2,294.51 | 824.84 | 319.48 | 507.49 |
| Tibetan | 7,521.56 | 3,103.22 | 850.52 | 426.09 | 429.67 |
| Tu | 6,473.72 | 2,358.14 | 712.11 | 365.51 | 549.79 |
| Tujia | 7,368.06 | 2,752.66 | 790.28 | 436.02 | 545.94 |
| Uygur | 6,219.03 | 2,261.60 | 825.87 | 310.93 | 499.93 |
| Uzbek | 6,258.43 | 2,277.71 | 823.69 | 313.77 | 501.77 |
| Va | 7,019.04 | 2,987.75 | 650.36 | 297.51 | 659.55 |
| Xibe | 7,138.65 | 2,702.99 | 773.42 | 313.86 | 694.01 |
| Yao | 7,514.95 | 2,952.88 | 617.75 | 432.26 | 534.48 |
| Yi | 6,891.39 | 2,860.10 | 651.45 | 334.07 | 573.83 |
| Yugur | 6,557.24 | 2,362.10 | 806.21 | 367.62 | 497.30 |
| Zhuang | 7,204.45 | 2,959.95 | 537.39 | 417.89 | 489.51 |

| Ethnic group | Transport and communications | Education, culture and recreation services | Housing | Water, electricity, fuels, and others | Miscellaneous goods and services |
|---|---|---|---|---|---|
| *National average* | *996.72* | *1,097.46* | *249.25* | *516.31* | *277.75* |
| Achang | 932.16 | 779.81 | 125.88 | 395.59 | 153.85 |
| Bai | 896.24 | 812.49 | 135.02 | 409.15 | 171.27 |
| Baonan | 647.65 | 930.72 | 221.51 | 421.82 | 248.48 |
| Blang | 932.27 | 782.08 | 126.88 | 395.84 | 154.28 |
| Buyi | 660.12 | 830.52 | 109.55 | 465.97 | 239.59 |
| Dai | 931.75 | 780.15 | 126.43 | 395.49 | 154.09 |
| Daur | 716.22 | 913.27 | 181.93 | 484.42 | 294.48 |
| Deang | 930.45 | 777.53 | 125.28 | 394.81 | 153.20 |
| Derung | 916.04 | 825.31 | 147.02 | 415.52 | 176.67 |
| Dong | 730.21 | 953.00 | 172.12 | 478.46 | 249.03 |
| Dongxiang | 653.13 | 919.78 | 213.92 | 421.62 | 249.00 |
| Ewenki | 764.59 | 966.94 | 193.12 | 481.03 | 319.72 |
| Gaoshan | 869.16 | 997.29 | 228.65 | 514.38 | 268.36 |
| Gelao | 653.33 | 828.94 | 107.80 | 466.92 | 240.40 |
| *Han* | *969.18* | *1,067.03* | *238.41* | *510.37* | *265.70* |
| Hani | 932.02 | 779.71 | 125.91 | 395.37 | 153.74 |

*Table 3.3* (cont.)

| Ethnic group | Transport and communications | Education, culture and recreation services | Housing | Water, electricity, fuels, and others | Miscellaneous goods and services |
|---|---|---|---|---|---|
| Hezhe | 656.98 | 847.26 | 172.81 | 510.19 | 249.07 |
| Hui | 779.92 | 894.21 | 203.56 | 467.23 | 250.09 |
| Jing | 733.00 | 996.73 | 220.37 | 510.65 | 246.60 |
| Jingpo | 931.99 | 780.15 | 125.81 | 396.12 | 154.17 |
| Jino | 931.80 | 779.69 | 126.16 | 395.41 | 153.73 |
| Kazak | 757.32 | 742.65 | 125.66 | 406.59 | 244.91 |
| Kirgiz | 756.53 | 743.29 | 125.89 | 407.65 | 244.96 |
| Korean | 738.50 | 842.35 | 200.50 | 575.58 | 279.05 |
| Lahu | 931.34 | 780.06 | 126.10 | 395.56 | 153.90 |
| Lhoba | 1,269.98 | 708.80 | 121.96 | 396.51 | 400.74 |
| Li | 734.87 | 669.45 | 160.60 | 394.85 | 183.28 |
| Lisu | 928.09 | 782.69 | 129.53 | 395.87 | 155.93 |
| Manchu | 768.43 | 873.43 | 192.52 | 565.89 | 291.92 |
| Maonan | 703.59 | 953.68 | 190.07 | 501.64 | 246.60 |
| Miao | 760.71 | 944.26 | 173.14 | 464.46 | 234.86 |
| Monba | 1,303.69 | 709.84 | 123.30 | 392.30 | 410.66 |
| Mongol | 764.36 | 941.47 | 192.69 | 491.49 | 312.80 |
| Mulao | 739.01 | 993.37 | 210.22 | 512.58 | 250.02 |
| Naxi | 931.84 | 784.42 | 129.81 | 396.07 | 157.41 |
| Nu | 939.46 | 782.51 | 127.23 | 396.76 | 158.90 |
| Oroqen | 701.98 | 901.32 | 181.74 | 495.89 | 283.90 |
| Pumi | 931.22 | 781.06 | 126.91 | 395.97 | 154.78 |
| Qiang | 829.64 | 911.29 | 256.37 | 408.88 | 233.44 |
| Russian | 785.11 | 859.99 | 161.75 | 440.16 | 278.85 |
| Salar | 697.09 | 824.97 | 223.40 | 399.39 | 222.88 |
| She | 1,270.02 | 1,256.40 | 336.62 | 613.79 | 326.98 |
| Shui | 655.81 | 830.10 | 111.91 | 464.80 | 237.98 |
| Tajik | 762.32 | 753.53 | 129.93 | 409.67 | 245.23 |
| Tatar | 766.12 | 768.18 | 135.48 | 411.12 | 247.37 |
| Tibetan | 1,005.91 | 786.49 | 180.03 | 397.54 | 310.85 |
| Tu | 731.76 | 849.99 | 225.13 | 410.37 | 226.07 |
| Tujia | 789.57 | 1,074.08 | 228.33 | 483.76 | 235.81 |
| Uygur | 758.56 | 743.82 | 126.01 | 407.04 | 245.08 |
| Uzbek | 765.93 | 751.66 | 128.31 | 409.18 | 245.99 |
| Va | 930.81 | 786.05 | 128.48 | 397.63 | 155.88 |
| Xibe | 754.02 | 844.87 | 179.24 | 543.93 | 305.56 |
| Yao | 872.26 | 1,068.79 | 232.55 | 512.45 | 254.19 |
| Yi | 870.90 | 820.46 | 159.93 | 406.86 | 185.33 |

Table 3.3 (cont.)

| Ethnic group | Transport and communications | Education, culture and recreation services | Housing | Water, electricity, fuels, and others | Miscellaneous goods and services |
|---|---|---|---|---|---|
| Yugur | 650.27 | 942.36 | 223.43 | 424.29 | 250.43 |
| Zhuang | 779.95 | 1,006.64 | 219.43 | 513.73 | 245.40 |

*Notes:* "Consumption expenditure" refers to total expenditure for consumption in daily life, including expenditure on nine categories such as food, clothing, household appliances and services, health care and medical services, transport and communications, education, recreation and cultural services, housing, miscellaneous goods and services.

Table 3.4 Number of major durable consumer goods owned per 100 urban households at the year-end

| Ethnic group | Composite furniture (sets) | Motorcycle (unit) | Bicycle (unit) | Helping hand car (unit) | Automobile (unit) |
|---|---|---|---|---|---|
| National Average | 77.55 | 25.00 | 120.04 | 9.54 | 3.37 |
| Achang | 70.45 | 22.14 | 114.04 | 9.04 | 7.87 |
| Bai | 71.30 | 20.18 | 99.49 | 7.79 | 6.76 |
| Baonan | 82.11 | 10.91 | 149.26 | 5.33 | 0.60 |
| Blang | 70.58 | 22.05 | 113.85 | 9.05 | 7.85 |
| Buyi | 67.92 | 8.82 | 22.93 | 0.82 | 2.05 |
| Dai | 70.59 | 21.99 | 113.81 | 9.01 | 7.86 |
| Daur | 62.43 | 20.58 | 142.09 | 4.63 | 2.94 |
| Deang | 70.39 | 21.98 | 114.02 | 9.00 | 7.89 |
| Derung | 71.37 | 22.13 | 114.18 | 8.58 | 6.82 |
| Dong | 75.53 | 15.70 | 41.47 | 2.86 | 1.81 |
| Dongxiang | 81.20 | 11.44 | 148.64 | 5.21 | 0.74 |
| Ewenki | 71.10 | 25.86 | 168.16 | 6.14 | 3.52 |
| Gaoshan | 75.32 | 28.16 | 125.82 | 9.63 | 2.73 |
| Gelao | 67.76 | 8.49 | 20.37 | 0.48 | 1.95 |
| Han | 78.81 | 27.14 | 121.76 | 10.34 | 3.28 |
| Hani | 70.45 | 22.04 | 114.03 | 9.05 | 7.88 |
| Hezhe | 44.10 | 10.76 | 89.49 | 1.92 | 1.89 |
| Hui | 63.81 | 19.53 | 130.30 | 7.14 | 2.58 |
| Jing | 87.98 | 45.94 | 119.57 | 9.94 | 2.14 |
| Jingpo | 70.44 | 22.11 | 113.88 | 8.99 | 7.86 |
| Jino | 70.45 | 21.96 | 113.81 | 8.99 | 7.87 |
| Kazak | 62.79 | 16.03 | 96.99 | 2.31 | 2.81 |
| Kirgiz | 62.56 | 16.01 | 96.85 | 2.30 | 2.80 |
| Korean | 33.88 | 14.45 | 104.26 | 2.61 | 1.70 |

*Table 3.4* *(cont.)*

| Ethnic group | Composite furniture (sets) | Motorcycle (unit) | Bicycle (unit) | Helping hand car (unit) | Automobile (unit) |
|---|---|---|---|---|---|
| Lahu | 70.50 | 22.08 | 114.18 | 9.07 | 7.86 |
| Lhoba | 86.69 | 8.13 | 131.08 | 0.51 | 2.97 |
| Li | 59.83 | 53.08 | 68.44 | 2.97 | 3.48 |
| Lisu | 71.31 | 21.67 | 113.10 | 8.98 | 7.72 |
| Manchu | 51.72 | 14.64 | 128.20 | 5.56 | 2.25 |
| Maonan | 82.99 | 36.37 | 92.46 | 7.34 | 1.97 |
| Miao | 75.77 | 14.51 | 45.49 | 3.20 | 2.47 |
| Monba | 88.05 | 7.50 | 134.65 | 0.52 | 3.03 |
| Mongol | 68.09 | 23.46 | 158.52 | 6.16 | 3.21 |
| Mulao | 86.37 | 42.76 | 108.56 | 8.88 | 2.10 |
| Naxi | 71.34 | 21.55 | 112.95 | 8.92 | 7.71 |
| Nu | 70.87 | 21.96 | 114.53 | 8.98 | 7.77 |
| Oroqen | 57.43 | 18.27 | 129.21 | 4.05 | 2.64 |
| Pumi | 70.56 | 22.01 | 114.06 | 9.04 | 7.83 |
| Qiang | 99.25 | 8.16 | 70.11 | 5.72 | 2.39 |
| Russian | 67.21 | 19.82 | 126.65 | 4.24 | 3.21 |
| Salar | 62.04 | 7.70 | 60.85 | 2.27 | 1.41 |
| She | 82.52 | 40.34 | 110.79 | 11.48 | 3.62 |
| Shui | 68.46 | 9.95 | 26.61 | 1.20 | 2.08 |
| Tajik | 63.40 | 16.37 | 97.29 | 2.49 | 2.80 |
| Tatar | 64.13 | 16.05 | 100.16 | 2.67 | 2.80 |
| Tibetan | 83.94 | 8.06 | 103.20 | 2.45 | 2.45 |
| Tu | 63.51 | 9.50 | 64.49 | 2.73 | 1.61 |
| Tujia | 85.18 | 13.68 | 48.76 | 3.20 | 1.34 |
| Uygur | 62.82 | 16.08 | 96.96 | 2.33 | 2.81 |
| Uzbek | 63.13 | 16.48 | 97.41 | 2.42 | 2.85 |
| Va | 70.88 | 22.27 | 114.33 | 9.10 | 7.76 |
| Xibe | 45.71 | 9.96 | 106.83 | 3.54 | 1.68 |
| Yao | 85.95 | 38.64 | 98.90 | 7.95 | 2.72 |
| Yi | 78.11 | 16.65 | 91.53 | 7.17 | 5.69 |
| Yugur | 82.90 | 11.20 | 153.07 | 5.52 | 0.61 |
| Zhuang | 87.90 | 46.92 | 122.05 | 10.03 | 2.60 |

| Ethnic group | Washing machine (set) | Electric fan (set) | Refrigerator (set) | Freezer (set) | Color TV set (set) |
|---|---|---|---|---|---|
| *National average* | *95.51* | *172.18* | *90.72* | *6.68* | *134.80* |
| Achang | 90.09 | 31.24 | 78.34 | 1.66 | 122.28 |

*Table 3.4* (cont.)

| Ethnic group | Washing machine (set) | Electric fan (set) | Refrigerator (set) | Freezer (set) | Color TV set (set) |
|---|---|---|---|---|---|
| Bai | 91.35 | 53.35 | 80.15 | 2.33 | 123.25 |
| Baonan | 97.99 | 53.60 | 88.43 | 3.97 | 117.42 |
| Blang | 90.17 | 31.90 | 78.45 | 1.67 | 122.41 |
| Buyi | 96.87 | 98.01 | 86.23 | 5.82 | 125.44 |
| Dai | 90.16 | 31.74 | 78.41 | 1.64 | 122.37 |
| Daur | 93.79 | 61.01 | 83.04 | 12.68 | 113.56 |
| Deang | 90.11 | 30.12 | 78.29 | 1.63 | 122.17 |
| Derung | 91.14 | 53.07 | 80.62 | 2.86 | 123.58 |
| Dong | 96.30 | 162.65 | 87.94 | 5.27 | 128.80 |
| Dongxiang | 97.24 | 54.80 | 87.98 | 4.16 | 116.62 |
| Ewenki | 94.90 | 65.79 | 85.13 | 13.46 | 114.40 |
| Gaoshan | 95.30 | 177.63 | 89.48 | 6.50 | 134.08 |
| Gelao | 97.01 | 98.05 | 86.30 | 5.86 | 125.31 |
| *Han* | *95.91* | *180.82* | *90.59* | *6.47* | *135.12* |
| Hani | 90.13 | 30.89 | 78.35 | 1.64 | 122.29 |
| Hezhe | 92.24 | 61.30 | 79.71 | 11.03 | 115.19 |
| Hui | 94.40 | 98.41 | 85.61 | 6.27 | 120.06 |
| Jing | 91.81 | 274.18 | 87.12 | 3.59 | 139.63 |
| Jingpo | 90.15 | 31.36 | 78.38 | 1.67 | 122.27 |
| Jino | 90.15 | 30.79 | 78.36 | 1.63 | 122.31 |
| Kazak | 88.57 | 53.52 | 79.76 | 7.70 | 105.78 |
| Kirgiz | 88.58 | 53.63 | 79.74 | 7.75 | 105.85 |
| Korean | 94.75 | 71.31 | 84.32 | 10.24 | 123.67 |
| Lahu | 90.16 | 31.44 | 78.39 | 1.67 | 122.30 |
| Lhoba | 95.08 | 23.11 | 88.12 | 6.92 | 134.75 |
| Li | 58.77 | 178.86 | 68.24 | 4.98 | 118.08 |
| Lisu | 90.35 | 35.83 | 78.78 | 1.73 | 122.72 |
| Manchu | 91.64 | 86.54 | 87.92 | 10.43 | 122.59 |
| Maonan | 93.32 | 231.00 | 87.00 | 4.24 | 135.93 |
| Miao | 95.72 | 141.85 | 87.51 | 4.86 | 129.10 |
| Monba | 95.12 | 19.44 | 88.30 | 6.88 | 135.49 |
| Mongol | 94.41 | 71.61 | 85.94 | 12.36 | 116.31 |
| Mulao | 92.56 | 260.66 | 87.30 | 3.86 | 138.60 |
| Naxi | 90.38 | 35.80 | 78.83 | 1.72 | 122.87 |
| Nu | 90.25 | 32.58 | 78.64 | 1.78 | 122.69 |
| Oroqen | 93.54 | 63.29 | 82.40 | 12.31 | 114.60 |
| Pumi | 90.19 | 32.24 | 78.47 | 1.69 | 122.39 |
| Qiang | 97.84 | 205.08 | 92.78 | 3.38 | 138.77 |
| Russian | 91.46 | 63.76 | 82.66 | 9.79 | 110.97 |

*Table 3.4  (cont.)*

| Ethnic group | Washing machine (set) | Electric fan (set) | Refrigerator (set) | Freezer (set) | Color TV set (set) |
|---|---|---|---|---|---|
| Salar | 98.02 | 19.23 | 81.86 | 6.18 | 112.66 |
| She | 96.90 | 234.98 | 96.35 | 3.05 | 161.70 |
| Shui | 96.66 | 101.81 | 86.08 | 5.70 | 125.64 |
| Tajik | 88.79 | 58.04 | 80.13 | 7.65 | 106.76 |
| Tatar | 89.17 | 57.48 | 80.52 | 7.54 | 107.35 |
| Tibetan | 96.52 | 62.36 | 87.56 | 5.63 | 129.52 |
| Tu | 98.02 | 30.00 | 82.51 | 5.92 | 114.68 |
| Tujia | 97.01 | 196.86 | 93.20 | 5.17 | 134.68 |
| Uygur | 88.58 | 54.15 | 79.79 | 7.70 | 105.88 |
| Uzbek | 88.61 | 56.69 | 79.93 | 7.65 | 106.41 |
| Va | 90.27 | 34.60 | 78.67 | 1.83 | 122.45 |
| Xibe | 88.80 | 70.21 | 86.23 | 8.37 | 119.06 |
| Yao | 93.29 | 252.16 | 87.86 | 3.59 | 136.92 |
| Yi | 93.03 | 86.56 | 83.23 | 2.60 | 127.16 |
| Yugur | 98.07 | 56.48 | 88.78 | 3.90 | 117.95 |
| Zhuang | 91.68 | 269.11 | 86.79 | 3.36 | 139.49 |

| Ethnic group | Video disc player (set) | Tape recorder (set) | Video recorder (set) | Computer (set) | Hi-Fi stereo component system (set) | Pickup camera (set) |
|---|---|---|---|---|---|---|
| National average | 68.07 | 39.26 | 15.49 | 41.52 | 28.79 | 4.32 |
| Achang | 80.36 | 40.11 | 18.12 | 29.60 | 36.54 | 2.89 |
| Bai | 79.63 | 37.35 | 16.88 | 29.63 | 36.50 | 2.89 |
| Baonan | 62.15 | 51.71 | 13.96 | 23.06 | 25.97 | 2.15 |
| Blang | 80.34 | 40.08 | 18.11 | 29.68 | 36.53 | 2.89 |
| Buyi | 79.09 | 22.35 | 11.40 | 25.14 | 38.58 | 2.86 |
| Dai | 80.41 | 40.06 | 18.10 | 29.61 | 36.54 | 2.89 |
| Daur | 54.76 | 42.51 | 10.20 | 25.15 | 14.62 | 3.61 |
| Deang | 80.39 | 40.13 | 18.13 | 29.50 | 36.54 | 2.88 |
| Derung | 77.20 | 39.81 | 17.32 | 30.86 | 34.48 | 3.07 |
| Dong | 77.35 | 24.86 | 11.18 | 31.23 | 36.84 | 2.95 |
| Dongxiang | 61.93 | 52.00 | 14.05 | 23.13 | 25.37 | 2.18 |
| Ewenki | 55.32 | 45.23 | 9.25 | 24.73 | 15.09 | 3.20 |
| Gaoshan | 67.70 | 36.36 | 13.61 | 39.38 | 27.20 | 3.99 |
| Gelao | 79.26 | 21.95 | 11.27 | 24.98 | 38.79 | 2.86 |

Table 3.4 *(cont.)*

| Ethnic group | Video disc player (set) | Tape recorder (set) | Video recorder (set) | Computer (set) | Hi-Fi stereo component system (set) | Pickup camera (set) |
|---|---|---|---|---|---|---|
| Han | 67.92 | 38.09 | 14.46 | 40.57 | 28.72 | 3.99 |
| Hani | 80.38 | 40.12 | 18.14 | 29.59 | 36.55 | 2.89 |
| Hezhe | 54.29 | 35.77 | 12.68 | 28.28 | 14.99 | 4.71 |
| Hui | 63.85 | 39.72 | 13.07 | 30.65 | 23.69 | 3.13 |
| Jing | 82.25 | 28.93 | 11.49 | 45.57 | 36.61 | 3.38 |
| Jingpo | 80.36 | 40.09 | 18.11 | 29.61 | 36.55 | 2.89 |
| Jino | 80.41 | 40.09 | 18.13 | 29.59 | 36.57 | 2.89 |
| Kazak | 61.75 | 50.04 | 13.44 | 23.89 | 16.15 | 3.12 |
| Kirgiz | 61.66 | 49.88 | 13.42 | 23.93 | 16.11 | 3.14 |
| Korean | 57.51 | 40.10 | 16.89 | 31.01 | 15.96 | 4.29 |
| Lahu | 80.32 | 40.12 | 18.11 | 29.61 | 36.50 | 2.89 |
| Lhoba | 76.48 | 56.75 | 40.35 | 20.64 | 31.86 | 5.80 |
| Li | 69.12 | 26.99 | 10.59 | 26.52 | 24.81 | 3.00 |
| Lisu | 80.35 | 39.84 | 17.92 | 29.66 | 36.31 | 2.88 |
| Manchu | 53.15 | 41.60 | 18.00 | 33.96 | 20.58 | 5.11 |
| Maonan | 81.86 | 26.73 | 11.27 | 40.29 | 37.47 | 3.24 |
| Miao | 77.80 | 26.46 | 12.20 | 31.37 | 36.95 | 2.96 |
| Monba | 77.00 | 58.14 | 41.71 | 20.43 | 32.07 | 5.96 |
| Mongol | 55.92 | 44.63 | 11.00 | 26.30 | 16.66 | 3.44 |
| Mulao | 82.40 | 28.11 | 11.40 | 44.07 | 37.36 | 3.37 |
| Naxi | 80.38 | 39.89 | 18.04 | 29.67 | 36.35 | 2.90 |
| Nu | 80.20 | 40.36 | 18.45 | 29.61 | 36.41 | 2.95 |
| Oroqen | 54.52 | 40.42 | 10.89 | 26.35 | 14.86 | 3.94 |
| Pumi | 80.27 | 40.10 | 18.10 | 29.64 | 36.44 | 2.90 |
| Qiang | 82.11 | 29.37 | 10.62 | 32.35 | 30.11 | 2.76 |
| Russian | 59.81 | 48.20 | 12.48 | 25.74 | 16.65 | 3.35 |
| Salar | 66.46 | 38.54 | 9.13 | 22.37 | 21.50 | 2.96 |
| She | 75.56 | 33.41 | 14.52 | 51.90 | 32.23 | 4.12 |
| Shui | 79.24 | 22.60 | 11.45 | 25.63 | 38.49 | 2.87 |
| Tajik | 62.00 | 49.55 | 13.46 | 24.47 | 16.62 | 3.15 |
| Tatar | 62.00 | 49.81 | 13.70 | 24.72 | 17.06 | 3.19 |
| Tibetan | 75.00 | 46.24 | 25.11 | 23.49 | 28.93 | 4.22 |
| Tu | 67.24 | 38.39 | 9.45 | 23.76 | 22.90 | 2.99 |
| Tujia | 75.92 | 26.79 | 11.54 | 38.83 | 35.53 | 2.85 |
| Uygur | 61.77 | 49.98 | 13.45 | 23.97 | 16.19 | 3.13 |
| Uzbek | 61.99 | 49.82 | 13.50 | 24.37 | 16.50 | 3.16 |

*Table 3.4 (cont.)*

| Ethnic group | Video disc player (set) | Tape recorder (set) | Video recorder (set) | Computer (set) | Hi-Fi stereo component system (set) | Pickup camera (set) |
|---|---|---|---|---|---|---|
| Va | 80.08 | 40.16 | 18.04 | 29.88 | 36.32 | 2.91 |
| Xibe | 53.80 | 43.08 | 18.74 | 31.33 | 20.28 | 5.14 |
| Yao | 80.03 | 30.46 | 12.02 | 43.67 | 37.17 | 3.42 |
| Yi | 80.70 | 35.11 | 15.28 | 29.80 | 34.97 | 2.84 |
| Yugur | 62.07 | 52.04 | 14.19 | 23.48 | 26.28 | 2.17 |
| Zhuang | 82.86 | 30.03 | 11.92 | 46.12 | 37.32 | 3.44 |

| Ethnic group | Camera (set) | Piano (set) | Other medium- and high-grade musical instrument (unit) | Oven (unit) | Air conditioner (unit) | Room heater (unit) |
|---|---|---|---|---|---|---|
| *National average* | *46.94* | *2.25* | *6.63* | *47.61* | *80.67* | *35.51* |
| Achang | 45.13 | 2.25 | 5.20 | 44.79 | 1.51 | 34.00 |
| Bai | 43.60 | 2.20 | 5.45 | 43.42 | 8.94 | 39.53 |
| Baonan | 42.63 | 1.88 | 8.40 | 28.34 | 3.96 | 16.31 |
| Blang | 45.17 | 2.25 | 5.20 | 44.90 | 2.10 | 34.09 |
| Buyi | 34.53 | 1.76 | 5.13 | 36.10 | 14.56 | 58.18 |
| Dai | 45.13 | 2.25 | 5.19 | 44.82 | 1.74 | 34.09 |
| Daur | 35.30 | 1.37 | 6.41 | 28.03 | 10.35 | 7.45 |
| Deang | 45.13 | 2.25 | 5.19 | 44.76 | 0.95 | 34.00 |
| Derung | 44.69 | 2.19 | 5.43 | 44.26 | 13.45 | 32.93 |
| Dong | 36.50 | 1.92 | 6.28 | 38.53 | 44.40 | 60.41 |
| Dongxiang | 42.19 | 1.92 | 8.33 | 27.33 | 4.15 | 15.32 |
| Ewenki | 36.10 | 1.23 | 6.76 | 27.79 | 11.68 | 6.97 |
| Gaoshan | 43.80 | 2.17 | 6.33 | 44.82 | 79.39 | 33.85 |
| Gelao | 34.34 | 1.76 | 5.12 | 35.91 | 14.14 | 58.69 |
| *Han* | *45.48* | *2.22* | *6.65* | *46.41* | *84.34* | *36.39* |
| Hani | 45.16 | 2.25 | 5.20 | 44.84 | 1.41 | 34.07 |
| Hezhe | 35.07 | 1.65 | 5.78 | 31.75 | 14.38 | 10.26 |
| Hui | 41.52 | 1.83 | 6.16 | 36.98 | 37.75 | 23.07 |
| Jing | 38.78 | 1.82 | 5.23 | 50.39 | 79.50 | 34.42 |
| Jingpo | 45.14 | 2.25 | 5.20 | 44.76 | 1.53 | 34.04 |
| Jino | 45.16 | 2.25 | 5.19 | 44.85 | 1.39 | 34.03 |

Table 3.4 (cont.)

| Ethnic group | Camera (set) | Piano (set) | Other medium- and high-grade musical instrument (unit) | Oven (unit) | Air conditioner (unit) | Room heater (unit) |
|---|---|---|---|---|---|---|
| Kazak | 37.46 | 2.23 | 5.98 | 19.76 | 7.12 | 6.89 |
| Kirgiz | 37.41 | 2.22 | 5.97 | 19.86 | 7.20 | 6.89 |
| Korean | 41.62 | 1.49 | 6.50 | 36.49 | 12.90 | 12.71 |
| Lahu | 45.15 | 2.25 | 5.20 | 44.81 | 1.74 | 34.07 |
| Lhoba | 54.81 | 0.20 | 2.38 | 35.01 | 10.37 | 56.15 |
| Li | 22.92 | 2.01 | 3.51 | 21.91 | 45.23 | 3.37 |
| Lisu | 45.02 | 2.25 | 5.18 | 44.74 | 3.57 | 34.32 |
| Manchu | 44.57 | 1.98 | 6.02 | 40.29 | 31.04 | 15.58 |
| Maonan | 37.38 | 1.79 | 5.17 | 46.56 | 62.37 | 40.81 |
| Miao | 38.07 | 1.94 | 5.98 | 40.56 | 43.43 | 56.25 |
| Monba | 55.92 | 0.13 | 2.22 | 35.13 | 9.58 | 57.24 |
| Mongol | 38.02 | 1.40 | 6.61 | 30.31 | 15.71 | 10.26 |
| Mulao | 38.49 | 1.83 | 5.25 | 49.14 | 74.62 | 36.69 |
| Naxi | 45.09 | 2.24 | 5.17 | 44.75 | 3.70 | 34.47 |
| Nu | 45.32 | 2.22 | 5.17 | 44.73 | 2.48 | 34.42 |
| Oroqen | 35.40 | 1.44 | 6.26 | 29.69 | 12.69 | 8.49 |
| Pumi | 45.14 | 2.25 | 5.20 | 44.81 | 2.04 | 34.06 |
| Qiang | 40.27 | 2.17 | 4.68 | 42.77 | 76.87 | 45.61 |
| Russian | 38.43 | 1.88 | 6.35 | 25.01 | 13.82 | 8.78 |
| Salar | 41.96 | 1.55 | 5.24 | 36.68 | 2.21 | 21.25 |
| She | 47.05 | 2.62 | 6.58 | 60.97 | 123.52 | 35.48 |
| Shui | 34.63 | 1.76 | 5.10 | 36.64 | 15.58 | 57.36 |
| Tajik | 37.69 | 2.22 | 5.99 | 20.68 | 9.80 | 7.86 |
| Tatar | 38.29 | 2.22 | 6.11 | 21.37 | 9.96 | 8.27 |
| Tibetan | 48.00 | 1.04 | 3.84 | 36.81 | 21.57 | 43.61 |
| Tu | 42.33 | 1.61 | 5.38 | 37.69 | 7.53 | 22.35 |
| Tujia | 40.39 | 1.91 | 6.62 | 46.21 | 88.40 | 61.98 |
| Uygur | 37.49 | 2.23 | 5.98 | 19.86 | 7.49 | 7.02 |
| Uzbek | 37.68 | 2.24 | 5.99 | 20.33 | 8.88 | 7.32 |
| Va | 45.25 | 2.26 | 5.24 | 44.81 | 3.54 | 34.09 |
| Xibe | 43.00 | 2.28 | 5.84 | 37.40 | 15.14 | 13.89 |
| Yao | 40.78 | 2.11 | 6.45 | 47.29 | 80.73 | 43.57 |
| Yi | 42.56 | 2.17 | 5.04 | 43.23 | 23.61 | 39.99 |
| Yugur | 42.89 | 1.90 | 8.53 | 28.52 | 5.17 | 16.34 |
| Zhuang | 39.76 | 1.89 | 5.29 | 50.85 | 79.22 | 32.74 |

*Table 3.4* (*cont.*)

| Ethnic group | Electric cooking appliances (unit) | Shower (unit) | Smoke absorber (unit) | Disinfection cupboard (unit) | Dishwasher (unit) | Drinking machine (unit) |
|---|---|---|---|---|---|---|
| *National average* | *107.20* | *72.65* | *67.93* | *15.77* | *0.64* | *42.40* |
| Achang | 114.38 | 64.95 | 73.03 | 11.89 | 0.83 | 62.69 |
| Bai | 109.57 | 64.48 | 66.86 | 14.28 | 0.76 | 59.91 |
| Baonan | 92.30 | 59.31 | 83.26 | 3.71 | 0.74 | 42.50 |
| Blang | 114.24 | 65.04 | 72.95 | 11.83 | 0.83 | 62.63 |
| Buyi | 99.10 | 56.84 | 38.91 | 26.89 | 0.23 | 55.52 |
| Dai | 114.40 | 65.06 | 72.87 | 11.84 | 0.83 | 62.60 |
| Daur | 152.79 | 40.63 | 69.00 | 3.16 | 0.42 | 32.28 |
| Deang | 114.32 | 64.84 | 73.05 | 11.75 | 0.83 | 62.73 |
| Derung | 112.01 | 65.00 | 71.27 | 12.01 | 0.77 | 58.04 |
| Dong | 94.43 | 65.37 | 41.15 | 29.16 | 0.43 | 47.81 |
| Dongxiang | 92.59 | 59.84 | 82.89 | 3.71 | 0.74 | 42.01 |
| Ewenki | 154.56 | 43.33 | 65.91 | 3.02 | 0.30 | 31.87 |
| Gaoshan | 104.71 | 70.99 | 63.16 | 19.42 | 0.60 | 41.62 |
| Gelao | 98.84 | 56.58 | 38.09 | 27.36 | 0.22 | 55.53 |
| *Han* | *103.10* | *72.88* | *66.25* | *16.66* | *0.65* | *42.85* |
| Hani | 114.37 | 64.93 | 73.04 | 11.80 | 0.83 | 62.73 |
| Hezhe | 154.52 | 35.71 | 75.27 | 5.43 | 0.65 | 33.91 |
| Hui | 99.31 | 61.54 | 71.20 | 6.78 | 0.58 | 41.42 |
| Jing | 132.91 | 94.40 | 57.10 | 51.17 | 0.49 | 42.68 |
| Jingpo | 114.30 | 64.92 | 72.96 | 11.95 | 0.83 | 62.66 |
| Jino | 114.41 | 64.95 | 72.98 | 11.80 | 0.83 | 62.67 |
| Kazak | 78.06 | 59.60 | 76.68 | 4.57 | 0.78 | 32.70 |
| Kirgiz | 78.89 | 59.34 | 76.64 | 4.59 | 0.78 | 32.68 |
| Korean | 126.99 | 44.82 | 78.84 | 5.73 | 0.55 | 31.47 |
| Lahu | 114.24 | 64.92 | 73.00 | 11.78 | 0.83 | 62.68 |
| Lhoba | 32.04 | 29.10 | 41.82 | 8.96 | 1.87 | 39.46 |
| Li | 126.02 | 69.14 | 53.07 | 50.90 | 0.67 | 31.81 |
| Lisu | 114.19 | 65.57 | 72.18 | 11.66 | 0.81 | 62.03 |
| Manchu | 98.79 | 57.81 | 77.14 | 5.16 | 0.63 | 31.49 |
| Maonan | 124.46 | 84.78 | 51.51 | 46.10 | 0.41 | 46.01 |
| Miao | 96.39 | 65.95 | 44.55 | 24.91 | 0.46 | 49.84 |
| Monba | 29.78 | 27.76 | 41.28 | 8.36 | 1.93 | 39.29 |
| Mongol | 137.66 | 47.72 | 67.49 | 3.51 | 0.36 | 32.07 |
| Mulao | 129.81 | 91.14 | 54.93 | 50.31 | 0.46 | 43.90 |
| Naxi | 113.93 | 65.43 | 72.03 | 11.72 | 0.81 | 61.92 |
| Nu | 113.02 | 64.56 | 72.55 | 11.85 | 0.84 | 62.20 |

*Table 3.4  (cont.)*

| Ethnic group | Electric cooking appliances (unit) | Shower (unit) | Smoke absorber (unit) | Disinfection cupboard (unit) | Dishwasher (unit) | Drinking machine (unit) |
|---|---|---|---|---|---|---|
| Oroqen | 154.70 | 39.34 | 70.58 | 3.98 | 0.47 | 32.76 |
| Pumi | 114.28 | 65.00 | 72.91 | 11.78 | 0.83 | 62.47 |
| Qiang | 111.32 | 87.83 | 41.09 | 9.83 | 0.14 | 38.70 |
| Russian | 107.19 | 54.86 | 72.54 | 4.28 | 0.59 | 33.18 |
| Salar | 59.82 | 46.77 | 79.81 | 5.27 | 0.73 | 35.55 |
| She | 123.33 | 93.11 | 67.63 | 30.85 | 0.66 | 42.81 |
| Shui | 100.39 | 57.92 | 39.68 | 27.43 | 0.24 | 55.31 |
| Tajik | 78.87 | 60.09 | 76.15 | 5.08 | 0.77 | 32.99 |
| Tatar | 79.89 | 60.15 | 76.71 | 4.97 | 0.77 | 33.51 |
| Tibetan | 59.69 | 47.93 | 52.86 | 7.69 | 1.16 | 38.92 |
| Tu | 63.74 | 48.92 | 79.01 | 7.27 | 0.72 | 36.60 |
| Tujia | 91.44 | 74.02 | 45.83 | 19.58 | 0.60 | 40.90 |
| Uygur | 78.12 | 59.65 | 76.60 | 4.64 | 0.78 | 32.71 |
| Uzbek | 78.80 | 60.07 | 76.48 | 5.21 | 0.78 | 32.86 |
| Va | 113.86 | 65.15 | 72.87 | 11.80 | 0.83 | 62.44 |
| Xibe | 90.28 | 58.95 | 78.05 | 5.10 | 0.65 | 28.05 |
| Yao | 114.30 | 86.84 | 54.39 | 44.23 | 0.63 | 42.08 |
| Yi | 111.80 | 70.30 | 60.28 | 12.93 | 0.57 | 55.23 |
| Yugur | 94.29 | 60.03 | 83.34 | 3.87 | 0.74 | 42.88 |
| Zhuang | 133.45 | 94.63 | 58.94 | 51.60 | 0.53 | 43.42 |

| Ethnic group | Dust catcher (unit) | Health equipment (set) | Telephone (unit) | Mobile telephone (unit) | Fax machine (unit) |
|---|---|---|---|---|---|
| National average | 13.57 | 4.68 | 94.40 | 137.00 | 1.17 |
| Achang | 8.69 | 3.96 | 83.33 | 130.90 | 0.73 |
| Bai | 8.13 | 3.91 | 84.19 | 130.27 | 0.77 |
| Baonan | 7.48 | 1.88 | 82.79 | 120.43 | 0.26 |
| Blang | 8.71 | 3.97 | 83.39 | 130.95 | 0.73 |
| Buyi | 5.59 | 2.88 | 89.61 | 120.84 | 0.63 |
| Dai | 8.68 | 3.96 | 83.33 | 130.89 | 0.73 |
| Daur | 13.27 | 2.51 | 88.48 | 124.23 | 0.69 |
| Deang | 8.67 | 3.95 | 83.23 | 130.79 | 0.72 |
| Derung | 9.35 | 3.96 | 85.26 | 130.66 | 0.76 |
| Dong | 5.74 | 3.61 | 88.51 | 129.80 | 0.96 |
| Dongxiang | 8.11 | 2.02 | 82.97 | 119.31 | 0.25 |
| Ewenki | 12.20 | 2.31 | 89.62 | 128.15 | 0.68 |

*Table 3.4 (cont.)*

| Ethnic group | Dust catcher (unit) | Health equipment (set) | Telephone (unit) | Mobile telephone (unit) | Fax machine (unit) |
|---|---|---|---|---|---|
| Gaoshan | 10.63 | 4.28 | 93.65 | 136.70 | 1.01 |
| Gelao | 5.48 | 2.86 | 89.62 | 120.61 | 0.62 |
| *Han* | *11.68* | *4.58* | *94.85* | *136.47* | *1.11* |
| Hani | 8.70 | 3.96 | 83.31 | 130.87 | 0.73 |
| Hezhe | 15.45 | 3.09 | 86.95 | 120.57 | 0.84 |
| Hui | 11.09 | 3.52 | 89.06 | 125.84 | 0.70 |
| Jing | 7.23 | 3.84 | 88.26 | 152.49 | 1.33 |
| Jingpo | 8.68 | 3.96 | 83.32 | 130.91 | 0.73 |
| Jino | 8.70 | 3.96 | 83.28 | 130.91 | 0.73 |
| Kazak | 16.22 | 3.89 | 87.23 | 108.70 | 0.37 |
| Kirgiz | 16.22 | 3.88 | 87.24 | 108.79 | 0.38 |
| Korean | 16.92 | 4.45 | 89.20 | 132.86 | 0.78 |
| Lahu | 8.69 | 3.96 | 83.33 | 130.88 | 0.73 |
| Lhoba | 7.39 | 1.31 | 89.42 | 113.88 | 0.09 |
| Li | 2.23 | 1.59 | 96.94 | 128.42 | 0.86 |
| Lisu | 8.66 | 3.95 | 83.51 | 130.74 | 0.72 |
| Manchu | 18.61 | 3.96 | 91.88 | 118.61 | 0.73 |
| Maonan | 6.68 | 3.57 | 88.49 | 144.37 | 1.15 |
| Miao | 6.27 | 3.69 | 88.42 | 129.96 | 0.89 |
| Monba | 7.61 | 1.23 | 89.33 | 113.71 | 0.09 |
| Mongol | 13.15 | 2.65 | 90.13 | 126.07 | 0.66 |
| Mulao | 7.09 | 3.81 | 88.45 | 150.13 | 1.30 |
| Naxi | 8.67 | 3.95 | 83.53 | 130.76 | 0.72 |
| Nu | 8.71 | 3.93 | 83.54 | 130.76 | 0.72 |
| Oroqen | 13.84 | 2.68 | 88.29 | 123.86 | 0.75 |
| Pumi | 8.72 | 3.96 | 83.41 | 130.84 | 0.73 |
| Qiang | 6.99 | 3.65 | 90.01 | 128.03 | 0.45 |
| Russian | 14.99 | 3.43 | 88.76 | 117.99 | 0.55 |
| Salar | 8.55 | 2.20 | 86.43 | 125.44 | 0.74 |
| She | 9.26 | 5.65 | 100.36 | 162.35 | 1.71 |
| Shui | 5.64 | 2.90 | 89.56 | 121.55 | 0.65 |
| Tajik | 16.03 | 3.90 | 87.44 | 109.67 | 0.39 |
| Tatar | 15.91 | 3.87 | 87.38 | 110.42 | 0.41 |
| Tibetan | 7.36 | 2.02 | 88.16 | 120.07 | 0.32 |
| Tu | 8.42 | 2.34 | 86.84 | 127.12 | 0.78 |
| Tujia | 6.78 | 4.12 | 89.93 | 135.64 | 0.97 |
| Uygur | 16.22 | 3.90 | 87.27 | 108.80 | 0.38 |
| Uzbek | 16.15 | 3.91 | 87.39 | 109.52 | 0.39 |
| Va | 8.77 | 3.99 | 83.51 | 131.10 | 0.73 |

*Table 3.4* (*cont.*)

| Ethnic group | Dust catcher (unit) | Health equipment (set) | Telephone (unit) | Mobile telephone (unit) | Fax machine (unit) |
|---|---|---|---|---|---|
| Xibe | 20.34 | 3.53 | 91.41 | 110.16 | 0.57 |
| Yao | 7.05 | 4.43 | 87.86 | 149.65 | 1.42 |
| Yi | 7.86 | 3.75 | 85.86 | 128.87 | 0.64 |
| Yugur | 7.50 | 1.90 | 82.78 | 120.83 | 0.26 |
| Zhuang | 7.44 | 3.99 | 88.05 | 153.53 | 1.37 |

*Table 3.5* Per capita net income of rural households (unit: yuan)

| Ethnic group | 2000 | 2002 | 2003 | 2004 | 2005 |
|---|---|---|---|---|---|
| *National average* | *2,253.42* | *2,475.63* | *2,622.24* | *2,936.40* | *3,254.93* |
| Achang | 1,492.68 | 1,624.54 | 1,714.08 | 1,883.21 | 2,063.04 |
| Bai | 1,543.03 | 1,679.74 | 1,771.71 | 1,950.90 | 2,137.30 |
| Baonan | 1,443.12 | 1,608.82 | 1,699.36 | 1,877.54 | 2,013.02 |
| Blang | 1,495.98 | 1,628.38 | 1,718.16 | 1,888.11 | 2,068.78 |
| Buyi | 1,438.81 | 1,563.06 | 1,642.94 | 1,808.01 | 1,973.10 |
| Dai | 1,492.20 | 1,624.06 | 1,713.46 | 1,882.79 | 2,062.84 |
| Daur | 2,092.15 | 2,232.56 | 2,391.31 | 2,775.55 | 3,101.75 |
| Deang | 1,484.52 | 1,615.43 | 1,704.39 | 1,872.44 | 2,051.15 |
| Derung | 1,641.15 | 1,793.26 | 1,894.50 | 2,093.76 | 2,301.74 |
| Dong | 1,760.53 | 1,914.06 | 2,012.91 | 2,229.70 | 2,435.63 |
| Dongxiang | 1,453.33 | 1,624.49 | 1,725.23 | 1,900.69 | 2,041.48 |
| Ewenki | 2,092.32 | 2,174.77 | 2,349.66 | 2,703.23 | 3,074.01 |
| Gaoshan | 2,372.79 | 2,628.15 | 2,758.58 | 3,080.05 | 3,414.65 |
| Gelao | 1,423.84 | 1,545.15 | 1,623.02 | 1,785.31 | 1,947.22 |
| *Han* | *2,491.84* | *2,756.15* | *2,908.77* | *3,249.62* | *3,590.78* |
| Hani | 1,491.26 | 1,622.97 | 1,712.41 | 1,881.45 | 2,061.27 |
| Hezhe | 2,211.18 | 2,479.77 | 2,597.55 | 3,076.48 | 3,325.73 |
| Hui | 1,980.70 | 2,210.67 | 2,342.98 | 2,615.92 | 2,887.72 |
| Jing | 1,892.74 | 2,045.91 | 2,132.46 | 2,347.98 | 2,545.06 |
| Jingpo | 1,491.98 | 1,623.63 | 1,712.93 | 1,881.90 | 2,061.56 |
| Jino | 1,489.06 | 1,620.61 | 1,709.90 | 1,878.77 | 2,058.35 |
| Kazak | 1,619.29 | 1,864.42 | 2,106.79 | 2,245.98 | 2,483.31 |
| Kirgiz | 1,626.22 | 1,871.61 | 2,113.05 | 2,255.82 | 2,493.52 |
| Korean | 2,161.66 | 2,455.26 | 2,650.42 | 3,105.72 | 3,393.99 |
| Lahu | 1,492.91 | 1,624.91 | 1,714.26 | 1,883.80 | 2,064.02 |
| Lhoba | 1,410.87 | 1,552.80 | 1,774.01 | 1,954.51 | 2,178.88 |
| Li | 2,156.90 | 2,392.74 | 2,553.53 | 2,781.29 | 2,968.81 |

*Table 3.5  (cont.)*

| Ethnic group | 2000 | 2002 | 2003 | 2004 | 2005 |
|---|---|---|---|---|---|
| Lisu | 1,503.77 | 1,637.66 | 1,728.24 | 1,900.93 | 2,083.93 |
| Manchu | 2,368.50 | 2,691.53 | 2,867.50 | 3,250.90 | 3,609.25 |
| Maonan | 1,751.15 | 1,892.97 | 1,974.73 | 2,172.37 | 2,355.57 |
| Miao | 1,720.67 | 1,874.73 | 1,973.94 | 2,188.37 | 2,395.71 |
| Monba | 1,411.82 | 1,553.06 | 1,780.29 | 1,958.84 | 2,189.68 |
| Mongol | 2,096.86 | 2,225.33 | 2,402.48 | 2,742.73 | 3,108.52 |
| Mulao | 1,857.68 | 2,007.79 | 2,092.69 | 2,301.47 | 2,494.13 |
| Naxi | 1,505.54 | 1,640.19 | 1,731.45 | 1,904.28 | 2,088.13 |
| Nu | 1,503.47 | 1,637.29 | 1,730.10 | 1,901.28 | 2,084.04 |
| Oroqen | 2,149.65 | 2,324.06 | 2,469.40 | 2,886.65 | 3,195.36 |
| Pumi | 1,497.79 | 1,630.58 | 1,720.49 | 1,891.11 | 2,072.17 |
| Qiang | 1,908.06 | 2,112.49 | 2,235.01 | 2,523.73 | 2,807.84 |
| Russian | 1,872.39 | 2,065.92 | 2,281.31 | 2,510.70 | 2,817.37 |
| Salar | 1,510.58 | 1,692.67 | 1,818.08 | 1,985.89 | 2,179.16 |
| She | 3,244.15 | 3,613.70 | 3,854.53 | 4,240.61 | 4,670.63 |
| Shui | 1,439.90 | 1,562.90 | 1,641.84 | 1,806.88 | 1,970.89 |
| Tajik | 1,643.32 | 1,888.33 | 2,127.09 | 2,272.46 | 2,512.33 |
| Tatar | 1,658.25 | 1,904.53 | 2,138.05 | 2,287.77 | 2,529.81 |
| Tibetan | 1,522.63 | 1,684.68 | 1,851.56 | 2,050.88 | 2,272.21 |
| Tu | 1,571.75 | 1,754.17 | 1,877.21 | 2,053.12 | 2,249.37 |
| Tujia | 2,063.06 | 2,248.94 | 2,369.83 | 2,654.12 | 2,902.13 |
| Uygur | 1,623.91 | 1,869.33 | 2,111.68 | 2,251.70 | 2,489.83 |
| Uzbek | 1,641.33 | 1,887.45 | 2,128.32 | 2,270.89 | 2,511.06 |
| Va | 1,510.96 | 1,645.37 | 1,735.99 | 1,908.76 | 2,092.58 |
| Xibe | 2,220.49 | 2,574.20 | 2,764.69 | 3,101.19 | 3,452.70 |
| Yao | 2,062.16 | 2,232.41 | 2,334.53 | 2,575.19 | 2,799.48 |
| Yi | 1,597.36 | 1,747.94 | 1,845.09 | 2,046.60 | 2,253.08 |
| Yugur | 1,458.91 | 1,625.65 | 1,713.78 | 1,895.74 | 2,033.33 |
| Zhuang | 1,908.62 | 2,061.25 | 2,147.15 | 2,359.76 | 2,555.24 |

*Notes:* "Rural households" refers to resident households in rural areas. Resident households in rural areas are the households residing for more than one year in the areas under the jurisdiction of administration of township governments (excluding county towns), and in the areas under the jurisdiction of administration of villages in county towns. Migrated households residing at their current addresses for over one year with their household registration in other places are included in the resident households of their current addresses. For households where their household registration is in one place but all members of the household have moved away to live in another place for over one year, they will not be included in the rural households of the area where they are registered, irrespective of whether they still keep their contracted land.

*Table 3.6* Per capita annual net income of rural households by sources (unit: yuan)

| Ethnic group | Net income | Income from wages and salaries | Income from household operations | Income from properties | Income from transfers |
|---|---|---|---|---|---|
| *National average* | *3,254.93* | *1,174.53* | *1,844.53* | *88.45* | *147.42* |
| Achang | 2,063.04 | 362.81 | 1,535.63 | 75.86 | 88.74 |
| Bai | 2,137.30 | 460.06 | 1,512.57 | 70.10 | 94.57 |
| Baonan | 2,013.02 | 576.42 | 1,300.99 | 23.55 | 112.06 |
| Blang | 2,068.78 | 368.02 | 1,535.91 | 75.81 | 89.03 |
| Buyi | 1,973.10 | 632.28 | 1,192.70 | 40.01 | 108.11 |
| Dai | 2,062.84 | 364.26 | 1,534.01 | 75.69 | 88.87 |
| Daur | 3,101.75 | 541.25 | 2,254.61 | 128.24 | 177.65 |
| Deang | 2,051.15 | 354.91 | 1,532.38 | 75.60 | 88.26 |
| Derung | 2,301.74 | 521.22 | 1,600.30 | 77.66 | 102.56 |
| Dong | 2,435.63 | 879.54 | 1,402.85 | 40.47 | 112.78 |
| Dongxiang | 2,041.48 | 546.71 | 1,361.81 | 22.67 | 110.30 |
| Ewenki | 3,074.01 | 574.15 | 2,221.17 | 91.80 | 186.88 |
| Gaoshan | 3,414.65 | 1,273.66 | 1,896.76 | 87.68 | 156.55 |
| Gelao | 1,947.22 | 624.82 | 1,176.32 | 38.54 | 107.54 |
| *Han* | *3,590.78* | *1,447.03* | *1,883.95* | *99.23* | *160.57* |
| Hani | 2,061.27 | 362.57 | 1,533.99 | 75.90 | 88.81 |
| Hezhe | 3,325.73 | 621.06 | 2,313.14 | 220.69 | 170.84 |
| Hui | 2,887.72 | 930.99 | 1,732.36 | 75.96 | 148.41 |
| Jing | 2,545.06 | 928.47 | 1,529.78 | 25.00 | 61.81 |
| Jingpo | 2,061.56 | 363.29 | 1,533.74 | 75.78 | 88.76 |
| Jino | 2,058.35 | 360.59 | 1,533.03 | 75.86 | 88.87 |
| Kazak | 2,483.31 | 199.27 | 2,137.73 | 34.10 | 112.20 |
| Kirgiz | 2,493.52 | 202.43 | 2,142.27 | 36.04 | 112.78 |
| Korean | 3,393.99 | 704.22 | 2,328.21 | 162.61 | 198.94 |
| Lahu | 2,064.02 | 363.96 | 1,535.67 | 75.73 | 88.66 |
| Lhoba | 2,178.88 | 620.37 | 1,239.51 | 205.15 | 113.84 |
| Li | 2,968.81 | 499.25 | 2,284.21 | 55.77 | 129.58 |
| Lisu | 2,083.93 | 379.33 | 1,540.03 | 74.91 | 89.66 |
| Manchu | 3,609.25 | 1,142.45 | 2,152.36 | 132.19 | 182.25 |
| Maonan | 2,355.57 | 839.86 | 1,418.17 | 26.16 | 71.38 |
| Miao | 2,395.71 | 812.39 | 1,424.99 | 44.71 | 113.62 |
| Monba | 2,189.68 | 649.73 | 1,207.06 | 214.78 | 118.11 |
| Mongol | 3,108.52 | 673.66 | 2,166.01 | 86.17 | 182.67 |
| Mulao | 2,494.13 | 919.25 | 1,481.47 | 26.52 | 66.89 |
| Naxi | 2,088.13 | 384.01 | 1,537.79 | 76.00 | 90.32 |

*Table 3.6  (cont.)*

| Ethnic group | Net income | Income from wages and salaries | Income from household operations | Income from properties | Income from transfers |
|---|---|---|---|---|---|
| Nu | 2,084.04 | 380.33 | 1,535.32 | 78.33 | 90.06 |
| Oroqen | 3,195.36 | 590.31 | 2,270.89 | 155.73 | 178.43 |
| Pumi | 2,072.17 | 369.76 | 1,537.11 | 76.04 | 89.27 |
| Qiang | 2,807.84 | 959.25 | 1,681.01 | 42.44 | 125.15 |
| Russian | 2,817.37 | 463.92 | 2,141.40 | 63.77 | 148.29 |
| Salar | 2,179.16 | 575.29 | 1,383.64 | 58.92 | 161.32 |
| She | 4,670.63 | 1,955.11 | 2,291.15 | 133.00 | 291.37 |
| Shui | 1,970.89 | 627.65 | 1,199.36 | 38.81 | 105.07 |
| Tajik | 2,512.33 | 236.71 | 2,126.66 | 35.73 | 113.23 |
| Tatar | 2,529.81 | 278.44 | 2,096.43 | 39.18 | 115.76 |
| Tibetan | 2,272.21 | 663.33 | 1,359.70 | 124.36 | 124.82 |
| Tu | 2,249.37 | 639.39 | 1,387.61 | 60.79 | 161.58 |
| Tujia | 2,902.13 | 1,054.14 | 1,686.41 | 37.25 | 124.32 |
| Uygur | 2,489.83 | 204.35 | 2,138.60 | 34.43 | 112.45 |
| Uzbek | 2,511.06 | 228.30 | 2,133.24 | 35.97 | 113.55 |
| Va | 2,092.58 | 382.89 | 1,544.28 | 75.75 | 89.66 |
| Xibe | 3,452.70 | 1,001.92 | 2,159.45 | 107.43 | 183.90 |
| Yao | 2,799.48 | 1,079.84 | 1,585.68 | 41.44 | 92.51 |
| Yi | 2,253.08 | 554.87 | 1,535.11 | 62.34 | 100.77 |
| Yugur | 2,033.33 | 601.58 | 1,294.92 | 24.77 | 112.05 |
| Zhuang | 2,555.24 | 931.97 | 1,531.26 | 28.85 | 63.16 |

*Notes:* "Net income" refers to the total income of rural households from all sources minus all corresponding expenses. The formula for calculation is as follows: Net income = total income – taxes and fees paid – household operation expenses – taxes and fees depreciation of fixed assets for production – subsidy for participating in household survey – gifts to non-rural relatives. Net income is mainly used as input for reproduction and as consumption expenditure of the year, and also used for savings and non-compulsory expenses of various forms. "Income from wages and salaries" refers to income from labor earned by the members of rural households employed by other units or individuals. "Income from household operations" refers to income by the rural households as units of production and operations. Operations by rural households are classified by economic activities as agriculture, forestry, animal husbandry, fishery, manufacturing, construction, transportation, post and telecommunications, wholesale, retail and catering, social service, culture, education, health, and other household operations. "Income from properties" refers to the income received as returns by owners of financial assets or tangible non-productive assets by providing capital or tangible non-productive assets to other institutional units. "Income from transfers" refers to the receipt by rural households and their members of goods, services, capital, or rights of assets without giving or repaying accordingly, excluding capital provided to them for the formation of fixed assets. In general, it refers to all income received by rural households through redistribution.

*Table 3.7* Per capita consumption expenditure of rural households (unit: yuan)

| Ethnic group | Consumption expenditure | Food | Clothing | Residence | Household appliances and services |
|---|---|---|---|---|---|
| National average | 2,555.40 | 1,162.16 | 148.57 | 370.16 | 111.44 |
| Achang | 1,801.66 | 979.47 | 81.15 | 227.98 | 67.79 |
| Bai | 1,856.35 | 999.29 | 85.22 | 236.52 | 71.21 |
| Baonan | 1,834.34 | 860.86 | 98.06 | 247.99 | 74.54 |
| Blang | 1,805.21 | 980.66 | 81.43 | 228.54 | 68.02 |
| Buyi | 1,628.08 | 849.43 | 83.21 | 246.13 | 65.31 |
| Dai | 1,802.44 | 980.36 | 81.21 | 227.83 | 67.87 |
| Daur | 2,485.84 | 1,008.79 | 164.77 | 404.30 | 83.07 |
| Deang | 1,794.42 | 976.98 | 80.84 | 226.84 | 67.36 |
| Derung | 1,941.11 | 1,007.23 | 96.03 | 253.43 | 75.09 |
| Dong | 2,082.21 | 1,073.63 | 98.37 | 285.06 | 85.34 |
| Dongxiang | 1,835.11 | 854.28 | 101.63 | 252.07 | 73.62 |
| Ewenki | 2,489.62 | 1,056.00 | 155.13 | 358.83 | 86.60 |
| Gaoshan | 2,572.52 | 1,158.58 | 150.65 | 385.26 | 113.38 |
| Gelao | 1,608.10 | 842.30 | 81.93 | 243.51 | 64.34 |
| *Han* | *2,730.44* | *1,223.48* | *155.75* | *400.21* | *121.77* |
| Hani | 1,801.28 | 979.32 | 81.15 | 227.98 | 67.77 |
| Hezhe | 2,598.26 | 964.21 | 185.32 | 509.85 | 82.82 |
| Hui | 2,239.95 | 981.13 | 147.54 | 350.67 | 94.94 |
| Jing | 2,349.71 | 1,183.31 | 83.30 | 374.03 | 95.77 |
| Jingpo | 1,800.79 | 978.87 | 81.19 | 228.04 | 67.73 |
| Jino | 1,799.49 | 979.03 | 81.08 | 227.42 | 67.67 |
| Kazak | 1,926.03 | 804.73 | 171.24 | 333.16 | 68.19 |
| Kirgiz | 1,933.58 | 806.43 | 171.54 | 335.29 | 68.30 |
| Korean | 2,484.93 | 1,024.88 | 180.20 | 345.58 | 88.31 |
| Lahu | 1,801.72 | 979.09 | 81.29 | 228.18 | 67.82 |
| Lhoba | 1,790.42 | 1,178.62 | 179.12 | 110.07 | 83.62 |
| Li | 1,969.56 | 1,125.88 | 68.30 | 155.09 | 91.62 |
| Lisu | 1,813.97 | 985.83 | 82.30 | 228.31 | 68.73 |
| Manchu | 2,638.36 | 1,058.80 | 197.60 | 395.39 | 101.24 |
| Maonan | 2,140.36 | 1,088.21 | 81.27 | 340.23 | 86.75 |
| Miao | 2,020.57 | 1,050.99 | 96.24 | 269.20 | 82.81 |
| Monba | 1,813.47 | 1,201.47 | 182.94 | 106.75 | 86.40 |
| Mongol | 2,469.81 | 1,052.67 | 160.61 | 347.72 | 88.88 |
| Mulao | 2,290.18 | 1,154.93 | 83.06 | 365.59 | 93.31 |
| Naxi | 1,818.52 | 988.24 | 82.99 | 228.58 | 69.05 |
| Nu | 1,815.01 | 986.47 | 83.66 | 228.78 | 68.78 |

*Table 3.7 (cont.)*

| Ethnic group | Consumption expenditure | Food | Clothing | Residence | Household appliances and services |
|---|---|---|---|---|---|
| Oroqen | 2,540.52 | 1,006.89 | 170.39 | 435.25 | 84.17 |
| Pumi | 1,807.42 | 981.07 | 81.83 | 228.86 | 68.15 |
| Qiang | 2,276.73 | 1,242.26 | 116.69 | 236.10 | 102.20 |
| Russian | 2,216.61 | 930.31 | 167.72 | 351.09 | 81.56 |
| Salar | 1,977.25 | 894.61 | 150.21 | 321.40 | 83.59 |
| She | 3,619.75 | 1,579.21 | 202.75 | 541.17 | 167.44 |
| Shui | 1,635.86 | 855.40 | 82.11 | 247.56 | 65.45 |
| Tajik | 1,947.74 | 817.73 | 170.28 | 334.36 | 69.64 |
| Tatar | 1,967.83 | 825.86 | 169.06 | 335.36 | 71.54 |
| Tibetan | 1,925.25 | 1,109.31 | 151.72 | 188.58 | 86.28 |
| Tu | 2,023.87 | 923.35 | 146.97 | 323.92 | 85.67 |
| Tujia | 2,380.99 | 1,212.02 | 115.31 | 291.86 | 102.55 |
| Uygur | 1,930.32 | 806.76 | 171.36 | 333.69 | 68.44 |
| Uzbek | 1,947.53 | 815.77 | 170.97 | 335.32 | 69.56 |
| Va | 1,817.17 | 982.45 | 82.54 | 231.15 | 68.87 |
| Xibe | 2,632.88 | 1,060.63 | 207.66 | 378.75 | 94.98 |
| Yao | 2,513.53 | 1,278.37 | 98.10 | 358.55 | 102.62 |
| Yi | 1,909.56 | 1,036.04 | 91.07 | 231.67 | 76.81 |
| Yugur | 1,849.23 | 865.99 | 96.76 | 248.76 | 75.55 |
| Zhuang | 2,361.50 | 1,193.12 | 82.80 | 373.79 | 95.82 |

| Ethnic group | Transport and communications | Education, culture and recreation services | Health care and medical services | Other goods and services |
|---|---|---|---|---|
| National average | 244.98 | 295.48 | 168.09 | 54.52 |
| Achang | 102.03 | 184.54 | 123.02 | 35.69 |
| Bai | 112.03 | 193.80 | 121.87 | 36.42 |
| Baonan | 158.58 | 248.72 | 117.76 | 27.83 |
| Blang | 102.53 | 185.06 | 123.24 | 35.73 |
| Buyi | 109.12 | 170.25 | 78.40 | 26.23 |
| Dai | 102.00 | 184.44 | 123.08 | 35.65 |
| Daur | 278.14 | 296.39 | 204.28 | 46.11 |
| Deang | 100.85 | 183.38 | 122.69 | 35.48 |
| Derung | 130.56 | 207.73 | 132.16 | 38.88 |
| Dong | 159.85 | 228.23 | 112.32 | 39.41 |
| Dongxiang | 158.67 | 246.19 | 120.67 | 27.97 |

*Table 3.7* (cont.)

| Ethnic group | Transport and communications | Education, culture and recreation services | Health care and medical services | Other goods and services |
|---|---|---|---|---|
| Ewenki | 291.87 | 310.00 | 185.62 | 45.57 |
| Gaoshan | 251.43 | 289.48 | 166.35 | 57.39 |
| Gelao | 106.80 | 167.39 | 76.14 | 25.69 |
| *Han* | *267.53* | *322.16* | *179.66* | *59.88* |
| Hani | 101.81 | 184.51 | 123.07 | 35.66 |
| Hezhe | 265.82 | 289.91 | 249.17 | 51.16 |
| Hui | 209.93 | 241.58 | 168.73 | 45.43 |
| Jing | 213.16 | 229.52 | 125.20 | 45.41 |
| Jingpo | 102.03 | 184.36 | 122.90 | 35.67 |
| Jino | 101.57 | 184.10 | 123.01 | 35.61 |
| Kazak | 183.14 | 159.92 | 169.25 | 36.40 |
| Kirgiz | 184.11 | 161.13 | 170.20 | 36.58 |
| Korean | 285.50 | 289.90 | 213.51 | 57.06 |
| Lahu | 102.03 | 184.58 | 123.07 | 35.65 |
| Lhoba | 93.06 | 50.95 | 55.02 | 39.96 |
| Li | 176.83 | 199.42 | 93.70 | 58.70 |
| Lisu | 103.90 | 185.64 | 123.65 | 35.61 |
| Manchu | 284.11 | 329.65 | 213.26 | 58.32 |
| Maonan | 183.87 | 210.36 | 110.15 | 39.51 |
| Miao | 149.36 | 220.76 | 113.39 | 37.83 |
| Monba | 92.52 | 47.81 | 54.65 | 40.91 |
| Mongol | 283.21 | 305.66 | 183.72 | 47.33 |
| Mulao | 205.17 | 224.06 | 120.24 | 43.82 |
| Naxi | 104.35 | 185.69 | 123.83 | 35.79 |
| Nu | 104.00 | 184.40 | 122.86 | 36.06 |
| Oroqen | 278.34 | 299.85 | 217.36 | 48.28 |
| Pumi | 103.03 | 185.26 | 123.46 | 35.77 |
| Qiang | 172.35 | 226.05 | 144.64 | 36.44 |
| Russian | 233.00 | 231.50 | 179.55 | 41.87 |
| Salar | 203.22 | 132.91 | 149.96 | 41.35 |
| She | 394.92 | 423.88 | 214.66 | 95.72 |
| Shui | 109.90 | 170.22 | 78.81 | 26.41 |
| Tajik | 185.13 | 164.48 | 169.12 | 37.00 |
| Tatar | 187.26 | 171.98 | 169.59 | 37.18 |
| Tibetan | 135.82 | 116.56 | 98.78 | 38.19 |
| Tu | 206.26 | 145.50 | 149.29 | 42.92 |
| Tujia | 196.10 | 272.79 | 140.28 | 50.07 |

*Table 3.7* (cont.)

| Ethnic group | Transport and communications | Education, culture and recreation services | Health care and medical services | Other goods and services |
|---|---|---|---|---|
| Uygur | 183.60 | 160.49 | 169.45 | 36.54 |
| Uzbek | 185.56 | 163.44 | 169.81 | 37.10 |
| Va | 105.05 | 187.20 | 124.03 | 35.89 |
| Xibe | 277.91 | 330.73 | 221.61 | 60.61 |
| Yao | 221.06 | 260.97 | 141.19 | 52.67 |
| Yi | 121.68 | 193.86 | 123.72 | 34.70 |
| Yugur | 159.50 | 256.57 | 118.28 | 27.83 |
| Zhuang | 213.45 | 229.22 | 126.77 | 46.54 |

*Note:* "Consumption expenditure" refers to total expenditure for consumption in daily life, including expenditure on eight categories such as food, clothing, household appliances and services, health care and medical services, transport and communications, education, culture and recreation services, housing, and miscellaneous goods and services.

*Table 3.8* Per capita cash consumption expenditure of rural households (yuan)

| Ethnic group | Consumption expenditure | Food | Clothing | Residence | Household appliances and services |
|---|---|---|---|---|---|
| National average | 2,134.58 | 770.69 | 147.94 | 342.33 | 110.92 |
| Achang | 1,271.01 | 491.00 | 81.10 | 186.11 | 67.73 |
| Bai | 1,329.97 | 510.42 | 85.15 | 199.41 | 71.14 |
| Baonan | 1,316.68 | 356.96 | 97.65 | 235.28 | 74.18 |
| Blang | 1,274.26 | 491.83 | 81.38 | 186.73 | 67.95 |
| Buyi | 1,171.27 | 406.57 | 83.20 | 233.23 | 65.26 |
| Dai | 1,270.77 | 490.88 | 81.17 | 185.96 | 67.79 |
| Daur | 2,111.48 | 687.80 | 162.91 | 354.03 | 82.99 |
| Deang | 1,262.98 | 487.81 | 80.79 | 184.89 | 67.30 |
| Derung | 1,434.77 | 540.46 | 95.83 | 214.47 | 74.96 |
| Dong | 1,585.41 | 596.82 | 98.24 | 265.83 | 85.30 |
| Dongxiang | 1,331.51 | 363.44 | 100.95 | 240.41 | 73.26 |
| Ewenki | 2,060.04 | 673.69 | 152.68 | 315.77 | 86.54 |
| Gaoshan | 2,175.07 | 796.56 | 150.23 | 351.09 | 113.14 |
| Gelao | 1,151.10 | 398.78 | 81.92 | 231.08 | 64.31 |
| Han | 2,320.27 | 843.30 | 155.26 | 371.57 | 121.21 |

*Table 3.8* (*cont.*)

| Ethnic group | Consumption expenditure | Food | Clothing | Residence | Household appliances and services |
|---|---|---|---|---|---|
| Hani | 1,270.31 | 490.55 | 81.11 | 186.10 | 67.71 |
| Hezhe | 2,336.49 | 771.79 | 185.22 | 440.75 | 82.77 |
| Hui | 1,834.97 | 598.30 | 146.75 | 330.44 | 94.55 |
| Jing | 1,862.18 | 746.77 | 83.28 | 323.19 | 95.75 |
| Jingpo | 1,270.43 | 490.67 | 81.14 | 186.20 | 67.66 |
| Jino | 1,268.01 | 489.82 | 81.03 | 185.47 | 67.60 |
| Kazak | 1,583.29 | 476.52 | 166.76 | 323.98 | 67.32 |
| Kirgiz | 1,592.05 | 480.03 | 167.09 | 325.46 | 67.44 |
| Korean | 2,183.02 | 772.59 | 179.94 | 296.32 | 88.26 |
| Lahu | 1,271.14 | 490.69 | 81.25 | 186.32 | 67.76 |
| Lhoba | 1,067.87 | 473.02 | 174.34 | 99.48 | 82.18 |
| Li | 1,523.78 | 709.65 | 68.30 | 125.60 | 91.62 |
| Lisu | 1,280.32 | 493.95 | 82.24 | 186.97 | 68.56 |
| Manchu | 2,341.07 | 789.17 | 196.93 | 368.63 | 101.19 |
| Maonan | 1,661.64 | 650.54 | 81.26 | 299.56 | 86.74 |
| Miao | 1,511.83 | 564.24 | 96.11 | 248.00 | 82.69 |
| Monba | 1,075.67 | 480.17 | 177.98 | 96.85 | 84.87 |
| Mongol | 2,051.97 | 675.40 | 158.39 | 310.99 | 88.76 |
| Mulao | 1,807.33 | 719.26 | 83.05 | 318.64 | 93.30 |
| Naxi | 1,284.12 | 495.56 | 82.91 | 187.30 | 68.88 |
| Nu | 1,282.49 | 495.63 | 83.54 | 187.51 | 68.69 |
| Oroqen | 2,196.45 | 721.25 | 169.12 | 379.03 | 84.13 |
| Pumi | 1,276.88 | 492.64 | 81.77 | 187.09 | 68.07 |
| Qiang | 1,629.25 | 625.11 | 116.35 | 210.13 | 98.38 |
| Russian | 1,841.95 | 581.64 | 164.20 | 329.88 | 81.01 |
| Salar | 1,456.32 | 412.49 | 148.78 | 290.67 | 82.41 |
| She | 3,251.08 | 1,256.57 | 202.63 | 497.27 | 167.41 |
| Shui | 1,176.69 | 411.47 | 82.10 | 233.31 | 65.41 |
| Tajik | 1,601.83 | 486.96 | 165.93 | 324.42 | 68.79 |
| Tatar | 1,618.07 | 491.05 | 164.90 | 325.44 | 70.71 |
| Tibetan | 1,268.44 | 477.98 | 148.99 | 169.15 | 84.38 |
| Tu | 1,502.70 | 441.00 | 145.71 | 292.59 | 84.56 |
| Tujia | 1,808.85 | 664.36 | 114.36 | 268.76 | 102.32 |
| Uygur | 1,587.64 | 478.68 | 166.89 | 324.44 | 67.57 |
| Uzbek | 1,603.78 | 486.96 | 166.57 | 325.64 | 68.71 |
| Va | 1,289.08 | 496.11 | 82.48 | 189.74 | 68.79 |
| Xibe | 2,314.80 | 768.25 | 206.17 | 354.79 | 94.78 |

*Table 3.8  (cont.)*

| Ethnic group | Consumption expenditure | Food | Clothing | Residence | Household appliances and services |
|---|---|---|---|---|---|
| Yao | 1,999.38 | 807.09 | 98.05 | 315.83 | 102.60 |
| Yi | 1,354.62 | 516.84 | 90.95 | 197.45 | 75.71 |
| Yugur | 1,333.38 | 363.21 | 96.44 | 236.42 | 75.23 |
| Zhuang | 1,870.78 | 754.58 | 82.79 | 321.70 | 95.81 |

| Ethnic group | Transport and communications | Education, culture and recreation services | Health care and medical services | Other goods and services |
|---|---|---|---|---|
| *National average* | *244.98* | *295.48* | *168.09* | *54.14* |
| Achang | 102.03 | 184.54 | 123.02 | 35.49 |
| Bai | 112.03 | 193.80 | 121.87 | 36.15 |
| Baonan | 158.58 | 248.72 | 117.76 | 27.55 |
| Blang | 102.53 | 185.06 | 123.24 | 35.53 |
| Buyi | 109.12 | 170.25 | 78.40 | 25.24 |
| Dai | 102.00 | 184.44 | 123.08 | 35.45 |
| Daur | 278.14 | 296.39 | 204.28 | 44.94 |
| Deang | 100.85 | 183.38 | 122.69 | 35.28 |
| Derung | 130.56 | 207.73 | 132.16 | 38.61 |
| Dong | 159.85 | 228.23 | 112.32 | 38.82 |
| Dongxiang | 158.67 | 246.19 | 120.67 | 27.91 |
| Ewenki | 291.87 | 310.00 | 185.62 | 43.85 |
| Gaoshan | 251.43 | 289.48 | 166.35 | 56.80 |
| Gelao | 106.80 | 167.39 | 76.14 | 24.69 |
| *Han* | *267.53* | *322.16* | *179.66* | *59.57* |
| Hani | 101.81 | 184.51 | 123.07 | 35.46 |
| Hezhe | 265.82 | 289.91 | 249.17 | 51.07 |
| Hui | 209.93 | 241.58 | 168.73 | 44.71 |
| Jing | 213.16 | 229.52 | 125.20 | 45.30 |
| Jingpo | 102.03 | 184.36 | 122.90 | 35.46 |
| Jino | 101.57 | 184.10 | 123.01 | 35.41 |
| Kazak | 183.14 | 159.92 | 169.25 | 36.40 |
| Kirgiz | 184.11 | 161.13 | 170.20 | 36.58 |
| Korean | 285.50 | 289.90 | 213.51 | 57.00 |
| Lahu | 102.03 | 184.58 | 123.07 | 35.45 |

*Table 3.8* (*cont.*)

| Ethnic group | Transport and communications | Education, culture and recreation services | Health care and medical services | Other goods and services |
|---|---|---|---|---|
| Lhoba | 93.06 | 50.95 | 55.02 | 39.82 |
| Li | 176.83 | 199.42 | 93.70 | 58.65 |
| Lisu | 103.90 | 185.64 | 123.65 | 35.41 |
| Manchu | 284.11 | 329.65 | 213.26 | 58.14 |
| Maonan | 183.87 | 210.36 | 110.15 | 39.16 |
| Miao | 149.36 | 220.76 | 113.39 | 37.29 |
| Monba | 92.52 | 47.81 | 54.65 | 40.81 |
| Mongol | 283.21 | 305.66 | 183.72 | 45.83 |
| Mulao | 205.17 | 224.06 | 120.24 | 43.62 |
| Naxi | 104.35 | 185.69 | 123.83 | 35.58 |
| Nu | 104.00 | 184.40 | 122.86 | 35.86 |
| Oroqen | 278.34 | 299.85 | 217.36 | 47.38 |
| Pumi | 103.03 | 185.26 | 123.46 | 35.57 |
| Qiang | 172.35 | 226.05 | 144.64 | 36.24 |
| Russian | 233.00 | 231.50 | 179.55 | 41.18 |
| Salar | 203.22 | 132.91 | 149.96 | 35.89 |
| She | 394.92 | 423.88 | 214.66 | 93.76 |
| Shui | 109.90 | 170.22 | 78.81 | 25.46 |
| Tajik | 185.13 | 164.48 | 169.12 | 36.99 |
| Tatar | 187.26 | 171.98 | 169.59 | 37.15 |
| Tibetan | 135.82 | 116.56 | 98.78 | 36.79 |
| Tu | 206.26 | 145.50 | 149.29 | 37.79 |
| Tujia | 196.10 | 272.79 | 140.28 | 49.87 |
| Uygur | 183.60 | 160.49 | 169.45 | 36.54 |
| Uzbek | 185.56 | 163.44 | 169.81 | 37.09 |
| Va | 105.05 | 187.20 | 124.03 | 35.68 |
| Xibe | 277.91 | 330.73 | 221.61 | 60.56 |
| Yao | 221.06 | 260.97 | 141.19 | 52.60 |
| Yi | 121.68 | 193.86 | 123.72 | 34.41 |
| Yugur | 159.50 | 256.57 | 118.28 | 27.72 |
| Zhuang | 213.45 | 229.22 | 126.77 | 46.47 |

*Note:* "Consumption expenditure" refers to total expenditure for consumption in daily life, including expenditure on eight categories such as food, clothing, household appliances and services, health care and medical services, transport and communications, education, culture and recreation services, housing, and miscellaneous goods and services.

*Table 3.9* Per capita consumption of major food in rural households (unit: kg)

| Ethnic group | Grain | Vegetables | Edible oil | Pork, beef, and mutton |
|---|---|---|---|---|
| *National average* | *208.85* | *102.28* | *6.01* | *17.09* |
| Achang | 192.30 | 98.34 | 3.30 | 28.37 |
| Bai | 195.03 | 105.30 | 3.77 | 28.01 |
| Baonan | 259.24 | 44.83 | 3.87 | 16.65 |
| Blang | 192.44 | 98.51 | 3.31 | 28.36 |
| Buyi | 187.18 | 133.61 | 4.07 | 30.01 |
| Dai | 192.42 | 98.68 | 3.30 | 28.43 |
| Daur | 199.58 | 89.77 | 6.37 | 19.68 |
| Deang | 192.35 | 98.30 | 3.29 | 28.43 |
| Derung | 195.35 | 100.20 | 3.87 | 26.36 |
| Dong | 202.98 | 132.66 | 5.60 | 25.49 |
| Dongxiang | 258.31 | 46.58 | 4.41 | 16.12 |
| Ewenki | 204.59 | 81.68 | 4.92 | 24.27 |
| Gaoshan | 202.09 | 106.30 | 5.67 | 15.73 |
| Gelao | 187.00 | 134.60 | 4.06 | 30.19 |
| *Han* | *207.18* | *106.15* | *6.15* | *16.29* |
| Hani | 192.30 | 98.40 | 3.30 | 28.40 |
| Hezhe | 183.84 | 112.18 | 8.84 | 10.72 |
| Hui | 217.38 | 81.07 | 5.74 | 15.03 |
| Jing | 190.92 | 103.22 | 5.04 | 16.30 |
| Jingpo | 192.32 | 98.46 | 3.31 | 28.37 |
| Jino | 192.29 | 98.55 | 3.29 | 28.44 |
| Kazak | 235.35 | 67.89 | 10.87 | 12.25 |
| Kirgiz | 234.76 | 68.40 | 10.86 | 12.22 |
| Korean | 180.37 | 133.50 | 7.38 | 14.00 |
| Lahu | 192.38 | 98.39 | 3.30 | 28.34 |
| Lhoba | 256.44 | 31.16 | 4.69 | 51.69 |
| Li | 188.99 | 74.71 | 4.35 | 19.04 |
| Lisu | 193.11 | 99.87 | 3.35 | 28.44 |
| Manchu | 192.50 | 131.97 | 7.16 | 15.04 |
| Maonan | 189.13 | 111.69 | 4.77 | 19.93 |
| Miao | 201.91 | 130.59 | 5.15 | 26.66 |
| Monba | 258.89 | 27.06 | 4.61 | 53.22 |
| Mongol | 204.90 | 91.72 | 5.19 | 22.96 |
| Mulao | 190.14 | 106.81 | 4.96 | 17.69 |
| Naxi | 193.30 | 99.65 | 3.35 | 28.57 |
| Nu | 193.43 | 97.30 | 3.35 | 28.64 |

Table 3.9 *(cont.)*

| Ethnic group | Grain | Vegetables | Edible oil | Pork, beef, and mutton |
|---|---|---|---|---|
| Oroqen | 194.21 | 97.21 | 6.91 | 17.36 |
| Pumi | 192.51 | 98.55 | 3.32 | 28.33 |
| Qiang | 220.65 | 155.13 | 4.89 | 31.42 |
| Russian | 221.47 | 74.31 | 8.39 | 17.10 |
| Salar | 235.25 | 45.55 | 3.81 | 20.04 |
| She | 196.31 | 97.97 | 5.30 | 19.05 |
| Shui | 187.14 | 132.36 | 4.07 | 29.60 |
| Tajik | 234.43 | 69.34 | 10.71 | 12.41 |
| Tatar | 234.58 | 68.33 | 10.45 | 12.61 |
| Tibetan | 244.14 | 62.64 | 4.32 | 38.37 |
| Tu | 233.83 | 49.61 | 3.73 | 20.28 |
| Tujia | 217.24 | 143.38 | 5.74 | 24.17 |
| Uygur | 235.19 | 68.14 | 10.87 | 12.25 |
| Uzbek | 234.63 | 68.52 | 10.79 | 12.34 |
| Va | 192.68 | 98.52 | 3.39 | 28.08 |
| Xibe | 201.71 | 146.26 | 7.91 | 16.43 |
| Yao | 205.58 | 113.74 | 6.06 | 18.44 |
| Yi | 199.56 | 118.14 | 3.82 | 29.42 |
| Yugur | 259.17 | 45.21 | 3.83 | 16.49 |
| Zhuang | 191.13 | 102.17 | 4.98 | 16.62 |

| Ethnic group | Poultry | Eggs and related products | Aquatic products | Sugar | Liquor |
|---|---|---|---|---|---|
| *National average* | *3.67* | *4.71* | *4.94* | *1.13* | *9.59* |
| Achang | 2.95 | 1.71 | 1.14 | 1.21 | 6.77 |
| Bai | 2.96 | 1.81 | 1.47 | 1.18 | 6.65 |
| Baonan | 0.85 | 1.61 | 0.25 | 0.78 | 4.71 |
| Blang | 2.95 | 1.74 | 1.14 | 1.21 | 6.79 |
| Buyi | 1.91 | 1.39 | 0.72 | 0.88 | 6.47 |
| Dai | 2.95 | 1.72 | 1.12 | 1.21 | 6.77 |
| Daur | 2.61 | 4.76 | 2.41 | 0.97 | 14.28 |
| Deang | 2.93 | 1.69 | 1.09 | 1.21 | 6.73 |
| Derung | 3.01 | 2.42 | 1.77 | 1.19 | 7.48 |
| Dong | 3.55 | 2.03 | 3.06 | 1.01 | 6.30 |
| Dongxiang | 0.92 | 1.59 | 0.25 | 0.73 | 4.49 |
| Ewenki | 2.46 | 4.50 | 2.04 | 1.06 | 13.73 |
| Gaoshan | 3.92 | 5.27 | 5.25 | 1.15 | 10.03 |

*Table 3.9* (*cont.*)

| Ethnic group | Poultry | Eggs and related products | Aquatic products | Sugar | Liquor |
|---|---|---|---|---|---|
| Gelao | 1.88 | 1.35 | 0.65 | 0.87 | 6.36 |
| *Han* | *3.97* | *5.34* | *5.78* | *1.15* | *10.39* |
| Hani | 2.94 | 1.71 | 1.12 | 1.21 | 6.77 |
| Hezhe | 3.33 | 5.89 | 3.90 | 0.86 | 16.75 |
| Hui | 2.16 | 4.00 | 2.12 | 1.03 | 7.08 |
| Jing | 8.66 | 1.22 | 4.31 | 1.18 | 7.39 |
| Jingpo | 2.95 | 1.71 | 1.13 | 1.21 | 6.76 |
| Jino | 2.94 | 1.71 | 1.11 | 1.21 | 6.76 |
| Kazak | 1.70 | 1.01 | 0.42 | 0.46 | 1.30 |
| Kirgiz | 1.72 | 1.06 | 0.46 | 0.46 | 1.46 |
| Korean | 3.75 | 7.87 | 4.31 | 0.77 | 15.07 |
| Lahu | 2.94 | 1.74 | 1.12 | 1.21 | 6.78 |
| Lhoba | 0.38 | 0.93 | 0.42 | 2.99 | 1.98 |
| Li | 9.60 | 1.27 | 14.31 | 1.09 | 4.95 |
| Lisu | 2.97 | 1.81 | 1.14 | 1.22 | 6.83 |
| Manchu | 2.20 | 7.54 | 4.48 | 0.77 | 13.25 |
| Maonan | 6.96 | 1.17 | 3.24 | 1.09 | 7.03 |
| Miao | 3.28 | 2.28 | 2.70 | 1.08 | 6.65 |
| Monba | 0.33 | 0.86 | 0.37 | 3.10 | 1.74 |
| Mongol | 2.32 | 4.95 | 2.33 | 1.00 | 12.77 |
| Mulao | 8.09 | 1.19 | 3.99 | 1.15 | 7.20 |
| Naxi | 2.97 | 1.80 | 1.15 | 1.23 | 6.81 |
| Nu | 2.92 | 1.73 | 1.17 | 1.24 | 6.76 |
| Oroqen | 2.86 | 5.23 | 2.96 | 0.96 | 15.33 |
| Pumi | 2.95 | 1.75 | 1.14 | 1.21 | 6.80 |
| Qiang | 4.38 | 4.82 | 2.22 | 1.45 | 8.29 |
| Russian | 2.04 | 2.60 | 1.29 | 0.72 | 6.42 |
| Salar | 0.69 | 0.76 | 0.42 | 1.38 | 3.25 |
| She | 5.81 | 3.56 | 12.58 | 1.69 | 17.66 |
| Shui | 2.11 | 1.36 | 0.75 | 0.88 | 6.43 |
| Tajik | 1.79 | 1.15 | 0.58 | 0.48 | 1.58 |
| Tatar | 1.76 | 1.22 | 0.62 | 0.49 | 1.83 |
| Tibetan | 1.36 | 1.76 | 0.69 | 2.17 | 3.76 |
| Tu | 0.98 | 0.92 | 0.88 | 1.39 | 3.64 |
| Tujia | 3.62 | 3.80 | 5.20 | 1.22 | 7.88 |
| Uygur | 1.71 | 1.03 | 0.44 | 0.46 | 1.33 |
| Uzbek | 1.80 | 1.06 | 0.57 | 0.47 | 1.44 |
| Va | 2.95 | 1.86 | 1.19 | 1.21 | 6.89 |
| Xibe | 2.14 | 6.90 | 4.55 | 0.68 | 11.56 |

*Table 3.9* (*cont.*)

| Ethnic group | Poultry | Eggs and related products | Aquatic products | Sugar | Liquor |
|---|---|---|---|---|---|
| Yao | 7.42 | 1.88 | 5.29 | 1.23 | 6.45 |
| Yi | 3.22 | 2.53 | 1.36 | 1.24 | 7.15 |
| Yugur | 0.90 | 1.70 | 0.30 | 0.76 | 4.92 |
| Zhuang | 8.70 | 1.19 | 4.39 | 1.21 | 7.19 |

*Table 3.10* Number of durable consumer goods owned per 100 rural households at the year-end

| Ethnic group | Large furniture (unit) | Washing machine (unit) | Electric fan (unit) | Refrigerator (unit) | Air conditioner (unit) |
|---|---|---|---|---|---|
| *National average* | *304.26* | *40.20* | *146.35* | *20.10* | *6.40* |
| Achang | 105.06 | 21.45 | 10.85 | 7.13 | 0.48 |
| Bai | 168.03 | 22.96 | 29.15 | 7.98 | 0.80 |
| Baonan | 317.10 | 38.87 | 25.67 | 8.02 | 1.04 |
| Blang | 106.30 | 21.54 | 11.59 | 7.19 | 0.51 |
| Buyi | 420.18 | 30.06 | 51.34 | 9.58 | 1.28 |
| Dai | 106.53 | 21.53 | 11.27 | 7.13 | 0.48 |
| Daur | 142.94 | 46.57 | 23.09 | 15.51 | 0.84 |
| Deang | 103.86 | 21.40 | 9.67 | 7.03 | 0.42 |
| Derung | 140.53 | 25.89 | 31.94 | 9.82 | 1.39 |
| Dong | 423.31 | 27.14 | 119.98 | 11.09 | 2.06 |
| Dongxiang | 311.99 | 37.93 | 25.47 | 8.59 | 1.00 |
| Ewenki | 166.17 | 39.58 | 24.81 | 14.35 | 0.97 |
| Gaoshan | 280.46 | 44.51 | 155.84 | 22.32 | 7.45 |
| Gelao | 425.81 | 29.94 | 50.50 | 9.34 | 1.14 |
| *Han* | *314.71* | *44.75* | *165.02* | *23.56* | *8.81* |
| Hani | 104.72 | 21.48 | 10.56 | 7.12 | 0.49 |
| Hezhe | 93.66 | 63.81 | 31.48 | 18.64 | 1.76 |
| Hui | 297.77 | 45.92 | 77.75 | 19.18 | 4.54 |
| Jing | 211.17 | 9.13 | 228.27 | 7.62 | 1.15 |
| Jingpo | 105.87 | 21.50 | 10.88 | 7.12 | 0.47 |
| Jino | 104.71 | 21.48 | 10.33 | 7.10 | 0.47 |
| Kazak | 242.02 | 28.34 | 17.22 | 20.12 | 0.41 |
| Kirgiz | 240.19 | 28.67 | 17.38 | 20.12 | 0.42 |
| Korean | 107.27 | 60.57 | 35.51 | 18.44 | 1.58 |

*Table 3.10  (cont.)*

| Ethnic group | Large furniture (unit) | Washing machine (unit) | Electric fan (unit) | Refrigerator (unit) | Air conditioner (unit) |
|---|---|---|---|---|---|
| Lahu | 105.53 | 21.56 | 11.13 | 7.14 | 0.49 |
| Lhoba | 515.32 | 9.60 | 10.96 | 6.25 | 0.65 |
| Li | 208.02 | 5.52 | 123.04 | 7.70 | 0.62 |
| Lisu | 116.40 | 22.14 | 15.17 | 7.31 | 0.49 |
| Manchu | 161.22 | 64.46 | 74.90 | 27.11 | 3.01 |
| Maonan | 270.92 | 14.20 | 183.86 | 7.76 | 0.98 |
| Miao | 387.25 | 27.03 | 102.47 | 10.87 | 1.87 |
| Monba | 525.61 | 8.75 | 9.19 | 6.11 | 1.11 |
| Mongol | 179.54 | 42.47 | 36.02 | 16.46 | 1.20 |
| Mulao | 239.75 | 11.22 | 214.57 | 7.90 | 1.32 |
| Naxi | 117.97 | 22.07 | 15.12 | 7.38 | 0.58 |
| Nu | 113.31 | 21.49 | 12.50 | 7.35 | 0.61 |
| Oroqen | 128.06 | 51.97 | 27.98 | 16.39 | 1.15 |
| Pumi | 107.24 | 21.72 | 11.86 | 7.24 | 0.52 |
| Qiang | 512.93 | 40.77 | 169.46 | 12.46 | 1.16 |
| Russian | 218.81 | 34.23 | 28.01 | 19.43 | 1.92 |
| Salar | 304.26 | 42.93 | 9.51 | 17.16 | 0.57 |
| She | 303.46 | 41.45 | 210.39 | 39.34 | 16.78 |
| Shui | 409.31 | 29.21 | 55.26 | 9.25 | 1.13 |
| Tajik | 244.13 | 28.66 | 22.17 | 20.12 | 0.62 |
| Tatar | 246.35 | 29.68 | 22.57 | 20.28 | 1.06 |
| Tibetan | 453.51 | 25.51 | 45.02 | 9.60 | 0.50 |
| Tu | 307.54 | 42.48 | 19.75 | 16.97 | 1.13 |
| Tujia | 419.32 | 27.15 | 160.11 | 13.99 | 3.19 |
| Uygur | 242.26 | 28.38 | 17.92 | 20.17 | 0.46 |
| Uzbek | 243.02 | 28.44 | 20.65 | 20.26 | 0.66 |
| Va | 110.77 | 21.91 | 14.44 | 7.44 | 0.57 |
| Xibe | 161.76 | 56.70 | 51.13 | 26.08 | 1.35 |
| Yao | 297.32 | 15.72 | 213.18 | 10.18 | 2.56 |
| Yi | 253.30 | 27.80 | 58.91 | 8.83 | 0.72 |
| Yugur | 317.05 | 39.12 | 28.15 | 7.98 | 1.30 |
| Zhuang | 203.75 | 9.11 | 225.14 | 7.59 | 1.34 |

| Ethnic group | Exhaust fan (unit) | Bicycle (unit) | Motorcycle (unit) | Telephone set (unit) | Black and white TV set (unit) |
|---|---|---|---|---|---|
| National average | 5.98 | 98.37 | 40.70 | 58.30 | 21.77 |
| Achang | 0.84 | 31.88 | 16.71 | 23.86 | 15.51 |

*Table 3.10  (cont.)*

| Ethnic group | Exhaust fan (unit) | Bicycle (unit) | Motorcycle (unit) | Telephone set (unit) | Black and white TV set (unit) |
|---|---|---|---|---|---|
| Bai | 1.03 | 31.32 | 17.64 | 27.42 | 16.57 |
| Baonan | 0.85 | 99.12 | 37.95 | 53.61 | 19.91 |
| Blang | 0.85 | 32.05 | 16.71 | 24.05 | 15.59 |
| Buyi | 1.54 | 11.82 | 15.83 | 34.11 | 13.36 |
| Dai | 0.83 | 31.74 | 16.62 | 23.90 | 15.59 |
| Daur | 3.29 | 68.76 | 44.24 | 51.81 | 14.54 |
| Deang | 0.78 | 31.46 | 16.46 | 23.58 | 15.52 |
| Derung | 1.67 | 42.83 | 21.89 | 31.65 | 16.36 |
| Dong | 1.87 | 33.44 | 25.70 | 44.13 | 20.94 |
| Dongxiang | 0.85 | 99.82 | 38.15 | 52.51 | 21.32 |
| Ewenki | 2.46 | 65.09 | 48.46 | 44.44 | 14.46 |
| Gaoshan | 5.77 | 100.78 | 47.62 | 65.18 | 20.59 |
| Gelao | 1.43 | 10.35 | 15.49 | 33.82 | 13.20 |
| *Han* | *7.13* | *105.19* | *47.02* | *68.31* | *21.87* |
| Hani | 0.84 | 31.76 | 16.58 | 23.80 | 15.53 |
| Hezhe | 5.99 | 77.70 | 36.08 | 71.45 | 12.10 |
| Hui | 3.72 | 105.01 | 46.87 | 56.66 | 20.58 |
| Jing | 1.50 | 83.24 | 55.05 | 55.92 | 27.97 |
| Jingpo | 0.83 | 31.84 | 16.71 | 23.88 | 15.50 |
| Jino | 0.82 | 31.48 | 16.51 | 23.75 | 15.52 |
| Kazak | 1.24 | 81.04 | 45.39 | 36.36 | 35.09 |
| Kirgiz | 1.29 | 80.95 | 45.32 | 36.67 | 34.88 |
| Korean | 3.66 | 78.25 | 42.79 | 73.51 | 10.91 |
| Lahu | 0.83 | 32.09 | 16.66 | 23.92 | 15.58 |
| Lhoba | 0.54 | 35.74 | 15.10 | 19.79 | 4.10 |
| Li | 1.14 | 47.03 | 74.11 | 43.67 | 4.13 |
| Lisu | 0.83 | 32.43 | 16.90 | 24.72 | 15.96 |
| Manchu | 6.40 | 112.19 | 46.92 | 79.41 | 11.09 |
| Maonan | 1.36 | 63.61 | 44.84 | 50.02 | 24.15 |
| Miao | 1.73 | 29.95 | 22.83 | 41.86 | 19.89 |
| Monba | 0.82 | 35.59 | 14.42 | 18.68 | 3.48 |
| Mongol | 2.82 | 72.84 | 47.98 | 49.58 | 14.83 |
| Mulao | 1.66 | 76.14 | 51.73 | 54.17 | 26.37 |
| Naxi | 0.90 | 32.24 | 16.83 | 24.67 | 15.89 |
| Nu | 0.94 | 32.70 | 16.97 | 24.26 | 15.44 |
| Oroqen | 4.13 | 71.93 | 42.30 | 58.30 | 13.29 |
| Pumi | 0.86 | 32.32 | 16.81 | 24.18 | 15.62 |
| Qiang | 0.97 | 43.41 | 25.05 | 52.99 | 30.71 |
| Russian | 2.57 | 78.30 | 46.78 | 41.53 | 26.45 |

*Table 3.10* (cont.)

| Ethnic group | Exhaust fan (unit) | Bicycle (unit) | Motorcycle (unit) | Telephone set (unit) | Black and white TV set (unit) |
|---|---|---|---|---|---|
| Salar | 1.48 | 49.08 | 50.54 | 47.51 | 14.33 |
| She | 15.15 | 84.72 | 64.68 | 86.33 | 17.84 |
| Shui | 1.38 | 13.82 | 16.75 | 34.33 | 13.89 |
| Tajik | 1.38 | 81.35 | 45.35 | 37.32 | 34.67 |
| Tatar | 1.67 | 82.97 | 45.14 | 38.39 | 33.80 |
| Tibetan | 0.65 | 42.78 | 26.10 | 34.66 | 13.12 |
| Tu | 1.88 | 51.05 | 50.23 | 48.65 | 14.15 |
| Tujia | 2.47 | 46.43 | 28.05 | 52.40 | 25.98 |
| Uygur | 1.27 | 81.10 | 45.41 | 36.46 | 35.07 |
| Uzbek | 1.42 | 81.42 | 45.66 | 36.94 | 34.78 |
| Va | 0.91 | 33.74 | 17.32 | 24.89 | 15.72 |
| Xibe | 6.22 | 98.35 | 45.02 | 75.74 | 14.31 |
| Yao | 2.39 | 73.04 | 48.47 | 55.74 | 27.40 |
| Yi | 0.92 | 32.62 | 18.77 | 32.99 | 19.49 |
| Yugur | 1.02 | 101.65 | 37.68 | 54.36 | 19.90 |
| Zhuang | 1.68 | 82.88 | 55.14 | 55.18 | 27.31 |

| Ethnic group | Color TV set (unit) | Video recorder (unit) | Radio cassette player (unit) | Camera (unit) | Computer (set) |
|---|---|---|---|---|---|
| *National average* | *84.00* | *3.00* | *10.98* | *4.05* | *2.10* |
| Achang | 70.71 | 2.39 | 8.35 | 1.87 | 0.74 |
| Bai | 70.81 | 2.12 | 7.56 | 1.79 | 0.78 |
| Baonan | 85.36 | 1.80 | 31.83 | 2.80 | 0.28 |
| Blang | 70.78 | 2.39 | 8.36 | 1.88 | 0.74 |
| Buyi | 68.18 | 0.77 | 2.84 | 0.83 | 0.64 |
| Dai | 70.73 | 2.39 | 8.34 | 1.87 | 0.74 |
| Daur | 90.02 | 1.37 | 15.12 | 3.06 | 0.72 |
| Deang | 70.57 | 2.38 | 8.39 | 1.85 | 0.72 |
| Derung | 74.26 | 2.47 | 9.06 | 2.30 | 1.00 |
| Dong | 72.11 | 0.87 | 3.88 | 1.36 | 0.90 |
| Dongxiang | 83.76 | 2.35 | 32.43 | 2.83 | 0.26 |
| Ewenki | 88.64 | 0.94 | 15.50 | 3.08 | 0.67 |
| Gaoshan | 90.92 | 2.72 | 9.04 | 4.15 | 2.83 |
| Gelao | 67.78 | 0.70 | 2.65 | 0.77 | 0.61 |
| *Han* | *92.45* | *3.17* | *9.96* | *4.46* | *3.06* |

*Table 3.10* (*cont.*)

| Ethnic group | Color TV set (unit) | Video recorder (unit) | Radio cassette player (unit) | Camera (unit) | Computer (set) |
|---|---|---|---|---|---|
| Hani | 70.69 | 2.39 | 8.35 | 1.87 | 0.74 |
| Hezhe | 97.30 | 1.58 | 10.82 | 3.38 | 1.43 |
| Hui | 87.39 | 2.58 | 18.57 | 4.08 | 1.66 |
| Jing | 80.99 | 0.73 | 5.71 | 1.74 | 0.74 |
| Jingpo | 70.70 | 2.38 | 8.34 | 1.87 | 0.74 |
| Jino | 70.68 | 2.38 | 8.35 | 1.86 | 0.74 |
| Kazak | 61.93 | 9.26 | 41.47 | 3.23 | 0.01 |
| Kirgiz | 62.25 | 9.20 | 41.16 | 3.23 | 0.02 |
| Korean | 98.50 | 2.22 | 10.03 | 3.54 | 1.14 |
| Lahu | 70.72 | 2.39 | 8.35 | 1.87 | 0.73 |
| Lhoba | 51.85 | 3.15 | 45.71 | 2.63 | 0.63 |
| Li | 77.19 | 7.66 | 10.96 | 1.55 | 1.54 |
| Lisu | 71.06 | 2.40 | 8.32 | 1.89 | 0.73 |
| Manchu | 100.86 | 3.44 | 10.38 | 5.36 | 2.45 |
| Maonan | 77.24 | 0.60 | 4.75 | 1.41 | 0.64 |
| Miao | 72.15 | 1.18 | 4.40 | 1.40 | 0.84 |
| Monba | 51.25 | 3.23 | 47.48 | 2.75 | 0.84 |
| Mongol | 89.24 | 1.63 | 15.33 | 3.44 | 0.89 |
| Mulao | 79.85 | 0.68 | 5.32 | 1.67 | 0.81 |
| Naxi | 71.02 | 2.41 | 8.49 | 1.91 | 0.76 |
| Nu | 70.68 | 2.43 | 8.97 | 1.92 | 0.77 |
| Oroqen | 93.08 | 1.22 | 12.99 | 3.18 | 0.97 |
| Pumi | 70.86 | 2.40 | 8.40 | 1.89 | 0.75 |
| Qiang | 81.83 | 2.61 | 6.79 | 2.60 | 0.67 |
| Russian | 74.14 | 5.96 | 30.48 | 3.64 | 0.82 |
| Salar | 81.26 | 2.38 | 34.63 | 2.69 | 0.18 |
| She | 109.16 | 5.16 | 8.31 | 5.72 | 5.98 |
| Shui | 68.29 | 0.75 | 2.94 | 0.83 | 0.58 |
| Tajik | 62.81 | 9.04 | 40.39 | 3.25 | 0.09 |
| Tatar | 64.21 | 8.78 | 40.00 | 3.42 | 0.29 |
| Tibetan | 67.00 | 2.67 | 33.59 | 2.56 | 0.42 |
| Tu | 82.29 | 2.27 | 32.58 | 2.71 | 0.40 |
| Tujia | 77.34 | 1.19 | 4.54 | 1.77 | 1.04 |
| Uygur | 62.00 | 9.25 | 41.36 | 3.24 | 0.03 |
| Uzbek | 62.52 | 9.17 | 40.90 | 3.29 | 0.13 |
| Va | 71.07 | 2.39 | 8.37 | 1.93 | 0.76 |
| Xibe | 94.32 | 5.07 | 15.31 | 5.50 | 2.19 |
| Yao | 79.86 | 1.12 | 5.95 | 2.09 | 1.36 |

*Table 3.10* (cont.)

| Ethnic group | Color TV set (unit) | Video recorder (unit) | Radio cassette player (unit) | Camera (unit) | Computer (set) |
|---|---|---|---|---|---|
| Yi | 73.45 | 2.26 | 7.28 | 1.94 | 0.69 |
| Yugur | 86.09 | 1.71 | 31.29 | 2.91 | 0.41 |
| Zhuang | 81.09 | 0.83 | 5.96 | 1.83 | 0.88 |

*Table 3.11* Engel coefficients by urban and rural areas

| Ethnic group | Urban | Rural |
|---|---|---|
| *National average* | *36.69* | *45.48* |
| Achang | 42.75 | 54.36 |
| Bai | 41.91 | 53.83 |
| Baonan | 36.07 | 46.93 |
| Blang | 42.71 | 54.32 |
| Buyi | 39.79 | 52.17 |
| Dai | 42.75 | 54.39 |
| Daur | 32.50 | 40.58 |
| Deang | 42.78 | 54.45 |
| Derung | 41.44 | 51.89 |
| Dong | 38.54 | 51.56 |
| Dongxiang | 36.07 | 46.55 |
| Ewenki | 31.91 | 42.42 |
| Gaoshan | 37.19 | 45.04 |
| Gelao | 39.79 | 52.38 |
| *Han* | *36.71* | *44.81* |
| Hani | 42.76 | 54.37 |
| Hezhe | 33.86 | 37.11 |
| Hui | 36.17 | 43.80 |
| Jing | 41.11 | 50.36 |
| Jingpo | 42.73 | 54.36 |
| Jino | 42.76 | 54.41 |
| Kazak | 36.36 | 41.78 |
| Kirgiz | 36.34 | 41.71 |
| Korean | 35.02 | 41.24 |
| Lahu | 42.73 | 54.34 |
| Lhoba | 43.90 | 65.83 |
| Li | 46.95 | 57.16 |
| Lisu | 42.64 | 54.35 |

*Table 3.11* (*cont.*)

| Ethnic group | Urban | Rural |
|---|---|---|
| Manchu | 36.51 | 40.13 |
| Maonan | 40.80 | 50.84 |
| Miao | 38.95 | 52.01 |
| Monba | 44.05 | 66.25 |
| Mongol | 33.16 | 42.62 |
| Mulao | 40.84 | 50.43 |
| Naxi | 42.64 | 54.34 |
| Nu | 42.70 | 54.35 |
| Oroqen | 32.85 | 39.63 |
| Pumi | 42.71 | 54.28 |
| Qiang | 39.29 | 54.56 |
| Russian | 34.60 | 41.97 |
| Salar | 36.28 | 45.24 |
| She | 38.29 | 43.63 |
| Shui | 39.95 | 52.29 |
| Tajik | 36.40 | 41.98 |
| Tatar | 36.34 | 41.97 |
| Tibetan | 41.26 | 57.62 |
| Tu | 36.43 | 45.62 |
| Tujia | 37.36 | 50.90 |
| Uygur | 36.37 | 41.79 |
| Uzbek | 36.39 | 41.89 |
| Va | 42.57 | 54.06 |
| Xibe | 37.86 | 40.28 |
| Yao | 39.29 | 50.86 |
| Yi | 41.50 | 54.26 |
| Yugur | 36.02 | 46.83 |
| Zhuang | 41.08 | 50.52 |

*Note:* "Engel coefficient" refers to the percentage of expenditure on food in the total consumption expenditure, using the following formula: Engel coefficient = (expenditure on food / total consumption expenditure) × 100%.

# 4 Agriculture and rural economy

The data in this chapter show the basic conditions of agriculture and the rural economy. Statistics on agriculture cover all agricultural production activities except horse raising for military purposes and activities undertaken by agricultural research institutions. Included in agriculture statistics are production activities in crop cultivation, forestry, animal husbandry, and fishery undertaken by rural economic units of various types and by rural households; production activities of farms specializing in crop cultivation, forestry, animal husbandry, and fishery; production activities undertaken by government agencies, institutions, schools, and military units; production activities in agriculture undertaken by collective farms run by townships and villages; and production activities in crop cultivation, forestry, animal husbandry, and fishery undertaken by manufacturing and mining enterprises.

*Comprehensive Statistical Reporting on Farming, Forestry, Animal Husbandry and Fishery* is a comprehensive reporting program reported by provincial statistical bureaus to the National Bureau of Statistics (NBS). Data required in this reporting program are collected by statistical offices at all levels by means of sample surveys, surveys of key units, or full enumeration depending on the local circumstances, or estimated by using information from other government agencies at the same level or from the sample survey of farm crops and rural household survey conducted by the NBS. For instance, some data on condition of agriculture production and on forestry and fishery are obtained from statistics collected by other government agencies at the same level.

The *Sample Survey of Farm Crops* is a nationwide survey designed by the NBS and implemented by sample survey teams throughout China with unified sample selection and estimation procedures, in order to obtain high quality data on grain production and related statistics. Using data from the agriculture census as a sampling frame, a total of 130,000 sample plots are selected from some 20,000 villages in the country through a comprehensive multi-stage and multi-phase stratified systematic sampling program. Actual crop cutting and measuring is conducted on these plots to estimate the national production. The survey is characterized by a multi-purpose probability proportional to size sample design that keeps sampling error to ±2 percent with the confidence probability as 95 percent. A rotation scheme is used in the sample survey on farm crops with the cycle of a complete rotation being five years. Data on crop production, cotton production, crop planting acreage, and production of major animal husbandry products are collected from the *Sample Survey of Farm Crops*.

The *Rural Social and Economic Survey* is a special survey designed by the NBS to understand the basic condition of social and economic activities at township level, the size and transfer of total rural labor force, and investment in fixed assets in rural areas. Under this survey program, a complete survey is conducted every year to collect information on the basic condition of social and economic activities for all towns. A similar survey is conducted every three years at township and village levels, while sample surveys are used to collect information on other items with the same sampling units as in the *Rural Household Survey Program*.

Data on the fixed assets and sales of farm products of rural households are collected and compiled by the Department of Rural Socio-economic Surveys at the NBS through the *Rural Household Survey Program*. Please refer to Chapter 3 (People's livelihood) of the book for a description of the *Rural Household Survey Program*.

*Table 4.1* Rural laborers at the year-end (unit: 1,000 persons)

| Ethnic group | Farming, forestry, animal husbandry, and fishery | Industry | Construction |
| --- | --- | --- | --- |
| 1990 China | 333,364.00 | 32,287.00 | 15,228.00 |
| 2000 China | 327,974.98 | 41,086.37 | 26,916.69 |
| 2005 China | 299,755.38 | 60,114.68 | 36,532.07 |
| Achang | 13.47 | 0.49 | 0.51 |
| Bai | 715.26 | 32.61 | 29.51 |
| Baonan | 4.91 | 0.23 | 0.41 |
| Blang | 36.42 | 1.34 | 1.40 |
| Buyi | 1,055.53 | 73.93 | 44.18 |
| Dai | 459.95 | 16.68 | 17.55 |
| Daur | 28.05 | 1.75 | 1.88 |
| Deang | 7.14 | 0.25 | 0.27 |
| Derung | 2.71 | 0.14 | 0.13 |
| Dong | 984.72 | 89.98 | 56.69 |
| Dongxiang | 148.95 | 6.85 | 11.87 |
| Ewenki | 6.76 | 0.40 | 0.44 |
| Gaoshan | 1.16 | 0.20 | 0.13 |
| Gelao | 206.20 | 14.13 | 8.49 |

*Table 4.1* (cont.)

| Ethnic group | Farming, forestry, animal husbandry, and fishery | Industry | Construction |
|---|---|---|---|
| *Han* | *269,556.39* | *57,622.55* | *34,416.45* |
| Hani | 571.94 | 20.69 | 21.69 |
| Hezhe | 0.89 | 0.08 | 0.07 |
| Hui | 2,538.94 | 314.81 | 289.94 |
| Jing | 7.60 | 0.49 | 0.49 |
| Jingpo | 52.45 | 1.90 | 1.99 |
| Jino | 8.30 | 0.30 | 0.31 |
| Kazak | 233.51 | 7.80 | 6.40 |
| Kirgiz | 30.00 | 1.02 | 0.83 |
| Korean | 357.10 | 31.58 | 31.33 |
| Lahu | 180.13 | 6.59 | 6.88 |
| Lhoba | 0.95 | 0.04 | 0.06 |
| Li | 324.60 | 16.76 | 14.71 |
| Lisu | 249.98 | 9.50 | 9.99 |
| Manchu | 1,981.42 | 356.66 | 238.08 |
| Maonan | 36.93 | 2.33 | 2.13 |
| Miao | 2,992.08 | 256.20 | 176.68 |
| Monba | 2.86 | 0.11 | 0.19 |
| Mongol | 1,279.10 | 99.23 | 94.90 |
| Mulao | 70.31 | 4.62 | 4.39 |
| Naxi | 121.48 | 4.62 | 4.84 |
| Nu | 11.34 | 0.43 | 0.44 |
| Oroqen | 1.70 | 0.12 | 0.12 |
| Pumi | 13.30 | 0.49 | 0.51 |
| Qiang | 86.07 | 9.66 | 11.14 |
| Russian | 3.12 | 0.17 | 0.15 |
| Salar | 27.93 | 2.08 | 3.10 |
| She | 147.91 | 58.71 | 18.66 |
| Shui | 145.01 | 9.79 | 6.10 |
| Tajik | 7.74 | 0.31 | 0.24 |
| Tatar | 0.94 | 0.04 | 0.03 |
| Tibetan | 1,639.50 | 97.70 | 147.58 |
| Tu | 65.14 | 5.34 | 7.16 |
| Tujia | 2,164.04 | 266.95 | 204.43 |
| Uygur | 1,568.21 | 53.84 | 43.46 |
| Uzbek | 2.32 | 0.09 | 0.07 |
| Va | 156.25 | 6.04 | 6.20 |
| Xibe | 32.45 | 4.06 | 3.01 |

*Table 4.1* (*cont.*)

| Ethnic group | Farming, forestry, animal husbandry, and fishery | Industry | Construction |
|---|---|---|---|
| Yao | 855.20 | 78.40 | 59.95 |
| Yi | 2,799.01 | 156.81 | 162.54 |
| Yugur | 4.09 | 0.20 | 0.34 |
| Zhuang | 5,493.28 | 348.84 | 350.32 |

| Ethnic group | Transport, storage, post and communication services | Wholesale and retail trade and catering services | Other non-agricultural trades |
|---|---|---|---|
| *1990 China* | *6,353.00* | *6,932.00* | *25,931.00* |
| *2000 China* | *11,705.77* | *17,518.44* | *54,419.17* |
| *2005 China* | *15,673.18* | *29,376.87* | *62,420.44* |
| Achang | 0.32 | 0.44 | 1.16 |
| Bai | 17.81 | 26.59 | 84.29 |
| Baonan | 0.16 | 0.26 | 1.00 |
| Blang | 0.88 | 1.20 | 3.17 |
| Buyi | 24.04 | 49.54 | 365.57 |
| Dai | 11.05 | 15.07 | 40.01 |
| Daur | 0.90 | 2.21 | 2.63 |
| Deang | 0.17 | 0.23 | 0.61 |
| Derung | 0.07 | 0.11 | 0.27 |
| Dong | 28.38 | 58.28 | 296.75 |
| Dongxiang | 4.85 | 7.66 | 29.45 |
| Ewenki | 0.20 | 0.52 | 0.67 |
| Gaoshan | 0.06 | 0.11 | 0.22 |
| Gelao | 4.62 | 9.60 | 72.43 |
| *Han* | *14,650.37* | *27,525.94* | *56,271.71* |
| Hani | 13.74 | 18.67 | 49.36 |
| Hezhe | 0.04 | 0.08 | 0.09 |
| Hui | 129.36 | 212.80 | 334.46 |
| Jing | 0.22 | 0.40 | 2.31 |
| Jingpo | 1.26 | 1.72 | 4.56 |
| Jino | 0.20 | 0.27 | 0.72 |
| Kazak | 7.52 | 12.28 | 7.09 |
| Kirgiz | 0.97 | 1.59 | 0.91 |
| Korean | 15.61 | 29.82 | 42.99 |

*Table 4.1  (cont.)*

| Ethnic group | Transport, storage, post and communication services | Wholesale and retail trade and catering services | Other non-agricultural trades |
|---|---|---|---|
| Lahu | 4.34 | 5.91 | 15.55 |
| Lhoba | 0.03 | 0.03 | 0.11 |
| Li | 11.87 | 30.21 | 37.59 |
| Lisu | 6.07 | 8.44 | 22.54 |
| Manchu | 121.77 | 207.16 | 281.88 |
| Maonan | 1.00 | 1.87 | 11.96 |
| Miao | 84.28 | 168.53 | 824.68 |
| Monba | 0.10 | 0.10 | 0.32 |
| Mongol | 44.03 | 101.71 | 143.15 |
| Mulao | 2.00 | 3.70 | 22.23 |
| Naxi | 2.95 | 4.10 | 10.99 |
| Nu | 0.28 | 0.38 | 0.99 |
| Oroqen | 0.06 | 0.14 | 0.17 |
| Pumi | 0.32 | 0.44 | 1.16 |
| Qiang | 2.83 | 7.02 | 24.37 |
| Russian | 0.10 | 0.21 | 0.22 |
| Salar | 1.20 | 2.28 | 3.59 |
| She | 9.77 | 20.97 | 45.22 |
| Shui | 3.30 | 6.70 | 49.64 |
| Tajik | 0.25 | 0.42 | 0.30 |
| Tatar | 0.03 | 0.05 | 0.04 |
| Tibetan | 58.56 | 90.39 | 256.55 |
| Tu | 2.77 | 5.32 | 9.01 |
| Tujia | 80.09 | 165.41 | 628.26 |
| Uygur | 50.67 | 82.91 | 48.00 |
| Uzbek | 0.08 | 0.12 | 0.08 |
| Va | 3.83 | 5.28 | 13.76 |
| Xibe | 1.81 | 2.95 | 4.83 |
| Yao | 27.95 | 53.84 | 218.01 |
| Yi | 72.10 | 125.18 | 441.80 |
| Yugur | 0.13 | 0.21 | 0.85 |
| Zhuang | 159.93 | 287.38 | 1,598.47 |

*Notes:* The number of laborers by sector in this table is classified by main economic activity. For example, those engaged primarily in agriculture and secondarily in commerce are classified as the laborers under farming, forestry, animal husbandry, and fishery. The number of employed persons of industry includes those working in enterprises at village and lower levels.

*Table 4.2* Original value of productive fixed assets of rural households at the year-end (unit: yuan/household)

| Ethnic group | Total original value | Agriculture | Industry | Construction |
|---|---|---|---|---|
| 1990 China | 1,258.06 | 898.93 | 82.56 | |
| 2000 China | 4,676.98 | 3,321.66 | 334.79 | 29.02 |
| 2005 China | 7,155.55 | 5,179.46 | 537.48 | 62.03 |
| Achang | 6,609.98 | 5,760.34 | 15.63 | 1.16 |
| Bai | 6,164.61 | 5,327.16 | 43.58 | 4.91 |
| Baonan | 7,332.17 | 6,231.36 | 93.23 | 3.39 |
| Blang | 6,604.95 | 5,752.30 | 17.57 | 1.42 |
| Buyi | 4,327.01 | 3,607.38 | 127.21 | 19.69 |
| Dai | 6,595.87 | 5,752.40 | 13.07 | 1.06 |
| Daur | 12,200.75 | 11,634.66 | 53.43 | 50.63 |
| Deang | 6,611.25 | 5,774.49 | 9.21 | 0.69 |
| Derung | 6,737.88 | 5,768.21 | 62.49 | 11.60 |
| Dong | 4,157.63 | 3,361.06 | 177.97 | 18.96 |
| Dongxiang | 7,612.50 | 6,533.02 | 90.07 | 2.93 |
| Ewenki | 12,979.03 | 12,397.69 | 62.46 | 70.53 |
| Gaoshan | 6,742.41 | 4,971.30 | 428.88 | 61.50 |
| Gelao | 4,232.87 | 3,553.52 | 107.32 | 19.11 |
| Han | 6,678.59 | 4,628.25 | 574.70 | 67.07 |
| Hani | 6,606.54 | 5,760.50 | 14.50 | 1.07 |
| Hezhe | 10,147.42 | 9,506.15 | 91.45 | 21.04 |
| Hui | 9,374.54 | 6,999.14 | 383.80 | 53.07 |
| Jing | 4,598.77 | 3,731.44 | 178.90 | 3.93 |
| Jingpo | 6,599.75 | 5,754.93 | 13.27 | 1.15 |
| Jino | 6,600.44 | 5,761.73 | 10.83 | 0.99 |
| Kazak | 11,957.42 | 11,025.28 | 35.66 | 0.26 |
| Kirgiz | 11,953.12 | 11,024.50 | 36.67 | 0.43 |
| Korean | 10,418.74 | 9,079.30 | 401.49 | 75.91 |
| Lahu | 6,608.81 | 5,758.34 | 16.52 | 1.25 |
| Lhoba | 29,108.88 | 25,510.66 | 60.00 | 134.31 |
| Li | 7,318.00 | 5,563.99 | 69.15 | 18.19 |
| Lisu | 6,580.11 | 5,723.63 | 19.36 | 1.66 |
| Manchu | 8,792.03 | 6,948.79 | 353.68 | 46.86 |
| Maonan | 4,420.87 | 3,632.18 | 153.17 | 6.76 |
| Miao | 4,440.57 | 3,640.09 | 151.17 | 16.80 |
| Monba | 30,133.27 | 26,430.72 | 48.23 | 138.09 |
| Mongol | 11,974.80 | 11,113.70 | 119.18 | 64.51 |
| Mulao | 4,483.38 | 3,637.00 | 178.31 | 5.36 |

*Table 4.2* (*cont.*)

| Ethnic group | Total original value | Agriculture | Industry | Construction |
|---|---|---|---|---|
| Naxi | 6,671.41 | 5,801.96 | 21.82 | 2.52 |
| Nu | 6,973.94 | 6,059.82 | 29.24 | 3.99 |
| Oroqen | 11,564.48 | 10,964.88 | 67.73 | 43.41 |
| Pumi | 6,621.39 | 5,767.24 | 17.00 | 1.72 |
| Qiang | 5,136.90 | 4,185.25 | 78.39 | 18.37 |
| Russian | 12,084.21 | 11,157.25 | 81.22 | 37.88 |
| Salar | 9,259.55 | 7,661.96 | 113.01 | 3.61 |
| She | 7,431.27 | 4,133.15 | 1,384.60 | 72.50 |
| Shui | 4,331.04 | 3,628.67 | 113.17 | 19.02 |
| Tajik | 11,753.87 | 10,802.98 | 44.34 | 2.10 |
| Tatar | 11,595.81 | 10,605.11 | 55.58 | 6.53 |
| Tibetan | 17,981.80 | 15,586.73 | 67.75 | 69.13 |
| Tu | 8,897.72 | 7,295.65 | 136.82 | 5.47 |
| Tujia | 3,931.19 | 3,071.63 | 211.50 | 20.98 |
| Uygur | 11,944.49 | 11,009.00 | 37.37 | 0.57 |
| Uzbek | 11,852.82 | 10,900.54 | 43.39 | 2.16 |
| Va | 6,614.94 | 5,738.92 | 26.74 | 2.30 |
| Xibe | 8,615.75 | 7,159.41 | 101.97 | 20.66 |
| Yao | 4,404.82 | 3,518.51 | 179.59 | 9.77 |
| Yi | 5,938.56 | 5,083.57 | 41.66 | 7.85 |
| Yugur | 7,194.67 | 6,087.47 | 99.05 | 5.64 |
| Zhuang | 4,648.61 | 3,788.15 | 164.33 | 2.87 |

| Ethnic group | Transport, post and tele-communication services | Wholesale and retail trade and catering services | Social services | Education, culture, and health care | Others |
|---|---|---|---|---|---|
| *1990 China* | *215.82* | | | | *60.45* |
| *2000 China* | *621.04* | *149.24* | *60.16* | *12.86* | *144.30* |
| *2005 China* | *863.38* | *310.71* | *107.41* | *43.00* | *52.07* |
| Achang | 751.23 | 46.38 | 14.73 | 0.86 | 19.64 |
| Bai | 691.95 | 56.83 | 17.07 | 3.01 | 20.10 |
| Baonan | 740.19 | 126.74 | 33.13 | 44.18 | 59.96 |
| Blang | 751.78 | 46.21 | 14.78 | 1.13 | 19.76 |
| Buyi | 423.06 | 87.77 | 25.42 | 8.76 | 27.70 |
| Dai | 748.86 | 45.24 | 14.59 | 0.91 | 19.74 |
| Daur | 279.09 | 90.69 | 18.18 | 11.41 | 62.65 |

*Table 4.2* (*cont.*)

| Ethnic group | Transport, post and tele-communication services | Wholesale and retail trade and catering services | Social services | Education, culture, and health care | Others |
|---|---|---|---|---|---|
| Deang | 749.83 | 42.78 | 14.24 | 0.55 | 19.44 |
| Derung | 737.83 | 95.41 | 27.60 | 9.10 | 25.64 |
| Dong | 429.33 | 108.08 | 26.15 | 12.27 | 23.82 |
| Dongxiang | 714.53 | 125.87 | 34.80 | 45.29 | 65.98 |
| Ewenki | 257.39 | 91.98 | 20.27 | 9.65 | 69.06 |
| Gaoshan | 778.51 | 335.61 | 74.70 | 50.27 | 41.63 |
| Gelao | 407.88 | 84.83 | 24.91 | 8.26 | 27.03 |
| *Han* | *854.59* | *344.92* | *112.00* | *48.45* | *48.61* |
| Hani | 751.19 | 44.40 | 14.55 | 0.78 | 19.54 |
| Hezhe | 347.53 | 117.05 | 14.16 | 13.35 | 36.68 |
| Hui | 1,389.52 | 293.28 | 94.03 | 35.60 | 126.07 |
| Jing | 522.25 | 98.74 | 19.95 | 10.51 | 33.06 |
| Jingpo | 749.44 | 45.72 | 14.90 | 0.81 | 19.55 |
| Jino | 748.83 | 43.55 | 14.47 | 0.63 | 19.41 |
| Kazak | 546.37 | 109.52 | 53.77 | 45.00 | 141.56 |
| Kirgiz | 543.33 | 109.50 | 53.35 | 44.67 | 140.66 |
| Korean | 585.64 | 200.50 | 27.24 | 19.27 | 29.40 |
| Lahu | 751.64 | 45.51 | 14.82 | 1.06 | 19.67 |
| Lhoba | 3,181.79 | 118.41 | 56.83 | 4.77 | 42.12 |
| Li | 495.77 | 1,062.95 | 24.62 | 31.56 | 51.76 |
| Lisu | 745.43 | 51.49 | 15.17 | 2.14 | 21.24 |
| Manchu | 847.55 | 421.02 | 65.88 | 71.03 | 37.23 |
| Maonan | 480.47 | 87.20 | 20.31 | 9.29 | 31.49 |
| Miao | 460.10 | 110.37 | 24.04 | 13.71 | 24.29 |
| Monba | 3,301.67 | 111.54 | 58.17 | 3.23 | 41.62 |
| Mongol | 399.69 | 157.06 | 30.49 | 23.76 | 66.41 |
| Mulao | 501.91 | 97.21 | 20.72 | 10.49 | 32.38 |
| Naxi | 755.26 | 51.04 | 15.57 | 2.01 | 21.23 |
| Nu | 793.38 | 49.69 | 15.93 | 1.39 | 20.49 |
| Oroqen | 301.21 | 105.01 | 17.03 | 12.23 | 52.98 |
| Pumi | 752.11 | 47.01 | 15.11 | 1.22 | 19.98 |
| Qiang | 461.19 | 249.51 | 28.07 | 42.11 | 74.02 |
| Russian | 489.14 | 123.92 | 52.67 | 32.28 | 109.85 |
| Salar | 1,198.15 | 134.28 | 34.95 | 14.59 | 98.99 |
| She | 1,077.32 | 570.22 | 72.38 | 51.78 | 69.32 |
| Shui | 427.16 | 82.62 | 24.49 | 8.40 | 27.51 |

*Table 4.2* (*cont.*)

| Ethnic group | Transport, post and tele-communication services | Wholesale and retail trade and catering services | Social services | Education, culture, and health care | Others |
|---|---|---|---|---|---|
| Tajik | 550.99 | 115.98 | 54.56 | 44.82 | 138.10 |
| Tatar | 571.19 | 122.22 | 55.83 | 44.76 | 134.60 |
| Tibetan | 1,990.91 | 146.27 | 41.96 | 16.62 | 62.43 |
| Tu | 1,166.51 | 147.41 | 36.88 | 16.02 | 92.96 |
| Tujia | 438.75 | 122.64 | 24.92 | 20.60 | 20.17 |
| Uygur | 546.91 | 110.38 | 53.99 | 45.01 | 141.28 |
| Uzbek | 550.94 | 116.33 | 54.97 | 44.81 | 139.68 |
| Va | 754.19 | 53.72 | 16.31 | 2.16 | 20.59 |
| Xibe | 732.70 | 404.93 | 53.04 | 82.15 | 60.90 |
| Yao | 494.27 | 137.52 | 25.45 | 14.78 | 24.93 |
| Yi | 632.22 | 105.30 | 19.44 | 13.06 | 35.47 |
| Yugur | 732.54 | 130.89 | 36.09 | 44.94 | 58.04 |
| Zhuang | 528.54 | 102.33 | 20.05 | 10.53 | 31.82 |

*Note:* Data in this table are obtained from the sample surveys on rural households.

*Table 4.3* Number of major productive fixed assets per 100 rural households at the year-end

| Ethnic group | Motor vehicles (set) | Large and medium tractors (set) | Mini and walking tractors (set) | Motorized threshing machines (set) |
|---|---|---|---|---|
| 1990 China | 0.28 | 0.45 | 5.30 | 3.55 |
| 1995 China | 0.51 | 0.77 | 9.93 | 6.33 |
| 2000 China | 1.32 | 1.41 | 16.72 | 9.59 |
| 2005 China | 1.76 | 2.13 | 20.24 | 8.69 |
| Achang | 1.79 | 0.64 | 8.09 | 4.74 |
| Bai | 1.69 | 0.58 | 6.98 | 5.96 |
| Baonan | 0.93 | 2.36 | 33.65 | 2.81 |
| Blang | 1.79 | 0.64 | 8.11 | 4.77 |
| Buyi | 1.40 | 0.36 | 1.30 | 5.60 |
| Dai | 1.79 | 0.63 | 8.04 | 4.81 |
| Daur | 1.66 | 5.33 | 46.82 | 3.55 |
| Deang | 1.79 | 0.64 | 8.10 | 4.70 |
| Derung | 1.77 | 0.97 | 10.79 | 5.21 |
| Dong | 1.16 | 0.44 | 3.14 | 11.53 |
| Dongxiang | 0.88 | 2.54 | 32.62 | 2.68 |

*Table 4.3* (cont.)

| Ethnic group | Motor vehicles (set) | Large and medium tractors (set) | Mini and walking tractors (set) | Motorized threshing machines (set) |
|---|---|---|---|---|
| Ewenki | 1.70 | 3.62 | 47.30 | 3.81 |
| Gaoshan | 1.69 | 2.47 | 21.66 | 8.54 |
| Gelao | 1.38 | 0.33 | 1.00 | 5.54 |
| *Han* | *1.72* | *2.06* | *19.36* | *9.13* |
| Hani | 1.79 | 0.63 | 8.08 | 4.73 |
| Hezhe | 1.62 | 8.72 | 45.63 | 3.67 |
| Hui | 2.19 | 2.70 | 33.65 | 4.25 |
| Jing | 0.81 | 1.32 | 13.47 | 19.37 |
| Jingpo | 1.79 | 0.64 | 8.09 | 4.73 |
| Jino | 1.79 | 0.63 | 8.05 | 4.74 |
| Kazak | 1.49 | 4.31 | 27.61 | 1.69 |
| Kirgiz | 1.49 | 4.37 | 27.80 | 1.71 |
| Korean | 1.52 | 4.76 | 38.53 | 3.83 |
| Lahu | 1.79 | 0.65 | 8.17 | 4.74 |
| Lhoba | 5.26 | 6.59 | 30.07 | 5.17 |
| Li | 0.54 | 0.81 | 8.69 | 13.30 |
| Lisu | 1.78 | 0.63 | 8.00 | 5.16 |
| Manchu | 2.25 | 3.69 | 26.50 | 2.39 |
| Maonan | 0.94 | 1.06 | 10.20 | 15.90 |
| Miao | 1.22 | 0.42 | 3.25 | 10.26 |
| Monba | 5.42 | 6.79 | 30.78 | 5.23 |
| Mongol | 1.80 | 3.18 | 41.64 | 3.71 |
| Mulao | 0.86 | 1.21 | 12.12 | 18.12 |
| Naxi | 1.80 | 0.65 | 8.01 | 5.17 |
| Nu | 1.85 | 0.74 | 8.49 | 4.81 |
| Oroqen | 1.66 | 6.23 | 46.63 | 3.67 |
| Pumi | 1.79 | 0.65 | 8.21 | 4.80 |
| Qiang | 1.21 | 0.24 | 2.18 | 20.75 |
| Russian | 1.67 | 3.82 | 34.10 | 2.66 |
| Salar | 3.39 | 1.29 | 49.83 | 3.47 |
| She | 1.74 | 0.85 | 3.16 | 9.83 |
| Shui | 1.38 | 0.38 | 1.74 | 5.98 |
| Tajik | 1.49 | 4.23 | 27.27 | 2.00 |
| Tatar | 1.51 | 4.15 | 27.50 | 1.96 |
| Tibetan | 3.70 | 3.66 | 28.64 | 8.29 |
| Tu | 3.24 | 1.21 | 47.22 | 3.91 |
| Tujia | 0.95 | 0.43 | 4.81 | 11.18 |
| Uygur | 1.49 | 4.31 | 27.55 | 1.73 |

*Table 4.3 (cont.)*

| Ethnic group | Motor vehicles (set) | Large and medium tractors (set) | Mini and walking tractors (set) | Motorized threshing machines (set) |
|---|---|---|---|---|
| Uzbek | 1.49 | 4.26 | 27.32 | 1.89 |
| Va | 1.79 | 0.68 | 8.44 | 4.81 |
| Xibe | 1.88 | 3.70 | 19.65 | 1.92 |
| Yao | 0.88 | 0.92 | 9.69 | 18.70 |
| Yi | 1.58 | 0.50 | 5.70 | 9.26 |
| Yugur | 0.87 | 2.37 | 33.02 | 2.85 |
| Zhuang | 0.84 | 1.29 | 13.44 | 19.02 |

| Ethnic group | Carts with rubber tyres (set) | Pumps (unit) | Draught animals (unit) | Commodity animals (unit) |
|---|---|---|---|---|
| *1990 China* | *7.89* | *3.86* | *57.27* | *30.91* |
| *1995 China* | *9.29* | *9.07* | *55.99* | *50.72* |
| *2000 China* | *13.26* | *17.73* | *41.75* | *41.56* |
| *2005 China* | *9.85* | *21.03* | *29.33* | *60.28* |
| Achang | 4.63 | 7.13 | 65.42 | 61.22 |
| Bai | 4.22 | 8.11 | 62.17 | 56.08 |
| Baonan | 18.53 | 6.87 | 74.36 | 68.48 |
| Blang | 4.64 | 7.17 | 65.20 | 61.20 |
| Buyi | 1.27 | 4.66 | 67.08 | 34.51 |
| Dai | 4.60 | 7.16 | 65.30 | 61.21 |
| Daur | 21.09 | 26.78 | 48.46 | 201.54 |
| Deang | 4.64 | 7.01 | 65.66 | 61.72 |
| Derung | 6.11 | 10.12 | 58.95 | 66.42 |
| Dong | 2.51 | 11.97 | 50.22 | 31.57 |
| Dongxiang | 21.16 | 6.67 | 74.51 | 94.53 |
| Ewenki | 26.38 | 30.05 | 59.36 | 242.84 |
| Gaoshan | 9.19 | 21.66 | 27.97 | 49.73 |
| Gelao | 1.13 | 4.39 | 67.62 | 33.89 |
| *Han* | *9.20* | *22.62* | *23.49* | *43.12* |
| Hani | 4.63 | 7.10 | 65.44 | 61.23 |
| Hezhe | 5.75 | 21.94 | 21.72 | 69.37 |
| Hui | 12.42 | 15.42 | 41.77 | 88.92 |
| Jing | 4.35 | 15.21 | 53.38 | 39.09 |
| Jingpo | 4.64 | 7.11 | 65.43 | 61.22 |
| Jino | 4.60 | 7.05 | 65.49 | 61.29 |
| Kazak | 47.14 | 1.84 | 69.36 | 441.41 |

Table 4.3 (cont.)

| Ethnic group | Carts with rubber tyres (set) | Pumps (unit) | Draught animals (unit) | Commodity animals (unit) |
|---|---|---|---|---|
| Kirgiz | 46.78 | 2.06 | 68.85 | 438.44 |
| Korean | 17.21 | 22.29 | 41.61 | 69.47 |
| Lahu | 4.65 | 7.19 | 65.26 | 61.17 |
| Lhoba | 11.75 | 1.24 | 233.63 | 692.60 |
| Li | 1.46 | 23.34 | 59.14 | 48.97 |
| Lisu | 4.56 | 7.66 | 64.18 | 61.07 |
| Manchu | 14.74 | 27.50 | 30.00 | 75.41 |
| Maonan | 3.36 | 12.21 | 57.82 | 37.28 |
| Miao | 2.55 | 11.05 | 50.88 | 35.77 |
| Monba | 11.61 | 0.78 | 242.14 | 719.59 |
| Mongol | 25.19 | 28.73 | 55.88 | 216.26 |
| Mulao | 3.88 | 14.07 | 54.87 | 37.81 |
| Naxi | 4.55 | 7.54 | 64.96 | 63.79 |
| Nu | 4.79 | 7.14 | 67.65 | 71.05 |
| Oroqen | 16.05 | 26.30 | 40.06 | 155.58 |
| Pumi | 4.67 | 7.26 | 65.15 | 61.58 |
| Qiang | 1.18 | 24.99 | 24.19 | 52.30 |
| Russian | 37.46 | 13.07 | 63.47 | 347.10 |
| Salar | 6.77 | 1.29 | 55.77 | 117.05 |
| She | 5.43 | 14.40 | 16.34 | 27.70 |
| Shui | 1.43 | 4.85 | 67.02 | 34.99 |
| Tajik | 45.79 | 2.50 | 67.91 | 428.17 |
| Tatar | 44.49 | 2.73 | 67.76 | 411.86 |
| Tibetan | 8.01 | 6.91 | 137.83 | 379.29 |
| Tu | 6.05 | 2.34 | 54.61 | 102.88 |
| Tujia | 4.73 | 17.24 | 30.36 | 28.56 |
| Uygur | 47.04 | 1.93 | 69.15 | 440.59 |
| Uzbek | 46.39 | 2.15 | 68.66 | 434.27 |
| Va | 4.77 | 7.67 | 64.31 | 60.75 |
| Xibe | 22.59 | 25.99 | 39.48 | 139.44 |
| Yao | 4.11 | 17.28 | 43.48 | 35.46 |
| Yi | 3.29 | 11.78 | 54.25 | 55.75 |
| Yugur | 18.42 | 7.26 | 74.10 | 61.18 |
| Zhuang | 4.34 | 15.03 | 53.70 | 39.98 |

*Note:* Data in this table are obtained from the sample surveys on rural households.

*Table 4.4* Per capita output of major farm products (kg)

| Ethnic group | Grain | Cotton | Oil-bearing crops | Pork, beef, and mutton | Total aquatic products | Milk |
|---|---|---|---|---|---|---|
| *1990 China* | *393.10* | *4.00* | *14.20* | | *10.90* | *3.70* |
| *2000 China* | *366.10* | *3.50* | *23.40* | *38.30* | *33.90* | *6.60* |
| *2005 China* | *371.26* | *4.38* | *23.60* | *47.23* | *39.18* | *21.12* |
| Achang | 341.41 | 0.05 | 8.36 | 62.04 | 6.09 | 7.06 |
| Bai | 343.55 | 0.29 | 10.99 | 60.60 | 7.53 | 6.11 |
| Baonan | 322.54 | 7.17 | 20.99 | 31.22 | 0.85 | 15.81 |
| Blang | 341.87 | 0.06 | 8.45 | 62.01 | 6.01 | 7.04 |
| Buyi | 309.52 | 0.09 | 22.33 | 41.96 | 5.01 | 1.50 |
| Dai | 341.68 | 0.03 | 8.41 | 62.09 | 5.83 | 7.02 |
| Daur | 709.31 | 4.09 | 36.73 | 64.47 | 8.01 | 211.72 |
| Deang | 341.72 | 0.10 | 8.31 | 62.14 | 5.55 | 7.11 |
| Derung | 356.38 | 1.09 | 11.50 | 59.85 | 12.05 | 16.34 |
| Dong | 341.96 | 1.11 | 22.04 | 51.00 | 19.85 | 1.38 |
| Dongxiang | 336.11 | 13.93 | 19.65 | 32.81 | 1.08 | 19.61 |
| Ewenki | 688.37 | 0.41 | 46.32 | 75.57 | 6.70 | 260.86 |
| Gaoshan | 384.72 | 3.75 | 24.77 | 51.84 | 46.25 | 22.96 |
| Gelao | 308.40 | 0.04 | 22.49 | 41.60 | 4.44 | 1.18 |
| *Han* | *379.42* | *3.85* | *24.63* | *47.83* | *40.64* | *20.27* |
| Hani | 341.70 | 0.04 | 8.35 | 62.06 | 5.80 | 7.02 |
| Hezhe | 762.55 | 0.70 | 16.70 | 39.73 | 14.38 | 103.89 |
| Hui | 398.68 | 10.69 | 26.45 | 47.80 | 17.17 | 46.55 |
| Jing | 319.80 | 0.14 | 13.96 | 44.66 | 58.58 | 1.90 |
| Jingpo | 341.48 | 0.06 | 8.39 | 61.98 | 5.94 | 7.08 |
| Jino | 342.02 | 0.02 | 8.30 | 62.10 | 5.63 | 7.02 |
| Kazak | 437.29 | 93.21 | 19.46 | 59.98 | 3.99 | 75.78 |
| Kirgiz | 441.16 | 92.41 | 19.44 | 59.85 | 4.14 | 76.44 |
| Korean | 810.00 | 0.41 | 18.20 | 54.41 | 20.40 | 37.01 |
| Lahu | 342.13 | 0.07 | 8.47 | 62.08 | 5.86 | 7.04 |
| Lhoba | 339.59 | 1.17 | 22.07 | 74.90 | 3.24 | 71.54 |
| Li | 192.43 | 0.03 | 10.98 | 49.46 | 171.75 | 0.38 |
| Lisu | 343.34 | 0.07 | 8.96 | 62.28 | 6.01 | 7.19 |
| Manchu | 498.62 | 2.04 | 15.59 | 57.48 | 56.74 | 46.63 |
| Maonan | 315.00 | 0.03 | 16.29 | 43.46 | 44.18 | 1.31 |
| Miao | 344.64 | 0.95 | 20.52 | 52.30 | 16.77 | 2.34 |
| Monba | 336.17 | 0.17 | 22.07 | 76.02 | 1.38 | 74.04 |
| Mongol | 625.78 | 2.95 | 41.14 | 72.95 | 16.75 | 209.82 |
| Mulao | 314.78 | 0.06 | 14.84 | 43.80 | 53.29 | 1.43 |
| Naxi | 342.59 | 0.06 | 8.93 | 62.24 | 5.96 | 7.39 |

*Table 4.4* (cont.)

| Ethnic group | Grain | Cotton | Oil-bearing crops | Pork, beef, and mutton | Total aquatic products | Milk |
|---|---|---|---|---|---|---|
| Nu | 341.34 | 0.12 | 8.68 | 62.09 | 6.35 | 8.19 |
| Oroqen | 727.44 | 0.41 | 31.50 | 57.71 | 11.27 | 183.27 |
| Pumi | 342.49 | 0.08 | 8.55 | 62.01 | 6.00 | 7.25 |
| Qiang | 391.11 | 0.41 | 28.23 | 68.26 | 12.26 | 7.36 |
| Russian | 516.65 | 53.83 | 29.52 | 65.09 | 6.55 | 141.09 |
| Salar | 201.12 | 3.88 | 52.21 | 45.07 | 0.84 | 40.95 |
| She | 224.33 | 0.41 | 10.81 | 36.66 | 122.33 | 4.89 |
| Shui | 310.88 | 0.12 | 21.96 | 42.25 | 6.18 | 1.48 |
| Tajik | 435.43 | 90.19 | 19.53 | 59.58 | 5.18 | 73.96 |
| Tatar | 428.89 | 86.41 | 19.50 | 58.37 | 5.12 | 71.84 |
| Tibetan | 316.74 | 0.55 | 30.42 | 64.62 | 3.43 | 46.37 |
| Tu | 204.95 | 1.74 | 49.87 | 44.35 | 3.88 | 37.62 |
| Tujia | 383.47 | 3.04 | 28.76 | 56.47 | 29.56 | 2.22 |
| Uygur | 437.40 | 93.02 | 19.47 | 60.01 | 4.15 | 75.69 |
| Uzbek | 434.31 | 91.56 | 19.36 | 59.70 | 5.15 | 74.78 |
| Va | 343.53 | 0.18 | 8.94 | 61.92 | 6.74 | 7.32 |
| Xibe | 446.02 | 17.29 | 12.23 | 56.63 | 73.21 | 37.68 |
| Yao | 336.22 | 0.88 | 15.34 | 52.41 | 48.76 | 1.71 |
| Yi | 352.13 | 0.13 | 15.45 | 61.53 | 7.38 | 6.53 |
| Yugur | 325.81 | 6.13 | 19.82 | 30.44 | 1.21 | 14.95 |
| Zhuang | 315.51 | 0.06 | 13.13 | 45.24 | 57.78 | 1.78 |

*Notes:* "Grain" includes rice, wheat, corn, sorghum, millet, and other miscellaneous grains as well as tubers and beans. Output of beans refers to dry beans without pods. The output of tubers (sweet potatoes and potatoes, not including taros and cassava) was converted into that of grain at the ratio of 5:1. Tubers supplied as vegetables (such as potatoes) in cities and suburbs are calculated as fresh vegetables and their output is not included in the output of grain. Output of all other grains refers to husked grain. "Cotton" refers to the cotton production in the whole country including cotton sown in spring and in autumn. Output is measured as the weight of ginned cotton. Ceiba is not included. "Oil-bearing crops" refers to the total production of oil-bearing crops of various kinds, including peanuts (dry, in shell), rapeseed, sesame, sunflower seeds, flax seeds, and other oil-bearing crops. Soybeans, oil-bearing woody plants, and wild oil-bearing crops are not included. "Aquatic products" refers to catches of both artificially cultured and naturally grown aquatic products, including fish, shrimps, crabs, and shellfish in sea and inland water as well as seaweed. Freshwater plants are not included. "Pork, beef, and mutton" refers to the meat of slaughtered hogs, cattle, sheep, and goats, with head, feet, and offal taken away.

*Table 4.5* Output of major farm products per agricultural laborer (kg)

| Ethnic group | Grain | Cotton | Oil-bearing crops | Pork, beef, and mutton | Total aquatic products | Milk |
|---|---|---|---|---|---|---|
| 1990 China | 1,357.00 | 13.40 | 47.90 | | 36.70 | 12.60 |
| 2000 China | 1,407.00 | 13.40 | 89.90 | 147.30 | 130.20 | 25.20 |
| 2005 China | 1,598.18 | 18.87 | 101.60 | 203.32 | 168.65 | 90.91 |
| Achang | 902.78 | 0.21 | 22.46 | 163.73 | 17.71 | 19.03 |
| Bai | 942.18 | 1.09 | 31.55 | 165.52 | 23.86 | 17.56 |
| Baonan | 1,140.23 | 32.33 | 74.72 | 112.89 | 3.50 | 62.18 |
| Blang | 906.59 | 0.30 | 22.86 | 163.92 | 17.49 | 18.96 |
| Buyi | 918.83 | 0.46 | 66.09 | 124.72 | 20.57 | 5.63 |
| Dai | 903.75 | 0.16 | 22.60 | 164.01 | 16.55 | 18.96 |
| Daur | 3,493.52 | 23.93 | 172.21 | 311.45 | 43.58 | 1,003.63 |
| Deang | 901.06 | 0.53 | 22.10 | 163.68 | 15.00 | 19.27 |
| Derung | 1,104.29 | 5.82 | 38.68 | 178.18 | 52.87 | 68.29 |
| Dong | 1,080.68 | 4.06 | 70.36 | 161.86 | 72.64 | 5.78 |
| Dongxiang | 1,260.96 | 72.37 | 72.22 | 127.94 | 4.93 | 87.77 |
| Ewenki | 3,196.72 | 2.33 | 211.17 | 349.80 | 35.28 | 1,195.43 |
| Gaoshan | 1,617.51 | 16.16 | 95.07 | 225.93 | 233.43 | 131.98 |
| Gelao | 910.45 | 0.23 | 66.22 | 123.25 | 17.64 | 4.38 |
| *Han* | *1,717.57* | *18.01* | *106.84* | *217.11* | *216.34* | *113.79* |
| Hani | 903.41 | 0.19 | 22.39 | 163.69 | 16.52 | 18.87 |
| Hezhe | 4,140.46 | 3.90 | 89.11 | 222.69 | 81.30 | 577.80 |
| Hui | 1,721.72 | 58.38 | 107.73 | 218.36 | 90.78 | 241.59 |
| Jing | 1,011.03 | 0.79 | 44.50 | 141.12 | 188.01 | 8.03 |
| Jingpo | 903.42 | 0.29 | 22.49 | 163.70 | 17.04 | 19.27 |
| Jino | 904.90 | 0.09 | 22.15 | 163.94 | 15.69 | 19.12 |
| Kazak | 2,559.69 | 546.05 | 113.81 | 351.27 | 23.38 | 444.16 |
| Kirgiz | 2,580.06 | 541.43 | 113.71 | 350.44 | 24.22 | 447.28 |
| Korean | 4,428.57 | 2.38 | 98.26 | 305.10 | 121.70 | 211.37 |
| Lahu | 904.90 | 0.29 | 22.79 | 163.77 | 16.68 | 18.85 |
| Lhoba | 1,140.66 | 6.75 | 73.24 | 248.70 | 17.61 | 238.15 |
| Li | 809.24 | 0.13 | 45.85 | 210.31 | 739.03 | 1.95 |
| Lisu | 918.45 | 0.32 | 24.80 | 166.12 | 17.32 | 19.66 |
| Manchu | 2,761.17 | 9.56 | 80.28 | 326.66 | 343.77 | 258.85 |
| Maonan | 964.52 | 0.23 | 49.59 | 133.60 | 139.81 | 4.81 |
| Miao | 1,083.40 | 3.64 | 65.86 | 164.31 | 63.24 | 8.61 |
| Monba | 1,118.06 | 0.95 | 73.18 | 251.37 | 11.70 | 245.91 |
| Mongol | 2,950.59 | 16.49 | 187.32 | 345.55 | 96.86 | 963.35 |
| Mulao | 981.48 | 0.35 | 46.27 | 137.53 | 171.44 | 6.04 |
| Naxi | 917.09 | 0.31 | 24.66 | 166.53 | 17.49 | 21.06 |

Table 4.5 (cont.)

| Ethnic group | Grain | Cotton | Oil-bearing crops | Pork, beef, and mutton | Total aquatic products | Milk |
|---|---|---|---|---|---|---|
| Nu | 912.68 | 0.65 | 23.92 | 165.50 | 19.62 | 23.27 |
| Oroqen | 3,677.78 | 2.17 | 150.11 | 285.47 | 62.05 | 888.68 |
| Pumi | 912.94 | 0.42 | 23.34 | 164.52 | 17.58 | 20.26 |
| Qiang | 1,371.48 | 1.65 | 98.94 | 239.36 | 43.75 | 26.74 |
| Russian | 2,716.13 | 315.30 | 149.29 | 351.16 | 39.83 | 713.76 |
| Salar | 839.28 | 21.53 | 216.60 | 190.54 | 4.53 | 177.62 |
| She | 1,102.16 | 2.07 | 52.72 | 182.86 | 635.98 | 26.72 |
| Shui | 922.31 | 0.71 | 65.13 | 124.98 | 22.61 | 5.32 |
| Tajik | 2,529.56 | 528.31 | 113.00 | 346.57 | 29.12 | 433.46 |
| Tatar | 2,474.37 | 505.90 | 111.34 | 340.46 | 30.16 | 425.06 |
| Tibetan | 1,087.00 | 2.19 | 111.49 | 222.49 | 12.85 | 159.92 |
| Tu | 830.58 | 8.77 | 205.95 | 183.39 | 21.10 | 159.13 |
| Tujia | 1,463.78 | 13.81 | 120.47 | 212.15 | 132.71 | 10.83 |
| Uygur | 2,559.61 | 544.96 | 113.83 | 351.34 | 24.28 | 443.71 |
| Uzbek | 2,536.78 | 536.41 | 112.91 | 349.41 | 29.06 | 439.60 |
| Va | 920.23 | 0.77 | 24.89 | 164.97 | 20.80 | 20.44 |
| Xibe | 2,653.74 | 101.29 | 71.15 | 342.94 | 449.03 | 222.57 |
| Yao | 1,077.35 | 2.96 | 49.86 | 169.21 | 169.38 | 6.18 |
| Yi | 1,035.55 | 0.55 | 48.49 | 180.21 | 23.79 | 19.72 |
| Yugur | 1,144.53 | 25.90 | 69.31 | 109.89 | 5.35 | 60.47 |
| Zhuang | 982.10 | 0.40 | 41.35 | 141.38 | 187.25 | 6.38 |

Notes: "Grain" includes rice, wheat, corn, sorghum, millet, and other miscellaneous grains as well as tubers and beans. Output of beans refers to dry beans without pods. The output of tubers (sweet potatoes and potatoes, not including taros and cassava) was converted into that of grain at the ratio of 5:1. Tubers supplied as vegetables (such as potatoes) in cities and suburbs are calculated as fresh vegetables and their output is not included in the output of grain. Output of all other grains refers to husked grain. "Cotton" refers to the cotton production in the whole country including cotton sown in spring and in autumn. Output is measured as the weight of ginned cotton. Ceiba is not included. "Oil-bearing crops" refers to the total production of oil-bearing crops of various kinds, including peanuts (dry, in shell), rapeseed, sesame, sunflower seeds, flax seeds, and other oil-bearing crops. Soybeans, oil-bearing woody plants, and wild oil-bearing crops are not included. "Aquatic products" refers to catches of both artificially cultured and naturally grown aquatic products, including fish, shrimps, crabs, and shellfish in sea and inland water as well as seaweed. Freshwater plants are not included. "Pork, beef, and mutton" refers to the meat of slaughtered hogs, cattle, sheep, and goats, with head, feet, and offal taken away.

*Table 4.6* Per capita major farm products sold by rural households (kg)

| Ethnic group | Grain | Cotton | Oil-bearing crops | Fiber crops | Tobacco | Vegetables | Fruits |
|---|---|---|---|---|---|---|---|
| *1990 China* | *180.24* | *4.31* | *12.87* | *1.56* | *2.67* | *65.07* | *13.17* |
| 2000 China | 264.74 | 5.59 | 18.43 | 0.47 | 2.73 | 132.07 | 46.43 |
| 2005 China | 375.79 | 22.06 | 20.09 | 0.69 | 3.69 | 167.93 | 61.62 |
| Achang | 102.13 | 0.24 | 10.76 | 3.78 | 25.18 | 147.18 | 21.94 |
| Bai | 105.77 | 1.94 | 11.02 | 3.19 | 23.01 | 137.04 | 22.26 |
| Baonan | 199.76 | 40.55 | 9.92 | 0.31 | 0.11 | 131.06 | 57.13 |
| Blang | 102.54 | 0.30 | 10.77 | 3.77 | 25.10 | 146.75 | 21.88 |
| Buyi | 71.40 | 0.39 | 11.65 | 0.10 | 16.59 | 100.17 | 8.39 |
| Dai | 101.61 | 0.16 | 10.78 | 3.78 | 25.14 | 146.63 | 21.82 |
| Daur | 1,209.44 | 9.23 | 62.62 | 0.62 | 2.32 | 187.91 | 15.01 |
| Deang | 101.79 | 0.29 | 10.75 | 3.81 | 25.30 | 146.46 | 21.74 |
| Derung | 177.33 | 4.12 | 14.00 | 3.14 | 20.87 | 153.96 | 29.42 |
| Dong | 117.32 | 7.96 | 11.68 | 0.61 | 12.18 | 99.33 | 25.06 |
| Dongxiang | 226.04 | 53.69 | 8.90 | 0.91 | 0.10 | 143.10 | 66.94 |
| Ewenki | 940.49 | 1.36 | 88.15 | 0.42 | 1.09 | 162.52 | 10.45 |
| Gaoshan | 387.94 | 14.60 | 18.02 | 0.63 | 4.49 | 165.29 | 63.24 |
| Gelao | 67.82 | 0.18 | 11.60 | 0.04 | 16.63 | 98.71 | 7.47 |
| *Han* | *383.19* | *19.64* | *19.49* | *0.45* | *3.28* | *174.86* | *60.42* |
| Hani | 102.31 | 0.21 | 10.76 | 3.79 | 25.24 | 146.64 | 21.74 |
| Hezhe | 1,825.45 | 2.61 | 9.10 | 0.09 | 5.18 | 235.68 | 9.54 |
| Hui | 389.96 | 33.10 | 22.60 | 1.07 | 2.88 | 181.13 | 73.87 |
| Jing | 133.76 | 0.63 | 4.81 | 2.41 | 1.87 | 133.82 | 47.57 |
| Jingpo | 102.67 | 0.28 | 10.76 | 3.78 | 25.17 | 146.96 | 21.93 |
| Jino | 102.98 | 0.11 | 10.73 | 3.79 | 25.24 | 146.45 | 21.69 |
| Kazak | 496.21 | 196.74 | 21.51 | 8.20 | 0.01 | 243.12 | 162.54 |
| Kirgiz | 510.99 | 195.02 | 21.45 | 8.13 | 0.07 | 243.34 | 161.14 |
| Korean | 1,860.24 | 2.23 | 20.36 | 0.11 | 2.89 | 211.45 | 21.40 |
| Lahu | 102.78 | 0.31 | 10.80 | 3.78 | 25.16 | 146.74 | 21.88 |
| Lhoba | 91.75 | 2.97 | 3.53 | 0.11 | 0.71 | 19.02 | 7.14 |
| Li | 62.36 | 0.12 | 7.88 | 0.15 | 0.83 | 387.89 | 107.10 |
| Lisu | 102.43 | 0.37 | 11.00 | 3.70 | 24.57 | 147.02 | 22.26 |
| Manchu | 1,114.59 | 13.32 | 22.64 | 0.06 | 2.49 | 274.05 | 73.93 |
| Maonan | 109.52 | 0.24 | 6.27 | 1.78 | 5.55 | 123.19 | 36.60 |
| Miao | 110.83 | 6.54 | 11.96 | 0.89 | 13.73 | 107.31 | 24.17 |
| Monba | 76.26 | 0.57 | 3.01 | 0.03 | 0.15 | 12.00 | 4.32 |
| Mongol | 880.75 | 7.96 | 76.25 | 0.57 | 1.34 | 176.98 | 27.63 |
| Mulao | 119.78 | 0.39 | 5.16 | 2.13 | 3.08 | 130.79 | 43.46 |
| Naxi | 101.57 | 0.24 | 10.92 | 3.69 | 24.49 | 146.02 | 22.25 |
| Nu | 103.35 | 0.50 | 10.69 | 3.70 | 24.61 | 145.21 | 22.10 |

*Table 4.6* (*cont.*)

| Ethnic group | Grain | Cotton | Oil-bearing crops | Fiber crops | Tobacco | Vegetables | Fruits |
|---|---|---|---|---|---|---|---|
| Oroqen | 1,391.91 | 1.75 | 48.61 | 0.24 | 3.17 | 200.46 | 10.41 |
| Pumi | 105.49 | 0.35 | 10.88 | 3.76 | 24.99 | 146.78 | 21.99 |
| Qiang | 83.03 | 0.54 | 18.16 | 0.94 | 3.62 | 142.16 | 32.96 |
| Russian | 631.77 | 114.57 | 46.34 | 4.88 | 0.48 | 208.60 | 102.15 |
| Salar | 100.63 | 11.43 | 59.85 | 0.31 | 0.08 | 54.61 | 21.45 |
| She | 136.95 | 2.03 | 7.09 | 0.03 | 8.68 | 162.85 | 120.52 |
| Shui | 72.94 | 0.39 | 11.41 | 0.22 | 16.33 | 100.34 | 8.98 |
| Tajik | 491.40 | 190.72 | 21.33 | 7.95 | 0.12 | 240.61 | 158.87 |
| Tatar | 480.71 | 183.82 | 20.85 | 7.60 | 0.15 | 236.73 | 154.30 |
| Tibetan | 86.37 | 3.44 | 20.31 | 0.32 | 1.47 | 58.70 | 16.16 |
| Tu | 98.82 | 7.54 | 56.53 | 0.17 | 0.72 | 60.56 | 20.82 |
| Tujia | 196.06 | 23.13 | 27.76 | 0.64 | 8.01 | 106.61 | 42.37 |
| Uygur | 496.48 | 196.34 | 21.51 | 8.19 | 0.02 | 243.03 | 162.33 |
| Uzbek | 490.64 | 193.35 | 21.30 | 8.07 | 0.05 | 242.45 | 160.88 |
| Va | 107.26 | 0.94 | 10.99 | 3.71 | 24.69 | 148.40 | 22.68 |
| Xibe | 1,069.07 | 36.93 | 24.29 | 1.53 | 2.61 | 292.24 | 101.57 |
| Yao | 137.85 | 6.18 | 6.21 | 2.02 | 5.10 | 129.07 | 45.43 |
| Yi | 94.20 | 0.28 | 12.92 | 2.58 | 18.28 | 139.93 | 23.26 |
| Yugur | 203.31 | 39.12 | 8.12 | 0.21 | 0.14 | 133.48 | 57.64 |
| Zhuang | 125.11 | 0.32 | 4.55 | 2.54 | 2.61 | 138.83 | 47.29 |

*Note:* Data in this table are obtained from the sample surveys on rural households (kg).

*Table 4.7* Sales of livestock, poultry, small animals, and fishery per capita rural household

| Ethnic group | Pork | Mutton | Beef | Poultry | Poultry eggs | Aquatic products |
|---|---|---|---|---|---|---|
| *1990 China* | *17.84* | *0.71* | *0.55* | *1.45* | *1.89* | *2.05* |
| *2000 China* | *30.19* | *2.06* | *2.40* | *4.60* | *6.32* | *5.82* |
| *2005 China* | *32.19* | *3.26* | *2.87* | *9.62* | *10.52* | *8.54* |
| Achang | 34.17 | 0.76 | 1.31 | 3.58 | 6.52 | 0.95 |
| Bai | 34.52 | 0.70 | 1.21 | 3.66 | 5.60 | 1.51 |
| Baonan | 5.29 | 5.07 | 4.42 | 0.70 | 1.75 | 0.17 |
| Blang | 34.22 | 0.76 | 1.31 | 3.60 | 6.54 | 0.92 |
| Buyi | 29.69 | 0.56 | 1.04 | 2.76 | 0.96 | 0.61 |
| Dai | 34.35 | 0.75 | 1.31 | 3.58 | 6.49 | 0.88 |
| Daur | 31.94 | 29.88 | 10.33 | 5.96 | 6.26 | 0.81 |
| Deang | 34.13 | 0.78 | 1.32 | 3.48 | 6.51 | 0.80 |
| Derung | 33.94 | 2.24 | 1.94 | 4.92 | 7.68 | 2.10 |

*Table 4.7* (cont.)

| Ethnic group | Pork | Mutton | Beef | Poultry | Poultry eggs | Aquatic products |
|---|---|---|---|---|---|---|
| Dong | 36.17 | 0.40 | 0.77 | 4.40 | 1.23 | 4.51 |
| Dongxiang | 5.01 | 5.85 | 4.76 | 0.81 | 2.40 | 0.15 |
| Ewenki | 23.95 | 41.92 | 12.60 | 3.90 | 5.21 | 0.86 |
| Gaoshan | 36.55 | 2.93 | 3.05 | 8.98 | 11.98 | 8.41 |
| Gelao | 29.54 | 0.53 | 1.02 | 2.68 | 0.74 | 0.54 |
| *Han* | *34.11* | *2.11* | *2.45* | *11.89* | *11.77* | *9.70* |
| Hani | 34.17 | 0.75 | 1.31 | 3.55 | 6.53 | 0.85 |
| Hezhe | 52.74 | 2.80 | 4.85 | 11.79 | 8.32 | 2.05 |
| Hui | 21.88 | 6.75 | 5.71 | 7.46 | 9.82 | 4.93 |
| Jing | 47.81 | 0.24 | 1.07 | 6.49 | 0.61 | 6.22 |
| Jingpo | 34.15 | 0.76 | 1.32 | 3.60 | 6.51 | 0.89 |
| Jino | 34.25 | 0.75 | 1.31 | 3.53 | 6.49 | 0.83 |
| Kazak | 1.69 | 19.80 | 10.57 | 1.94 | 9.84 | 0.01 |
| Kirgiz | 2.23 | 19.69 | 10.52 | 2.05 | 9.84 | 0.04 |
| Korean | 46.15 | 2.52 | 7.57 | 14.21 | 13.11 | 2.64 |
| Lahu | 34.20 | 0.76 | 1.32 | 3.58 | 6.55 | 0.87 |
| Lhoba | 3.55 | 2.90 | 7.48 | 0.73 | 0.90 | 0.58 |
| Li | 32.92 | 0.64 | 2.19 | 4.61 | 0.15 | 68.60 |
| Lisu | 35.13 | 0.77 | 1.31 | 3.78 | 6.50 | 0.98 |
| Manchu | 47.19 | 4.96 | 6.59 | 19.11 | 33.20 | 6.61 |
| Maonan | 43.32 | 0.29 | 1.05 | 5.48 | 0.36 | 4.38 |
| Miao | 36.28 | 0.47 | 0.86 | 4.28 | 1.94 | 4.46 |
| Monba | 2.46 | 2.86 | 7.65 | 0.45 | 0.44 | 0.41 |
| Mongol | 26.79 | 34.68 | 11.52 | 6.43 | 10.67 | 1.98 |
| Mulao | 46.14 | 0.23 | 1.04 | 6.55 | 0.36 | 5.57 |
| Naxi | 34.99 | 0.77 | 1.33 | 3.74 | 6.41 | 1.00 |
| Nu | 33.70 | 0.81 | 1.41 | 3.62 | 6.49 | 0.94 |
| Oroqen | 38.67 | 22.36 | 8.74 | 7.91 | 7.12 | 1.31 |
| Pumi | 34.27 | 0.78 | 1.33 | 3.62 | 6.56 | 0.92 |
| Qiang | 68.36 | 0.83 | 0.95 | 10.94 | 2.48 | 6.03 |
| Russian | 11.14 | 27.19 | 10.92 | 3.21 | 8.77 | 0.86 |
| Salar | 4.17 | 14.61 | 8.27 | 0.43 | 0.77 | 1.08 |
| She | 33.62 | 0.34 | 0.45 | 8.62 | 2.52 | 11.91 |
| Shui | 30.20 | 0.55 | 1.04 | 2.69 | 1.06 | 0.66 |
| Tajik | 2.87 | 19.21 | 10.29 | 2.23 | 9.81 | 0.35 |
| Tatar | 3.13 | 18.59 | 10.03 | 2.34 | 9.72 | 0.50 |
| Tibetan | 18.83 | 5.09 | 5.96 | 2.89 | 1.05 | 1.75 |
| Tu | 6.14 | 13.40 | 7.66 | 1.37 | 0.84 | 1.85 |
| Tujia | 38.55 | 0.33 | 0.52 | 5.30 | 4.23 | 12.44 |

*Table 4.7* (*cont.*)

| Ethnic group | Pork | Mutton | Beef | Poultry | Poultry eggs | Aquatic products |
|---|---|---|---|---|---|---|
| Uygur | 1.84 | 19.76 | 10.54 | 1.99 | 9.86 | 0.06 |
| Uzbek | 2.32 | 19.48 | 10.40 | 2.17 | 9.78 | 0.38 |
| Va | 34.32 | 0.79 | 1.37 | 3.87 | 6.66 | 1.01 |
| Xibe | 48.90 | 6.88 | 7.95 | 21.34 | 35.14 | 8.52 |
| Yao | 45.40 | 0.22 | 0.79 | 8.30 | 0.97 | 8.00 |
| Yi | 43.16 | 0.76 | 1.18 | 5.47 | 4.78 | 2.23 |
| Yugur | 5.78 | 4.58 | 4.19 | 0.84 | 1.85 | 0.26 |
| Zhuang | 47.57 | 0.22 | 1.06 | 7.25 | 0.68 | 6.39 |

*Notes:* (1) Data in this table are obtained from the sample surveys on rural households. (2) Sales of poultry eggs before 1992 excluded egg products, and sales of aquatic products only referred to the sales of fish and shrimp.

# 5    Education and science and technology

The data on education cover the situations on postgraduates, higher education (universities and colleges), secondary education (senior and junior high schools), elementary education (primary schools), preschool education, special education (schools for the blind, profoundly deaf, and disabled), and expenditure on education. The main indicators cover the number of schools, the number of students enrolled, the number of new students enrolled, the number of graduates, the number of staff and workers, the number of full-time teachers, sources and outlay of education funds, and education expenditure from the state budget.

The Ministry of Education mainly provides statistical data on education and education funds. Detailed information can be found in the *Statistical Yearbook on China Educational Undertakings* compiled by the Department of Planning and Development, Ministry of Education; and the *Communiqué on the Implementation of National Education Funds* compiled jointly by the Ministry of Education, the National Bureau of Statistics, and the Ministry of Finance.

Data on patents are provided by the State Intellectual Property Office.

*Table 5.1* Number of students enrolled in undergraduate or specialized courses in institutions of higher education (unit: persons)

| Ethnic group | Graduates | Degrees awarded | Entrants |
|---|---|---|---|
| National total | 3,067,956.00 | 1,309,692.00 | 5,044,581.00 |
| Achang | 38.72 | 17.44 | 68.49 |
| Bai | 2,307.20 | 1,009.28 | 4,040.58 |
| Baonan | 32.65 | 13.30 | 46.99 |
| Blang | 105.30 | 47.42 | 186.22 |
| Buyi | 3,405.38 | 1,436.63 | 6,012.83 |
| Dai | 1,323.62 | 597.40 | 2,341.64 |
| Daur | 286.76 | 136.29 | 481.82 |

Table 5.1 (cont.)

| Ethnic group | Graduates | Degrees awarded | Entrants |
|---|---|---|---|
| Deang | 20.37 | 9.19 | 36.02 |
| Derung | 10.31 | 4.57 | 17.73 |
| Dong | 4,740.60 | 1,831.80 | 8,158.13 |
| Dongxiang | 1,019.95 | 413.86 | 1,473.54 |
| Ewenki | 57.35 | 24.55 | 100.09 |
| Gaoshan | 10.45 | 4.42 | 17.27 |
| Gelao | 655.46 | 276.82 | 1,160.45 |
| *Han* | *2,869,215.85* | *1,225,916.59* | *4,716,410.73* |
| Hani | 1,642.45 | 740.45 | 2,903.14 |
| Hezhe | 13.38 | 7.42 | 21.27 |
| Hui | 22,223.08 | 10,085.32 | 34,517.47 |
| Jing | 34.00 | 10.84 | 61.22 |
| Jingpo | 150.88 | 67.98 | 266.77 |
| Jino | 23.86 | 10.78 | 42.17 |
| Kazak | 2,499.85 | 905.61 | 3,780.79 |
| Kirgiz | 322.72 | 117.70 | 488.68 |
| Korean | 6,044.59 | 3,337.99 | 9,258.91 |
| Lahu | 518.43 | 233.38 | 916.66 |
| Lhoba | 3.88 | 1.24 | 8.82 |
| Li | 1,932.90 | 608.75 | 3,979.66 |
| Lisu | 735.58 | 332.99 | 1,303.78 |
| Manchu | 34,604.98 | 17,127.87 | 49,633.80 |
| Maonan | 148.40 | 49.79 | 265.88 |
| Miao | 13,876.80 | 5,608.72 | 24,162.87 |
| Monba | 11.68 | 3.72 | 26.71 |
| Mongol | 12,086.21 | 5,279.73 | 19,984.73 |
| Mulao | 303.15 | 97.99 | 543.29 |
| Naxi | 359.47 | 162.92 | 636.95 |
| Nu | 33.23 | 14.86 | 59.00 |
| Oroqen | 19.46 | 9.81 | 32.17 |
| Pumi | 38.72 | 17.47 | 68.38 |
| Qiang | 520.29 | 263.69 | 994.65 |
| Russian | 32.49 | 13.04 | 51.31 |
| Salar | 186.27 | 67.20 | 266.18 |
| She | 1,536.21 | 589.21 | 2,999.12 |
| Shui | 467.13 | 195.32 | 825.35 |
| Tajik | 82.56 | 30.09 | 125.42 |
| Tatar | 10.07 | 3.76 | 15.20 |
| Tibetan | 8,143.17 | 3,109.01 | 15,585.06 |

*Table 5.1* (*cont.*)

| Ethnic group | Graduates | Degrees awarded | Entrants |
|---|---|---|---|
| Tu | 428.34 | 155.04 | 622.07 |
| Tujia | 18,369.30 | 7,864.22 | 31,481.43 |
| Uygur | 16,816.76 | 6,096.01 | 25,448.57 |
| Uzbek | 24.90 | 9.07 | 37.74 |
| Va | 462.32 | 207.66 | 817.45 |
| Xibe | 596.11 | 297.23 | 847.64 |
| Yao | 4,559.76 | 1,544.02 | 8,012.72 |
| Yi | 10,051.56 | 4,708.74 | 18,292.38 |
| Yugur | 27.63 | 11.43 | 39.75 |
| Zhuang | 23,957.62 | 7,605.69 | 43,139.53 |

| Ethnic group | Enrollment | Anticipated graduates for next year |
|---|---|---|
| *National total* | *15,617,767.00* | *3,881,031.00* |
| Achang | 206.47 | 52.20 |
| Bai | 12,193.60 | 3,100.79 |
| Baonan | 150.05 | 37.69 |
| Blang | 561.45 | 141.85 |
| Buyi | 18,147.27 | 4,708.69 |
| Dai | 7,058.83 | 1,783.61 |
| Daur | 1,581.11 | 393.38 |
| Deang | 108.60 | 27.47 |
| Derung | 54.04 | 13.58 |
| Dong | 24,563.54 | 6,376.12 |
| Dongxiang | 4,731.10 | 1,185.07 |
| Ewenki | 326.10 | 81.89 |
| Gaoshan | 53.30 | 13.28 |
| Gelao | 3,498.77 | 908.82 |
| *Han* | *14,607,460.65* | *3,626,625.72* |
| Hani | 8,754.74 | 2,213.64 |
| Hezhe | 70.29 | 17.30 |
| Hui | 109,057.14 | 27,062.52 |
| Jing | 178.53 | 46.23 |
| Jingpo | 804.32 | 203.40 |
| Jino | 127.17 | 32.16 |
| Kazak | 12,328.93 | 3,016.89 |
| Kirgiz | 1,593.98 | 390.03 |
| Korean | 29,635.54 | 7,460.68 |
| Lahu | 2,763.75 | 698.50 |

*Table 5.1* (*cont.*)

| Ethnic group | Enrollment | Anticipated graduates for next year |
|---|---|---|
| Lhoba | 22.65 | 4.75 |
| Li | 11,407.50 | 2,951.84 |
| Lisu | 3,925.13 | 988.18 |
| Manchu | 160,849.02 | 40,529.40 |
| Maonan | 778.55 | 202.66 |
| Miao | 72,778.87 | 18,687.49 |
| Monba | 68.20 | 14.18 |
| Mongol | 64,686.43 | 16,232.70 |
| Mulao | 1,584.79 | 411.98 |
| Naxi | 1,917.84 | 482.61 |
| Nu | 177.38 | 44.68 |
| Oroqen | 105.70 | 26.21 |
| Pumi | 206.24 | 52.10 |
| Qiang | 2,890.70 | 653.17 |
| Russian | 167.17 | 41.49 |
| Salar | 769.25 | 197.47 |
| She | 8,888.49 | 2,153.66 |
| Shui | 2,487.52 | 645.54 |
| Tajik | 407.94 | 99.88 |
| Tatar | 49.47 | 12.14 |
| Tibetan | 42,627.31 | 9,610.80 |
| Tu | 1,800.33 | 461.07 |
| Tujia | 96,942.24 | 25,318.52 |
| Uygur | 82,964.02 | 20,302.44 |
| Uzbek | 122.90 | 30.09 |
| Va | 2,463.30 | 621.22 |
| Xibe | 2,772.22 | 672.92 |
| Yao | 23,575.04 | 6,066.93 |
| Yi | 54,402.61 | 13,246.38 |
| Yugur | 127.43 | 32.02 |
| Zhuang | 125,380.37 | 32,499.77 |

*Notes:* "Institutions of higher learning" refers to educational establishments set up according to the government evaluation and approval procedures, enrolling graduates from senior secondary schools and providing higher education courses and training for senior professionals. They include full-time universities, colleges, high professional schools, high professional vocational schools, and others. Universities and colleges are mainly providing undergraduate courses; those high professional schools and high professional vocational schools are mainly providing professional training; and "others" refers to educational establishments that are responsible for enrolling students but not covered in the total number of schools, including: branch schools of universities and colleges, and universities and colleges that have been approved and prepared for construction.

*Table 5.2* Conditions on students in secondary vocational schools (institutions) (unit: person)

| Ethnic group | Graduates | New enrollment | Total enrollment | Graduates for next year |
|---|---|---|---|---|
| *National* | *3,491,921.00* | *5,372,922.00* | *13,247,421.00* | *3,919,519.00* |
| Achang | 72.81 | 91.68 | 237.87 | 70.79 |
| Bai | 3,931.20 | 5,368.35 | 13,374.92 | 3,889.29 |
| Baonan | 34.95 | 51.96 | 126.01 | 35.46 |
| Blang | 197.62 | 248.90 | 645.88 | 192.30 |
| Buyi | 3,940.55 | 8,575.02 | 17,677.13 | 4,465.59 |
| Dai | 2,485.94 | 3,134.72 | 8,127.44 | 2,418.38 |
| Daur | 296.91 | 462.10 | 1,077.58 | 311.94 |
| Deang | 38.40 | 48.29 | 125.28 | 37.29 |
| Derung | 16.75 | 21.99 | 56.40 | 16.78 |
| Dong | 5,682.77 | 10,654.08 | 23,186.21 | 6,174.20 |
| Dongxiang | 1,081.73 | 1,613.35 | 3,916.43 | 1,099.46 |
| Ewenki | 71.90 | 110.10 | 260.91 | 77.50 |
| Gaoshan | 12.77 | 19.24 | 47.66 | 14.28 |
| Gelao | 748.83 | 1,658.78 | 3,393.34 | 850.82 |
| *Han* | *3,263,409.33* | *5,013,190.17* | *12,392,293.97* | *3,670,576.76* |
| Hani | 3,088.76 | 3,887.08 | 10,087.86 | 3,002.13 |
| Hezhe | 9.79 | 15.43 | 35.24 | 9.63 |
| Hui | 25,579.25 | 39,878.09 | 94,038.92 | 28,180.11 |
| Jing | 50.05 | 76.25 | 188.86 | 56.36 |
| Jingpo | 283.23 | 356.83 | 925.33 | 275.39 |
| Jino | 44.80 | 56.35 | 146.22 | 43.53 |
| Kazak | 1,939.25 | 3,479.23 | 7,865.68 | 2,246.26 |
| Kirgiz | 250.23 | 448.43 | 1,013.68 | 289.33 |
| Korean | 4,194.67 | 5,893.49 | 14,818.35 | 4,657.63 |
| Lahu | 975.77 | 1,228.24 | 3,187.00 | 949.11 |
| Lhoba | 3.66 | 3.98 | 9.74 | 3.31 |
| Li | 2,075.40 | 3,993.51 | 9,574.99 | 2,440.45 |
| Lisu | 1,367.52 | 1,744.09 | 4,500.88 | 1,338.74 |
| Manchu | 29,890.02 | 42,621.18 | 107,962.10 | 32,626.64 |
| Maonan | 208.84 | 343.95 | 815.59 | 235.28 |
| Miao | 17,732.44 | 31,084.64 | 69,477.73 | 18,945.81 |
| Monba | 10.76 | 11.02 | 27.46 | 9.52 |
| Mongol | 14,113.98 | 21,317.88 | 51,333.12 | 15,423.82 |
| Mulao | 437.88 | 684.88 | 1,669.89 | 491.98 |
| Naxi | 664.14 | 845.98 | 2,183.90 | 649.62 |
| Nu | 61.58 | 77.64 | 201.30 | 59.99 |

Table 5.2 (cont.)

| Ethnic group | Graduates | New enrollment | Total enrollment | Graduates for next year |
|---|---|---|---|---|
| Oroqen | 18.37 | 28.58 | 66.47 | 18.99 |
| Pumi | 72.19 | 91.18 | 236.35 | 70.32 |
| Qiang | 715.27 | 1,279.96 | 2,908.31 | 843.27 |
| Russian | 30.51 | 49.72 | 116.62 | 34.09 |
| Salar | 142.38 | 294.09 | 580.49 | 182.65 |
| She | 2,410.33 | 3,659.55 | 9,324.87 | 2,833.18 |
| Shui | 547.35 | 1,174.74 | 2,440.11 | 619.36 |
| Tajik | 65.34 | 116.05 | 263.67 | 75.47 |
| Tatar | 7.96 | 13.94 | 31.90 | 9.12 |
| Tibetan | 8,409.49 | 12,953.07 | 29,131.32 | 9,055.65 |
| Tu | 347.68 | 695.04 | 1,402.72 | 436.96 |
| Tujia | 20,059.65 | 34,144.51 | 77,988.51 | 21,560.64 |
| Uygur | 13,067.95 | 23,425.44 | 52,986.76 | 15,136.11 |
| Uzbek | 19.46 | 34.71 | 78.75 | 22.51 |
| Va | 861.57 | 1,086.23 | 2,818.47 | 841.72 |
| Xibe | 491.56 | 683.31 | 1,775.62 | 538.59 |
| Yao | 6,346.38 | 9,870.49 | 23,661.36 | 6,839.71 |
| Yi | 16,328.07 | 24,295.12 | 58,770.67 | 17,096.01 |
| Yugur | 29.76 | 43.72 | 106.88 | 30.02 |
| Zhuang | 36,000.52 | 53,590.66 | 133,839.90 | 40,036.60 |

Table 5.3 Number of teachers and staff in secondary vocational schools (institutions) (unit: person)

| Ethnic group | Teachers and staff | Teachers and staff in headquarters | Employees in school-run enterprises | Personnel in other subsidiary units | Engaged from other schools |
|---|---|---|---|---|---|
| National total | 889,171.00 | 867,655.00 | 10,868.00 | 10,648.00 | 82,306.00 |
| Achang | 18.99 | 18.81 | 0.05 | 0.13 | 2.09 |
| Bai | 1,013.75 | 1,002.05 | 3.69 | 8.02 | 110.59 |
| Baonan | 11.43 | 11.26 | 0.10 | 0.07 | 0.78 |
| Blang | 51.48 | 50.99 | 0.13 | 0.36 | 5.65 |
| Buyi | 1,117.43 | 1,095.85 | 6.17 | 15.41 | 144.99 |
| Dai | 648.41 | 642.27 | 1.60 | 4.53 | 71.24 |
| Daur | 99.23 | 97.25 | 0.72 | 1.26 | 4.75 |
| Deang | 10.02 | 9.93 | 0.02 | 0.07 | 1.10 |
| Derung | 4.40 | 4.34 | 0.02 | 0.03 | 0.46 |

*Table 5.3  (cont.)*

| Ethnic group | Teachers and staff | Teachers and staff in headquarters | Employees in school-run enterprises | Personnel in other subsidiary units | Engaged from other schools |
|---|---|---|---|---|---|
| Dong | 1,440.56 | 1,403.09 | 13.34 | 24.14 | 157.19 |
| Dongxiang | 360.78 | 355.67 | 3.01 | 2.10 | 25.18 |
| Ewenki | 23.87 | 23.47 | 0.18 | 0.21 | 1.10 |
| Gaoshan | 3.23 | 3.14 | 0.04 | 0.05 | 0.31 |
| Gelao | 213.74 | 209.58 | 1.16 | 3.00 | 28.02 |
| *Han* | *821,739.40* | *801,789.86* | *10,285.98* | *9,663.56* | *76,149.96* |
| Hani | 805.55 | 797.97 | 1.98 | 5.60 | 88.57 |
| Hezhe | 3.20 | 3.10 | 0.02 | 0.07 | 0.16 |
| Hui | 6,702.68 | 6,565.79 | 76.39 | 60.50 | 583.04 |
| Jing | 14.94 | 14.25 | 0.12 | 0.56 | 1.67 |
| Jingpo | 73.92 | 73.22 | 0.18 | 0.52 | 8.12 |
| Jino | 11.69 | 11.59 | 0.03 | 0.08 | 1.29 |
| Kazak | 915.83 | 905.50 | 7.79 | 2.54 | 70.39 |
| Kirgiz | 117.71 | 116.36 | 1.00 | 0.35 | 9.02 |
| Korean | 1,685.32 | 1,652.78 | 15.41 | 17.13 | 78.71 |
| Lahu | 254.14 | 251.72 | 0.64 | 1.77 | 27.90 |
| Lhoba | 1.42 | 1.42 | 0.00 | 0.00 | 0.05 |
| Li | 676.82 | 647.29 | 2.39 | 27.14 | 73.49 |
| Lisu | 356.36 | 352.90 | 0.94 | 2.51 | 38.77 |
| Manchu | 9,316.45 | 9,105.14 | 107.01 | 104.30 | 720.60 |
| Maonan | 62.52 | 59.87 | 0.47 | 2.17 | 7.24 |
| Miao | 4,417.36 | 4,318.28 | 36.74 | 62.35 | 487.37 |
| Monba | 4.28 | 4.27 | 0.00 | 0.00 | 0.15 |
| Mongol | 4,620.23 | 4,540.53 | 40.76 | 38.94 | 252.46 |
| Mulao | 131.15 | 125.29 | 1.02 | 4.83 | 14.87 |
| Naxi | 173.21 | 171.54 | 0.45 | 1.22 | 18.85 |
| Nu | 16.12 | 15.96 | 0.04 | 0.11 | 1.75 |
| Oroqen | 6.02 | 5.89 | 0.04 | 0.09 | 0.29 |
| Pumi | 18.84 | 18.66 | 0.05 | 0.13 | 2.06 |
| Qiang | 179.04 | 176.04 | 1.19 | 1.81 | 14.24 |
| Russian | 11.92 | 11.75 | 0.10 | 0.07 | 0.80 |
| Salar | 52.75 | 51.22 | 0.93 | 0.59 | 2.81 |
| She | 510.06 | 500.80 | 6.36 | 2.89 | 66.86 |
| Shui | 156.48 | 153.24 | 0.86 | 2.37 | 20.21 |
| Tajik | 30.00 | 29.65 | 0.26 | 0.10 | 2.32 |
| Tatar | 3.59 | 3.55 | 0.03 | 0.01 | 0.28 |
| Tibetan | 2,798.77 | 2,763.48 | 18.51 | 16.77 | 148.41 |

*Table 5.3 (cont.)*

| Ethnic group | Teachers and staff | Teachers and staff in headquarters | Employees in school-run enterprises | Personnel in other subsidiary units | Engaged from other schools |
|---|---|---|---|---|---|
| Tu | 122.78 | 119.33 | 2.09 | 1.37 | 7.04 |
| Tujia | 4,662.25 | 4,541.70 | 58.65 | 61.91 | 493.64 |
| Uygur | 6,152.96 | 6,083.24 | 52.47 | 17.25 | 473.41 |
| Uzbek | 9.06 | 8.96 | 0.08 | 0.03 | 0.70 |
| Va | 223.79 | 221.55 | 0.65 | 1.59 | 24.32 |
| Xibe | 158.10 | 155.04 | 1.63 | 1.44 | 13.75 |
| Yao | 1,694.47 | 1,631.73 | 15.05 | 47.69 | 175.58 |
| Yi | 4,234.57 | 4,182.21 | 16.63 | 35.74 | 433.89 |
| Yugur | 9.63 | 9.48 | 0.08 | 0.06 | 0.67 |
| Zhuang | 10,747.99 | 10,269.96 | 81.30 | 396.74 | 1,201.49 |

*Table 5.4* Student–teacher ratio by level of regular schools (unit: %)

| Ethnic group | Primary school | Junior secondary school | Regular senior secondary school |
|---|---|---|---|
| *National total* | *19.43* | *17.80* | *18.54* |
| Achang | 20.12 | 18.80 | 16.26 |
| Bai | 20.50 | 18.80 | 16.79 |
| Baonan | 22.74 | 19.41 | 19.13 |
| Blang | 20.13 | 18.79 | 16.27 |
| Buyi | 25.51 | 20.96 | 19.21 |
| Dai | 20.14 | 18.80 | 16.27 |
| Daur | 13.67 | 15.38 | 18.56 |
| Deang | 20.12 | 18.80 | 16.24 |
| Derung | 19.83 | 18.50 | 16.76 |
| Dong | 22.66 | 19.23 | 19.30 |
| Dongxiang | 22.37 | 19.20 | 18.97 |
| Ewenki | 13.67 | 15.34 | 19.32 |
| Gaoshan | 19.11 | 18.04 | 19.20 |
| Gelao | 25.66 | 21.04 | 19.26 |
| *Han* | *19.37* | *17.83* | *18.74* |
| Hani | 20.12 | 18.80 | 16.25 |
| Hezhe | 13.82 | 15.61 | 17.33 |
| Hui | 18.98 | 17.73 | 18.28 |
| Jing | 22.09 | 19.90 | 19.64 |

*Table 5.4* (*cont.*)

| Ethnic group | Primary school | Junior secondary school | Regular senior secondary school |
|---|---|---|---|
| Jingpo | 20.14 | 18.80 | 16.27 |
| Jino | 20.12 | 18.80 | 16.25 |
| Kazak | 15.93 | 15.59 | 15.43 |
| Kirgiz | 15.89 | 15.59 | 15.44 |
| Korean | 13.07 | 15.31 | 19.27 |
| Lahu | 20.12 | 18.79 | 16.27 |
| Lhoba | 22.67 | 19.26 | 17.42 |
| Li | 21.12 | 22.03 | 17.99 |
| Lisu | 20.19 | 18.78 | 16.34 |
| Manchu | 15.31 | 15.37 | 19.05 |
| Maonan | 23.20 | 20.29 | 19.64 |
| Miao | 22.55 | 19.23 | 18.88 |
| Monba | 22.76 | 19.27 | 17.38 |
| Mongol | 14.40 | 15.49 | 19.32 |
| Mulao | 22.64 | 20.09 | 19.68 |
| Naxi | 20.21 | 18.79 | 16.34 |
| Nu | 20.15 | 18.79 | 16.28 |
| Oroqen | 13.70 | 15.45 | 18.34 |
| Pumi | 20.12 | 18.79 | 16.28 |
| Qiang | 23.23 | 18.61 | 19.10 |
| Russian | 15.17 | 15.52 | 17.02 |
| Salar | 18.89 | 17.11 | 15.81 |
| She | 18.95 | 17.57 | 16.60 |
| Shui | 25.36 | 20.93 | 19.19 |
| Tajik | 16.06 | 15.67 | 15.54 |
| Tatar | 16.25 | 15.78 | 15.66 |
| Tibetan | 22.03 | 18.68 | 17.51 |
| Tu | 19.28 | 17.35 | 16.04 |
| Tujia | 20.62 | 17.99 | 19.31 |
| Uygur | 15.92 | 15.59 | 15.44 |
| Uzbek | 16.00 | 15.64 | 15.48 |
| Va | 20.10 | 18.75 | 16.32 |
| Xibe | 16.00 | 15.01 | 18.57 |
| Yao | 20.98 | 18.74 | 19.22 |
| Yi | 21.59 | 18.99 | 17.38 |
| Yugur | 22.86 | 19.48 | 19.27 |
| Zhuang | 22.09 | 19.90 | 19.48 |

*Table 5.4* (*cont.*)

| Ethnic group | Vocational senior secondary school | Regular specialized secondary school | Regular institution of higher education |
|---|---|---|---|
| *National total* | *20.62* | *31.02* | *16.85* |
| Achang | 16.76 | 24.87 | 16.08 |
| Bai | 17.41 | 27.58 | 16.13 |
| Baonan | 13.70 | 19.25 | 17.17 |
| Blang | 16.79 | 24.93 | 16.09 |
| Buyi | 19.13 | 31.86 | 15.91 |
| Dai | 16.79 | 24.87 | 16.09 |
| Daur | 14.18 | 27.19 | 15.65 |
| Deang | 16.74 | 24.81 | 16.07 |
| Derung | 17.04 | 26.14 | 16.16 |
| Dong | 20.34 | 37.31 | 16.34 |
| Dongxiang | 13.38 | 19.45 | 17.09 |
| Ewenki | 14.75 | 26.61 | 15.36 |
| Gaoshan | 17.98 | 33.93 | 16.75 |
| Gelao | 19.14 | 31.91 | 15.90 |
| *Han* | *20.15* | *33.85* | *16.92* |
| Hani | 16.77 | 24.86 | 16.08 |
| Hezhe | 13.58 | 29.61 | 16.48 |
| Hui | 18.63 | 32.00 | 15.69 |
| Jing | 21.31 | 25.49 | 16.93 |
| Jingpo | 16.76 | 24.86 | 16.08 |
| Jino | 16.76 | 24.83 | 16.08 |
| Kazak | 11.54 | 17.40 | 14.70 |
| Kirgiz | 11.56 | 17.54 | 14.71 |
| Korean | 14.74 | 24.67 | 16.46 |
| Lahu | 16.79 | 24.91 | 16.09 |
| Lhoba | 1.57 | 11.28 | 14.32 |
| Li | 11.18 | 40.85 | 15.84 |
| Lisu | 16.90 | 25.03 | 16.15 |
| Manchu | 15.89 | 27.20 | 16.59 |
| Maonan | 20.83 | 26.69 | 16.67 |
| Miao | 19.80 | 35.94 | 16.38 |
| Monba | 0.90 | 10.27 | 14.27 |
| Mongol | 15.26 | 26.33 | 15.54 |
| Mulao | 21.18 | 25.65 | 16.85 |
| Naxi | 16.83 | 24.97 | 16.14 |
| Nu | 16.56 | 24.73 | 16.06 |

*Table 5.4* (cont.)

| Ethnic group | Vocational senior secondary school | Regular specialized secondary school | Regular institution of higher education |
|---|---|---|---|
| Oroqen | 14.14 | 28.20 | 15.92 |
| Pumi | 16.79 | 24.90 | 16.09 |
| Qiang | 21.35 | 31.24 | 18.56 |
| Russian | 13.15 | 21.50 | 15.06 |
| Salar | 18.70 | 13.32 | 14.01 |
| She | 11.02 | 32.55 | 16.66 |
| Shui | 19.17 | 31.58 | 15.94 |
| Tajik | 11.83 | 17.99 | 14.77 |
| Tatar | 11.89 | 18.07 | 14.88 |
| Tibetan | 10.69 | 16.41 | 15.38 |
| Tu | 18.76 | 14.46 | 14.25 |
| Tujia | 21.70 | 40.19 | 17.00 |
| Uygur | 11.57 | 17.48 | 14.70 |
| Uzbek | 11.66 | 17.69 | 14.74 |
| Va | 16.85 | 25.09 | 16.10 |
| Xibe | 14.29 | 24.21 | 16.23 |
| Yao | 21.11 | 32.43 | 16.89 |
| Yi | 18.30 | 27.41 | 16.75 |
| Yugur | 13.65 | 19.73 | 17.30 |
| Zhuang | 21.11 | 24.56 | 16.94 |

*Notes:* Number of teachers is set as 1. Of the student–teacher ratio of regular institutions of higher education, full-time teachers include those from other schools.

*Table 5.5* Basic statistics on educational funds (unit: 1,000 yuan)

| Ethnic group | Total | Government appropriation for education | Of which, budgetary for education |
|---|---|---|---|
| *1995 China* | *187,795,011.0* | *141,152,333.0* | *102,839,300.0* |
| *2000 China* | *384,908,058.0* | *256,260,557.0* | *208,567,920.0* |
| *2004 China* | *724,259,892.0* | *446,585,748.0* | *402,781,580.0* |
| Achang | 14,101.2 | 11,160.1 | 10,545.9 |
| Bai | 765,458.8 | 583,223.6 | 549,120.1 |
| Baonan | 7,032.4 | 5,001.6 | 4,533.1 |
| Blang | 38,215.7 | 30,204.7 | 28,540.2 |
| Buyi | 1,011,941.0 | 716,143.2 | 659,370.1 |
| Dai | 481,458.0 | 380,846.4 | 359,944.1 |

*Table 5.5* (cont.)

| Ethnic group | Total | Government appropriation for education | Of which, budgetary for education |
|---|---|---|---|
| Daur | 72,555.0 | 51,563.5 | 45,488.1 |
| Deang | 7,436.9 | 5,898.3 | 5,576.4 |
| Derung | 3,291.1 | 2,484.2 | 2,324.0 |
| Dong | 1,134,554.7 | 715,172.6 | 657,864.3 |
| Dongxiang | 229,213.8 | 161,504.8 | 144,991.5 |
| Ewenki | 15,632.3 | 11,604.6 | 10,485.6 |
| Gaoshan | 2,536.7 | 1,617.1 | 1,474.3 |
| Gelao | 195,099.2 | 138,191.6 | 127,346.5 |
| *Han* | *671,820,957.9* | *410,452,642.3* | *369,758,611.4* |
| Hani | 598,266.8 | 473,627.2 | 447,622.8 |
| Hezhe | 2,943.1 | 1,912.1 | 1,621.1 |
| Hui | 5,690,597.0 | 3,937,762.2 | 3,600,450.8 |
| Jing | 8,599.3 | 5,665.4 | 5,264.0 |
| Jingpo | 54,908.4 | 43,453.0 | 41,067.5 |
| Jino | 8,690.6 | 6,881.2 | 6,504.2 |
| Kazak | 901,764.7 | 626,315.5 | 537,596.9 |
| Kirgiz | 115,847.6 | 80,411.4 | 69,001.0 |
| Korean | 1,155,464.1 | 767,631.2 | 680,623.3 |
| Lahu | 188,280.4 | 148,991.9 | 140,808.8 |
| Lhoba | 2,578.9 | 2,398.8 | 2,378.0 |
| Li | 635,605.9 | 406,247.3 | 340,649.0 |
| Lisu | 262,761.9 | 206,715.7 | 195,265.4 |
| Manchu | 6,803,111.8 | 4,494,127.0 | 4,032,469.7 |
| Maonan | 38,896.7 | 26,146.1 | 24,263.1 |
| Miao | 3,499,912.5 | 2,272,226.4 | 2,094,391.5 |
| Monba | 8,033.6 | 7,488.2 | 7,427.9 |
| Mongol | 3,053,578.2 | 2,224,160.3 | 2,016,310.9 |
| Mulao | 78,626.7 | 52,009.1 | 48,275.9 |
| Naxi | 129,391.6 | 101,825.8 | 96,207.6 |
| Nu | 12,216.6 | 9,691.6 | 9,168.9 |
| Oroqen | 4,639.0 | 3,206.4 | 2,801.7 |
| Pumi | 14,008.1 | 11,065.1 | 10,454.7 |
| Qiang | 116,145.8 | 68,873.7 | 63,454.1 |
| Russian | 10,526.1 | 7,406.0 | 6,505.5 |
| Salar | 50,469.1 | 41,242.5 | 39,490.9 |
| She | 508,452.0 | 305,278.3 | 271,121.9 |
| Shui | 137,921.6 | 97,825.7 | 90,218.8 |
| Tajik | 29,357.8 | 20,329.1 | 17,470.1 |

*Table 5.5 (cont.)*

| Ethnic group | Total | Government appropriation for education | Of which, budgetary for education |
|---|---|---|---|
| Tatar | 3,526.7 | 2,441.0 | 2,104.5 |
| Tibetan | 3,440,903.6 | 2,977,947.9 | 2,916,145.0 |
| Tu | 115,376.0 | 92,866.8 | 88,841.2 |
| Tujia | 3,658,619.7 | 2,045,785.4 | 1,867,079.9 |
| Uygur | 6,059,629.7 | 4,206,466.7 | 3,610,953.3 |
| Uzbek | 8,950.2 | 6,203.7 | 5,331.1 |
| Va | 165,132.5 | 129,933.2 | 122,679.3 |
| Xibe | 127,029.5 | 84,455.4 | 74,859.7 |
| Yao | 1,121,954.3 | 697,260.0 | 646,936.4 |
| Yi | 3,075,019.8 | 2,249,234.0 | 2,109,549.7 |
| Yugur | 5,921.2 | 4,171.9 | 3,776.2 |
| Zhuang | 6,309,298.5 | 4,194,058.9 | 3,905,135.5 |

| Ethnic group | Funds of social organizations and citizens for running schools | Donations and fund-raising for running schools | Tuition and miscellaneous fees | Other educational funds |
|---|---|---|---|---|
| *1995 China* | *2,036,715.0* | *16,284,140.0* | *20,124,225.0* | *8,197,598.0* |
| *2000 China* | *8,585,372.0* | *11,395,569.0* | *59,483,043.0* | *49,183,517.0* |
| *2004 China* | *34,785,288.0* | *9,342,038.0* | *134,655,173.0* | *98,891,645.0* |
| Achang | 349.8 | 116.2 | 1,389.1 | 1,086.0 |
| Bai | 22,131.0 | 6,272.3 | 88,044.1 | 65,787.7 |
| Baonan | 139.2 | 44.8 | 1,167.8 | 679.0 |
| Blang | 949.6 | 318.2 | 3,777.7 | 2,965.5 |
| Buyi | 33,561.1 | 5,891.5 | 150,634.5 | 105,710.6 |
| Dai | 11,912.0 | 3,952.7 | 47,472.0 | 37,275.0 |
| Daur | 1,365.8 | 241.7 | 11,608.8 | 7,775.4 |
| Deang | 182.0 | 60.4 | 726.5 | 569.7 |
| Derung | 94.7 | 29.1 | 390.3 | 292.8 |
| Dong | 52,264.6 | 8,609.2 | 218,467.5 | 140,040.8 |
| Dongxiang | 4,576.7 | 1,375.7 | 36,769.5 | 24,987.1 |
| Ewenki | 247.2 | 54.3 | 2,364.3 | 1,361.8 |
| Gaoshan | 113.5 | 27.9 | 450.4 | 327.8 |
| Gelao | 6,403.2 | 1,072.7 | 29,171.5 | 20,260.3 |
| *Han* | *33,295,949.0* | *8,970,781.6* | *126,628,052.9* | *92,473,532.2* |
| Hani | 14,813.5 | 4,924.2 | 58,808.1 | 46,093.8 |

*Table 5.5 (cont.)*

| Ethnic group | Funds of social organizations and citizens for running schools | Donations and fund-raising for running schools | Tuition and miscellaneous fees | Other educational funds |
|---|---|---|---|---|
| Hezhe | 75.7 | 15.3 | 538.6 | 401.4 |
| Hui | 134,343.0 | 41,044.8 | 868,020.9 | 709,426.1 |
| Jing | 205.6 | 48.1 | 1,655.2 | 1,025.0 |
| Jingpo | 1,362.7 | 448.7 | 5,419.9 | 4,224.2 |
| Jino | 214.0 | 71.5 | 853.3 | 670.6 |
| Kazak | 15,861.6 | 2,133.7 | 90,627.2 | 166,826.7 |
| Kirgiz | 2,049.7 | 275.1 | 11,721.2 | 21,390.1 |
| Korean | 24,724.2 | 20,020.3 | 192,692.8 | 150,395.6 |
| Lahu | 4,667.3 | 1,550.0 | 18,558.5 | 14,512.7 |
| Lhoba | 7.0 | 7.9 | 93.0 | 72.2 |
| Li | 29,299.5 | 16,673.7 | 115,094.3 | 68,291.1 |
| Lisu | 6,527.6 | 2,171.5 | 26,428.7 | 20,918.4 |
| Manchu | 235,170.1 | 43,364.0 | 1,222,605.0 | 807,845.7 |
| Maonan | 958.9 | 196.1 | 7,136.4 | 4,459.1 |
| Miao | 144,912.2 | 33,894.8 | 616,686.8 | 432,192.3 |
| Monba | 21.5 | 24.8 | 280.0 | 219.1 |
| Mongol | 61,002.7 | 13,028.6 | 468,139.0 | 287,247.7 |
| Mulao | 1,963.0 | 429.6 | 14,980.0 | 9,245.0 |
| Naxi | 3,201.0 | 1,071.0 | 12,941.5 | 10,352.4 |
| Nu | 299.9 | 100.0 | 1,190.6 | 934.5 |
| Oroqen | 100.4 | 18.7 | 789.7 | 523.8 |
| Pumi | 347.1 | 115.7 | 1,389.0 | 1,091.3 |
| Qiang | 3,591.1 | 1,203.2 | 21,311.2 | 21,166.5 |
| Russian | 192.0 | 40.3 | 1,254.7 | 1,633.1 |
| Salar | 398.9 | 125.5 | 5,524.2 | 3,178.0 |
| She | 44,272.0 | 9,109.2 | 85,371.1 | 64,421.3 |
| Shui | 4,377.1 | 785.5 | 20,544.4 | 14,388.9 |
| Tajik | 536.8 | 77.8 | 3,019.3 | 5,394.8 |
| Tatar | 64.2 | 10.6 | 370.0 | 640.9 |
| Tibetan | 24,157.2 | 13,256.0 | 243,525.2 | 182,017.4 |
| Tu | 1,422.3 | 383.6 | 13,512.9 | 7,190.4 |
| Tujia | 181,616.9 | 48,068.2 | 801,232.4 | 581,916.8 |
| Uygur | 107,350.6 | 14,536.7 | 610,552.1 | 1,120,723.6 |
| Uzbek | 162.1 | 23.3 | 912.8 | 1,648.3 |
| Va | 4,172.2 | 1,379.3 | 16,690.1 | 12,957.7 |
| Xibe | 4,870.8 | 373.2 | 20,964.0 | 16,366.1 |

*Table 5.5* (*cont.*)

| Ethnic group | Funds of social organizations and citizens for running schools | Donations and fund-raising for running schools | Tuition and miscellaneous fees | Other educational funds |
|---|---|---|---|---|
| Yao | 47,912.3 | 8,722.8 | 231,940.0 | 136,119.2 |
| Yi | 83,172.0 | 26,141.6 | 386,334.9 | 330,137.3 |
| Yugur | 120.7 | 40.4 | 1,001.7 | 586.5 |
| Zhuang | 156,622.7 | 35,956.8 | 1,197,796.2 | 724,863.8 |

*Notes:* "Government appropriation for education" refers to the state budgetary fund for education, taxes and fees collected by governments at all levels that are used for education purposes, education fund for enterprise-run schools, income from school-run enterprises, work-study programs, and social services that are used for education purposes. "Budgetary fund for education" refers to an education fund that is planned to be allocated to various schools and education institutions by central and local financial departments at various levels within the reference year, which is within the state budgetary expenditure, including: appropriate funds for education, science and research, capital construction, and others.

*Table 5.6* Patent applications examined and granted (unit: item)

| Ethnic group | Number of patent applications examined | Inventions | Utility models | Designs |
|---|---|---|---|---|
| National total | 383,157 | 93,485 | 138,085 | 151,587 |
| Achang | 2 | 1 | 1 | 1 |
| Bai | 137 | 41 | 51 | 45 |
| Baonan | 1 | 0 | 1 | 0 |
| Blang | 6 | 2 | 2 | 2 |
| Buyi | 236 | 74 | 103 | 59 |
| Dai | 74 | 22 | 26 | 26 |
| Daur | 16 | 4 | 8 | 4 |
| Deang | 1 | 0 | 0 | 0 |
| Derung | 1 | 0 | 0 | 0 |
| Dong | 330 | 93 | 135 | 101 |
| Dongxiang | 38 | 14 | 18 | 6 |
| Ewenki | 3 | 1 | 1 | 1 |
| Gaoshan | 1 | 0 | 0 | 0 |
| Gelao | 45 | 14 | 20 | 11 |
| Han | 345,862 | 80,431 | 121,588 | 143,844 |
| Hani | 92 | 27 | 32 | 32 |
| Hezhe | 1 | 0 | 0 | 0 |
| Hui | 1,816 | 577 | 724 | 515 |

*Table 5.6 (cont.)*

| Ethnic group | Number of patent applications examined | Inventions | Utility models | Designs |
|---|---|---|---|---|
| Jing | 2 | 0 | 1 | 0 |
| Jingpo | 8 | 3 | 3 | 3 |
| Jino | 1 | 0 | 0 | 0 |
| Kazak | 126 | 22 | 76 | 28 |
| Kirgiz | 16 | 3 | 10 | 4 |
| Korean | 416 | 123 | 195 | 98 |
| Lahu | 29 | 9 | 10 | 10 |
| Lhoba | 0 | 0 | 0 | 0 |
| Li | 90 | 31 | 31 | 29 |
| Lisu | 41 | 12 | 15 | 15 |
| Manchu | 3,142 | 828 | 1,535 | 778 |
| Maonan | 7 | 2 | 3 | 2 |
| Miao | 990 | 267 | 400 | 324 |
| Monba | 1 | 0 | 0 | 0 |
| Mongol | 740 | 183 | 350 | 207 |
| Mulao | 17 | 4 | 7 | 5 |
| Naxi | 21 | 6 | 7 | 7 |
| Nu | 2 | 1 | 1 | 1 |
| Oroqen | 1 | 0 | 1 | 0 |
| Pumi | 2 | 1 | 1 | 1 |
| Qiang | 40 | 9 | 14 | 18 |
| Russian | 2 | 1 | 1 | 1 |
| Salar | 6 | 3 | 2 | 1 |
| She | 302 | 47 | 94 | 161 |
| Shui | 30 | 10 | 13 | 7 |
| Tajik | 4 | 1 | 3 | 1 |
| Tatar | 1 | 0 | 0 | 0 |
| Tibetan | 369 | 91 | 117 | 161 |
| Tu | 19 | 7 | 7 | 5 |
| Tujia | 1,394 | 304 | 553 | 537 |
| Uygur | 857 | 151 | 512 | 194 |
| Uzbek | 1 | 0 | 1 | 0 |
| Va | 27 | 8 | 10 | 9 |
| Xibe | 60 | 13 | 31 | 16 |
| Yao | 372 | 88 | 135 | 149 |
| Yi | 643 | 171 | 230 | 242 |
| Yugur | 1 | 0 | 0 | 0 |
| Zhuang | 1,392 | 335 | 559 | 498 |

*Table 5.6* (cont.)

| Ethnic group | Number of patent applications granted | Inventions | Utility models | Designs |
|---|---|---|---|---|
| National total | 171,619 | 20,705 | 78,137 | 72,777 |
| Achang | 1 | 0 | 0 | 0 |
| Bai | 69 | 14 | 30 | 25 |
| Baonan | 0 | 0 | 0 | 0 |
| Blang | 3 | 1 | 1 | 1 |
| Buyi | 101 | 15 | 52 | 33 |
| Dai | 39 | 9 | 16 | 15 |
| Daur | 8 | 1 | 5 | 2 |
| Deang | 1 | 0 | 0 | 0 |
| Derung | 0 | 0 | 0 | 0 |
| Dong | 143 | 19 | 73 | 50 |
| Dongxiang | 13 | 2 | 8 | 3 |
| Ewenki | 2 | 0 | 1 | 1 |
| Gaoshan | 0 | 0 | 0 | 0 |
| Gelao | 19 | 3 | 10 | 6 |
| *Han* | *151,815* | *17,319* | *66,582* | *67,914* |
| Hani | 49 | 11 | 20 | 18 |
| Hezhe | 0 | 0 | 0 | 0 |
| Hui | 746 | 145 | 389 | 211 |
| Jing | 1 | 0 | 0 | 0 |
| Jingpo | 5 | 1 | 2 | 2 |
| Jino | 1 | 0 | 0 | 0 |
| Kazak | 63 | 6 | 36 | 20 |
| Kirgiz | 8 | 1 | 5 | 3 |
| Korean | 188 | 34 | 116 | 38 |
| Lahu | 15 | 3 | 6 | 6 |
| Lhoba | 0 | 0 | 0 | 0 |
| Li | 37 | 6 | 14 | 17 |
| Lisu | 22 | 5 | 9 | 8 |
| Manchu | 1,326 | 234 | 839 | 254 |
| Maonan | 4 | 0 | 2 | 1 |
| Miao | 447 | 59 | 219 | 169 |
| Monba | 0 | 0 | 0 | 0 |
| Mongol | 352 | 52 | 201 | 99 |
| Mulao | 8 | 1 | 4 | 3 |
| Naxi | 11 | 2 | 4 | 4 |
| Nu | 1 | 0 | 0 | 0 |
| Oroqen | 1 | 0 | 0 | 0 |

*Table 5.6* (*cont.*)

| Ethnic group | Number of patent applications granted | Inventions | Utility models | Designs |
| --- | --- | --- | --- | --- |
| Pumi | 1 | 0 | 0 | 0 |
| Qiang | 17 | 2 | 7 | 8 |
| Russian | 1 | 0 | 1 | 0 |
| Salar | 2 | 1 | 1 | 1 |
| She | 145 | 8 | 51 | 86 |
| Shui | 13 | 2 | 7 | 4 |
| Tajik | 2 | 0 | 1 | 1 |
| Tatar | 0 | 0 | 0 | 0 |
| Tibetan | 154 | 19 | 57 | 77 |
| Tu | 8 | 1 | 3 | 3 |
| Tujia | 605 | 73 | 296 | 237 |
| Uygur | 425 | 41 | 247 | 137 |
| Uzbek | 1 | 0 | 0 | 0 |
| Va | 14 | 3 | 6 | 5 |
| Xibe | 24 | 4 | 16 | 4 |
| Yao | 181 | 17 | 78 | 85 |
| Yi | 309 | 55 | 132 | 122 |
| Yugur | 0 | 0 | 0 | 0 |
| Zhuang | 710 | 71 | 329 | 311 |

*Notes:* "Patent" is an abbreviation for the patent right and refers to the exclusive right of ownership by the inventors or designers for the creation of inventions, given from the patent offices after due process of assessment and approval in accordance with the Patent Law. Patents are granted for inventions, utility models, and designs. This indicator reflects the achievements of S&T and design with independent intellectual property. "Inventions" refers to the new technical proposals to the products or methods or their modifications. This is a universal core indicator reflecting the technologies with independent intellectual property. "Utility models" refers to the practical and new technical proposals on the shape and structure of the product or the combination of both. This indicator reflects the condition of technological results with certain technical content. "Designs" refers to the aesthetics and industrially applicable new designs for the shape, pattern, and color of the product, or their combinations. The detailed description of the term "appearance design" can be found in the preceding sentence.

# 6 Culture and public health

Data in this chapter mainly show the development of culture and public health. Data on culture cover a number of textbooks and books published for children, publication of video products, and publication of audio products. Data on public health include number of employed persons in health institutions.

Data are collected and tabulated in accordance with the statistical reporting schemes stipulated by the departments concerned. Data on news and publication are mainly provided by the State Agency of News and Publication. Data on public health are mainly from the Ministry of Public Health.

For detailed information please refer to *China Cultural Relics Yearbook* (Department of Financial Management, Ministry of Culture), *Collection of China News and Publication Statistical Information* (Department of Financial Management, State Agency of News and Publication), *Collection of Broadcasting, Film and Television Statistics* (Department of Financial Management, State Administration of Broadcasting, Film and Television), and *Annual Statistical Yearbook on National Health Care* (Information Center, Ministry of Public Health).

*Table 6.1* Number of books for children and textbooks published

| Ethnic group | Printed copies (1,000 copies) | | Printed sheets (1,000 sheets) | |
|---|---|---|---|---|
| | Books for children | Textbooks | Books for children | Textbooks |
| National total | 229,260 | 3,529,490 | 955,545 | 25,393,488 |
| Center publishing | 30,080 | 681,120 | 158,664 | 7,188,463 |
| Local publishing | 199,180 | 2,848,370 | 796,881 | 18,205,025 |
| Achang | 0.08 | 75.54 | 0.33 | 452.16 |
| Bai | 16.51 | 4,197.22 | 51.14 | 24,921.58 |

*Table 6.1 (cont.)*

| Ethnic group | Printed copies (1,000 copies) | | Printed sheets (1,000 sheets) | |
| --- | --- | --- | --- | --- |
| | Books for children | Textbooks | Books for children | Textbooks |
| Baonan | 0.98 | 38.36 | 2.19 | 241.93 |
| Blang | 0.26 | 204.71 | 0.91 | 1,225.73 |
| Buyi | 60.37 | 4,473.75 | 175.23 | 29,011.57 |
| Dai | 3.17 | 2,576.39 | 11.05 | 15,431.36 |
| Daur | 12.91 | 292.80 | 57.33 | 2,051.50 |
| Deang | 0.03 | 39.94 | 0.08 | 238.96 |
| Derung | 0.21 | 16.55 | 0.79 | 100.65 |
| Dong | 219.09 | 6,756.94 | 727.43 | 39,358.92 |
| Dongxiang | 41.03 | 1,256.12 | 110.64 | 7,922.56 |
| Ewenki | 3.60 | 79.06 | 15.76 | 554.78 |
| Gaoshan | 0.76 | 9.87 | 3.13 | 61.94 |
| Gelao | 10.27 | 861.38 | 26.32 | 5,596.07 |
| *Han* | *182,310.27* | *2,607,142.08* | *731,683.08* | *16,696,572.41* |
| Hani | 3.02 | 3,207.67 | 10.91 | 19,198.74 |
| Hezhe | 0.24 | 5.74 | 1.27 | 40.80 |
| Hui | 973.69 | 21,578.25 | 4,091.27 | 137,266.12 |
| Jing | 8.52 | 50.57 | 31.19 | 300.59 |
| Jingpo | 0.29 | 293.81 | 1.05 | 1,758.74 |
| Jino | 0.05 | 46.54 | 0.19 | 278.65 |
| Kazak | 388.42 | 4,524.48 | 1,496.72 | 28,941.55 |
| Kirgiz | 49.58 | 578.37 | 191.18 | 3,701.40 |
| Korean | 635.84 | 4,053.45 | 3,264.62 | 27,193.41 |
| Lahu | 0.94 | 1,010.60 | 3.41 | 6,047.92 |
| Lhoba | 0.07 | 7.84 | 0.22 | 47.05 |
| Li | 460.44 | 2,951.33 | 2,165.36 | 19,487.67 |
| Lisu | 3.33 | 1,399.97 | 11.08 | 8,416.43 |
| Manchu | 1,884.14 | 16,943.23 | 8,505.83 | 113,326.17 |
| Maonan | 30.65 | 217.39 | 111.36 | 1,313.26 |
| Miao | 513.27 | 19,915.90 | 1,646.08 | 118,422.50 |
| Monba | 0.22 | 24.07 | 0.72 | 145.26 |
| Mongol | 825.10 | 14,424.49 | 3,600.62 | 99,757.82 |
| Mulao | 70.99 | 446.47 | 259.22 | 2,669.38 |
| Naxi | 1.93 | 681.87 | 6.97 | 4,099.48 |
| Nu | 0.14 | 64.22 | 0.55 | 384.77 |
| Oroqen | 0.65 | 15.57 | 3.04 | 109.79 |
| Pumi | 0.12 | 74.73 | 0.46 | 447.62 |
| Qiang | 36.73 | 465.83 | 115.55 | 3,376.93 |

*Table 6.1* (cont.)

| Ethnic group | Printed copies (1,000 copies) | | Printed sheets (1,000 sheets) | |
|---|---|---|---|---|
| | Books for children | Textbooks | Books for children | Textbooks |
| Russian | 3.73 | 49.63 | 14.91 | 327.56 |
| Salar | 2.71 | 181.35 | 9.81 | 1,210.67 |
| She | 154.24 | 1,443.49 | 712.87 | 9,749.18 |
| Shui | 12.49 | 625.95 | 38.37 | 4,033.19 |
| Tajik | 12.55 | 146.70 | 48.31 | 938.02 |
| Tatar | 1.45 | 17.17 | 5.60 | 109.82 |
| Tibetan | 221.61 | 11,594.28 | 664.73 | 73,486.43 |
| Tu | 6.10 | 418.23 | 21.49 | 2,785.63 |
| Tujia | 683.68 | 21,595.93 | 1,884.44 | 131,529.46 |
| Uygur | 2,608.86 | 30,382.84 | 10,055.43 | 194,331.35 |
| Uzbek | 3.83 | 44.48 | 14.80 | 284.44 |
| Va | 1.44 | 882.21 | 5.18 | 5,289.42 |
| Xibe | 40.15 | 316.89 | 165.90 | 2,113.71 |
| Yao | 665.26 | 7,003.38 | 2,388.01 | 39,706.27 |
| Yi | 284.41 | 15,130.17 | 891.32 | 95,335.67 |
| Yugur | 0.83 | 31.87 | 1.87 | 200.73 |
| Zhuang | 5,897.15 | 36,406.32 | 21,544.65 | 216,004.39 |

*Table 6.2* Publication of video products

| Ethnic group | Videotapes (1,000 cassettes) | VCD (1,000 disks) | DVD-V (1,000 disks) |
|---|---|---|---|
| National total | 54.0 | 268,803.1 | 115,116.8 |
| Center publishing house | 14.5 | 69,716.5 | 35,228.8 |
| Local publishing house | 39.5 | 199,086.6 | 79,888.0 |
| Achang | 0.000 | 0.930 | 0.235 |
| Bai | 0.001 | 65.962 | 19.716 |
| Baonan | 0.000 | 0.286 | 0.014 |
| Blang | 0.000 | 2.527 | 0.637 |
| Buyi | 0.004 | 130.062 | 81.280 |
| Dai | 0.001 | 31.225 | 7.741 |
| Daur | 0.000 | 9.276 | 1.952 |
| Deang | 0.000 | 0.466 | 0.111 |
| Derung | 0.000 | 0.343 | 0.111 |
| Dong | 0.027 | 217.050 | 90.896 |

*Table 6.2* (cont.)

| Ethnic group | Videotapes (1,000 cassettes) | VCD (1,000 disks) | DVD-V (1,000 disks) |
|---|---|---|---|
| Dongxiang | 0.000 | 8.596 | 0.339 |
| Ewenki | 0.000 | 1.006 | 0.333 |
| Gaoshan | 0.000 | 0.571 | 0.198 |
| Gelao | 0.001 | 26.251 | 16.629 |
| *Han* | *38.014* | *191,767.691* | *77,833.407* |
| Hani | 0.001 | 38.720 | 9.483 |
| Hezhe | 0.000 | 0.825 | 0.155 |
| Hui | 0.125 | 1,130.454 | 188.935 |
| Jing | 0.002 | 1.110 | 0.325 |
| Jingpo | 0.000 | 3.731 | 0.980 |
| Jino | 0.000 | 0.557 | 0.134 |
| Kazak | 0.000 | 0.409 | 0.069 |
| Kirgiz | 0.000 | 0.330 | 0.070 |
| Korean | 0.011 | 339.442 | 43.486 |
| Lahu | 0.000 | 12.310 | 3.074 |
| Lhoba | 0.000 | 0.640 | 0.012 |
| Li | 0.000 | 44.893 | 6.854 |
| Lisu | 0.000 | 16.799 | 4.038 |
| Manchu | 0.020 | 1,284.175 | 327.770 |
| Maonan | 0.006 | 5.027 | 1.957 |
| Miao | 0.045 | 549.541 | 228.237 |
| Monba | 0.000 | 1.990 | 0.020 |
| Mongol | 0.015 | 219.702 | 67.058 |
| Mulao | 0.013 | 12.006 | 4.601 |
| Naxi | 0.000 | 8.354 | 1.917 |
| Nu | 0.000 | 0.897 | 0.207 |
| Oroqen | 0.000 | 0.862 | 0.178 |
| Pumi | 0.000 | 0.926 | 0.227 |
| Qiang | 0.000 | 6.134 | 1.146 |
| Russian | 0.000 | 0.332 | 0.086 |
| Salar | 0.000 | 0.595 | 0.089 |
| She | 0.002 | 186.897 | 63.506 |
| Shui | 0.001 | 16.438 | 10.078 |
| Tajik | 0.000 | 0.217 | 0.087 |
| Tatar | 0.000 | 0.040 | 0.011 |
| Tibetan | 0.004 | 592.103 | 9.981 |
| Tu | 0.001 | 6.198 | 2.928 |
| Tujia | 0.011 | 654.456 | 196.075 |
| Uygur | 0.004 | 9.063 | 2.996 |

*Table 6.2 (cont.)*

| Ethnic group | Videotapes (1,000 cassettes) | VCD (1,000 disks) | DVD-V (1,000 disks) |
|---|---|---|---|
| Uzbek | 0.000 | 0.065 | 0.028 |
| Va | 0.000 | 12.459 | 3.464 |
| Xibe | 0.000 | 19.510 | 6.716 |
| Yao | 0.112 | 321.272 | 140.888 |
| Yi | 0.004 | 203.524 | 60.318 |
| Yugur | 0.000 | 0.282 | 0.017 |
| Zhuang | 1.075 | 1,091.324 | 427.531 |

*Table 6.3* Publication of audio products

| Ethnic group | Audiotapes (1,000 cassettes) | CDs (1,000 pieces) | DVD-A and others (1,000 pieces) |
|---|---|---|---|
| *National total* | *151,568.7* | *71,119.3* | *239.0* |
| *Center publishing house* | *82,142.6* | *21,957.0* | *66.7* |
| *Local publishing house* | *69,426.1* | *49,162.3* | *172.3* |
| Achang | 0.073 | 0.269 | 0.004 |
| Bai | 13.888 | 16.372 | 0.186 |
| Baonan | 0.057 | 0.015 | 0.000 |
| Blang | 0.217 | 0.734 | 0.011 |
| Buyi | 10.492 | 13.881 | 0.040 |
| Dai | 2.835 | 9.116 | 0.137 |
| Daur | 0.664 | 5.555 | 0.001 |
| Deang | 0.034 | 0.136 | 0.002 |
| Derung | 0.082 | 0.099 | 0.001 |
| Dong | 78.145 | 38.391 | 0.087 |
| Dongxiang | 1.638 | 0.510 | 0.000 |
| Ewenki | 0.175 | 1.853 | 0.000 |
| Gaoshan | 0.199 | 0.128 | 0.001 |
| Gelao | 2.168 | 2.814 | 0.008 |
| *Han* | *67,728.908* | *47,471.026* | *165.979* |
| Hani | 3.623 | 11.371 | 0.170 |
| Hezhe | 0.052 | 0.047 | 0.000 |
| Hui | 247.502 | 315.835 | 0.341 |
| Jing | 0.311 | 0.234 | 0.001 |
| Jingpo | 0.306 | 1.069 | 0.016 |
| Jino | 0.055 | 0.164 | 0.002 |
| Kazak | 0.215 | 0.082 | 0.000 |

*Table 6.3* (cont.)

| Ethnic group | Audiotapes (1,000 cassettes) | CDs (1,000 pieces) | DVD-A and others (1,000 pieces) |
|---|---|---|---|
| Kirgiz | 0.027 | 0.028 | 0.000 |
| Korean | 27.401 | 88.249 | 0.785 |
| Lahu | 1.008 | 3.590 | 0.053 |
| Lhoba | 0.013 | 0.080 | 0.000 |
| Li | 48.217 | 7.912 | 0.009 |
| Lisu | 1.343 | 4.930 | 0.072 |
| Manchu | 272.963 | 173.987 | 0.731 |
| Maonan | 1.108 | 0.888 | 0.005 |
| Miao | 188.249 | 99.515 | 0.312 |
| Monba | 0.174 | 0.280 | 0.000 |
| Mongol | 50.682 | 297.262 | 0.155 |
| Mulao | 2.980 | 2.370 | 0.014 |
| Naxi | 0.791 | 2.392 | 0.035 |
| Nu | 0.071 | 0.243 | 0.003 |
| Oroqen | 0.067 | 0.287 | 0.000 |
| Pumi | 0.081 | 0.268 | 0.004 |
| Qiang | 1.461 | 2.078 | 0.001 |
| Russian | 0.206 | 0.409 | 0.000 |
| Salar | 0.164 | 0.071 | 0.000 |
| She | 17.624 | 30.076 | 0.483 |
| Shui | 1.245 | 1.663 | 0.005 |
| Tajik | 0.092 | 0.055 | 0.000 |
| Tatar | 0.019 | 0.008 | 0.000 |
| Tibetan | 12.582 | 78.472 | 0.026 |
| Tu | 1.513 | 1.272 | 0.007 |
| Tujia | 308.503 | 112.795 | 0.193 |
| Uygur | 5.284 | 2.458 | 0.006 |
| Uzbek | 0.024 | 0.015 | 0.000 |
| Va | 1.241 | 3.637 | 0.046 |
| Xibe | 4.655 | 1.762 | 0.003 |
| Yao | 97.799 | 68.919 | 0.327 |
| Yi | 23.430 | 54.576 | 0.571 |
| Yugur | 0.067 | 0.021 | 0.000 |
| Zhuang | 261.361 | 229.328 | 1.461 |

*Table 6.4* Number of employed persons in health institutions (unit: person)

| Ethnic group | Total | Medical technical personnel | Of which, doctors | Of which, nurses |
|---|---|---|---|---|
| *National total* | *5,426,851* | *4,460,187* | *1,938,272* | *1,349,589* |
| Achang | 114 | 95 | 45 | 31 |
| Bai | 6,242 | 5,212 | 2,448 | 1,640 |
| Baonan | 66 | 56 | 24 | 15 |
| Blang | 309 | 258 | 121 | 83 |
| Buyi | 8,229 | 7,065 | 3,503 | 2,051 |
| Dai | 3,901 | 3,249 | 1,530 | 1,041 |
| Daur | 703 | 579 | 270 | 162 |
| Deang | 60 | 50 | 24 | 16 |
| Derung | 27 | 22 | 10 | 7 |
| Dong | 9,698 | 8,181 | 3,780 | 2,410 |
| Dongxiang | 2,131 | 1,809 | 770 | 504 |
| Ewenki | 159 | 134 | 64 | 36 |
| Gaoshan | 20 | 16 | 7 | 5 |
| Gelao | 1,589 | 1,366 | 679 | 396 |
| *Han* | *4,976,326* | *4,088,763* | *1,771,803* | *1,234,651* |
| Hani | 4,845 | 4,036 | 1,901 | 1,294 |
| Hezhe | 25 | 20 | 9 | 6 |
| Hui | 46,923 | 38,661 | 16,957 | 11,851 |
| Jing | 81 | 67 | 28 | 23 |
| Jingpo | 445 | 371 | 175 | 119 |
| Jino | 70 | 59 | 28 | 19 |
| Kazak | 7,928 | 6,514 | 2,803 | 2,074 |
| Kirgiz | 1,019 | 837 | 360 | 266 |
| Korean | 11,142 | 8,884 | 3,937 | 2,783 |
| Lahu | 1,527 | 1,272 | 599 | 408 |
| Lhoba | 12 | 10 | 5 | 2 |
| Li | 6,003 | 4,861 | 1,926 | 1,744 |
| Lisu | 2,138 | 1,782 | 840 | 568 |
| Manchu | 61,560 | 49,196 | 21,770 | 15,699 |
| Maonan | 360 | 298 | 131 | 98 |
| Miao | 29,116 | 24,537 | 11,438 | 7,231 |
| Monba | 37 | 31 | 16 | 7 |
| Mongol | 30,801 | 25,643 | 12,148 | 7,225 |
| Mulao | 731 | 599 | 258 | 202 |
| Naxi | 1,043 | 869 | 410 | 277 |
| Nu | 97 | 81 | 38 | 26 |
| Oroqen | 43 | 35 | 16 | 10 |
| Pumi | 113 | 94 | 44 | 30 |

*Table 6.4*  (*cont.*)

| Ethnic group | Total | Medical technical personnel | Of which, doctors | Of which, nurses |
|---|---|---|---|---|
| Qiang | 1,047 | 880 | 423 | 229 |
| Russian | 92 | 76 | 34 | 23 |
| Salar | 494 | 420 | 182 | 135 |
| She | 2,754 | 2,323 | 1,023 | 748 |
| Shui | 1,135 | 972 | 480 | 285 |
| Tajik | 257 | 211 | 91 | 67 |
| Tatar | 30 | 25 | 11 | 8 |
| Tibetan | 21,943 | 18,378 | 8,822 | 4,737 |
| Tu | 1,111 | 943 | 409 | 303 |
| Tujia | 30,130 | 25,077 | 11,094 | 7,387 |
| Uygur | 53,231 | 43,734 | 18,820 | 13,925 |
| Uzbek | 78 | 64 | 28 | 20 |
| Va | 1,341 | 1,117 | 525 | 357 |
| Xibe | 1,182 | 941 | 411 | 318 |
| Yao | 9,893 | 8,140 | 3,481 | 2,628 |
| Yi | 25,704 | 21,531 | 10,257 | 6,467 |
| Yugur | 54 | 46 | 20 | 13 |
| Zhuang | 58,726 | 47,966 | 20,382 | 16,429 |

# Appendix A: Methodology used in this book

In theory, multi-ethnic data can be derived and sorted directly based on the sampled information about the Chinese economy. In practice, however, it is almost impossible to measure them, due to the large number of ethnic minorities and the wide distribution of them throughout China, both of which would result in high cost for the sampling surveys.

For example, China's 55 ethnic minorities have been identified as having their permanent residences in 698 county-level administrative divisions, which are under the jurisdiction of 77 prefecture-level administrative divisions and, further, of 20 provincial-level administrative divisions (see Appendix C for more details). As a result, any meaningful multi-ethnic surveys of socioeconomic data must be based on a huge amount of samples.

However, if the socioeconomic indicators are uniformly distributed within each region, we can estimate the multi-ethnic data based on a weighted-mean approach. To illustrate this analytical framework, let $x(i)$ and $X(i)$ denote relative and absolute values of the $i$th administrative division, respectively; $y(j)$ and $Y(j)$ denote relative and absolute values of the $j$th ethnic group, respectively; and $n(i, j)$=number of people for the $j$th ethnic group of the $i$th administrative division ($i$=1, 2, 3,..., $L$ and $j$=1, 2, 3,..., $M$, where $L$ is the total number of administrative divisions and $M$ is the total number of ethnic groups).

In order to estimate different types of socioeconomic indicators, we build two equations:

$$y(j) = \sum_{i=1}^{L} \frac{n(i, j)}{\sum_{i=1}^{L} n(i, j)} x(i), \text{for a relative indicator;} \tag{1}$$

$$Y(j) = \sum_{i=1}^{L} \frac{n(i, j)}{\sum_{j=1}^{M} n(i, j)} X(i), \text{for an absolute indicator.} \tag{2}$$

It should be noted that the effectiveness of Equations 1 and 2 depends closely on the assumption that the socioeconomic indicators are uniformly distributed within each region. As a matter of fact, the greater the intra-regional differences, *ceteris paribus*, the larger the estimation errors derived from Equations 1 and 2. In theory, the intra-regional differences can be reduced when the region selected becomes smaller in size. However, smaller regions will also result in higher cost and other possible difficulties in data collection, when the number of regions and, naturally, the number of regional data needed to be collected also increase accordingly.

Given the task of estimating $N$ indicators of $M$ ethnic groups from $L$ regions, the total times of computations (that is, the number of computational signs such as "+," "–," "×," or "÷" appearing in Equation 1 or 2) are $[(L-1)+L \times (L+1)] \times M \times N$ (for a relative indicator), or $[(L-1)+L \times (M+1)] \times M \times N$ (for an absolute indicator).

According to the above formulas, we may sum up the total times of computation for the estimation of each one indicator for 56 ethnic groups (that is, $M=56$) from 2,135 county-level administrative divisions in China (that is, $L=2,135$):[1]

> 1.21939244×10$^7$ (for a relative indicator) or
> 2.6291244×10$^6$ (for an absolute indicator).

Even though the work of the huge data processing can be done with the help of electronic means, the collection of the multi-regional data still meets many difficulties, as, when the lower-level administrative divisions are selected, the total number of sampled data will increase dramatically. Therefore, the art of scientifically collecting regional data lies in the fact that the regional samples are kept to a certain size, for which the spatial data can be collected without too many difficulties and to which the final estimated results are not statistically sensitive.

Another factor that may possibly produce estimation errors is ethnic diversity. It is not difficult to understand that the estimation errors are positively related to the number of ethnic groups involved. In the case of only one ethnic group ($M=1$), for example, does there exist no estimation errors in Equations 1 and 2, as the socioeconomic indicators of each region also represent completely those of the monopolized ethnic group involved in that region.[2] On the other hand, if the ethnic diversity increases, given the existence of intra-regional differences, so do the errors produced.

---

1 For example, there existed 332 prefecture-level administrative divisions and 2,135 county-level administrative divisions in China – see *China Statistical Yearbook* (2010: 3).
2 As a matter of fact, when $M=1$, Equations 1 and 2 become

$$y(1) = \sum_{i=1}^{L} n(i)x(i) / \sum_{i=1}^{L} n(i) \text{ and } Y(1) = \sum_{i=1}^{L} x(i), \text{ respectively.}$$

After having clarified the factors by which the derivation of multi-ethnic data from multi-regional data may be affected, we can go further to take measures so as to reduce their influences.

First, we stipulate that only the provinces (or other provincial regions) with the highest intra-provincial inequalities might affect seriously the estimated results and, therefore, the choice of the subprovincial data of these provinces is desirable. According to an estimation based on a national sample survey, the GINI coefficient (here it is used to express the intra-provincial inequalities) of per capita income is the highest in the rural areas of Qinghai (0.35240), Shanxi (0.35146), Guangdong (0.34877), Guangxi (0.33426), and Jiangsu (0.32916).[3]

Second, we stipulate that only the provinces with the greatest ethnic diversities might affect seriously the estimated results and, therefore, the choice of the subprovincial data of those provinces is desirable. According to Appendix B, among all provinces, Xinjiang, Qinghai, Guangxi, Ningxia, and Guizhou are the most ethnically diversified, while Shanxi, Guangdong, and Jiangsu are the least ethnically diversified. Since the latter's intra-provincial inequalities may not, or at least not very much, falsify the estimated results, we thus don't divide these provinces into subprovincial divisions. Finally, the sampled regions in our research are selected as follows:

- 25 provincial divisions (including provinces, autonomous regions, and centrally administrative municipalities) except for Qinghai, Ningxia, Guizhou, Xinjiang, and Guangxi;
- 51 subprovincial divisions (prefectures, cities, and other prefecture-level divisions, if any) of 5 provincial divisions, including 8 subprovincial divisions of Qinghai, 4 subprovincial divisions of Ningxia, 9 subprovincial divisions of Guizhou, 15 subprovincial divisions of Xinjiang, and 15 subprovincial divisions of Guangxi.

Finally, the total number of the sampled regions is 76.

3  This result is obtained from a research project entitled "The Income Distribution in Urban and Rural China" directed by Professor Renwei Zhao, Institute of Economics, Chinese Academy of Social Sciences (CASS), Beijing, China. Even though the inequalities are also very high in urban China, we stipulate that the GINI coefficients used here can better reflect the intra-provincial inequalities. For more literature on China's intra-provincial inequalities, see, for example, Griffin and Zhao (eds.): *The Distribution of Income in China*, New York: St. Martin's Press, 1993; and Tsui (1994): "Decomposition of China's Regional Inequalities," *Journal of Comparative Economics*, vol. 18.

# Appendix B: China's ethnic population shares

| Province | Achang | Bai | Baonan | Blang |
|----------|--------|-----|--------|-------|
| Anhui | 0.00000 | 0.00001 | 0.00000 | 0.00000 |
| Beijing | 0.00000 | 0.00011 | 0.00000 | 0.00000 |
| Chongqing | 0.00000 | 0.00004 | 0.00000 | 0.00001 |
| Fujian | 0.00000 | 0.00002 | 0.00000 | 0.00000 |
| Gansu | 0.00000 | 0.00001 | 0.00060 | 0.00000 |
| Guangdong | 0.00000 | 0.00007 | 0.00000 | 0.00000 |
| Guangxi | 0.00000 | 0.00002 | 0.00000 | 0.00000 |
| Guizhou | 0.00000 | 0.00532 | 0.00000 | 0.00000 |
| Hainan | 0.00001 | 0.00003 | 0.00000 | 0.00000 |
| Hebei | 0.00000 | 0.00001 | 0.00000 | 0.00000 |
| Heilongjiang | 0.00000 | 0.00001 | 0.00000 | 0.00000 |
| Henan | 0.00000 | 0.00001 | 0.00000 | 0.00000 |
| Hubei | 0.00000 | 0.00012 | 0.00000 | 0.00000 |
| Hunan | 0.00000 | 0.00198 | 0.00000 | 0.00000 |
| Inner Mongolia | 0.00000 | 0.00001 | 0.00000 | 0.00000 |
| Jiangsu | 0.00000 | 0.00003 | 0.00000 | 0.00000 |
| Jiangxi | 0.00000 | 0.00001 | 0.00000 | 0.00000 |
| Jilin | 0.00000 | 0.00001 | 0.00000 | 0.00000 |
| Liaoning | 0.00000 | 0.00001 | 0.00000 | 0.00000 |
| Ningxia | 0.00000 | 0.00001 | 0.00000 | 0.00000 |
| Qinghai | 0.00000 | 0.00005 | 0.00013 | 0.00000 |
| Shaanxi | 0.00000 | 0.00001 | 0.00000 | 0.00000 |
| Shandong | 0.00000 | 0.00003 | 0.00000 | 0.00000 |
| Shanghai | 0.00000 | 0.00003 | 0.00000 | 0.00000 |
| Shanxi | 0.00000 | 0.00001 | 0.00000 | 0.00000 |
| Sichuan | 0.00000 | 0.00009 | 0.00000 | 0.00000 |
| Tianjin | 0.00000 | 0.00002 | 0.00000 | 0.00000 |
| Tibet | 0.00000 | 0.00028 | 0.00001 | 0.00001 |
| Xinjiang | 0.00000 | 0.00002 | 0.00003 | 0.00000 |
| Yunnan | 0.00079 | 0.03554 | 0.00000 | 0.00213 |
| Zhejiang | 0.00000 | 0.00006 | 0.00000 | 0.00000 |

| Province | Buyi | Dai | Daur | Deang |
|---|---|---|---|---|
| Anhui | 0.00005 | 0.00001 | 0.00000 | 0.00000 |
| Beijing | 0.00008 | 0.00002 | 0.00006 | 0.00000 |
| Chongqing | 0.00008 | 0.00002 | 0.00000 | 0.00000 |
| Fujian | 0.00012 | 0.00000 | 0.00000 | 0.00000 |
| Gansu | 0.00003 | 0.00000 | 0.00000 | 0.00000 |
| Guangdong | 0.00027 | 0.00001 | 0.00000 | 0.00000 |
| Guangxi | 0.00047 | 0.00002 | 0.00000 | 0.00000 |
| Guizhou | 0.07939 | 0.00002 | 0.00000 | 0.00000 |
| Hainan | 0.00020 | 0.00003 | 0.00001 | 0.00000 |
| Hebei | 0.00006 | 0.00000 | 0.00001 | 0.00000 |
| Heilongjiang | 0.00002 | 0.00000 | 0.00120 | 0.00000 |
| Henan | 0.00002 | 0.00001 | 0.00000 | 0.00000 |
| Hubei | 0.00002 | 0.00000 | 0.00000 | 0.00000 |
| Hunan | 0.00005 | 0.00001 | 0.00000 | 0.00000 |
| Inner Mongolia | 0.00004 | 0.00000 | 0.00331 | 0.00000 |
| Jiangsu | 0.00011 | 0.00001 | 0.00000 | 0.00000 |
| Jiangxi | 0.00004 | 0.00000 | 0.00000 | 0.00000 |
| Jilin | 0.00004 | 0.00000 | 0.00002 | 0.00000 |
| Liaoning | 0.00003 | 0.00000 | 0.00003 | 0.00000 |
| Ningxia | 0.00001 | 0.00000 | 0.00000 | 0.00000 |
| Qinghai | 0.00004 | 0.00000 | 0.00001 | 0.00000 |
| Shaanxi | 0.00001 | 0.00000 | 0.00000 | 0.00000 |
| Shandong | 0.00003 | 0.00002 | 0.00001 | 0.00000 |
| Shanghai | 0.00006 | 0.00001 | 0.00001 | 0.00000 |
| Shanxi | 0.00003 | 0.00000 | 0.00000 | 0.00000 |
| Sichuan | 0.00010 | 0.00008 | 0.00000 | 0.00000 |
| Tianjin | 0.00005 | 0.00000 | 0.00004 | 0.00000 |
| Tibet | 0.00017 | 0.00001 | 0.00000 | 0.00000 |
| Xinjiang | 0.00005 | 0.00000 | 0.00030 | 0.00000 |
| Yunnan | 0.00129 | 0.02696 | 0.00000 | 0.00042 |
| Zhejiang | 0.00047 | 0.00001 | 0.00000 | 0.00000 |

| Province | Derung | Dong | Dongxiang | Ewenki |
|---|---|---|---|---|
| Anhui | 0.00000 | 0.00003 | 0.00000 | 0.00000 |
| Beijing | 0.00000 | 0.00012 | 0.00001 | 0.00001 |
| Chongqing | 0.00000 | 0.00008 | 0.00000 | 0.00000 |
| Fujian | 0.00000 | 0.00017 | 0.00000 | 0.00000 |
| Gansu | 0.00000 | 0.00002 | 0.01798 | 0.00000 |
| Guangdong | 0.00000 | 0.00066 | 0.00000 | 0.00000 |
| Guangxi | 0.00000 | 0.00691 | 0.00000 | 0.00000 |

| Province | Derung | Dong | Dongxiang | Ewenki |
|---|---|---|---|---|
| Guizhou | 0.00000 | 0.04620 | 0.00001 | 0.00000 |
| Hainan | 0.00000 | 0.00018 | 0.00000 | 0.00001 |
| Hebei | 0.00000 | 0.00003 | 0.00000 | 0.00000 |
| Heilongjiang | 0.00000 | 0.00003 | 0.00000 | 0.00007 |
| Henan | 0.00000 | 0.00001 | 0.00000 | 0.00000 |
| Hubei | 0.00000 | 0.00118 | 0.00000 | 0.00000 |
| Hunan | 0.00000 | 0.01331 | 0.00000 | 0.00000 |
| Inner Mongolia | 0.00001 | 0.00002 | 0.00001 | 0.00112 |
| Jiangsu | 0.00000 | 0.00013 | 0.00000 | 0.00000 |
| Jiangxi | 0.00000 | 0.00004 | 0.00000 | 0.00000 |
| Jilin | 0.00000 | 0.00002 | 0.00000 | 0.00000 |
| Liaoning | 0.00000 | 0.00002 | 0.00000 | 0.00001 |
| Ningxia | 0.00000 | 0.00002 | 0.00040 | 0.00000 |
| Qinghai | 0.00000 | 0.00003 | 0.00052 | 0.00000 |
| Shaanxi | 0.00000 | 0.00001 | 0.00000 | 0.00000 |
| Shandong | 0.00000 | 0.00001 | 0.00000 | 0.00000 |
| Shanghai | 0.00000 | 0.00012 | 0.00000 | 0.00000 |
| Shanxi | 0.00000 | 0.00002 | 0.00000 | 0.00000 |
| Sichuan | 0.00000 | 0.00002 | 0.00000 | 0.00000 |
| Tianjin | 0.00000 | 0.00005 | 0.00001 | 0.00001 |
| Tibet | 0.00000 | 0.00003 | 0.00004 | 0.00000 |
| Xinjiang | 0.00000 | 0.00005 | 0.00303 | 0.00000 |
| Yunnan | 0.00014 | 0.00008 | 0.00000 | 0.00000 |
| Zhejiang | 0.00000 | 0.00039 | 0.00000 | 0.00000 |

| Province | Gaoshan | Gelao | Han | Hani |
|---|---|---|---|---|
| Anhui | 0.00000 | 0.00000 | 0.99326 | 0.00001 |
| Beijing | 0.00001 | 0.00002 | 0.95685 | 0.00001 |
| Chongqing | 0.00000 | 0.00004 | 0.93532 | 0.00003 |
| Fujian | 0.00001 | 0.00002 | 0.98288 | 0.00000 |
| Gansu | 0.00000 | 0.00000 | 0.91247 | 0.00000 |
| Guangdong | 0.00000 | 0.00007 | 0.98511 | 0.00001 |
| Guangxi | 0.00001 | 0.00009 | 0.61624 | 0.00000 |
| Guizhou | 0.00001 | 0.01586 | 0.62165 | 0.00003 |
| Hainan | 0.00001 | 0.00001 | 0.82621 | 0.00001 |
| Hebei | 0.00000 | 0.00000 | 0.95647 | 0.00000 |
| Heilongjiang | 0.00000 | 0.00000 | 0.95109 | 0.00000 |
| Henan | 0.00001 | 0.00000 | 0.98747 | 0.00000 |
| Hubei | 0.00000 | 0.00001 | 0.95636 | 0.00000 |

| Province | Gaoshan | Gelao | Han | Hani |
|---|---|---|---|---|
| Hunan | 0.00000 | 0.00001 | 0.89868 | 0.00002 |
| Inner Mongolia | 0.00001 | 0.00000 | 0.79172 | 0.00000 |
| Jiangsu | 0.00000 | 0.00001 | 0.99644 | 0.00003 |
| Jiangxi | 0.00000 | 0.00000 | 0.99689 | 0.00000 |
| Jilin | 0.00000 | 0.00000 | 0.90846 | 0.00001 |
| Liaoning | 0.00001 | 0.00000 | 0.83937 | 0.00000 |
| Ningxia | 0.00000 | 0.00000 | 0.65445 | 0.00000 |
| Qinghai | 0.00000 | 0.00000 | 0.54034 | 0.00000 |
| Shaanxi | 0.00000 | 0.00000 | 0.99501 | 0.00000 |
| Shandong | 0.00000 | 0.00000 | 0.99297 | 0.00003 |
| Shanghai | 0.00000 | 0.00001 | 0.99367 | 0.00002 |
| Shanxi | 0.00000 | 0.00000 | 0.99682 | 0.00000 |
| Sichuan | 0.00000 | 0.00001 | 0.94999 | 0.00001 |
| Tianjin | 0.00000 | 0.00001 | 0.97289 | 0.00000 |
| Tibet | 0.00000 | 0.00001 | 0.06061 | 0.00001 |
| Xinjiang | 0.00000 | 0.00001 | 0.40575 | 0.00000 |
| Yunnan | 0.00000 | 0.00007 | 0.66575 | 0.03364 |
| Zhejiang | 0.00000 | 0.00005 | 0.99139 | 0.00002 |

| Province | Hezhe | Hui | Jing | Jingpo |
|---|---|---|---|---|
| Anhui | 0.00000 | 0.00572 | 0.00000 | 0.00000 |
| Beijing | 0.00001 | 0.01738 | 0.00000 | 0.00000 |
| Chongqing | 0.00000 | 0.00033 | 0.00000 | 0.00000 |
| Fujian | 0.00000 | 0.00322 | 0.00000 | 0.00000 |
| Gansu | 0.00000 | 0.04716 | 0.00000 | 0.00000 |
| Guangdong | 0.00000 | 0.00030 | 0.00000 | 0.00000 |
| Guangxi | 0.00000 | 0.00074 | 0.00046 | 0.00000 |
| Guizhou | 0.00000 | 0.00479 | 0.00002 | 0.00001 |
| Hainan | 0.00000 | 0.00111 | 0.00002 | 0.00000 |
| Hebei | 0.00000 | 0.00814 | 0.00000 | 0.00000 |
| Heilongjiang | 0.00011 | 0.00342 | 0.00000 | 0.00000 |
| Henan | 0.00000 | 0.01045 | 0.00000 | 0.00000 |
| Hubei | 0.00000 | 0.00131 | 0.00000 | 0.00000 |
| Hunan | 0.00000 | 0.00154 | 0.00000 | 0.00000 |
| Inner Mongolia | 0.00000 | 0.00900 | 0.00000 | 0.00000 |
| Jiangsu | 0.00000 | 0.00182 | 0.00000 | 0.00000 |
| Jiangxi | 0.00000 | 0.00025 | 0.00001 | 0.00000 |
| Jilin | 0.00001 | 0.00469 | 0.00000 | 0.00000 |

| Province | Hezhe | Hui | Jing | Jingpo |
|---|---|---|---|---|
| Liaoning | 0.00000 | 0.00632 | 0.00000 | 0.00000 |
| Ningxia | 0.00000 | 0.33947 | 0.00000 | 0.00000 |
| Qinghai | 0.00000 | 0.15621 | 0.00000 | 0.00000 |
| Shaanxi | 0.00000 | 0.00394 | 0.00000 | 0.00000 |
| Shandong | 0.00000 | 0.00553 | 0.00000 | 0.00000 |
| Shanghai | 0.00000 | 0.00351 | 0.00000 | 0.00000 |
| Shanxi | 0.00000 | 0.00190 | 0.00000 | 0.00000 |
| Sichuan | 0.00000 | 0.00134 | 0.00000 | 0.00000 |
| Tianjin | 0.00000 | 0.01750 | 0.00000 | 0.00000 |
| Tibet | 0.00000 | 0.00345 | 0.00000 | 0.00000 |
| Xinjiang | 0.00000 | 0.04550 | 0.00000 | 0.00000 |
| Yunnan | 0.00000 | 0.01519 | 0.00001 | 0.00307 |
| Zhejiang | 0.00000 | 0.00043 | 0.00000 | 0.00000 |

| Province | Jino | Kazak | Kirgiz | Korean |
|---|---|---|---|---|
| Anhui | 0.00000 | 0.00000 | 0.00000 | 0.00005 |
| Beijing | 0.00000 | 0.00003 | 0.00000 | 0.00150 |
| Chongqing | 0.00000 | 0.00000 | 0.00000 | 0.00003 |
| Fujian | 0.00000 | 0.00000 | 0.00000 | 0.00005 |
| Gansu | 0.00000 | 0.00012 | 0.00000 | 0.00006 |
| Guangdong | 0.00000 | 0.00000 | 0.00000 | 0.00012 |
| Guangxi | 0.00000 | 0.00000 | 0.00000 | 0.00005 |
| Guizhou | 0.00000 | 0.00001 | 0.00000 | 0.00003 |
| Hainan | 0.00000 | 0.00000 | 0.00000 | 0.00010 |
| Hebei | 0.00000 | 0.00000 | 0.00000 | 0.00018 |
| Heilongjiang | 0.00000 | 0.00000 | 0.00004 | 0.01072 |
| Henan | 0.00000 | 0.00000 | 0.00000 | 0.00005 |
| Hubei | 0.00000 | 0.00000 | 0.00000 | 0.00005 |
| Hunan | 0.00000 | 0.00000 | 0.00000 | 0.00004 |
| Inner Mongolia | 0.00000 | 0.00000 | 0.00001 | 0.00094 |
| Jiangsu | 0.00000 | 0.00000 | 0.00000 | 0.00007 |
| Jiangxi | 0.00000 | 0.00000 | 0.00000 | 0.00004 |
| Jilin | 0.00000 | 0.00000 | 0.00000 | 0.04275 |
| Liaoning | 0.00000 | 0.00000 | 0.00000 | 0.00576 |
| Ningxia | 0.00000 | 0.00001 | 0.00000 | 0.00009 |
| Qinghai | 0.00000 | 0.00008 | 0.00000 | 0.00009 |
| Shaanxi | 0.00000 | 0.00000 | 0.00000 | 0.00005 |
| Shandong | 0.00000 | 0.00000 | 0.00000 | 0.00031 |

| Province | Jino | Kazak | Kirgiz | Korean |
|---|---|---|---|---|
| Shanghai | 0.00000 | 0.00000 | 0.00000 | 0.00031 |
| Shanxi | 0.00000 | 0.00000 | 0.00000 | 0.00006 |
| Sichuan | 0.00000 | 0.00000 | 0.00000 | 0.00004 |
| Tianjin | 0.00000 | 0.00000 | 0.00000 | 0.00112 |
| Tibet | 0.00000 | 0.00000 | 0.00000 | 0.00002 |
| Xinjiang | 0.00000 | 0.06745 | 0.00860 | 0.00008 |
| Yunnan | 0.00049 | 0.00000 | 0.00000 | 0.00004 |
| Zhejiang | 0.00000 | 0.00000 | 0.00000 | 0.00004 |

| Province | Lahu | Lhoba | Li | Lisu |
|---|---|---|---|---|
| Anhui | 0.00000 | 0.00000 | 0.00000 | 0.00000 |
| Beijing | 0.00000 | 0.00000 | 0.00003 | 0.00000 |
| Chongqing | 0.00002 | 0.00000 | 0.00001 | 0.00001 |
| Fujian | 0.00000 | 0.00000 | 0.00002 | 0.00000 |
| Gansu | 0.00000 | 0.00000 | 0.00000 | 0.00000 |
| Guangdong | 0.00000 | 0.00000 | 0.00008 | 0.00000 |
| Guangxi | 0.00000 | 0.00000 | 0.00007 | 0.00000 |
| Guizhou | 0.00000 | 0.00000 | 0.00159 | 0.00000 |
| Hainan | 0.00000 | 0.00000 | 0.15507 | 0.00000 |
| Hebei | 0.00000 | 0.00000 | 0.00000 | 0.00002 |
| Heilongjiang | 0.00000 | 0.00000 | 0.00000 | 0.00000 |
| Henan | 0.00001 | 0.00000 | 0.00000 | 0.00000 |
| Hubei | 0.00000 | 0.00000 | 0.00001 | 0.00000 |
| Hunan | 0.00001 | 0.00000 | 0.00001 | 0.00000 |
| Inner Mongolia | 0.00000 | 0.00000 | 0.00002 | 0.00001 |
| Jiangsu | 0.00001 | 0.00000 | 0.00001 | 0.00001 |
| Jiangxi | 0.00000 | 0.00000 | 0.00001 | 0.00000 |
| Jilin | 0.00000 | 0.00000 | 0.00001 | 0.00000 |
| Liaoning | 0.00000 | 0.00000 | 0.00001 | 0.00000 |
| Ningxia | 0.00000 | 0.00000 | 0.00000 | 0.00000 |
| Qinghai | 0.00000 | 0.00000 | 0.00000 | 0.00001 |
| Shaanxi | 0.00000 | 0.00000 | 0.00000 | 0.00000 |
| Shandong | 0.00002 | 0.00000 | 0.00000 | 0.00002 |
| Shanghai | 0.00000 | 0.00000 | 0.00001 | 0.00000 |
| Shanxi | 0.00000 | 0.00000 | 0.00000 | 0.00000 |
| Sichuan | 0.00001 | 0.00000 | 0.00000 | 0.00023 |
| Tianjin | 0.00000 | 0.00000 | 0.00001 | 0.00000 |
| Tibet | 0.00001 | 0.00103 | 0.00000 | 0.00001 |
| Xinjiang | 0.00000 | 0.00000 | 0.00001 | 0.00000 |

| Province | Lahu | Lhoba | Li | Lisu |
|---|---|---|---|---|
| Yunnan | 0.01057 | 0.00000 | 0.00003 | 0.01439 |
| Zhejiang | 0.00001 | 0.00000 | 0.00004 | 0.00001 |

| Province | Manchu | Maonan | Miao | Monba |
|---|---|---|---|---|
| Anhui | 0.00015 | 0.00000 | 0.00012 | 0.00000 |
| Beijing | 0.01845 | 0.00000 | 0.00039 | 0.00000 |
| Chongqing | 0.00010 | 0.00000 | 0.01647 | 0.00000 |
| Fujian | 0.00021 | 0.00000 | 0.00065 | 0.00000 |
| Gansu | 0.00069 | 0.00000 | 0.00006 | 0.00000 |
| Guangdong | 0.00021 | 0.00001 | 0.00142 | 0.00000 |
| Guangxi | 0.00022 | 0.00168 | 0.01056 | 0.00000 |
| Guizhou | 0.00062 | 0.00089 | 0.12199 | 0.00000 |
| Hainan | 0.00022 | 0.00001 | 0.00810 | 0.00000 |
| Hebei | 0.03177 | 0.00000 | 0.00012 | 0.00000 |
| Heilongjiang | 0.02862 | 0.00000 | 0.00009 | 0.00000 |
| Henan | 0.00068 | 0.00000 | 0.00006 | 0.00000 |
| Hubei | 0.00024 | 0.00000 | 0.00360 | 0.00000 |
| Hunan | 0.00013 | 0.00000 | 0.03037 | 0.00000 |
| Inner Mongolia | 0.02143 | 0.00000 | 0.00009 | 0.00000 |
| Jiangsu | 0.00016 | 0.00000 | 0.00030 | 0.00000 |
| Jiangxi | 0.00013 | 0.00000 | 0.00013 | 0.00000 |
| Jilin | 0.03705 | 0.00000 | 0.00006 | 0.00000 |
| Liaoning | 0.12876 | 0.00000 | 0.00007 | 0.00000 |
| Ningxia | 0.00400 | 0.00000 | 0.00007 | 0.00000 |
| Qinghai | 0.00161 | 0.00000 | 0.00009 | 0.00000 |
| Shaanxi | 0.00045 | 0.00000 | 0.00004 | 0.00000 |
| Shandong | 0.00037 | 0.00000 | 0.00008 | 0.00000 |
| Shanghai | 0.00055 | 0.00000 | 0.00029 | 0.00001 |
| Shanxi | 0.00042 | 0.00000 | 0.00009 | 0.00000 |
| Sichuan | 0.00017 | 0.00000 | 0.00179 | 0.00000 |
| Tianjin | 0.00574 | 0.00000 | 0.00016 | 0.00000 |
| Tibet | 0.00006 | 0.00000 | 0.00015 | 0.00324 |
| Xinjiang | 0.00106 | 0.00000 | 0.00038 | 0.00000 |
| Yunnan | 0.00029 | 0.00000 | 0.02463 | 0.00000 |
| Zhejiang | 0.00011 | 0.00000 | 0.00116 | 0.00000 |

| Province | Mongol | Mulao | Naxi | Nu |
|---|---|---|---|---|
| Anhui | 0.00024 | 0.00000 | 0.00000 | 0.00000 |
| Beijing | 0.00276 | 0.00001 | 0.00002 | 0.00000 |

| Province | Mongol | Mulao | Naxi | Nu |
|---|---|---|---|---|
| Chongqing | 0.00026 | 0.00000 | 0.00001 | 0.00000 |
| Fujian | 0.00018 | 0.00000 | 0.00000 | 0.00000 |
| Gansu | 0.00063 | 0.00000 | 0.00000 | 0.00000 |
| Guangdong | 0.00024 | 0.00006 | 0.00000 | 0.00000 |
| Guangxi | 0.00020 | 0.00388 | 0.00000 | 0.00000 |
| Guizhou | 0.00135 | 0.00081 | 0.00001 | 0.00000 |
| Hainan | 0.00025 | 0.00002 | 0.00000 | 0.00000 |
| Hebei | 0.00255 | 0.00001 | 0.00000 | 0.00000 |
| Heilongjiang | 0.00390 | 0.00000 | 0.00000 | 0.00000 |
| Henan | 0.00090 | 0.00000 | 0.00000 | 0.00000 |
| Hubei | 0.00018 | 0.00000 | 0.00000 | 0.00000 |
| Hunan | 0.00025 | 0.00001 | 0.00000 | 0.00000 |
| Inner Mongolia | 0.17130 | 0.00000 | 0.00000 | 0.00000 |
| Jiangsu | 0.00019 | 0.00000 | 0.00000 | 0.00000 |
| Jiangxi | 0.00022 | 0.00000 | 0.00000 | 0.00000 |
| Jilin | 0.00642 | 0.00000 | 0.00000 | 0.00000 |
| Liaoning | 0.01602 | 0.00000 | 0.00000 | 0.00000 |
| Ningxia | 0.00089 | 0.00000 | 0.00000 | 0.00000 |
| Qinghai | 0.01789 | 0.00000 | 0.00000 | 0.00000 |
| Shaanxi | 0.00017 | 0.00000 | 0.00000 | 0.00000 |
| Shandong | 0.00026 | 0.00000 | 0.00000 | 0.00000 |
| Shanghai | 0.00039 | 0.00001 | 0.00000 | 0.00000 |
| Shanxi | 0.00029 | 0.00000 | 0.00000 | 0.00000 |
| Sichuan | 0.00051 | 0.00000 | 0.00011 | 0.00000 |
| Tianjin | 0.00115 | 0.00000 | 0.00000 | 0.00000 |
| Tibet | 0.00026 | 0.00000 | 0.00047 | 0.00016 |
| Xinjiang | 0.00812 | 0.00000 | 0.00000 | 0.00000 |
| Yunnan | 0.00066 | 0.00001 | 0.00698 | 0.00065 |
| Zhejiang | 0.00008 | 0.00002 | 0.00001 | 0.00000 |

| Province | Oroqen | Pumi | Qiang | Russian |
|---|---|---|---|---|
| Anhui | 0.00000 | 0.00000 | 0.00000 | 0.00000 |
| Beijing | 0.00001 | 0.00000 | 0.00001 | 0.00002 |
| Chongqing | 0.00000 | 0.00000 | 0.00001 | 0.00000 |
| Fujian | 0.00000 | 0.00000 | 0.00000 | 0.00000 |
| Gansu | 0.00000 | 0.00000 | 0.00000 | 0.00000 |
| Guangdong | 0.00000 | 0.00000 | 0.00000 | 0.00000 |
| Guangxi | 0.00000 | 0.00000 | 0.00000 | 0.00000 |

| Province | Oroqen | Pumi | Qiang | Russian |
|---|---|---|---|---|
| Guizhou | 0.00000 | 0.00000 | 0.00004 | 0.00000 |
| Hainan | 0.00000 | 0.00000 | 0.00001 | 0.00000 |
| Hebei | 0.00000 | 0.00000 | 0.00000 | 0.00000 |
| Heilongjiang | 0.00011 | 0.00000 | 0.00000 | 0.00001 |
| Henan | 0.00000 | 0.00000 | 0.00000 | 0.00000 |
| Hubei | 0.00000 | 0.00000 | 0.00000 | 0.00000 |
| Hunan | 0.00000 | 0.00000 | 0.00000 | 0.00000 |
| Inner Mongolia | 0.00015 | 0.00000 | 0.00000 | 0.00022 |
| Jiangsu | 0.00000 | 0.00000 | 0.00000 | 0.00000 |
| Jiangxi | 0.00000 | 0.00000 | 0.00001 | 0.00000 |
| Jilin | 0.00000 | 0.00000 | 0.00000 | 0.00000 |
| Liaoning | 0.00000 | 0.00000 | 0.00000 | 0.00000 |
| Ningxia | 0.00000 | 0.00000 | 0.00001 | 0.00000 |
| Qinghai | 0.00000 | 0.00000 | 0.00002 | 0.00001 |
| Shaanxi | 0.00000 | 0.00000 | 0.00000 | 0.00000 |
| Shandong | 0.00000 | 0.00000 | 0.00000 | 0.00000 |
| Shanghai | 0.00000 | 0.00000 | 0.00000 | 0.00000 |
| Shanxi | 0.00000 | 0.00000 | 0.00000 | 0.00000 |
| Sichuan | 0.00000 | 0.00000 | 0.00365 | 0.00000 |
| Tianjin | 0.00000 | 0.00000 | 0.00000 | 0.00001 |
| Tibet | 0.00000 | 0.00001 | 0.00001 | 0.00001 |
| Xinjiang | 0.00000 | 0.00000 | 0.00002 | 0.00048 |
| Yunnan | 0.00000 | 0.00078 | 0.00001 | 0.00000 |
| Zhejiang | 0.00000 | 0.00000 | 0.00000 | 0.00000 |

| Province | Salar | She | Shui | Tajik |
|---|---|---|---|---|
| Anhui | 0.00000 | 0.00003 | 0.00001 | 0.00000 |
| Beijing | 0.00003 | 0.00005 | 0.00001 | 0.00000 |
| Chongqing | 0.00000 | 0.00000 | 0.00000 | 0.00001 |
| Fujian | 0.00000 | 0.01100 | 0.00001 | 0.00000 |
| Gansu | 0.00047 | 0.00001 | 0.00000 | 0.00000 |
| Guangdong | 0.00000 | 0.00033 | 0.00002 | 0.00000 |
| Guangxi | 0.00000 | 0.00001 | 0.00035 | 0.00000 |
| Guizhou | 0.00000 | 0.00127 | 0.01049 | 0.00000 |
| Hainan | 0.00001 | 0.00004 | 0.00001 | 0.00001 |
| Hebei | 0.00000 | 0.00000 | 0.00001 | 0.00000 |
| Heilongjiang | 0.00000 | 0.00000 | 0.00000 | 0.00000 |
| Henan | 0.00000 | 0.00000 | 0.00000 | 0.00000 |

| Province | Salar | She | Shui | Tajik |
|---|---|---|---|---|
| Hubei | 0.00000 | 0.00004 | 0.00000 | 0.00000 |
| Hunan | 0.00000 | 0.00005 | 0.00000 | 0.00000 |
| Inner Mongolia | 0.00000 | 0.00000 | 0.00000 | 0.00000 |
| Jiangsu | 0.00000 | 0.00001 | 0.00004 | 0.00000 |
| Jiangxi | 0.00000 | 0.00192 | 0.00000 | 0.00000 |
| Jilin | 0.00000 | 0.00000 | 0.00000 | 0.00000 |
| Liaoning | 0.00000 | 0.00000 | 0.00000 | 0.00000 |
| Ningxia | 0.00001 | 0.00002 | 0.00000 | 0.00000 |
| Qinghai | 0.01805 | 0.00000 | 0.00000 | 0.00000 |
| Shaanxi | 0.00000 | 0.00000 | 0.00000 | 0.00000 |
| Shandong | 0.00000 | 0.00000 | 0.00000 | 0.00000 |
| Shanghai | 0.00000 | 0.00005 | 0.00001 | 0.00000 |
| Shanxi | 0.00000 | 0.00001 | 0.00000 | 0.00000 |
| Sichuan | 0.00000 | 0.00000 | 0.00000 | 0.00000 |
| Tianjin | 0.00000 | 0.00001 | 0.00000 | 0.00000 |
| Tibet | 0.00009 | 0.00000 | 0.00000 | 0.00000 |
| Xinjiang | 0.00020 | 0.00001 | 0.00002 | 0.00214 |
| Yunnan | 0.00000 | 0.00001 | 0.00030 | 0.00000 |
| Zhejiang | 0.00000 | 0.00372 | 0.00003 | 0.00000 |

| Province | Tatar | Tibetan | Tu | Tujia |
|---|---|---|---|---|
| Anhui | 0.00000 | 0.00004 | 0.00000 | 0.00004 |
| Beijing | 0.00000 | 0.00022 | 0.00003 | 0.00062 |
| Chongqing | 0.00000 | 0.00008 | 0.00001 | 0.04668 |
| Fujian | 0.00000 | 0.00004 | 0.00003 | 0.00085 |
| Gansu | 0.00001 | 0.01764 | 0.00121 | 0.00005 |
| Guangdong | 0.00000 | 0.00008 | 0.00005 | 0.00159 |
| Guangxi | 0.00000 | 0.00005 | 0.00001 | 0.00011 |
| Guizhou | 0.00000 | 0.00005 | 0.00008 | 0.04058 |
| Hainan | 0.00000 | 0.00006 | 0.00003 | 0.00044 |
| Hebei | 0.00000 | 0.00005 | 0.00001 | 0.00010 |
| Heilongjiang | 0.00000 | 0.00005 | 0.00000 | 0.00006 |
| Henan | 0.00000 | 0.00004 | 0.00000 | 0.00006 |
| Hubei | 0.00000 | 0.00003 | 0.00001 | 0.03659 |
| Hunan | 0.00000 | 0.00005 | 0.00002 | 0.04172 |
| Inner Mongolia | 0.00000 | 0.00009 | 0.00002 | 0.00007 |
| Jiangsu | 0.00000 | 0.00004 | 0.00001 | 0.00023 |
| Jiangxi | 0.00000 | 0.00004 | 0.00000 | 0.00004 |

| Province | Tatar | Tibetan | Tu | Tujia |
| --- | --- | --- | --- | --- |
| Jilin | 0.00000 | 0.00006 | 0.00000 | 0.00003 |
| Liaoning | 0.00000 | 0.00005 | 0.00000 | 0.00009 |
| Ningxia | 0.00000 | 0.00009 | 0.00003 | 0.00014 |
| Qinghai | 0.00000 | 0.22530 | 0.03889 | 0.00020 |
| Shaanxi | 0.00000 | 0.00009 | 0.00001 | 0.00005 |
| Shandong | 0.00000 | 0.00003 | 0.00000 | 0.00003 |
| Shanghai | 0.00000 | 0.00010 | 0.00001 | 0.00032 |
| Shanxi | 0.00000 | 0.00005 | 0.00001 | 0.00007 |
| Sichuan | 0.00000 | 0.01541 | 0.00001 | 0.00050 |
| Tianjin | 0.00000 | 0.00013 | 0.00002 | 0.00037 |
| Tibet | 0.00000 | 0.92770 | 0.00013 | 0.00012 |
| Xinjiang | 0.00024 | 0.00033 | 0.00015 | 0.00086 |
| Yunnan | 0.00000 | 0.00303 | 0.00007 | 0.00009 |
| Zhejiang | 0.00000 | 0.00002 | 0.00002 | 0.00120 |

| Province | Uygur | Uzbek | Va | Xibe |
| --- | --- | --- | --- | --- |
| Anhui | 0.00003 | 0.00000 | 0.00001 | 0.00000 |
| Beijing | 0.00023 | 0.00000 | 0.00000 | 0.00011 |
| Chongqing | 0.00004 | 0.00000 | 0.00005 | 0.00000 |
| Fujian | 0.00003 | 0.00000 | 0.00000 | 0.00000 |
| Gansu | 0.00008 | 0.00000 | 0.00001 | 0.00001 |
| Guangdong | 0.00004 | 0.00000 | 0.00001 | 0.00000 |
| Guangxi | 0.00004 | 0.00000 | 0.00001 | 0.00000 |
| Guizhou | 0.00003 | 0.00000 | 0.00000 | 0.00000 |
| Hainan | 0.00005 | 0.00000 | 0.00000 | 0.00000 |
| Hebei | 0.00003 | 0.00000 | 0.00000 | 0.00001 |
| Heilongjiang | 0.00003 | 0.00000 | 0.00000 | 0.00025 |
| Henan | 0.00005 | 0.00000 | 0.00002 | 0.00000 |
| Hubei | 0.00002 | 0.00000 | 0.00000 | 0.00000 |
| Hunan | 0.00013 | 0.00000 | 0.00001 | 0.00000 |
| Inner Mongolia | 0.00005 | 0.00000 | 0.00001 | 0.00013 |
| Jiangsu | 0.00003 | 0.00000 | 0.00001 | 0.00000 |
| Jiangxi | 0.00003 | 0.00000 | 0.00000 | 0.00000 |
| Jilin | 0.00006 | 0.00000 | 0.00000 | 0.00012 |
| Liaoning | 0.00006 | 0.00000 | 0.00000 | 0.00317 |
| Ningxia | 0.00006 | 0.00000 | 0.00000 | 0.00004 |
| Qinghai | 0.00009 | 0.00000 | 0.00000 | 0.00003 |
| Shaanxi | 0.00003 | 0.00000 | 0.00000 | 0.00001 |

| Province | Uygur | Uzbek | Va | Xibe |
|---|---|---|---|---|
| Shandong | 0.00003 | 0.00000 | 0.00005 | 0.00000 |
| Shanghai | 0.00010 | 0.00000 | 0.00001 | 0.00001 |
| Shanxi | 0.00003 | 0.00000 | 0.00000 | 0.00000 |
| Sichuan | 0.00003 | 0.00000 | 0.00002 | 0.00000 |
| Tianjin | 0.00010 | 0.00000 | 0.00000 | 0.00003 |
| Tibet | 0.00027 | 0.00000 | 0.00000 | 0.00000 |
| Xinjiang | 0.45210 | 0.00066 | 0.00000 | 0.00187 |
| Yunnan | 0.00003 | 0.00000 | 0.00904 | 0.00000 |
| Zhejiang | 0.00002 | 0.00000 | 0.00001 | 0.00000 |

| Province | Yao | Yi | Yugur | Zhuang |
|---|---|---|---|---|
| Anhui | 0.00001 | 0.00010 | 0.00000 | 0.00007 |
| Beijing | 0.00008 | 0.00014 | 0.00000 | 0.00054 |
| Chongqing | 0.00002 | 0.00015 | 0.00000 | 0.00009 |
| Fujian | 0.00004 | 0.00008 | 0.00000 | 0.00032 |
| Gansu | 0.00001 | 0.00007 | 0.00052 | 0.00005 |
| Guangdong | 0.00238 | 0.00010 | 0.00000 | 0.00669 |
| Guangxi | 0.03356 | 0.00022 | 0.00000 | 0.32396 |
| Guizhou | 0.00126 | 0.02393 | 0.00000 | 0.00148 |
| Hainan | 0.00092 | 0.00008 | 0.00000 | 0.00668 |
| Hebei | 0.00002 | 0.00006 | 0.00000 | 0.00031 |
| Heilongjiang | 0.00001 | 0.00006 | 0.00000 | 0.00007 |
| Henan | 0.00000 | 0.00006 | 0.00000 | 0.00005 |
| Hubei | 0.00003 | 0.00004 | 0.00000 | 0.00013 |
| Hunan | 0.01114 | 0.00007 | 0.00000 | 0.00037 |
| Inner Mongolia | 0.00001 | 0.00009 | 0.00000 | 0.00008 |
| Jiangsu | 0.00002 | 0.00011 | 0.00000 | 0.00012 |
| Jiangxi | 0.00003 | 0.00006 | 0.00000 | 0.00008 |
| Jilin | 0.00001 | 0.00008 | 0.00000 | 0.00006 |
| Liaoning | 0.00001 | 0.00006 | 0.00000 | 0.00009 |
| Ningxia | 0.00001 | 0.00002 | 0.00001 | 0.00010 |
| Qinghai | 0.00002 | 0.00006 | 0.00003 | 0.00013 |
| Shaanxi | 0.00001 | 0.00002 | 0.00000 | 0.00006 |
| Shandong | 0.00001 | 0.00007 | 0.00000 | 0.00006 |
| Shanghai | 0.00005 | 0.00009 | 0.00000 | 0.00018 |
| Shanxi | 0.00001 | 0.00008 | 0.00000 | 0.00006 |
| Sichuan | 0.00001 | 0.02577 | 0.00000 | 0.00008 |

| Province | Yao | Yi | Yugur | Zhuang |
|---|---|---|---|---|
| Tianjin | 0.00004 | 0.00008 | 0.00000 | 0.00041 |
| Tibet | 0.00001 | 0.00011 | 0.00000 | 0.00007 |
| Xinjiang | 0.00004 | 0.00009 | 0.00002 | 0.00031 |
| Yunnan | 0.00450 | 0.11109 | 0.00000 | 0.02701 |
| Zhejiang | 0.00004 | 0.00014 | 0.00000 | 0.00041 |

*Source: The Fifth National Population Census*, 2000.

# Appendix C: Statistics of ethnic minority autonomous areas – administrative divisions and population

| Provinces and autonomous regions | Number of regions at prefecture level | Number of cities at prefecture level | Number of autonomous prefectures | Number of regions at county level |
|---|---|---|---|---|
| National total | 77 | 31 | 30 | 698 |
| Chongqing | | | | 4 |
| Gansu | 2 | | 2 | 21 |
| Guangdong | | | | 3 |
| Guangxi | 14 | 14 | | 109 |
| Guizhou | 3 | | 3 | 46 |
| Hainan | | | | 6 |
| Hebei | | | | 6 |
| Heilongjiang | | | | 1 |
| Hubei | 1 | | 1 | 10 |
| Hunan | 1 | | 1 | 15 |
| Inner Mongolia | 12 | 9 | | 101 |
| Jilin | 1 | | 1 | 11 |
| Liaoning | | | | 8 |
| Ningxia | 5 | 5 | | 21 |
| Qinghai | 6 | | 6 | 35 |
| Sichuan | 3 | | 3 | 51 |
| Tibet | 7 | 1 | | 73 |
| Xinjiang | 14 | 2 | 5 | 98 |
| Yunnan | 8 | | 8 | 78 |
| Zhejiang | | | | 1 |

Source: China Statistical Yearbook (2011).

| Cities at county level | Autonomous counties (Qi) | Total population in minority areas (10,000 persons) | Ethnic minority population (10,000 persons) | Ethnic minority population as percentage of total population in minority areas (%) |
|---|---|---|---|---|
| *65* | *120* | *18,494.30* | *8,851.74* | *47.86* |
|  | 4 | 270.81 | 187.96 | 69.41 |
| 2 | 7 | 345.10 | 198.19 | 57.43 |
|  | 3 | 49.98 | 18.52 | 37.06 |
| 7 | 12 | 5,159.00 | 1,957.00 | 37.93 |
| 4 | 11 | 1,718.57 | 1,034.97 | 60.22 |
|  | 6 | 177.51 | 88.75 | 49.99 |
|  | 6 | 204.38 | 121.19 | 59.29 |
|  | 1 | 25.52 | 5.28 | 20.70 |
| 2 | 2 | 458.86 | 258.28 | 56.29 |
| 1 | 7 | 515.77 | 397.84 | 77.14 |
| 11 | 3 | 2,472.18 | 505.56 | 20.45 |
| 6 | 3 | 335.16 | 114.47 | 34.15 |
|  | 8 | 334.15 | 179.09 | 53.59 |
| 2 |  | 632.71 | 233.21 | 36.86 |
| 2 | 7 | 322.93 | 275.92 | 85.44 |
| 1 | 4 | 734.12 | 437.52 | 59.60 |
| 1 |  | 300.21 | 275.69 | 91.83 |
| 19 | 6 | 2,181.33 | 1,306.72 | 59.90 |
| 7 | 29 | 2,238.82 | 1,253.70 | 56.00 |
|  | 1 | 17.19 | 1.88 | 10.94 |

# Appendix D: Selected indicators on social and economic development in ethnic minority autonomous areas

*Table D1* Aggregate data

| Item | 1990 | 1995 | 2000 | 2005 | 2009 | 2010 |
|---|---|---|---|---|---|---|
| Population at year-end (10,000 persons) | 15,296 | 16,044 | 16,818 | 17,499 | 18,318 | 18,494 |
| Ethnic minority population (10,000 persons) | 6,880 | 7,232 | 7,767 | 8,239 | 8,714 | 8,852 |
| Persons employed in various units (10,000 persons) | 1,543 | 1,672 | 1,733 | 1,202 | 1,257 | 1,963 |
| **GRP (100 million yuan)** | | **4,901** | **7,486** | **15,706** | **27,940** | **38,989** |
| Primary industry | | 1,629 | 2,022 | 3,300 | 5,002 | 6,198 |
| Secondary industry | | 1,747 | 2,834 | 6,419 | 13,202 | 18,809 |
| Tertiary industry | | 1,526 | 2,629 | 5,987 | 9,736 | 13,982 |
| **Per capita gross domestic product** | | **3,055** | **4,451** | **8,991** | **15,889** | **22,061** |
| **Investment in fixed assets (100 million yuan)** | | | | | | |
| Total investment in fixed assets | | 1,444 | 2,477 | 8,358 | 17,285 | 29,876 |
| State-owned units | 259 | 983 | 1,553 | 3,767 | 6,655 | 12,046 |
| **Public finance (100 million yuan)** | | | | | | |
| Local governments revenue | 167 | 248 | 476 | 1,026 | 2,100 | 3,257 |
| Local governments expenditures | 304 | 595 | 1,173 | 3,050 | 6,497 | 10,512 |
| **Agriculture** | | | | | | |
| Cultivated areas (10,000 hectares) | 1,763 | 1,508 | 2,086 | 2,033 | 2,303 | 2,380 |
| Irrigated areas (10,000 hectares) | 764 | 838 | 936 | 1,027 | 1,114 | 1,156 |

*Table D1* (*cont.*)

| Item | 1990 | 1995 | 2000 | 2005 | 2009 | 2010 |
|---|---|---|---|---|---|---|
| Gross output value of farming, forestry, animal husbandry, and fishery (100 million yuan) | | 2,537 | 3,200 | 5,349 | 8,260 | 10,374 |
| *Output of major farm products* | | | | | | |
| Grain output (10,000 tons) | 5,373 | 5,801 | 6,381 | 7,187 | 7,925 | 8,308 |
| Cotton output (10,000 tons) | 47 | 95 | 146 | 188 | 303 | 248 |
| Oil-bearing crops output (10,000 tons) | 208 | 264 | 353 | 372 | 397 | 422 |
| Large domestic animals (10,000 head) | 5,286 | 5,618 | 5,566 | 6,153 | 5,599 | 6,068 |
| Goats and sheep (10,000 head) | 11,362 | 11,906 | 13,076 | 16,391 | 14,467 | 14,885 |
| Hogs (10,000 head) | 5,668 | 7,240 | 8,201 | 8,526 | 7,697 | 8,141 |
| **Industry** | | | | | | |
| Gross industrial output value above designated size (100 million yuan) | | | 3,923 | 10,654 | 29,145 | 42,787 |
| *Output of major industrial products* | | | | | | |
| Cloth (100 million m) | 7.4 | 6.9 | 5.0 | 3.5 | 3.1 | 3.6 |
| Machine-made paper and paperboards (10,000 tons) | 94 | 191 | 175 | 273 | 500 | 385 |
| Refined sugar (10,000 tons) | 223 | 240 | 498 | 678 | 1,047 | 907 |
| Coal (100 million tons) | 1.2 | 1.7 | 1.5 | 3.8 | 8.3 | 10.5 |
| Crude oil (10,000 tons) | 1,265 | 1,610 | 2,292 | 2,833 | 4,649 | 3,247 |
| Electricity (100 million kwh) | 739 | 1,187 | 1,712 | 3,052 | 5,911 | 6,805 |
| Crude steel (10,000 tons) | 368 | 700 | 647 | 1,846 | 3,469 | 4,005 |
| Pig iron (10,000 tons) | 417 | 555 | 725 | 2,087 | 3,946 | 4,447 |
| Cement (10,000 tons) | 1,958 | 4,296 | 5,703 | 10,156 | 21,376 | 21,653 |
| Timber (10,000 cu.m) | 1,761 | 3,257 | 1,052 | 169 | 401 | 417 |
| **Construction** | | | | | | |
| Number of employed persons (10,000 persons) | | | 132 | 142 | 184 | 194 |
| Gross output value (100 million yuan) | | | 754 | 1,656 | 3,962 | 5,203 |

*Table D1　(cont.)*

| Item | 1990 | 1995 | 2000 | 2005 | 2009 | 2010 |
|---|---|---|---|---|---|---|
| Floor space of buildings under construction (10,000 sq.m) | | | 9,232 | 15,964 | 28,156 | 35,052 |
| Floor space of buildings completed (10,000 sq.m) | | | 5,326 | 8,072 | 13,167 | 15,418 |
| **Transportation, post, and telecommunication** | | | | | | |
| Railways in operation (10,000 km) | 1.31 | 1.70 | 1.43 | 1.69 | 2.09 | 2.12 |
| Highways (10,000 km) | 29 | 33 | 42 | 59 | 88 | 91 |
| Total value of telecommunications services (100 million yuan) | 9 | 78 | 297 | 892 | 2,142 | 2,456 |
| Total length of postal routes and rural delivery routes (10,000 km) | 88 | 107 | 110 | 110 | 123 | 127 |
| **Domestic trade** | | | | | | |
| Total value of retail sales (100 million yuan) | 682 | 1,692 | 2,570 | 4,874 | 9,857 | 11,685 |
| **Foreign trade** | | | | | | |
| Total exports and imports (USD 100 million) | | | 86 | 222 | 416 | 533 |
| Exports | | | 50 | 126 | 266 | 331 |
| Imports | | | 36 | 95 | 150 | 202 |
| **International tourism** | | | | | | |
| Number of foreign tourists (10,000 persons) | | | 348 | 532 | 751 | 939 |
| Foreign exchange earnings from tourism (USD 100 million) | | | 8 | 13 | 27 | 30 |
| **Finance** | | | | | | |
| Deposits of national banking system (100 million yuan) | | | 7,906 | 16,324 | 37,098 | 46,622 |
| Loans of national banking system (100 million yuan) | | | 6,548 | 11,300 | 24,494 | 30,579 |

*Table D1* (cont.)

| Item | 1990 | 1995 | 2000 | 2005 | 2009 | 2010 |
|---|---|---|---|---|---|---|
| **Education** | | | | | | |
| *Student enrollment (10,000 persons)* | | | | | | |
| Regular institutions of higher education | 13.6 | 18.6 | 34.2 | 100.0 | 148.5 | 161.9 |
| Regular secondary schools | 610 | 632 | 873 | 1,082 | 1,050 | 1,050 |
| Regular primary schools | 1,853 | 1,889 | 1,886 | 1,668 | 1,581 | 1,536 |
| *Full-time teachers (10,000 persons)* | | | | | | |
| Regular institutions of higher education | 2.8 | 3.7 | 3.6 | 6.3 | 8.7 | 9.5 |
| Regular secondary schools | 41.5 | 41.5 | 47.9 | 61.1 | 66.2 | 67.4 |
| Regular primary schools | 84.8 | 85.8 | 89.9 | 88.1 | 90.6 | 90.7 |
| **Culture** | | | | | | |
| *Publications* | | | | | | |
| Number of books published (10,000 copies) | 30,166 | 42,275 | 42,310 | 41,958 | 47,690 | 54,799 |
| Number of magazines issued (10,000 copies) | 7,866 | 7,881 | 8,332 | 10,280 | 7,366 | 8,279 |
| Number of newspapers issued (10,000 copies) | 79,120 | 94,985 | 123,277 | 169,518 | 165,395 | 175,251 |
| **Health care** | | | | | | |
| Number of hospitals and health centers (10,000 units) | 1.06 | 1.23 | 1.25 | 1.18 | 1.18 | 1.20 |
| Number of beds of hospitals and health centers (10,000 units) | 33.2 | 35.7 | 36.1 | 38.4 | 51.6 | 55.7 |
| **Social services** | | | | | | |
| Number of beds in social welfare institutions (10,000 units) | | | | | 24.3 | 27.3 |
| Number of urban community services facilities (units) | | | | | 1,795.0 | 6,188.0 |
| Number of persons receiving minimum living allowance in urban and rural areas (10,000 persons) | | | | | 1,677.8 | 1,907.4 |

*Source: China Statistical Yearbook* (2011).

*Table D2* Indices and growth rates

| Item | (2010 as percentage of the following years) | | | | | Annual growth rate | | |
|---|---|---|---|---|---|---|---|---|
| | *1990* | *1995* | *2000* | *2005* | *2009* | *1991– 2010* | *1996– 2010* | *2001– 2010* |
| Population at year-end (10,000 persons) | 120.9 | 115.3 | 110.0 | 105.7 | 101.0 | 1.0 | 1.0 | 1.0 |
| Ethnic minority population (10,000 persons) | 128.7 | 122.4 | 114.0 | 107.4 | 101.6 | 1.3 | 1.4 | 1.3 |
| Persons employed in various units (10,000 persons) | 127.2 | 117.4 | 113.2 | 163.3 | 156.2 | 1.2 | 1.1 | 1.3 |
| **Macroeconomic indicators** | | | | | | | | |
| **GRP (100 million yuan)** | | **524.4** | **340.0** | **195.4** | **114.0** | | **11.7** | **13.0** |
| Primary industry | | 228.8 | 174.2 | 132.1 | 105.6 | | 5.7 | 5.7 |
| Secondary industry | | 823.9 | 489.3 | 234.8 | 118.3 | | 15.1 | 17.2 |
| Tertiary industry | | 515.0 | 320.3 | 186.6 | 112.1 | | 11.5 | 12.3 |
| **Investment in fixed assets (100 million yuan)** | | | | | | | | |
| Total investment in fixed assets | | 2,069.0 | 1,206.1 | 357.5 | 172.8 | | 22.4 | 28.3 |
| State-owned units | 4,643.7 | 1,225.9 | 775.9 | 319.7 | 181.0 | 21.2 | 18.2 | 22.7 |
| **Public finance (100 million yuan)** | | | | | | | | |
| Local governments revenue | 1,953.8 | 1,312.8 | 684.9 | 317.3 | 155.1 | 16.0 | 18.7 | 21.2 |
| Local governments expenditures | 3,453.2 | 1,766.3 | 896.2 | 344.6 | 161.8 | 19.4 | 21.1 | 24.5 |
| **Agriculture** | | | | | | | | |
| Cultivated areas (10,000 hectares) | 135.0 | 157.9 | 114.1 | 117.1 | 103.4 | 1.5 | 3.1 | 1.3 |
| Irrigated areas (10,000 hectares) | 151.3 | 138.0 | 123.6 | 112.5 | 103.8 | 2.1 | 2.2 | 2.1 |
| Gross output value of farming, forestry, animal husbandry, and fishery (100 million yuan) | 351.0 | 251.8 | 191.8 | 140.7 | 107.6 | 6.5 | 6.3 | 6.7 |

*Table D2 (cont.)*

| Item | (2010 as percentage of the following years) | | | | | Annual growth rate | | |
|---|---|---|---|---|---|---|---|---|
| | *1990* | *1995* | *2000* | *2005* | *2009* | *1991– 2010* | *1996– 2010* | *2001– 2010* |
| *Output of major farm products* | | | | | | | | |
| Grain output (10,000 tons) | 154.6 | 143.2 | 130.2 | 115.6 | 104.8 | 2.2 | 2.4 | 2.7 |
| Cotton output (10,000 tons) | 528.7 | 262.6 | 169.9 | 132.2 | 81.9 | 8.7 | 6.6 | 5.4 |
| Oil-bearing crops output (10,000 tons) | 203.0 | 160.0 | 119.6 | 113.5 | 106.5 | 3.6 | 3.2 | 1.8 |
| Large domestic animals (10,000 head) | 114.8 | 108.0 | 109.0 | 98.6 | 108.4 | 0.7 | 0.5 | 0.9 |
| Goats and sheep (10,000 head) | 131.0 | 125.0 | 113.8 | 90.8 | 102.9 | 1.4 | 1.5 | 1.3 |
| Hogs (10,000 head) | 143.6 | 112.4 | 99.3 | 95.5 | 105.8 | 1.8 | 0.8 | −0.1 |
| **Industry** | | | | | | | | |
| *Output of major industrial products* | | | | | | | | |
| Cloth (100 million m) | 49.1 | 52.6 | 72.5 | 103.8 | 117.6 | −3.5 | −4.2 | −3.2 |
| Machine-made paper and paperboards (10,000 tons) | 409.4 | 201.5 | 219.6 | 141.2 | 77.0 | 7.3 | 4.8 | 8.2 |
| Refined sugar (10,000 tons) | 407.4 | 378.7 | 182.0 | 133.7 | 86.6 | 7.3 | 9.3 | 6.2 |
| Coal (100 million tons) | 871.1 | 634.9 | 720.8 | 277.4 | 126.5 | 11.4 | 13.1 | 21.8 |
| Crude oil (10,000 tons) | 256.6 | 201.6 | 141.7 | 114.6 | 69.8 | 4.8 | 4.8 | 3.5 |
| Electricity (100 million kwh) | 921.1 | 573.5 | 397.4 | 223.0 | 115.1 | 11.7 | 12.3 | 14.8 |
| Crude steel (10,000 tons) | 1,087.4 | 572.4 | 618.9 | 216.9 | 115.5 | 12.7 | 12.3 | 20.0 |
| Pig iron (10,000 tons) | 1,066.5 | 801.8 | 613.6 | 213.1 | 112.7 | 12.6 | 14.9 | 19.9 |
| Cement (10,000 tons) | 1,106.0 | 504.0 | 379.7 | 213.2 | 101.3 | 12.8 | 11.4 | 14.3 |
| Timber (10,000 cu.m) | 23.7 | 12.8 | 39.6 | 246.2 | 104.1 | −6.9 | −12.8 | −8.8 |
| **Construction** | | | | | | | | |
| Number of employed persons (10,000 persons) | | | 147.6 | 137.1 | 105.6 | | | 4.0 |
| Gross output value (100 million yuan) | | | 689.8 | 314.2 | 131.3 | | | 21.3 |

*Table D2  (cont.)*

| Item | (2010 as percentage of the following years) | | | | | Annual growth rate | | |
|---|---|---|---|---|---|---|---|---|
| | *1990* | *1995* | *2000* | *2005* | *2009* | *1991–2010* | *1996–2010* | *2001–2010* |
| Floor space of buildings under construction (10,000 sq.m) | | | 379.7 | 219.6 | 124.5 | | | 14.3 |
| Floor space of buildings completed (10,000 sq.m) | | | 289.5 | 191.0 | 117.1 | | | 11.2 |
| **Transportation, post, and telecommunication** | | | | | | | | |
| Railways in operation (10,000 km) | | | 148.7 | 125.7 | 101.4 | | | 4.1 |
| Highways (10,000 km) | 310.5 | 274.6 | 215.3 | 154.7 | 103.6 | 5.8 | 7.0 | 8.0 |
| Total value of telecommunications services (100 million yuan) | 28,562.4 | 3,149.2 | 827.4 | 275.4 | 114.7 | 32.7 | 25.9 | 23.5 |
| **Domestic trade** | | | | | | | | |
| Total value of retail sales (100 million yuan) | 1,713.9 | 690.5 | 454.7 | 239.7 | 118.5 | 15.3 | 13.7 | 16.4 |
| **Foreign trade** | | | | | | | | |
| Total exports and imports (USD 100 million) | | | 622.7 | 240.8 | 128.2 | | | 20.1 |
| Exports | | | 667.2 | 262.2 | 124.7 | | | 20.9 |
| Imports | | | 561.2 | 212.2 | 134.5 | | | 18.8 |
| **International tourism** | | | | | | | | |
| Number of foreign tourists (10,000 persons) | | | 269.7 | 176.5 | 125.0 | | | 10.4 |
| Foreign exchange earnings from tourism (USD 100 million) | | | 395.2 | 233.1 | 111.4 | | | 14.7 |
| **Finance** | | | | | | | | |
| Deposits of national banking system (100 million yuan) | | | 589.7 | 285.6 | 125.7 | | | 19.4 |

*Table D2  (cont.)*

| Item | (2010 as percentage of the following years) | | | | | Annual growth rate | | |
|---|---|---|---|---|---|---|---|---|
| | *1990* | *1995* | *2000* | *2005* | *2009* | *1991–2010* | *1996–2010* | *2001–2010* |
| Loans of national banking system (100 million yuan) | | | 467.0 | 270.6 | 124.8 | | | 16.7 |
| **Education** | | | | | | | | |
| *Student enrollment (10,000 persons)* | | | | | | | | |
| Regular institutions of higher education | 1,190.3 | 870.3 | 473.3 | 161.9 | 109.0 | 13.2 | 15.5 | 16.8 |
| Regular secondary schools | 172.3 | 166.2 | 120.3 | 97.0 | 100.0 | 2.8 | 3.4 | 1.9 |
| Regular primary schools | 82.9 | 81.3 | 81.5 | 92.1 | 97.2 | -0.9 | -1.4 | -2.0 |
| *Full-time teachers (10,000 persons)* | | | | | | | | |
| Regular institutions of higher education | 338.2 | 255.9 | 260.2 | 150.3 | 108.9 | 6.3 | 6.5 | 10.0 |
| Regular secondary schools | 162.5 | 162.6 | 140.8 | 110.4 | 101.9 | 2.5 | 3.3 | 3.5 |
| Regular primary schools | 107.0 | 105.7 | 100.9 | 103.0 | 100.2 | 0.3 | 0.4 | 0.1 |
| **Culture** | | | | | | | | |
| *Publications* | | | | | | | | |
| Number of books published (10,000 copies) | 181.7 | 129.6 | 129.5 | 130.6 | 114.9 | 3.0 | 1.7 | 2.6 |
| Number of magazines issued (10,000 copies) | 105.3 | 105.1 | 99.4 | 80.5 | 112.4 | 0.3 | 0.3 | -0.1 |
| Number of newspapers issued (10,000 copies) | 221.5 | 184.5 | 142.2 | 103.4 | 106.0 | 4.1 | 4.2 | 3.6 |
| **Health care** | | | | | | | | |
| Number of hospitals and health centers (10,000 units) | 113.1 | 97.0 | 95.7 | 101.0 | 101.0 | 0.6 | -0.2 | -0.4 |
| Number of beds of hospitals and health centers (10,000 units) | 167.9 | 156.1 | 154.3 | 145.0 | 108.0 | 2.6 | 3.0 | 4.4 |

*Table D2* (*cont.*)

| Item | (2010 as percentage of the following years) | | | | | Annual growth rate | | |
|---|---|---|---|---|---|---|---|---|
| | 1990 | 1995 | 2000 | 2005 | 2009 | 1991– 2010 | 1996– 2010 | 2001– 2010 |
| **Social services** | | | | | | | | |
| Number of beds in social welfare institutions (10,000 units) | | | | | 112.6 | | | |
| Number of urban community services facilities (units) | | | | | 344.7 | | | |
| Number of persons receiving minimum living allowance in urban and rural areas (10,000 persons) | | | | | 113.7 | | | |

*Source: China Statistical Yearbook* (2011).

# Appendix E: Geocultural conditions of the 55 ethnic minorities in China

| Name | Population (1,000 persons) | Geographic distribution | Language(s) | Religion(s) |
|------|------|------|------|------|
| Achang | 33.94 | Yunnan | Achang | Buddhism |
| Bai | 1,858.06 | Yunnan, Guizhou | Bai, most also speak Chinese | Animism |
| Baonan | 91.88 | Gansu | Baonan, Chinese (spoken and written) | Islam |
| Blang | 16.51 | Yunnan | Blang, Dai | Buddhism |
| Buyi | 2,971.46 | Guizhou, Yunnan, Guangxi | Dai | Buddhism |
| Dai | 1,158.99 | Yunnan | Dai, most also speak Chinese | Buddhism |
| Daur | 132.39 | Inner Mongolia, Heilongjiang, Xinjiang | Daur (spoken), Chinese (written) | Lamaism |
| Deang | 17.94 | Yunnan | Deang | Buddhism |
| Derung | 7.43 | Yunnan | Derung | |
| Dong | 2,960.29 | Guizhou, Hunan, Guangxi | Dong, Chinese | Animism |
| Dongxiang | 513.81 | Gansu, Xinjiang | Dongxiang, most also speak Chinese | Islam |
| Ewenki | 30.51 | Inner Mongolia, Heilongjiang | Ewenki (spoken), Mongolian (written), Chinese (written) | Shamanism |
| Gaoshan | 458.00 | Taiwan, Fujian | Gaoshan (spoken), Chinese | |
| Gelao | 579.36 | Guizhou, Guangxi | Gelao, Chinese | Islam |
| Hani | 22.52 | Yunnan | Hani | Animism |

| Name | Population (1,000 persons) | Geographic distribution | Language(s) | Religion(s) |
|------|------|------|------|------|
| Hezhe | 1,439.67 | Heilongjiang | Hezhe (spoken), Chinese | |
| Hui | 4.64 | Ningxia, Gansu, Henan, Hebei, Qinghai, Shandong | Chinese | Islam |
| Jing | 9,816.80 | Guangxi | Jing, Chinese (spoken and written) | |
| Jingpo | 132.14 | Yunnan | Jingpo | Animism |
| Jino | 20.90 | Yunnan | Jino | |
| Kazak | 1,420.46 | Xinjiang, Gansu, Qinghai | Kazaki | Islam |
| Kirgiz | 160.82 | Xinjiang, Heilongjiang | Kirgiz, Uygur (written), Kazaki (written) | Islam, Lamaism |
| Korean | 1,923.84 | Jilin, Liaoning, Heilongjiang | Korean, Chinese | Individual choice |
| Lahu | 453.71 | Yunnan | Lahu | Animism |
| Lhoba | 2.97 | Tibet | Lhoba (spoken) | Lamaism |
| Li | 1,247.81 | Hainan | Li, some also speak Chinese | Animism |
| Lisu | 634.91 | Yunnan, Sichuan | Lisu | |
| Manchu | 10,682.26 | Liaoning, Jilin, Heilongjiang, Beijing, Inner Mongolia | Most speak Chinese; only a small portion speak Manchu | Individual choice |
| Maonan | 107.17 | Guangxi | Maonan, Zhuang, Chinese (written) | Islam |
| Miao | 8,940.12 | Guizhou, Sichuan, Hunan, Hubei, Guangdong | Miao; the majority also assimilated into Chinese language | Animism |
| Monba | 8.92 | Tibet | Monba, Tibetan | Lamaism |
| Mongol | 5,813.95 | Inner Mongolia, Xinjiang, Liaoning, Jilin, Heilongjiang, Gansu, Hebei, Henan, Qinghai | Mongolian, Mandarin | Lamaism |
| Mulao | 207.35 | Guangxi | Mulam and Zhuang (spoken), Chinese (written) | Lamaism |
| Naxi | 308.84 | Yunnan, Sichuan | Naxi, most also speak Chinese | Dongba |
| Nu | 28.76 | Yunnan | Nu | |

| Name | Population (1,000 persons) | Geographic distribution | Language(s) | Religion(s) |
|---|---|---|---|---|
| Oroqen | 8.20 | Inner Mongolia, Heilongjiang | Oroqen (spoken), Chinese (written) | Shamanism |
| Pumi | 33.60 | Yunnan | Pumi | |
| Qiang | 306.07 | Sichuan | Qiang (spoken) | Lamaism |
| Russian | 15.61 | Xinjiang, Heilongjiang | Russian | Eastern Orthodox |
| Salar | 104.50 | Qinghai, Gansu | Salar (spoken), Chinese (spoken and written) | Islam |
| She | 709.59 | Fujian, Zhejiang, Jiangxi, Guangdong | Chinese | Animism |
| Shui | 406.90 | Guizhou, Guangxi | Shui, most also speak Chinese | Animism |
| Tajik | 41.03 | Xinjiang | Tajik (spoken), Uygur | Islam |
| Tatar | 4.89 | Xinjiang | Tatar, Uygur, Kazaki | Islam |
| Tibetan | 5,416.02 | Tibet, Qinghai, Sichuan, Gansu, Yunnan, Xinjiang | Tibetan | Lamaism |
| Tu | 241.20 | Qinghai, Gansu | Tu, Chinese | Lamaism |
| Tujia | 8,028.13 | Hunan, Hubei | Tujia, most also speak Chinese | Animism |
| Uygur | 8,399.39 | Xinjiang | Uygur | Islam |
| Uzbek | 12.37 | Xinjiang | Uzbek, Uygur, Kazaki | Islam |
| Va | 396.61 | Yunnan | Va | Animism |
| Xibe | 188.82 | Xinjiang, Liaoning, Jilin | Xibe | Islam |
| Yao | 2,637.42 | Guangxi, Hunan, Yunnan, Guangdong | Yao, most also speak Chinese | Animism |
| Yi | 7,762.29 | Sichuan, Hunan, Guizhou, Guangxi | Yi (spoken), males also speak and write Chinese | Animism |
| Yugur | 13.72 | Gansu | Yugur, Chinese (spoken and written) | Lamaism |
| Zhuang | 16,178.81 | Guangxi, Guangdong, Yunnan, Guizhou | Zhuang (spoken), most also speak and write Chinese | Animism |

*Sources: China Statistical Yearbook* (2011) for the data of population and author for others.

For Product Safety Concerns and Information please contact our EU
representative  GPSR@taylorandfrancis.com
Taylor & Francis Verlag GmbH, Kaufingerstraße 24, 80331 München, Germany

www.ingramcontent.com/pod-product-compliance
Lightning Source LLC
Chambersburg PA
CBHW050419280326
41932CB00013BA/1921